Helping Children Become Readers Through Writing

A Guide to Writing Workshop in Kindergarten

Arlene C. Schulze

INTERNATIONAL
Reading Association
800 BARKSDALE ROAD, PO BOX 8139
NEWARK, DE 19714-8139, USA
www.reading.org

The International Reading Association attempts, through its publications, to provide a forum for a wide spectrum of opinions on reading. This policy permits divergent viewpoints without implying the endorsement of the Association.

Executive Editor, Books   Corinne M. Mooney
Developmental Editor   Charlene M. Nichols
Developmental Editor   Tori Mello Bachman
Developmental Editor   Stacey Lynn Sharp
Editorial Production Manager   Shannon T. Fortner
Production Manager   Iona Muscella
Supervisor, Electronic Publishing   Anette Schuetz

Project Editors   Charlene M. Nichols and Amy Messick

Cover   Design, Linda Steere; Photo, © Blend Images, LLC/Veer.com.

Web addresses in this book were correct as of the publication date but may have become inactive or otherwise modified since that time. If you notice a deactivated or changed Web address, please e-mail books@reading.org with the words "Website Update" in the subject line. In your message, specify the Web link, the book title, and the page number on which the link appears.

Library of Congress Cataloging-in-Publication Data

Schulze, Arlene C., 1941-

  Helping children become readers through writing : a guide to writing workshop in kindergarten / Arlene C. Schulze.

       p. cm.

  Includes bibliographical references and index.

  ISBN-13: 978-0-87207-566-5

  1. English language--Composition and exercises--Study and teaching (Preschool) I. Title.

  LB1181.S28 2006

  372.62'3--dc22

                                                                                      2006013534

To Dr. Kathleen Buss—first my teacher, then my mentor, and now my friend. This book would not have been possible without your guidance.

And to my family—Gary, my husband, who not only took over many household duties but, along with our children, Robyn, Randy, Stacey, and Ray, always believed this book was necessary and possible. You all offered encouragement and support whenever and however I needed it.

CONTENTS

PREFACE   vii

ABOUT THE AUTHOR   xv

CHAPTER 1   1

Writing and Writing Workshop in Kindergarten

CHAPTER 2   29

Developmental Letter Formation and Developmental Stages of Spelling

CHAPTER 3   60

Developmental Sequence of Learning Written Language and Understanding Genres

CHAPTER 4   98

Planning a Comprehensive Literacy Program

CHAPTER 5   147

Getting Ready and Writing Workshop

CHAPTER 6   181

Minilessons for Writing Workshop

CHAPTER 7   231

Assessment, Evaluation, and Reporting

CHAPTER 8   269

Reflections on Writing Workshop in Kindergarten

APPENDIX A   277

Phonemic Awareness Activities and Additional Minilesson Topics

APPENDIX B   299
Booklists

APPENDIX C   313
Letters and Charts

APPENDIX D   320
Common Lists and How to Teach Them

APPENDIX E   331
Reproducible Forms

REFERENCES   343

AUTHOR AND SUBJECT INDEX   351

"It's a miracle!" exclaims Mrs. Carlton, a kindergarten teacher, as she proudly shows her student Jestin's paper to me. Jestin, on his own initiative, not only has written his name, but next to his picture of Santa and Santa's bag he also has written *B the bg is fl* (But the bag is full). Upon entering school in September, Jestin could not and would not even attempt to write his name, not even the first letter. He did not know any of the letters of the alphabet and he could not hear individual sounds in words. So this event that took place in December indeed was a miracle.

Through implementing a writing workshop that was based on Graves's (1994) and Calkins's (1994) approaches, this event—this miracle—was possible. Jestin's teacher and I were ecstatic. Both of us were veteran teachers with more than 60 years of teaching experience between us, yet we had never had such success with teaching kindergartners to hear sounds (i.e., phonemic awareness) and learn sound–letter relationships (i.e., the alphabetic principle), which are prerequisites for conventional reading.

After Mrs. Carlton had implemented a writing workshop approach for one year, I asked her to reflect on why writing workshop had worked so well. Her answer was in agreement with most of the kindergarten teachers with whom I've worked:

> First of all, it actually teaches the process of writing, and it has predictable structure. Also, it's an individual approach. I can assess and guide each child in his or her particular needs. Of course it employs all of Cambourne's [1988] conditions of language learning. [She said this with a chuckle for my benefit, but she did appreciate their value.] And the best thing of all is my kids absolutely love it!

I also asked her to reflect on writing methods she'd used in the absence of a writing workshop:

> Studying one letter each week is too isolated from meaningful reading and writing to transfer to the process of real reading and writing. Also, the writing process develops differently in each child, so the child needs to do it independently and he needs guidance. While I think group writing procedures are useful to teaching certain points, they don't allow each child to use his active mind for himself, and they don't allow me to know what the child knows about writing. On the other hand, while personal journal writing and writing centers are independent activities, they didn't really help me teach writing, because Cambourne's conditions of learning are not a part of their structure like they are in a writing workshop.

Nothing has succeeded like a writing workshop to teach children how to communicate in written language and read written language. It immerses children in meaningful writing, and its very predictable three-part structure is built on Cambourne's (1988) conditions of learning language (which will be discussed in detail in chapter 1). The first part of writing workshop is the minilesson, which consists of the teacher demonstrating his or her own writing. The second part of the workshop focuses on each child independently writing his or her own message while the teacher offers guidance to each child's writing needs. During this part of the workshop, students are given the time and responsibility to "approximate," or attempt, writing in the best way they can. The third part of the workshop consists of students sharing their writings; a few children share their precious words with a responsive, appreciative audience who expects and encourages them to succeed.

In a writing workshop, each child is allowed and encouraged to develop his or her own voice, which promotes engagement in literacy. Voluntary engagement in a task is the key ingredient to learning and the key to success in school and in life. The kindergarten and first- and second-grade teachers whom I have instructed in a writing workshop approach report that their students are really enthusiastic about writing workshop and request it if they miss even one day. As Holdaway (1979) asserts, children know when they are learning.

The Impact of Writing Workshop in Kindergarten

As a university literacy instructor for the past 12 years and a literacy coach to school systems for the past 13 years, I have seen many failing readers in kindergarten and grades one through nine who have been unable to analyze words by their sounds; they could not decode printed text. Other readers who could decode did not read for sense or meaning. Decoding and comprehending a message are the two basic elements of reading (Gough & Tunmer, 1986). A message is the reason for reading and the reason for writing. Therefore, as writers learn to write, or encode, to communicate their own messages, they also learn that reading is about comprehending others' messages. Thus, writing workshop, in conjunction with reading workshop, provides the approach teachers need to help children experience reading success and enable them to reach their full literacy potential (Calkins, 2001; Clay, 2001).

When kindergarten teachers provide instruction within a quality literacy curriculum that focuses on writing and reading workshops, all kindergartners' reading achievement improves. Even lower achieving students (Smith & Elley, 1997; Stires, 1991) and students with learning disabilities can learn to write in writing workshops (Hallenbeck, 1995; Lewis, Ashton, & Kieley, 1996; Morocco, 1987; Morocco, Dalton, & Tivan, 1992; Storeyard, Simmons, Stumpf, & Pavloglou, 1993). And writing is a precursor to reading (Clay, 2001).

I first began implementing writing workshop in the early 1990s as a research experiment. I asked my local superintendent, Ralph Neale, and the personnel director, John Ader, if I could set up a writing workshop with a couple of teachers. These administrators listened to and supported my plan. Two interested teachers volunteered: a kindergarten teacher and a first-grade teacher. The results I gained from pre- and posttesting the children in these two classrooms on Clay's (1993a) Dictation Test, which tests a child's ability to hear individual sounds in words (i.e., phonemic awareness) and represent these sounds with appropriate letters (i.e., alphabetic principle), were amazing—they indicated significant improvement for *all* of the children. The following year I was asked to work with an entire K–5 elementary school.

Again, I pretested and posttested the kindergarten children to verify the remarkable results I'd gotten the year before. Had I known the school's reading teacher also used Clay's Dictation Test to test all kindergarten students at the end of the year, I would have inquired as to which of five forms of this test she would be using, so my pretest would have been the same as her posttest. (I needed to use the same test for my research purposes.) As it was, the reading teacher did use a different form of the test than I did. I first heard about her scores through the principal, Debra Olson. She called me to tell me the reading teacher's test results were so astounding compared to the results of previous years that the reading teacher had shown her the tests. Now, they both wanted to show them to the superintendent. Next, the results were shown to the school board, whose members decided that I should work with all eight K–5 elementary schools in the implementation of writing workshop. I enlisted fellow reading specialist and poet Linda Scaffidi to work in grades 3–5, while I chose to concentrate on grades K–2 because a quality literacy program in the K–2 level is critical to preventing future reading and writing difficulties.

A quality literacy program is a necessity in schools because many children have not had the preschool literacy exposure and immersion they should have had. Clay (1993b) explains that the best literacy training for the young child should incorporate the following:

- Preschool literacy experiences that immerse children in quality literature and expose them to meaningful print.
- Curriculum for literacy learning in the early years of school that is based on the conditions of learning language (Cambourne, 1988), which allows children to be active constructors of their own learning within meaningful writing and reading.
- Early intervention (end of kindergarten) for children who are being left behind by fast-learning classmates.

Although educators do not have control over students' preschool literacy experiences, they do have control over what happens once formal schooling begins in kindergarten. A quality literacy program that includes writing and reading workshops at all grade levels, especially kindergarten, can give all students the opportunity to be literate.

After helping kindergarten teachers implement writing workshop in 17 kindergartens in and near my hometown, I found the students' results on Clay's Dictation Test (1993a)—and progress on writing samples charted throughout the year—to be astounding. Principals, like Jeff Reiche, called me one year after I had worked in their schools, citing the remarkable progress their previous kindergartners were making in first-grade reading. In fact, many of these children had entered first grade as early or fluent readers because they understood and could apply the alphabetic principle.

Principals, first-grade teachers, and school district personnel expect that kindergartners will learn the alphabetic principle; however, until the advent of the writing workshop approach, kindergarten teachers often did not feel successful in teaching the alphabetic principle, especially with children like Jestin who had not had good preschool literacy experiences. Jestin's teacher had wanted to try a writing workshop, but she never could find enough research and information on its application to effectively implement the approach. Given the limitations of a kindergarten teacher's time (or any teacher's time for that matter), scouring hundreds of sources for theory and application was not a possibility. As a literacy coach, I had the time to learn about and implement writing workshop in the classroom, and I decided to write this book to provide an introduction to writing workshop for busy teachers.

Who Should Read This Book?

Anyone who wants to understand why and how young children become readers (and writers) should read this book. Although this book was specifically written for kindergarten teachers so they could gain knowledge of how to help children become readers through writing, it also is for policymakers, administrators, first- and second-grade teachers, preschool teachers, parents, and anyone else who wants to understand the best way to teach young children to become readers. (To read the reflections of other teachers and administrators concerning implementing a writing workshop, see chapter 8.)

This book was written to answer questions that kindergarten teachers, other teachers, administrators, and policymakers have about *how to help* young children progress from scribble writing, to learning the alphabetic principle as they try to write, to writing readable print, to finally becoming conventional readers through writing. This book also explains *why* this progression happens through explanations of current research.

First- and second-grade teachers will find many useful literacy teaching activities and minilessons that could prove helpful in implementing their writing and reading workshops in this book. The theory section (chapters 1 through 3) will help first- and second-grade teachers better understand and teach those readers, writers, and spellers who may be struggling in their classrooms. Also, the informal assessments and forms in chapter 7 have proven useful to first- and second-grade teachers as well as kindergarten teachers.

Kindergarten teachers do not have to read the entire book before they begin implementing a writing workshop. As well as explaining how to implement a writing workshop, this book is a resource for questions that arise during implementation. This book can serve as a guide—teachers can learn as they "go." Ray and Cleaveland (2004) reinforce the concept of learning as you go: "No matter what, just let students write every day. Even if you're not sure what to teach, just let them write" (p. ix). First, begin a writing workshop (chapter 5 tells you how); then, read the rest of this book as time permits and your students' needs dictate. As you learn to use the writing workshop approach in your classroom, this book will serve as both a guide and a resource for your questions regarding writing workshop in kindergarten.

An Explanation of This Book's Structure

This book is organized into seven chapters. Although the chapters are filled with a wealth of information related to writing workshop in kindergarten, readers can choose to first read the sections that most pertain to them.

Chapter 1, "Writing and Writing Workshop in Kindergarten," highlights the effective application of writing workshop in kindergarten. The three focal points are (1) Ferreiro and Teberosky's (1982) development of young children's written language concepts, (2) Clay's (1991) three stages of reading and four emergent literacy behaviors (highlighting phonemic awareness), and (3) Cambourne's (1988) conditions of learning language.

Chapter 2, "Developmental Letter Formation and Developmental Stages of Spelling," defines developmental learning and how it applies to letter formation and spelling in kindergarten. Understanding developmental learning is essential in planning appropriate literacy instruction of letter formation and spelling skills. Gentry and Gillet's (1993) stages of spelling are the focus of this chapter.

Chapter 3, "Developmental Sequence of Learning Written Language and Understanding Genres," begins with information about children's development of written language prior to kindergarten. Next, the chapter outlines the five stages of kindergartners' written language development in kindergarten with student samples from each stage. These stages assess the development of "content" in kindergartners' written language, whereas spelling stages only assess the development of spelling skills. Knowing these stages of written language acquisition can aid teachers in planning appropriate instruction to improve kindergartners' quality of writing.

Finally, the chapter highlights genres appropriate for the kindergarten and provides initial instruction ideas and samples for each genre.

Chapter 4, "Planning a Comprehensive Literacy Program," presents a possible daily kindergarten schedule, highlighting writing workshops, reading workshops, and read-alouds. Other valuable literacy approaches are also discussed, with explanations of how they might be incorporated into the daily kindergarten curriculum. These approaches include language experience, interactive writing, shared reading and writing, guided reading, the morning message, sign-in, the class newspaper, and more.

Chapter 5, "Getting Ready and Writing Workshop," focuses on how to get ready for and structure this literacy approach. This chapter begins with a description and discussion of the two parts of Getting Ready, which provides the groundwork for children's progression in writing readable print: (1) working with the alphabet and (2) learning phonemic awareness. Next, the chapter describes and discusses the three parts of writing workshop, which enable children to progress in communicating meaning: (1) teacher demonstration and minilesson, (2) teacher observation and conferring while students write, and (3) teacher and classmates encouraging and celebrating the writings of children who share their writing through Author's Chair.

A written demonstration of a typical day with an entire kindergarten class in the beginning of the year is used to describe Getting Ready and Writing Workshop, and a discussion section follows. According to teachers who have used this book in rough draft form, this format has proven to be helpful to those teachers implementing a writing workshop for the first time as well as those teachers attempting to improve existing workshops.

Chapter 6, "Minilessons for Writing Workshop," explains the importance of teachers' demonstrations of their own writing to their students' writing success. The chapter presents several teacher minilesson demonstrations and discusses the importance of teachers observing the needs of their students in regard to the scheduling, design, and implementation of minilessons. The minilessons presented are based on kindergarten teachers' choices. They serve as models for kindergarten teachers to construct their own minilessons as their students' needs dictate. Minilessons are grouped according to the following categories: procedures, content, strategies, and skills.

Chapter 7, "Assessment, Evaluation, and Reporting," highlights what to observe and what to record during writing conferences. Sample anecdotal records of actual conferences are presented. This chapter also focuses on how kindergarten teachers collect students' work, save it, evaluate it using rubrics and checklists to document students' literacy development, and report these findings. Furthermore, valuable kindergarten literacy tests are discussed, and Clay's (1993a) Dictation Test (with student samples) is highlighted as an important evaluation tool.

Chapter 8, "Reflections on Writing Workshop in Kindergarten," includes reflections and reactions from teachers, administrators, and students concerning the benefits of a writing workshop.

Throughout the book, student writing samples are included to reinforce and demonstrate specific points. In addition, Appendixes A–E include helpful resources for kindergarten teachers who choose to implement writing workshop. Appendix A offers phonemic awareness activities, which can be used prior to writing workshop to teach kindergartners how to hear individual sounds in words and manipulate these sounds, as well as additional kindergarten minilesson topics. Appendixes B–E include recommended booklists, wordlists, sample letters, and reproducible forms.

Summary

All kindergarten teachers deserve to know how to provide their students with the success of becoming writers and readers via a writing workshop based on sound research. All kindergarten children can be readers and writers if we teach writing (and reading) through the workshop approach. Writing in writing workshop allows emergent writers and readers to become early writers and readers by teaching the alphabetic principle as children strive to communicate messages.

Acknowledgments

First, I would like to thank former Editorial Director Matt Baker, Corinne Mooney, and the reviewers of the International Reading Association (IRA) who were patient and helpful during the writing process. They heard my voice and believed others should hear it, too.

I also would like to give special thanks to Charlene Nichols, my editor at IRA, who was not only patient with my process of writing, but also greatly enhanced it with her insightful questions, advice, and her encouragement to draw on my own experiences to exemplify the research.

Next, I wish to express my gratitude and appreciation for teachers, friends, and relatives who gave so unselfishly of their time as readers and support staff. I would especially like to thank Karen Clark, kindergarten teacher at Marathon Elementary, Marathon, Wisconsin, USA, who believed in writing workshop from the start. She supported this book from its inception and graciously produced necessary materials for it whenever needed. Gratitude is also extended to Teri Williams, another kindergarten teacher at Marathon Elementary, who was most helpful in providing comments and materials for this book.

In addition to Karen and Teri, the following kindergarten teachers—all located in the state of Wisconsin—were instrumental in acting as readers of the draft form of this book. Their advice and support was necessary and is greatly appreciated.

- Joan Scheirer and Diane Poirier, who faithfully read every chapter and offered comments and ideas that I incorporated into the book.
- Cindy Lentz, Eileen Richardson, Ann Neale, and Amy Neuenfeldt, who read and offered comments and teaching ideas on selected chapters of the book.

A special note of thanks is due to my sister, Janet Zielinski, multimedia specialist in the Denver, Colorado, USA, school system, who took the time from her busy schedule to help me compile book recommendations and search for references, and Judi Weaver, a friend and retired computer resource teacher from Merrill, Wisconsin, USA, who provided information on computer programs that support literacy in kindergarten.

Finally, appreciation is due Linda Scaffidi, a colleague and friend who offered support and acted as a reader; Ardis Marquis, a retired first-grade teacher, who on her own initiative retyped my phonemic awareness activities on her computer, so I could give other teachers handouts that were more readable than those photocopied from my original typewritten version had been; and Leslie McClain-Ruelle, who supported and believed in my knowledge of emergent literacy enough to hire me as an instructor at the University of Wisconsin–Stevens Point.

Please send comments and questions along with a self-addressed, stamped envelope to me at 1105 Michler Crest, Merrill, WI 54452, USA.

Arlene Schulze received her Bachelor of Science degree in elementary education from the University of Wisconsin–Madison in 1963. Observing her own children become early readers through immersion and exposure to meaningful print made Arlene even more curious about how reading should be taught in schools. In 1989, Arlene returned to college at the University of Wisconsin–Stevens Point (UWSP) to obtain a master's degree with a focus on reading teacher and reading specialist titles. During this time, she thoroughly researched phonemic awareness and then presented her findings to the Wisconsin State Reading Association in 1993. All of the activities she created for this study have been used by hundreds of kindergarten teachers over the past 13 years.

Arlene then worked as an instructor for UWSP in the College of Professional Studies School of Education. She taught on and off campus successfully for the past 12 years and was recognized by the university as a master teacher. During this time, she also worked as a literacy consultant to the Merrill, Wisconsin, and Marathon, Wisconsin, school systems to help their K–2 teachers implement writing workshops.

Arlene received a lifetime teaching certificate from the state of Wisconsin for successful teaching. Although Arlene recently retired from coaching, she remains active as a language arts instructor at UWSP and a speaker promoting writing's value to reading, especially on the emergent level.

Writing and Writing Workshop in Kindergarten

"Children have shown to us that they need to reconstruct the written system in order to make it their own. Let us allow them the time and the opportunities for such a tremendous task."

—Ferreiro (1981, p. 56)

Approximately 80% of children learn to read regardless of the teacher's methodology (Clay, as cited by Calkins, 2001, p. 256). However, based on my experience it takes children longer to become proficient at reading without a writing workshop because of the reciprocity that exists between writing and reading (Clay, 2001; Shanahan, 1990)—and because of the proper learning conditions that exist in a writing workshop (Cambourne, 1988).

And what about the remaining 20%? Robinson's (1973) research shows that writing is the main predictor of early reading progress for children between the ages of 5.6 and 6.0 and again between 6.0 and 6.5. Based on this research, Clay (2001) discovered that writing is crucial to early reading interventions because it prevents learners from overlooking many things they need to know about print and reveals things about the learner's processing of print that the teacher needs to know.

Thus, this chapter explains the importance of and provides the research to support incorporating daily writing workshops based on Cambourne's (1988) conditions of language learning, as Calkins (1994) and Graves (1994) describe, so all children can reach their full literacy potential.

(Chapter 5, "Getting Ready and Writing Workshop," explains the practice of this chapter.)

What Children and Researchers Know About Writing Development

Writing workshop helps foster young children's developing awareness of literacy. Researchers have studied emergent literacy, and their findings have helped teachers understand young children's developing awareness of print (Chomsky, 1971; Clay, 1975, 1991; Dyson, 1989; Ferreiro & Teberosky, 1982; Graves, 1975; Harste, Burke, & Woodward, 1981, 1983; Temple, Nathan, Burris, & Temple, 1988). Clay (2001) explains, "Writing can contribute to building almost every kind of inner control of literacy learning that is needed by the successful reader" (p. 12). Therefore, educators must understand what children know about the complexity of written language when they enter kindergarten. Two studies—one by Ferreiro and Teberosky (1982) with 108 middle and lower class 4-, 5-, and 6-year-old children, and one by Harste, Burke, and Woodward (1981) with children as young as 3 years old—explain some of the concepts that must be learned before young children can begin to read print. The children must learn to distinguish

- drawing from writing—Harste and colleagues (1981) discovered that most 3-year-olds can see the difference between drawing and writing; however, they do not understand that writing represents speech.

- pictures from print—Ferreiro and Teberosky (1982) discovered that a majority of 4- and 5-year-olds could indicate that pictures were for "looking at" and print was "for reading."

- letters from numerals—Ferreiro and Teberosky (1982) indicated that a significant number of children from lower class homes confused numerals with letters of the alphabet. Only a few middle class children didn't know the difference between letters and numerals, and they tended to be younger than 5 years old. (Some beginning kindergartners do not know the difference.)

- letters from punctuation—Ferreiro and Teberosky (1982) indicated that the middle class group of children who were able to differentiate punctuation marks from letters had been provided extensive practice with texts by people who read to them. Unfortunately, most lower class children did not have the benefit of this extensive exposure to text and, therefore, did not distinguish punctuation from letters. (Some beginning kindergartners do not make this distinction.)

- letters from words (which involves spatial orientation)—Ferreiro and Teberosky (1982) concluded that children who could make distinctions between letters and words had been involved with someone who had read to them and helped them make this distinction. (Many beginning kindergartners do not make distinctions between letters and words.)

Ferreiro and Teberosky's (1982) cross-age study also determined that most 4-year-olds did not understand the spatial orientation of the page or print (i.e., directionality) unless some informant (e.g., a proficient reader) either told them about spatial orientation and/or pointed to the print while reading to them. (Many beginning kindergartners have trouble with spatial orientation of page and print.)

When 4-, 5-, and 6-year-old children were confronted with a picture and a sentence over a period of time, Ferreiro and Teberosky (1982) discovered a developmental sequence of change as the children learned to pay attention to print. The sequence they reported represents children's gradual growing awareness of the importance of print, especially as it represented oral language:

- Level One—Children do not differentiate between the picture and the sentence. The picture and the print are one unit that cannot be separated; it is not understood that print represents oral language.

- Level Two—Children begin to distinguish a difference between the sentence and the picture (usually around 3 years old), but they have no understanding that print represents oral language. The print is looked at as one large unit that directly represents the picture. Individual graphic symbols or cues in the sentence are not considered.

- Level Three—Children begin to consider or think about the individual graphic symbols of print in the sentence, but they continue to rely on the picture to predict the text. They still do not understand that print represents oral language.

- Level Four—Children begin to focus on the individual graphic symbols in the sentence. Children expect that the print in the sentence is associated with the picture, but they also begin to look for a correspondence between graphic symbols of print and sound segments (alphabetic principle). Watching the children's early reading of the print shows some measure of correspondence between print and the sounds it represents. Finally, children begin to understand the alphabetic principle and how print can represent oral language.

Before children become aware that other people's oral language and their own oral language can be analyzed into words and letter patterns, they attempt to "pretend" read and write following their own logic (Clay, 2001). Preschoolers and most new kindergarten entrants "often explore writing without connecting it to reading, as if it were quite a different code" (Clay, 2001, p. 13). Therefore, Clay (1991) states that it is imperative for teachers of young children to understand that "[visual attention to print]...and correspondence with sound segments is the final step in a progression, not the entry point to understanding what written language is" (p. 33). Independent approximated writing at a student's own pace, with guidance from the teacher at points of need, fosters visual attention to print and its corresponding sound segments.

Through rigorous analysis, Robinson's (1973) study shows writing in the first 18 months of learning to read to be of major importance to early reading progress. When writing, "the eye and ear and hand are jointly involved in the management of a task, [and] they send three different messages to the brain" (Clay, 2001, p. 16). These messages, sent by these three different senses, help the child initially recognize objects like toys and eventually familiar words. Joint involvement of eye, ear, and hand not only provides a way to check on the way each of these senses receives message, but it is also a necessary "precursor [for young children] to being able to use their eyes alone to do the searching at a later stage" (p. 16). When writing their own stories, children are given the opportunity, time, and guidance at their point of need to gain control of literacy concepts that help build processes, strategies, and sources of knowledge that readers use. Clay (2001) adds that writing not only provides "an awareness of how to construct messages" (p. 17), but it also forces children to pay attention to important features of print, for they must

- attend very closely to features of letters;
- construct their own words, letter by letter;
- direct attention to spatial concepts;
- work within the order and sequence constraints of print;
- break down the task into its smallest segments while at the same time synthesizing these segments into words and sentences; and
- engage in their own form of segmenting sounds in words (phonemic awareness) to write them (with invented spelling) (Clay, 1991).

Writing is described by Clay (1991) as a "building-up process" and a great complement to the "breaking-down process" of reading's visual analysis (p. 109). The constructive nature of writing's building-up process makes the task of learning the alphabetic principle (sound-to-letter relationships) more obvious to the young child. Because children know sounds (phonemes) already, or they wouldn't be able to talk, it is easier for them to learn sound-to-letter relationships (as in writing) over letter-to-sound relationships (as in conventional reading). When children write, they only have to

- learn to isolate the individual sounds in words (phonemic awareness) and
- then search for an appropriate English letter to represent the targeted sound (phoneme).

In conventional reading, children must begin with a letter (which they often don't know), then try to connect it to a sound (which they know and only need to learn to isolate). Beginning conventional reading before *approximated* writing does not make sense developmentally. Developmental learning means going from what one knows to what one doesn't; students' strengths need to be identified and used to teach to students' needs (Holdaway, 1979).

Because it is familiar, children's own writing is often the easiest to read (Clay, 1991). Avery (1993) describes this writing–reading connection further: "Children naturally incorporate context, visual, and phonetic clues to decipher their own writing, then transfer these strategies to the reading of books by professional authors" (p. 381). Furthermore, in conventional reading there is not much time for young children to grapple with the various shapes of unfamiliar letters and punctuation. Independent approximated writing provides the time and opportunity to closely attend to the features of print and "prevents learners from neglecting or overlooking many things that they must know about print" (Clay, 2001, p. 18).

Writing not only aids the teaching of reading but also provides a window into students' literacy knowledge. Teachers can gain an understanding of what a student knows about literacy by analyzing writing samples and closely examining which features of these extremely complex activities (reading and writing) the child is attending to or not attending to (Clay, 2001). This assessment provides a guide to the teacher's instruction.

Because reading and writing "occur in parallel alongside each other," Clay (2001, p. 12) advises they be learned that way. However, guiding young children to read and write requires teachers to understand and initially support approximated or pretend attempts to read and write until children learn to read and write conventionally (Calkins, 1994, 2001; Clay, 1991, 2001). Two separate research studies (McNaughton, 1974; Wotherspoon, 1974) capture the importance of teaching writing and reading concurrently. These researchers documented positive change over time in both reading and writing behaviors as writing supported or contributed to reading and vice versa. Numerous other research studies also support the positive effect writing and reading have on each other in kindergarten through 12th grade (Birnbaum, 1982; McGinley, 1992; Shanahan & Lomax, 1986).

Sampson (1986) agrees:

> The young child's reading and writing abilities mutually reinforce each other, developing concurrently and interrelatedly rather than sequentially. The child develops as a reader/writer; therefore, it is more appropriate to speak of *literacy development* [italics added].... Furthermore, reading and writing have intimate connections with oral language. Truly, the child develops as a speaker/reader/ writer with each role supporting the other [as he becomes a literate being]. (p. 5)

Neither learning to be literate nor teaching literacy is a simple task; they are both very complex (Clay, 2001). Even in their simplest definitions, reading involves listening comprehension as well as decoding (Gough & Tunmer, 1986), and writing, a psycho-motor task, requires listening comprehension as well as encoding (Dahl & Farnan, 1998). Writing is not simply copying a model; writing is dependent on a range of skills and components that require coordination, just like reading (Dyson & Freedman, 1991; Ferreiro & Teberosky, 1982).

Learning to be literate takes time. However, if young children are allowed to write in a writing workshop at the same time they are learning to read in a reading workshop where their approximations (pretend reading and invented spelling) are valued and guided, they can achieve Ferreiro and Teberosky's developmental sequence of change in their awareness of print while they are still in kindergarten (Calkins, 1994, 2001).

Writing begins with intent (Calkins, 1994; Graves, 1994; Harste, Burke, & Woodward, 1983). Children want to write, especially children from literate homes where oral communication, reading, and writing are valued. They leave evidence of their desire to write on walls, pavements, books, and newspapers with crayons, pens, markers, chalk, and stones—and anything else that makes a mark—long before they enter formal schooling. Calkins (1994) states that "ninety percent of children come to school believing they can write" (p. 62). Children believe they can do many things long before they can actually do them conventionally. It is this belief that makes them want to keep trying until they can do something conventionally (Calkins, 1994).

Writing as a Process and Product

When children make marks in an effort to communicate, they are writing. Previously, adults' false perception of writing—not as a learning process, but as a finished, polished product—led parents and teachers to ignore children's early attempts to make meaning through print. Until the late 1980s, teaching writing in kindergarten seemed absurd because teachers did not yet fully appreciate young writers' intent or their attempts (i.e., approximations) to learn the process (Calkins, 1994; Graves, 1983). However, students' approximations need to be valued, learned from, and guided (Calkins, 1994, 2001; Clay, 2001; Graves, 1983). Writing is the act of composing, and the process of writing refers to everything writers do from the time they conceive the idea and make their first marks, letters, or words on paper until they complete the finished, polished text (Graves, 1994).

Emig (1971) is credited with first looking at writing as a process as well as a product. She researched the composing processes of 12th-grade students and found little contemplation of what was being written or attention to revision when these students wrote to the teacher as their primary audience (extensive writing). In contrast, when students cared about their message and their audience while writing poetry or letters to their friends (reflexive writing), they gave a lot of thought to the content and the mechanics.

Research from the mid-1960s to the mid-1980s shows that teaching writing as a process has a more positive effect on students' writing progress than simply analyzing a final product. (See Hillocks, 1986, for a comprehensive review of writing research from 1963 to 1982.) In 1996, Goldstein and Carr published their findings from examining the 1992 National Assessment of Educational Progress writing drafts of 7,000 fourth graders, 11,000 eighth graders, and 11,500 twelfth graders. Their research confirmed earlier research that students who participated in writing process classrooms performed better than those who did not. In addition, those students who learned *strategies* of how to plan their writing by defining their purpose and audience in their classroom did better than those students who did not participate in learning such knowledge in their classrooms. In other words, the effect of teaching writing as a process was heightened when teachers designed instructional strategies that specifically targeted their corrective comments. For example, when a student was having difficulty expanding his brief and lackluster sentences, his teacher helped him to make significant progress by showing him a sentence expansion strategy. (See chapter 3, Stage Four of Written Language Development—"Taking Inventory and Adding Description," p. 78, for a detailed description of this technique.)

Graves (1983) also helped educators understand writing as a process. However, Graves (1994) states, "I've found that some teachers have misunderstood the writing process. They deliberately take children through phases of making a choice, rehearsing, composing and then rewriting" (p. 82). Writing as a process is not a step-by-step procedure; it is recursive. As an author, I know this to be true. I do not write my whole piece and then revise it; I am constantly revising as I write. Each writer uses the parts of the writing process in his or her own way. Some writers find a more tantalizing subject to write about in the middle of writing a less interesting piece. They should be allowed to follow their passion, their voice. Indeed, Graves recommends that teachers encourage their students to let their voice "breathe through the entire [recursive] process: rehearsal, topic choice, selection of information, composing, reading, and rewriting" (p. 82).

One of the earliest studies of primary children's writing processes was done by Graves in 1975. In 1981, Graves did another extensive research project that spanned two years with both primary and intermediate students. His research included direct observations of students as they wrote; interviews with children before, during, and after their writing; and analysis of written products. Based on this research, Graves (1981) defined children's writing process as "a series of operations leading to the solution of a problem. The process begins when the writer consciously or unconsciously starts a topic and is finished when the written piece is published" (p. 4). Graves emphasizes that composing can begin before the physical process of writing begins, even with writers as young as 6 years old. Graves also found that the youngest children's "[writing] process resembles spontaneous play" (p. 7).

When kindergarten teachers employ a writing workshop, they observe their students experimenting with letters, words, spacing, and writing materials in their desire to communicate meaning. Most kindergartners are secure in their belief that they are communicating meaning, and they are eager to read or tell their message to others who may not know what their writing says.

As children develop as writers, they begin to understand that they will not always be available to explain their work to an audience; their writing must stand on its own. Sharing their work with an appreciative audience gives young authors the incentive to work hard to write meaningful and readable print. However, even when kindergartners produce readable invented spelling, they may experience difficulty reading it conventionally at first (Kamberelis & Sulzby, 1988). This ability develops over time with daily reading and writing workshops where approximation is valued.

Although young children can compose stories before they can write, the *task* of actually printing their words can inhibit the creativity of the child (Temple et al., 1988). Beginning and struggling writers need to have access to strategies for composing, planning, and starting a piece of written language. Drawing pictures is essential to young children. Calkins (1994) explains, "The act of drawing and the picture itself both provide a supportive scaffolding within which he can construct his piece of writing" (p. 85). There are many children who prefer to do their composing as they draw. Calkins provides a classic example: When a 5-year-old boy was asked what he would write, he replied, "How should I know? I haven't even drawed it yet" (p. 84).

A teacher's demonstration of his or her own writing process is one of the most effective ways of teaching these writing process strategies. As young authors' writing develops, evidence of their planning and thinking about ideas prior to writing begins to appear, and talking aloud before and during composing is no longer needed. The emphasis shifts from talking to focusing on letter formation and spelling and finally to focusing on context. With time every day to practice their writing, young authors also become quite adept at choosing topics and selecting information for their writing (Graves, 1994).

Graves (1994) and Calkins (1994) strongly advise all teachers, especially kindergarten and primary teachers, to promote and guide process writing in their classrooms on a daily basis, and to closely observe what young children do as they try to gain control over the process. Of course this process needs to be simplified for kindergartners. (See chapter 3 for a simplified version of the writing process.)

As educators began to think about teaching writing as a process and teaching writing strategies to aid this process, they generated an instructional approach that set aside a special time daily for writing practice (Atwell, 1987; Calkins, 1986; Graves, 1983; Parry & Hornsby, 1985); this writing time is often referred to as a "conference approach" (Parry & Hornsby, 1985) because of the importance of the teacher working one-on-one with individual authors to improve their writing skills. This is a time for the teacher to listen, listen hard, guide, and encourage. Calkins (1986) coined the more popular term "writing workshop" for this instructional time of process writing. She based the structure of her workshop around the research of writing process and language acquisition. Calkins's (1994) writing workshop has three components:

Teacher-led minilessons to inspire and instruct

Practice time where students write, confer, and receive writing guidance from their teacher and classmates

Share sessions where students share their writings (which may include finished rough drafts, rough drafts in process, or students' published work) (pp. 188–191)

Because students write on topics that they choose themselves in writing workshop, they assume "ownership" and care about their writing and spelling (Calkins, 1994; Graves, 1983, 1994). Graves (1983) strongly advises that

> Above all, [the teacher] wants to maintain [the student's] ownership in the selection. [The teacher] wants [the student] to feel in control, to learn how to make her own decisions when she is writing, and to control her standards of what is a clear piece of writing. (p. 9)

The teacher guides the student to become *responsible* for his or her own learning. The teacher teaches him- or herself out of a job. Clay (2001) explains the teacher's role as a "challenge…to understand what is going on before their eyes, as [children's] reading and writing come together and influence each other" (p. 12). The teacher's role changes from being a provider of knowledge to serving as a guide and a cheerleader in the children's process of writing (Calkins, 1986; Murray, 1985).

For the last four decades, research concerning writing has shifted from studying not only the finished text but also the thought processes that lead to the finished text. Dahl and Farnan (1998) state, "Research…suggests that when teachers help students think about and use writing strategies related to writing process, students' writing improves [as does their reading]" (p. 18). This is especially true for the beginning or emergent reader (Clay, 2001).

To understand why writing is so crucial to emergent readers, it is necessary to understand how young children become readers.

Stages of Reading and Emergent Reading Behaviors

Clay (2001) defines reading "as a message-getting, problem-solving activity, which increases in power and flexibility the more it is practiced" (p. 1). Simple theories of reading (literacy) are not sufficient to help beginning and struggling readers become literate (Clay, 1991). Just teaching word attack, using knowledge of sounds to letters, is not enough to teach reading. Reading is about understanding a message, not just pronunciation. Readers use multiple sources of information embedded in the text to read and understand the message. Meaning is not only the result of reading but also the facilitator of reading (Clay, 1991).

There is no specific age to begin teaching reading. Although educators once believed that a child could only begin reading in the first grade, Durkin's (1966) research refuted this concept. Quite a few children from literate homes come to kindergarten already reading; my siblings, my children, and I are living proof of it.

The complex process of learning to read develops over time when children are allowed to use their active, constructive minds as they individually experiment with and explore meaningful print with a knowledgeable literacy teacher to guide their efforts (Calkins, 1994, 2001; Clay, 1991, 2001). This complex reading process develops in three broad stages (Holdaway, 1979; Ministry of Education, New Zealand, 1992; Tompkins & Hoskisson, 1995) as outlined and explained in the next section.

The Three Stages of Reading

Emergent Stage

Children do not suddenly learn to read. Rather, children accumulate knowledge about print and stories as they interact with their world from the time they are born. When they enter school and begin formal literacy instruction, they build on this knowledge, especially their knowledge of language (Clay, 1967; Galda et al., 1997; Morrow & Strickland, 1989). The emergent stage begins early in life, prior to formal schooling, and it is sometimes referred to as the "pretend" stage of reading and writing in which children approximate reading and writing behaviors (Clay, 1991; Morrow, 1989). Clay (1991) explains that four emergent behaviors must be learned and used in relationship with each other (i.e., interrelatedly) for emergent readers to become early readers. These behaviors, which will be discussed in detail later in the chapter, include

> 1. using language abilities,
> 2. understanding basic concepts of print,
> 3. hearing individual sounds in words (phonemic awareness), and
> 4. visually attending to graphic symbols of print.

See Figure 1 for a graphic display of these behaviors.

Early Stage

During the early stage of reading, children understand that their oral language can be represented with written language and they have acquired the alphabetic principle through learning to interrelate Clay's (1991) four emergent reading behaviors within meaningful print. However, they must now learn to interrelate the four cues of reading:

> 1. prior knowledge of a subject,
> 2. semantics (meaning),
> 3. syntax (sentence structure), and
> 4. graphophonics (written symbols of print) (May, 1990).

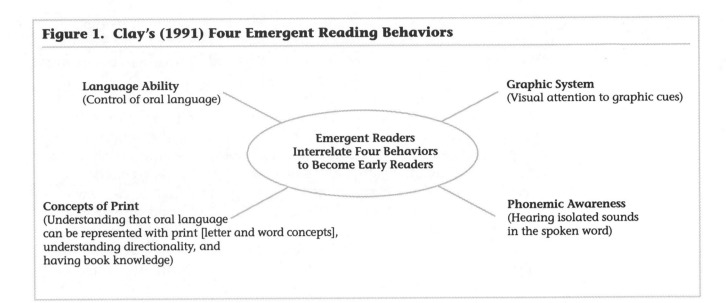

Figure 1. Clay's (1991) Four Emergent Reading Behaviors

Language Ability
(Control of oral language)

Graphic System
(Visual attention to graphic cues)

Emergent Readers
Interrelate Four Behaviors
to Become Early Readers

Concepts of Print
(Understanding that oral language
can be represented with print [letter and word concepts],
understanding directionality, and
having book knowledge)

Phonemic Awareness
(Hearing isolated sounds
in the spoken word)

Being able to interrelate these four cues takes some practice; therefore, early readers' initial attempts at conventional reading are slow, halting, and hopefully include some self-correction for the miscues they often make at this stage. They read aloud, and they need and should be encouraged to point to words as they read (Bear, Invernizzi, Templeton, & Johnston, 2000; Clay, 1991). Clay strongly advises teachers not to be in a hurry to discourage pointing; let the child's active, constructive mind make the decision. During this early stage, teachers must observe the process of reading closely to be sure early readers are using all four cues interrelatedly, or they may become overly dependent on only one or two of them. For example, using some of the cues and ignoring others results in miscues like reading the word *lady* as *woman*.

Fluent Stage
During the fluent stage, children can read silently. They are adept at interrelating the four cues of reading. They develop a variety of reading styles and can read at a conversational rate with appropriate expression. They also can reflect on the message or meaning of their reading (Bear et al., 2000; Clay, 1991; Hudson, Mercer, & Lane, 2000).

When teachers observe their students reading and look for the interrelationship of all four behaviors in emergent readers and all four cues in early and fluent readers, they can begin to understand how the child is processing printed material, which is necessary for implementing the right instruction. Thus, kindergarten and first-grade teachers need to thoroughly understand Clay's (1991) four emergent behaviors.

Clay first observed these emergent behaviors in 1963 when she systematically observed and took note of everything New Zealand school entrants, 5 to 6 years old, said and did as they progressed with reading behaviors. Researchers made notes at school, and mothers kept notes at home. Following this intensive documentation, follow-up observations were made when these children reached the ages of 7 and 8. In 1967, Clay did a longitudinal research study similar to the one done in 1963 with children from very different backgrounds: non-English and English speaking. This study reaffirmed the findings from her earlier study and the importance of interrelating the four emergent reading behaviors. Although it is difficult to observe the interrelationship of the four behaviors in kindergartners' approximated reading, it is possible to observe this interrelationship with their process of writing. For example, when I was conferring with Toby, I noticed he wrote the word *bee* as *de*. If I had only looked at his writing, I would have thought he lacked phonemic awareness and visual attention to graphic cues; however, I heard him say "buh" for the *b* and then print *d*. Because I knew he was capable of using his ABC chart as a strategy when searching for a letter, I said, "Toby, could you show me a *b* on your chart?" He sang the ABC song as he pointed to the letters, and when he came to the *b*, he said, "Oh, yeah. That's it!" and happily made the correction on his own initiative.

An in-depth study of Clay's four emergent reading behaviors and how they are learned is not only necessary but also should be a priority for all educators involved with teaching young children to be literate.

Clay's Emergent Reading Behaviors

Language Ability

Language ability refers to children's control over their oral language. When children learn to talk, they implicitly develop an understanding of the four systems of language: (1) the sound system (phonological), (2) the structural system (syntactic), (3) the meaning system (semantic), and (4) the social or cultural system (pragmatic) (Tompkins & Hoskisson, 1995). These four systems need to be used simultaneously in order for children to talk conventionally. As children develop their language abilities in order to communicate, it is interesting to observe their active, constructive minds working out the interrelationship of these four systems. For example, Hanah, my 1-year-old grandchild, lacking full-blown sentence structure, communicates whole sentences with one or only a few words. Her favorite phrases are "All done" and "der you go." In the case of *der* for *there*, Hanah is also still working on the phonological or sound system of language. Her parents delight in her talk and encourage her to talk more. They do not say, "No, the word isn't *der*, it's *there*." The only form of tutoring they use is to repeat the approximated word correctly with delight. A lot of miscued words are simply allowed because Hanah's parents know and can expect that Hanah will work it out for herself eventually with more time spent in meaningful conversations.

Young children move through a series of developmental stages as they learn to use these systems to the best of their ability to meet their needs (Galda, Cullinan, & Strickland, 1997; Glazer, 1980; Halliday, 1978). In a period of three to four years, children master the exceedingly complex system of their native language. They can understand sentences they have never heard before and create sentences they have never said before. Learning language is a byproduct of pursuing some other purpose—for example, wanting a cookie or a toy and needing a way to request it.

Language is not learned simply by imitation (Temple et al., 1988). While partially true, just imitating speech does not help us develop the ability to interrelate sounds, meaning, syntax, and our knowledge of the social and linguistic rules that govern our language (Galda et al., 1997). Children's minds are very active as they try to figure out (construct) the complexities of speech. Temple et al. (1988) explains this process:

> They attempt—through a sort of gradual [developmental] trial and error process—to construct a system of rules that will allow them to produce sentences like those they hear others use. "Rules" [generalizations] is used in a loose sense, they are not consciously saying to themselves: "Hmm...whenever I mean more than one, I must put an S on the end of the noun. Yet some sort of unspoken assumption close to this must have been made or else why would the three year old boy say 'gooses' and 'foots.'" (p. 3)

Children's language is extremely important to reading because the more they know about language and the more their vocabulary is developed, the better they can comprehend and predict during the reading and writing processes (Clay, 1991; Galda et al., 1997; Roth, Speece, & Cooper, 2002). It is the first emergent reading behavior that Clay (1991) emphasizes because it has "two powerful bases for prediction: its structures and its meanings" (p. 235). A third base exists in the sound system of language, but children are not conscious of using this system except for their use of inflection and rhyming (Clay, 1991)—until they are taught to be conscious of isolating individual sounds, or phonemes, which will be discussed more in this chapter.

Galda and colleagues (1997) describe and laud the many opportunities for language enhancement that exist in a writing workshop: Language abilities are greatly enhanced in individual writing conferences as the young author talks and writes about his or her chosen topic with guidance from a knowledgeable literacy teacher. The teacher is able to praise the child's approximations by facing the child and repeating phrases to the child with interest and correct pronunciation, when necessary. Talking one on one with a proficient language provider is the best way to learn language (Clay, 1991).

As children work independently in a writing workshop, they talk to themselves to guide their writing as they communicate meaning, and they learn that print can represent their speech. They talk to others to seek help in this endeavor, too (Galda et al., 1997). Talk is also encouraged when some writers share their work with the entire class and receive encouraging feedback, otherwise known as Author's Chair. Galda and colleagues (1997) explain that young authors are not told to write silently (but quietly) because they need to "talk to support their language learning as they take chances and grow as writers" (p. 189). Children's daily speech strongly influences the fluency with which they will read and write (Galda et al., 1997).

Clay (1991) informs educators,

> If children have been slow to acquire speech or offered fewer opportunities to have conversations (for many different reasons), or have had health problems...[that has affected their] auditory discrimination of sounds, words, and sentence structures... when learning to read these children can have particular difficulty in breaking up language into its parts or in synthesizing sounds into whole words. (p. 38)

This is also true for learning to write, but writing is beneficial for this problem (Clay, 2001).When children understand that writing is for recording a message based on their oral language, they understand that reading is also about understanding a message based on the author's oral language (Clay, 1991; Galda et al., 1997). If children have not had the daily opportunity of writing in a writing workshop, they may not apply their oral language skills (prior knowledge, semantics, and syntax) to reading and become overly dependent on using the cue of graphophonics alone (Clay, 2001).

Clay (1991, p. 15) provides an example of such a reader: A failing young reader, being tested as he read a paragraph, was to point to each word in the paragraph and say "Yes" or "No" to indicate his ability to read the word(s). When he came to the end of the paragraph he said, "I can read [the word] 'bear,' but I can't read [the word] 'polar.'" He did not understand the value of using his oral language abilities to predict the author's message.

A writing workshop promotes and requires prediction and teaches children to use their oral language as a base to predict both their writing and reading (Clay, 2001). Because children want to communicate meaning and are guided by a knowledgeable literacy teacher as they write in writing workshop, they learn that print represents oral language. Clay (2001) sums up the symbiotic relationship between writing and oral language as follows: As children work toward composing a simple message in writing, "oral language is both a resource and a beneficiary" (p. 95).

Concepts of Print

For young children to be able to think about and understand that sounds, letters, and words can represent oral speech, they need to develop certain basic understandings about print. These understandings are called concepts of print, the second emergent reading behavior noted by Clay. Tompkins and Hoskisson (1995) state the three types of concepts of print that must be acquired:

1. Book orientation concepts—Students learn how to handle a book and turn its pages properly, and learn that print, not the pictures, carries the message.

2. Directional concepts—Students learn that print is written and read from left to right whether it is a word, line, or page, and from top to bottom on a page.

3. Letter and word concepts—Students learn to identify letter names and match upper- and lowercase letters. They also learn that words are composed of letters; sentences are composed of words; spaces mark boundaries between words and sentences; and capital letters highlight the first word in a sentence.

The concept of word is very difficult to understand for many beginning kindergartners. Papandroupolou and Sinclair's (1974) research with 102 students ages 4–10 supports this statement. Initially, the youngest children in this study did not appear to make any distinction between words and things. Young children think objects, but also actions, are words because the objects or actions that words refer to really exist. When children were asked, "What is a word?" they gave the following answers: "Strawberry, because it grows in the garden" (4.9 yrs.) and "Pencil, because it writes" (4.8 yrs.). Another child answered, "A word, that's saying something...." Then the child said, "'The' is not a word, because you'd need something else, a truck." But when the researcher asked if a truck was a word, the child answered, "No the truck that's not enough, for a word you need two things...the truck...well, it goes" (5.4 yrs.).

Templeton (1980) provides a developmental example of two children's reactions to the concept of word:

> When asked if "dog" were a word, a four year old...jumped up...began barking ferociously, and charged through the house panting and woofing. Confronted with the same question, an eight year old responded, "Of course 'dog' is a word..." [and explained] the word "dog" stood for a particular kind of animal. (p. 454)

Understanding the concept of directionality is also difficult for young children. Although some children learn directionality quickly, probably because many stories have been read to them and the print pointed to, Clay (1979) informs teachers, "It takes the average child nearly six months to establish consistency in this behavior" (p. 131). Clay (1991) explains why:

> Until he reached school, the child was free to scan objects, people, scenes, pictures and even books, in any direction that he chose.... [However, when he tried to read and write, he discovered] there are one-way routes to be learned. He must learn to go from a top-left position across to the right and then to return to the next top-left position after a downward movement and again go across to the right. (p. 95)

The child knows a chair in any position is a chair, but letters, words, and print require one position. For example, when Larry first used the lowercase letter *d*, he could hear the correct phoneme and he knew the letter's form. However, his mind alone did not have a stable enough image of the letter's directional constraints, so he often represented the letter *d* as a *p* or a *b*.

With experience and the use of his individual ABC chart in writing workshop, Larry learned how to write *d* correctly.

Clay (1991) also believes the terms teachers use for positions of letters and words in print, like *first, last, beginning, start, end,* and *next,* can be confusing concepts to the child when applied to print. Teachers need to explain these terms as they demonstrate them, and they must be consistent in how they use the terms or the desired learning will not take place. (See chapter 4, p. 122, for the Elkonin Sound Boxes strategy, which can be used to teach positional terms.)

Reid (1966) and Downing (1970) found that children learn concepts of print slowly over the first year at school through meaningful reading and writing activities. Following the claims of Reid and Downing—that children learn letters before words and words before sentences, and these concepts are learned after the children are already reading—one can derive a developmental progression of how children learn concepts of print. It is the experience of reading that helped them learn the concepts and not vice versa (Clay, 2001; Durkin, 1987; Harste et al., 1981; Temple et al., 1988). Clay (1991, 2001) states that it is imperative to foster children's desire to explore writing at the same time that they are exploring reading to enhance their understanding of concepts of print because writing teaches concepts as one learns to write, not after they are already writing.

By modeling writing and minilessons in a writing workshop, teachers can provide many meaningful opportunities to teach and reinforce concepts of print. For example, children can make their own books to learn how print is arranged in books and other reading materials. They also learn the concept that their oral language can be represented by print and read by others.

Through examining students' writing, teachers can determine whether or not children understand directionality and the alphabetic principle, but teachers may only get a rough idea of what students understand about the concept of word (Bear et al., 2000; Clay, 1991; Temple et al., 1988). Leaving spaces between words is a highly abstract procedure for children to manage; it has to do with the "negative" use of space—a difficult concept even for adults. Children will often improvise some kind of demarcation (e.g., dots, lines) between words; it is easier for them to fill the space ("positive use of space") than use "negative space" (Temple et al., 1988). If no demarcation exists between words, Bear and colleagues (2000) recommend that teachers observe students' written words for initial and final consonants because this probably indicates a concept of word. To facilitate the concept of word, teachers should encourage students to point to their words as they read, especially in their writing in Author's Chair. This is beneficial to developing one-to-one correspondence between oral language and print and cementing a concept of word; Clay (1991) refers to this as "reading the spaces" (p. 164).

Writing is invaluable to teaching concepts of print because writing allows the teacher to teach these abstract concepts in a nonverbal manner, rather than through explanations that young children do not understand.

Demonstrations often are more helpful than explanations. Also, children are afforded the opportunity to use the concepts on their own initiative and at their own pace before they have to learn to talk about them (Clay, 1991).

Phonemic Awareness

Phonemic awareness, the third emergent reading behavior noted by Clay, is defined in its simplest terms by Ball and Blachman (1991) as "the ability to recognize that a spoken word consists of a sequence of individual sounds [phonemes]" (p. 51). Not knowing the definition of phonemic awareness has caused some educators, including myself, to initially confuse phonemic awareness with phonics. Clay (1991) addresses the distinction between phonemic awareness and phonics:

> A strategy of analyzing spoken words into sounds [phonemic awareness] and then going from those sounds to letters [via invented spelling] may be a precursor of the ability to utilize....phonics [letters to sounds]. And many children may not need phonics instruction once they acquire and use a sound sequence analysis [phonemic awareness] strategy. (p. 85)

Other educators have mistakenly believed that phonemic awareness is the same as phonological awareness. However, phonological awareness, one of the four systems of language, refers to a sensitivity to *any* size unit of sound—such as the ability to hear and rhyme words, count syllables, separate words into onset and rime, and identify each of the phonemes in a word. Thus, phonemic awareness, the ability to identify each of the phonemes in a word, is a *subset* of phonological awareness.

In the 1970s and 1980s, researchers began to study phonemic awareness. They began to think it might be the missing link to teaching reading (literacy)—not because it was more important than Clay's other three emergent reading behaviors, but because it had not been understood and, therefore, not taught.

After Clay (1979) emphasized the importance of phonemic awareness, Bradley and Bryant conducted a two-year research project (1983) that revealed that children who are poor readers tend to be lower in phonemic awareness than in any other factor related to reading. Bradley and Bryant's study seemed to initiate many other phonemic awareness studies. For example, the Lundberg study (Lundberg, Frost, & Peterson, 1988) reported that poor readers entering first grade without phonemic awareness remained poor readers with little understanding of the alphabetic principle at the end of the fourth grade if, by then, they still lacked phonemic awareness skills. According to Morris, Bloodgood, Lomax, and Perney (2003), another benefit of phonemic awareness is that it enables readers to monitor or check their sound-to-letter expectations, which leads to self-correction. This increased independence in both searching and monitoring strategies is sorely needed by beginning and struggling readers.

In addition, Chall (1983) and Gough and Tunmer (1986) report that their studies have shown phonemic awareness does not develop in some children unless explicitly taught; indeed this may also be the missing link in reading acquisition for the child who eventually becomes diagnosed as learning disabled. Cunningham (1990) informs teachers that "the degree of improvement in the reading ability in first grade children depended strongly on the *type* [italics added] of phonemic instruction received" (p. 442). The Lundberg study (Lundberg et al., 1988) showed that phonemic awareness training based on the use of songs and playful language (literature readings, and games and riddles that deal playfully with the sounds of language through rhyme, manipulation of phonemes, alliteration, and assonance) had better transfer value to the act of reading than skill-and-drill activities. Other researchers agree (Griffith & Olson, 1992).

A good way for all children to practice transference of sounds to visual symbols, once they can hear individual sounds and can recognize most of their letters, is to use inventive spelling (Chomsky, 1979; Griffith & Olson, 1992; Yopp, 1992). Invented spelling does not correspond to conventional spelling; instead, words are spelled the way they sound. For example, *you* might be spelled as *u*. Young children would not be able to write without invented spelling. It is essential to the development and practice of phonemic awareness (Clay, 1991, 2001). Indeed, Gillet and Temple (1990) state that "invented spelling, when measured as a test of phonemic segmentation in kindergarten, significantly predicted reading ability in first grade" (p. 105).

Clay (1991) asks, "How can we get young children to *want* to hear the sound segments in words and to *search* [italics added] for these on their own initiative?" (p. 86). Writing workshop (according to Cambourne's conditions, 1988) provides purpose and *engagement* for young authors to want to write and thereby use their phonemic awareness abilities (Richgels, 1995). Therefore, Routman (2000) states, "The most effective kindergarten and first-grade teachers demonstrate and promote daily writing as well as verbal word play" (p. 101). (See Appendix A for phonemic awareness activities.)

Early writing and reading cannot begin properly without an understanding of the alphabetic principle. Writing with invented spelling in writing workshop helps early writers and readers practice the alphabetic principle (sound-to-letter relationships) in a developmentally appropriate manner, and it allows the teacher to get a rough idea of what children are thinking as they learn to write and read. Writing with invented spelling is the "stepping stone" to early reading. Phonemic awareness is best taught, then, with playful language (see phonemic awareness activities in Appendix A) and practiced when children use invented spelling in writing workshop.

Visual Attention to Graphic Cues

The fourth emergent reading behavior is looking at and paying attention to written or graphic cues. Clay (1991, 2001) lists the graphic cues that the beginning reader may be attending to: shape or features of letters (e.g., dots or tails hanging down); clusters of letters; sequence of letters; certain letters; certain words; repeated phrases; spaces; punctuation; and arrangement of text in short lines, illustrations, or both. To read conventionally, emergent readers must learn to differentiate each letter and each graphic cue that is unknown from those already known, which they do slowly at first.

Emergent readers tend to look at print as a whole at first, and only much later do they look at the individual parts of print (Clay, 1975). They do not learn to be sensitive to graphemes (written letters) by learning letters one by one but by first becoming sensitive to the features of graphemes in meaningful written language (Temple et al., 1988).

Emergent readers only attend to some features of print until they gain familiarity with them (Temple et al., 1988). Juel (1991) calls this the Selective-Cue stage, during which children first recognize words by attending to the environment in which the words are placed (e.g., a stop sign), or they may use selected print but nonalphabetic features of the word (e.g., two circles in moon). Using selected print is explained by Ehri (2002) as the Prealphabetic stage of emergent reading, during which there is no understanding of the alphabetic principle. For example, a child may identify the word *monkey* solely from associating the letter *y* with a monkey's tail. This causes some confusion when, by the same reasoning, the child may also identify the word *pony* as *monkey* (Ehri, 2002).

In Ehri's next stage of reading, the Partial Alphabetic stage, readers understand that sounds and letters are related, but they are not able to make complete use of letter–sound relations (alphabetic principle). Thus, they concentrate on the most salient parts of a word, usually initial letters first and then final letters. An example of this is identifying the word *boat* by focusing on the first letter *b* and the sound it represents (/b/) to identify the word; however, with this limited focus, *bat* and *bunny* might also be identified as *boat* (Clay, 2001). Ehri's third stage of reading, the Fully Alphabetic stage, requires children to have become more familiar with letters and sounds. Even though they might not have seen the word *mug* before, they know the sounds commonly associated with the letters, and they can pronounce the word. (If *mug* is in their speaking vocabulary, they will also understand its meaning. Simply pronouncing a word with no understanding of its meaning is not reading.)

It is the careful processing of graphic cues in the Fully Alphabetic stage that leads to Ehri's fourth and final stage, the Consolidated Alphabetic stage. At this stage, readers store words as units and repeated encounters with words allow them to store letter patterns across words. For example, knowing the words *sent* and *went* will allow the reader to connect the letter pattern *ent* (rime) to *d* (onset) and pronounce the new word *dent* without having to sound out every letter of *dent*. In a syllable like *dent*, the onset is the letter *d*, and the rime is the vowel and the letters that follow it, *ent*. Johnston (1999) states, "Rimes are the basic units for reading and spelling words by analogy" (p. 66). Other researchers agree (Gaskins et al., 1988; Gaskins, Ehri, Cress, O'Hara, & Donnelly, 1997).

Children's early reading is dysfluent until they gain the ability to explore all the details in words and letter patterns quickly. Also, children need to increase their sight recognition of words through practice with meaningful reading and writing because it is even faster than blending patterns of words. To do this fluently usually takes several years, and it takes approximated writing and reading in the early years (Clay, 1991, 2001). Initially, reading requires familiar picture books; the print in these books should offer only minimal challenge and be predictable (using rhyme, rhythm, and repetition).

Adults tend to forget how much information (interrelating the four emergent reading behaviors and then the four cues while focusing on meaning) has been used when they read because much of this information is automatic for them. However, all of these perceptions take conscious effort on the part of the emergent or early reader. Teachers need to discover what children know and need to know as they become literate. Children's writing can show the teacher where perceptions about reading are going wrong (Clay, 2001).

As children write independently and at their own pace, they are taught and guided to visually attend to all the graphic symbols, and teachers are able to discover what graphic symbols they know and what they need to learn. As kindergartners attempt to communicate their thoughts in writing, their writing develops in the following general manner: They move away from using scribbles to using a few uppercase letters, and then they add some lowercase letters. Next, they attempt to write words with letters, and finally they attempt to write full sentences—both individual words and words in sentences will be spelled with invented spelling (Calkins, 1994; Clay, 1975; Gentry & Gillet, 1993; Schickedanz, 1990)—until they reach the middle to end of third grade or fourth grade. Then invented spelling becomes conventional spelling (Routman, 1991).

In writing workshop, children experiment and progress from using periods anywhere on the paper, to the end of a line of writing, to finally using them at the end of a sentence, which takes many years to develop properly (Temple et al., 1988). With a knowledgeable literacy teacher guiding their progress, they begin to learn about other end-of-the-sentence markers, too, such as question marks and exclamation points (Tompkins & Hoskisson, 1995). Learning about these graphic cues and what they mean in writing also enhances children's early reading and later fluent reading.

Individual writing is essential to get children to attend to print, especially low literacy achievers and those who rely heavily on memorization (Clay, 2001). Clay (2001) explains, "It is mandatory in writing to write letter by letter, so this is a naturally-occurring training situation" (p. 22). In addition, "When writing we attend to every feature of every letter in correct sequence and to words in text, one after the other, and to composing language (just as we do in reading)" (pp. 91–92).

In summary, language abilities must interrelate with concepts of print, phonemic awareness, and graphic cues as young children actively construct knowledge about literacy with their teacher's guidance (Clay, 1991). It is a teacher's job to assess what children know about integrating these four emergent reading behaviors so the children can be guided to use their strengths to teach their weaknesses.

Requirements for Effective Teaching of Literacy

Literacy is a process that begins long before formal schooling and continues into adulthood. Literacy involves thinking, listening, speaking, writing, and reading (Tompkins & Hoskisson, 1995). Children learn to talk not simply by imitating language but by constructing a set of rules that enable them to produce and understand sentences as they engage in meaningful conversation with and communicate their needs to proficient language users (Clay, 1991; Galda et al., 1997). In the 1970s, Cambourne carefully observed children becoming successful language users. Although there are many conditions that contribute to this amazing accomplishment of learning to talk, Cambourne (1988) explains that seven conditions are most relevant to learning language.

The Seven Conditions of Learning Language

When children are immersed in meaningful language with proficient language users who demonstrate language, they should be given the time to use and the responsibility to choose what to say and what conventions to master. Children's approximations should be given positive and encouraging responses. Then, it can be expected that children will learn to talk. These seven conditions—immersion, demonstration, approximation, time or use, responsibility, encouraging response, and expectation—are the major characteristics of developmental learning (Holdaway, 1979). When these conditions are present, the child's own constructive mind "acts as an amazingly sensitive teaching machine" (Holdaway, 1979, p. 23). These conditions should be seriously considered when children are learning to write and read. Keeping this thought in mind, Holdaway (1979) asks educators, "What explanation can we give for the continuing difficulties experienced by so many children in learning the tasks of literacy? Are reading and writing intrinsically more difficult even than learning to talk?" (p. 11).

To answer Holdaway's questions, it is necessary to look more closely at Cambourne's (1988) conditions of learning language and think about the implications they have for learning to read and write. Although the stage for language learning is set with immersion and demonstration, these conditions should interrelate, and there is no particular order to my discussion of them.

Immersion

From the moment a baby is born, it is hoped that he or she is immersed in a flood of meaningful language demonstrated by proficient users of the language. For the first five years of the child's life, his or her oral language is entirely dependent on what and how much people say to the child—and what kind of responses are given to the child's approximations. Children develop language abilities as they actively use language to learn about their world. Galda and colleagues (1997) explain that parents generally know their children so well that they help them to "link new ideas about language to those that already exist in their conceptual frameworks" (p. 23).

When teaching emergent literacy, teachers should saturate, or immerse, children in and expose them to meaningful print in the classroom through meaningful reading and writing. Nursery rhymes, songs, poems, and stories need to be read on a daily basis; some of these texts should be posted in the classroom, along with children's names, and objects in the room should be labeled. This posted print, reread and referred to often, helps link new ideas about reading and writing to those that already exist in the children's minds. The children should also be allowed to explore and experiment with writing and reading on a daily basis in any way they can (Morrow, 1989).

Demonstration

In the process of learning to talk, young children receive thousands of meaningful whole demonstrations of speech, not little bits and pieces. For example, perhaps a young child sees and hears his older brother ask for a cookie, and then he sees his mother give his brother one. As he sees this kind of meaningful modeling repeatedly, he learns to choose and adopt the conventions he needs to talk.

When teaching emergent literacy, teachers need to demonstrate on a daily basis how one learns to read and write. For example, pointing to the words in a shared book experience is a good way to begin the process of demonstrating reading. Writing should be demonstrated daily as the teacher uses his or her own writing as examples during the minilesson part of writing workshop. Other good methods of demonstrating writing—such as the language experience approach, shared writing, and interactive writing—should be utilized, too.

Once children demonstrate in their writing that they can interrelate the four emergent reading behaviors and that they understand the alphabetic principle, teachers should demonstrate and begin guided early reading in a reading workshop. Prior to this time, reading should be about approximation (i.e., pretending).

Approximation

Young children use approximations, or come close to saying actual words, at first. Children do not pronounce the words perfectly, and parents should reward them both for their attempts and for being right. All children make errors in speech as they are learning to talk. It is a sign of remarkable progress when children say *writed* because this shows that they have acquired a rule for past-tense verb endings that is often used in English. Children need to be praised for such approximations, even though they applied the rule incorrectly (Clay, 1991). Parents know that they can expect that attempts will become correct over time if they respond with joyful enthusiasm to the message of the sentence and repeat the incorrect word correctly (e.g., "Oh, you *wrote* about the kitty? How wonderful, let me see your writing!").

When teaching emergent literacy, teachers should allow children to use approximations when writing and reading. Teachers cannot expect young children to get reading and writing attempts correct on the first try. As children become writers and readers, they will pretend to write and read. Initially, they will make errors because they must weigh everything they are learning against what they have already learned. Looking for what is correct in their approximated attempts to interrelate the four emergent reading behaviors, and eventually the four cues of early reading, requires teachers to guide young children from what they know to what they need to know. This is the challenge for literacy teachers (Clay, 1991).

Employment or Use

Parents do not force children to wait until it is "talking time" two or three days a week to have experiences with language. Teachers too should allow students plenty of opportunities to independently use meaningful speech, reading, and writing every day. As Clay (1991) states, "Children need frequent opportunities to test the rules of language that they are discovering" (p. 70); they will attempt to hold an adult's attention as they do so.

When teaching emergent literacy, teachers should allow children plenty of time to practice writing and reading independently with some teacher guidance. Kindergarten teachers should make writing and reading workshops of approximation a priority every day. In fact, Graves (1994) explains that if a writing workshop cannot be employed at least four days a week for 35–40 minutes, it should not be done at all because writers need to be in a constant state of composition to learn and grow as writers.

Responsibility

Children should be able to decide what topic and what conventions of language to master based on their needs. Children should be responsible for the direction and assessment of their own language learning. However, how well they will be able to follow their direction or assess the correctness of their developing language ability is dependent on the availability of a proficient language user to scaffold and guide their language needs.

When teaching emergent literacy, teachers should allow children some choice in writing (and reading) so they are engaged with the print. Choice is also essential to writing with "voice," or a personal style. Writers cannot show their insights and feelings about a topic that they care little about. When writers care about their writing, they want to make it better. Thus, it makes sense to teach children self-monitoring strategies in reading and writing so they can take some responsibility in assessing their developing literacy abilities. (See the strategy minilessons "Choosing Topics," "Identifying Good Writing Traits," and "Choosing My Best Writing" in chapter 6, pp. 212, 215, and 218, for self-monitoring strategies.)

Feedback or Response

Cambourne (1987) asks, "How do we get young children who say 'Yesterday, I goed downtown' [to progress to] 'Yesterday, I went downtown?'" (p. 9). He explains that feedback or response of a special kind is necessary. When a parent receives this message, he or she says, "You went downtown? When you went downtown, what did you do?" The message is received, acknowledged positively, and it is repeated in correct, expanded form in a noncritical, accepting manner.

When teaching emergent literacy in reading and writing workshops, teachers should acknowledge writing and reading approximations in a positive manner as parents do when their children learn to talk. A correcting or tutoring approach to language is fraught with danger. If parents were to correct every "approximated" word that their children use, the children would become afraid to try to talk, and thus their ability to do so would be severely hampered. For example, when my daughter said, "The kitty bited me," I did not say, "No, that's wrong. It's *bit* me." She might not have kept trying to actively construct language if I'd done that. Covington (1992) explains that children can become "failure acceptors." These children took risks in learning when they were young, and when they weren't successful (in the conventional way), they were condescendingly corrected for it. Soon they lost the confidence to keep trying because they didn't want to risk the pain again. Confidence is the key to success in learning (Stiggens, 2001). Teachers, like parents, need to be cheerleaders and encourage young students' approximated attempts to write and read. It is through trying and appropriate, encouraging feedback that children want to learn.

Expectation

When teaching emergent literacy, do teachers truly expect all children to be able to write and read? When teachers use writing workshops—and reading workshops—that implement Cambourne's (1988) conditions of learning language, they can *expect* that children will be able to write and read, just as they learned to talk. Clay (1991) explains:

> [Teachers] must do more than provide the child with stimulating experiences and opportunities for growth. If she [the teacher] works alongside a child letting him do all that he can, but supporting the [literacy] activity when he reaches some limit by sharing the task she is more likely to uncover the cutting edges of his learning. (pp. 65–66)

In this way the teacher will be able to provide the most valuable instruction for children to make good progress in their process of learning to write and read.

Cambourne (1988) states that all children can be literate in the fullest sense of the word if teachers transfer his seven conditions of language learning to the classroom for teaching writing and reading. Graves (1994) agrees and cites the use of these conditions in renowned writing teacher Nancie Atwell's classroom as being the reason for her remarkable work. Because Cambourne's conditions (1988) are essential for literacy learning, writing workshop is based on them as well.

How Writing Workshop Employs Cambourne's Conditions of Language Learning

Writing should be taught within the context of meaningful, authentic writing opportunities that teach it as a process. Graves (1994) described writing as a process and Calkins (1994) developed the writing workshop around Cambourne's (1988) seven conditions of language learning. Writing workshop is the only writing structure or approach that is designed to incorporate all of Cambourne's conditions; these are the same "right" conditions that Clay (1991) refers to when she discusses becoming literate.

Clay (1991) states, "Because of what we know about language acquisition, we have to accept that children can be active constructors of their own language competencies [and learning]…provided conditions are right for them" (p. 61). These conditions provide support for the children and their teacher to facilitate the children's attempts to teach themselves as they experiment with and explore print (Clay, 1991). This is, in essence, a description of writing workshop.

In support of writing workshops, Ray and Cleaveland (2004) ask and answer their own question:

> Why do we believe a daily, hour-long writing workshop is essential for our teaching of writing to young children? The answer to this question really comes down to a belief that two things are essential for children's development as writers: *experience and teaching* [italics added]. A writing workshop creates a space for both to happen naturally, side by side. (pp. 23–24)

In a writing workshop, teachers immerse children in independent, meaningful writing on a daily basis. Kindergartners are allowed the responsibility to practice writing on their own initiative, with minimal guidance from their teacher and classmates. In a writing workshop, kindergartners are allowed to choose their own topics and are taught to be responsible and to assess their own work.

Choice is a powerful motivator; it affects students' desire to read and write, understanding of the goals of literacy, and self-regulation as a writer–reader (Graves, 1994; Schiefele, 1991). When students select their own topics that have personal value to them, they are more likely to use learning strategies rather than shortcuts such as copying or guessing. Choice allows students the chance to make decisions about organizing information and creating unique products. It provides engagement to do the laborious parts of writing (and reading). As students write, they are encouraged to communicate and discuss their topics of choice with other children and their teacher using the best approximations they can. Their finished approximated work can be responded to positively by their classmates and teacher through sharing during Author's Chair, posting their work on walls and bulletin boards, or publishing their edited work as short books, if desired.

Writing workshop is an open-ended structure, and students will make miscues as they experiment. Encouraging approximated responses is most important. Almost-correct approximations should be praised for being nearly right. Incorrect approximations should not be reinforced. Errors should not be seen as evidence of failure but as evidence of insufficient learning. For students to adapt their strategies rather than give up, mistakes need to be treated as pathways to learning by the students and their teacher (Cambourne, 1988; Clay, 2001; Holdaway, 1979).

When teachers demonstrate their own writing for their students and confer individually with them, teachers guide their students' writing efforts. By repeating what children tell them in conferences, praising, and guiding children's approximated efforts to write, teachers help children develop as writers and readers (Vygotsky, 1934/1986). When all seven conditions are in place, teachers can expect kindergartners to become literate. I can attest to this, and so would the more than 60 kindergarten teachers with whom I've had the good fortune to work.

Many of the kindergarten teachers with whom I worked were originally using the letter-of-the week approach and journaling to teach literacy. The letter-of-the-week approach did not employ Cambourne's conditions nor did it teach literacy as a process. Although the letter-of-the-week approach can teach children to recognize letters in isolation, this knowledge often does not transfer to reading and writing text that makes sense, especially for lower achieving students. Clay (2001) agrees and states,

> Teaching letters, sounds, words and isolated skills first, while downplaying the need to work at understanding messages, does not seem to impede the progress of proficient learners, but could make it harder for some learners to incorporate the (hidden) linguistic relationships into the patterning of processing at some later time. (p. 93)

Becoming literate cannot be learned in isolation. "Building a literacy processing system only begins when a child is expected to compose and write a simple message or read a simple continuous text" (Clay, 2001, p. 97), and this independent process needs "*explicit daily teacher guidance* [italics added]" (Routman, 2000, p. 234).

Journaling is an independent method of writing. While there are various types of journals, most young children usually begin journaling in personal journals. Personal journals are like diary writing, and they are not intended for display (Tompkins & Hoskisson, 1995). Personal journaling is what most of the teachers with whom I worked promoted. Because the concept of personal journaling did not require teachers to have an understanding of the process of writing or use all of Cambourne's conditions as writing workshop does, for the most part, kindergartners' process of writing did not improve.

There are several useful methods to teach the process of writing to emergent readers and writers such as language experience approach, shared writing, and interactive writing. However, writing workshop is the only approach that allows children to be "active constructors of their own learning" as they explore print for themselves with a knowledgeable literacy teacher offering minimal guidance (Clay, 1991, p. 61). Writing workshop allows each child to think creatively and be guided to write his or her own way into understanding print. Group writing situations do not support this individual thinking, and they do not allow the teacher to know what the individual is thinking or learning (Clay, 1991, 2001).

As Clay (2001) states, "Often the child's attention is not where the teacher expects it to be" (p. 19). The writing workshop approach provides a daily assessment that enables the teacher to learn what each child knows and is learning about literacy. No other writing method or approach does this. Comparing kindergartners' writing samples from one day to the next shows teachers what children are learning and how effective the teachers' writing instruction is every day (Clay, 2001; Ray & Cleveland, 2004). Dated writing samples not only guide teachers' instruction but also provide verification of students' literacy progress (Clay, 1993a). Formal tests also will show the same results as writing samples. However, the best form of verification is watching children as they happily write and read their own work.

Summary

Educators have not always understood what young children know about writing (and reading)—especially how they learn to be literate—and literacy instruction has suffered because of this lack of knowledge. Emergent literacy research has opened educators' eyes to two extremely important understandings regarding instruction:

1. Children use their active, constructive minds (with minimal guidance from proficient language users) to figure out how to write (and read), just like they have figured out how to talk.

2. Guided, conventional early reading, which requires the interrelation of four cues, should not begin until children have demonstrated

control of interrelating four emergent reading behaviors in their approximated writing.

For all children to learn the alphabetic principle and become literate, kindergarten entrants need to be allowed and encouraged to write and read in any way they can at first. This means implementing writing and reading workshops based on Cambourne's (1988) conditions of learning language in which process and approximations are valued and guided. Reading and writing need to be concurrent sources in learning about print because development in one area of literacy relates to and advances the development in other areas. Writing enhances reading and reading enhances writing, and they both enhance spelling and formation of letters of the alphabet. The next chapter provides a discussion of developmentally appropriate learning that focuses on letter formation and spelling.

Developmental Letter Formation and Developmental Stages of Spelling

As Ms. Kitell, a kindergarten teacher, observes her students' writing, she is concerned because many of her students are not leaving spaces between their words. She wonders, Is this developmentally appropriate behavior?

Before a teacher can determine whether or not teaching word spacing to a student is appropriate, the teacher must know the *individual* child's current stage of thinking about print. Then, the teacher needs to provide encouragement, modeling, and instruction that are directed toward that stage (Temple et al., 1988).

According to Holdaway (1979), developmental learning involves the same characteristics or conditions as learning language (for a list and description of these conditions, see chapter 1, pp. 21–25). Two of these conditions—expectation and responsibility—need to be emphasized when discussing developmental learning: (1) "development tends to proceed continuously in an orderly sequence [but there are] considerable differences from individual to individual" and (2) "what aspect of the task will be practiced, at what pace, and for how long is determined largely by the learner" (p. 23). For students to learn to write and read at their developmental level, teachers need to find a place where they can "begin using something the child can do and moving out from there in whatever directions the learner can go in both writing and reading" (Clay, 2001, p. 17). This is referred to by Routman (1991) as relating the "known to the unknown" (p. 144). To better understand this concept, it is necessary to have some understanding of how a child learns to talk.

When children learn to talk, they do not simply imitate what they hear. Instead, they appear to be constructing a set of generalizations based on what they know about language (known) to understand and produce words and sentences they've never heard (unknown) (Temple et al., 1988). With encouragement and minimal guidance from proficient language users, they revise their generalizations as their needs dictate. As this learning develops, considerable differences can be observed from one child to the next; therefore, this learning is of a highly independent and noncompetitive developmental nature. Although this development proceeds continuously in an orderly sequence, sometimes it is perfectly natural for a period of regression to occur where a child reverts briefly to a lower stage (Holdaway, 1979).

Holdaway (1979) informs teachers that the way children develop oral language can be used as a developmental model for all literacy learning. His model is an abbreviated form of Cambourne's (1988) conditions of learning language, and it "includes only cooperation, acceptance, approval, and an invitation to join in" (Routman, 1991, p. 11). Routman (1991) explains, "Implicit in Holdaway's model are teachers as real readers and writers; a curriculum and materials that are interesting, meaningful, whole, and relevant to the learners; and a safe, nurturing environment that promotes social interaction and collaboration" (p. 11).

When Holdaway's model for learning literacy is not utilized, the student is often forced into a predesignated literacy program that proves unsuccessful (Clay, 1991; Routman, 1991). Morrow (1989) explains why: "Problems arise when the developmental, social, and natural environments in which literacy flourishes are exchanged for a systematic presentation of skills that do not reflect a child's stage of development socially, emotionally, physically, or intellectually" (p. 15).

Developmental literacy learning emphasizes instruction designed for the individual student's needs wherever he or she happens to be in the developmental literacy process of meaningful communication (Cambourne, 1988; Clay, 1991; Holdaway, 1979). It focuses on using a child's strengths to teach his or her weaknesses (Routman, 1991), and it capitalizes on Cambourne's conditions of learning language.

Letter Formation Is Developmental

In virtually every kindergarten in which I have served as a literacy coach, the question of teaching letter formation has arisen. Well-intentioned first-grade teachers often demand that formal or proper letter formation be taught in kindergarten because they do not understand the concepts of developmentally appropriate instruction and approximation. Therefore, kindergarten teachers often feel forced to set aside time in their busy schedules to teach proper letter formation.

Morrow (1989) informs teachers that although "[w]riting requires dexterity...it is unnecessary and often unwise to bog down preschoolers and kindergartners with the particulars of proper letter formation" (p. 166). Rather, she suggests that they be encouraged to use self-stimulating manipulatives (e.g., puzzles and sewing cards) to strengthen their fine motor coordination.

There are two impediments to mastering letter formation. First, when taught separately from meaningful writing, it is boring and laborious; however, writing workshop brings motivation and reward to this tedious task (Holdaway, 1979). Based on the findings from the 1978–1980 National Institute of Education study in Atkinson, New Hampshire, Graves (1983) reports that poor letter formation and handwriting improved in a little over a month when children were allowed to compose and share topics of their own choosing in a writing workshop approach. The second problem centers on what letter formation looks like in its earliest form and what developmental stages it goes through to reach conventional form (Holdaway, 1979). As young as three years old, children begin to differentiate between drawing and writing; they begin to use different marks for their writing than for their drawings, even though both may appear as scribbling to an adult's eyes (Harste et al., 1981, 1983). One of the first writing features that appears is called linearity—that is, writing is arranged horizontally (Gentry & Gillet, 1993; Lavine, 1972). As children's exposure to print increases, Gentry and Gillet (1993) explain that "a fundamental change occurs when children's writing moves away from scribbling toward character writing" (p. 24). Children's first attempts at forming letters of the alphabet look something like letters (mock letters), but they are made up of other kinds of characters, referred to as "character writing" by Gentry and Gillet (1993, p. 24). This stage may not last long; indeed, some children skip this stage and go directly from scribbling to writing letters.

When children first begin to use letters, they do so at random until they discover the alphabetic principle, which is the next major discovery about print (Temple et al., 1988). Making letters of the alphabet often results from children making discriminations about letter forms as they play around with letters hoping they will say something with them (Clay, 1991). Children usually attempt to make uppercase letters first, because they are easier to make than lowercase letters (Stennett, Smithe, & Hardy, 1972). In fact, according to Stennett and colleagues (1972), lowercase letters are not totally mastered until the end of third grade, and some students still have problems then with certain letters like *r*, *u*, *h*, and *t*.

Children select certain features of letters (e.g., straight lines, curves, open, closed, rotated) as they learn to differentiate them one from the other, which is why they often initially confuse *E* with *F*, *O* with *Q*, and *M* with *W* (Gibson, Osser, Schiff, & Smith, 1963). During this time of experimentation, children "may be constantly surprised that letters they know can be varied to produce new letters" (Temple et al., 1988, pp. 32–33). They often make comments like a *d* can be turned around to make a *b* or a *W* is an upside-down *M*. When children share their discoveries with teachers, it is a sign that they are learning (Holdaway, 1979).

Children do not learn alphabetical letters in any particular order, although letters in their name usually take precedence (Clay, 1991; McGee & Richgels, 1990). Over a period of months in writing workshop, as kindergartners individually explore and experiment with letters, they establish a more stable image of letters in their minds so they can write them at will and are less confused about them; however, it takes years before they learn to use all the letter forms (Clay, 2001). Clay (1991) explains that because the sequence of writing a letter can change directions at any one of several change points, children must learn how to put a set of instructions together, store these instructions for the future, and access the instructions for each letter they wish to write. Initially, this is slow work. According to Clay, "Each newly learned letter in English (54 in English when considering the variant forms of 'a' and 'g' printers use) has to find an identity among a rapidly growing set of letters" (p. 21); the magnitude of this task is much greater than most parents and teachers realize.

Researchers recognize that it is more difficult to see letters embedded in text, as one does in conventional reading, than see them in isolation as one does when he or she writes or prints (Clay, 1991). Although it might seem reasonable for teachers to think that copying isolated letters contributes to learning about them, Morrow (1989) states, "Tracing, copying, drilling—all such activities do not work well when given as external assignments" (p. 145). However, based on my observations and as noted by Morrow, Clay (1991), and Holdaway (1979), when a child voluntarily decides to copy or trace a letter it can contribute to his or her learning it.

To illustrate the point that copying letters given as an external assignment, as in a handwriting class, is not the best way to learn letter formation, Clay (1991) cites a series of experiments conducted by Russian researchers with children learning to write Russian letters. In this study, children were taught by the following three different methods:

1. Model Only

The first method was to simply copy a letter as the researcher wrote the letter and gave general directions. More than 50 representations were required per letter for the average child to gain mastery over it.

2. A Model Plus Presenter's Detailed Instructions

The second method was for the researcher to point out all the basic points of the contour and explain the shifts from point to point as he modeled the letter's formation. This method reduced the training to 10 sessions per letter.

3. A Model and Self-Directed Search

The third method proved the most successful and reduced the training to four sessions per letter. The researcher wrote a letter in front of each child and encouraged the child to look at a model of the letter and independently analyze and identify supportive points of the letter for him- or herself. The researchers believed mastery was accomplished as each child practiced and gradually refined the image of the actions he or she used to produce the letter—the child's attention was directed to the sequence of movements in the action being learning, not just the product of that action.

Futhermore, when the children in this study were allowed to organize and learn sequential steps of letter formation for themselves, they could shift to writing their newly learned letters in varied settings without much difficulty. In the other two methods mentioned, children could learn to write letters, but whatever they learned was unstable and sensitive to changes in the surroundings such as a shift from the blackboard to a book, or to writing on paper that had lines of different width (Clay, 1991).

Based on these findings, kindergartners need to be allowed to explore, experiment, and organize the sequential steps in letter formation without the *added pressure* of formal or proper letter formation as is done in a handwriting class (Clay, 1991; McGee & Richgels, 1990). Writing letters can contribute to the child's early attempts to learn letter formation, but this must be handled sensitively and meaningfully within creative writing to provide "for that focus on letters without undue emphasis on these letters" (Clay, 1991, p. 282). Readable letters are the goal for kindergartners, not perfection. Readable letters develop out of the young child's intent, not the teacher's (Harste et al., 1981, 1983).

As teachers watch children learn to form letters, they must recall that students' individual differences play a great part in this learning due to the differences in their literacy preparation before formal schooling (Clay, 1991). These differences can be easily seen when children first enter school and try to write their names. For example, on the first day of school, Phoebe wrote her name in perfectly legible print, while it took Eddie six months to reach the same control over his name.

When young children ask for aid or seem to be having difficulty in making a particular letter, especially in their names, results of the Russian study (as cited by Clay, 1991) can be applied to instruct developmentally appropriate letter formation:

The teacher should model printing the letter in manuscript on a separate piece of paper from the student's. A moving model is the best model. Then, the teacher should ask the child to try to make the letter. As he or she tries, the student should "think out loud" about how he or she is making the letter. For example, while attempting to make the letter *B*, a kindergartner stated that you make a *B* with a stick and two humps (sequence of movement). After he made the letter, he was asked what he might think of that would help him remember this letter, and he replied, "It looks like a camel [association once the letter was made]." This child actively constructed his own associations, and they proved to be most helpful to him in printing the letter *B* in the future.

If a beginning kindergartner is having great difficulty in writing the first letter of his or her name, the teacher should guide the child's hand through a manual analysis of the letter. Clay (1991) explains, "He may be able to discriminate better the shapes that he can handle or make movement with, rather than the ones he can merely look at" (p. 285). Mrs. Clark suggests that if children, especially English-language learners, have difficulty with terminology as they attempt to make the letter and "think out loud," the teacher can reguide their hand and demonstrate how he or she would briefly describe the sequence of motion using the terms sticks and circles (or parts of). These shapes (and usually the terminology) are familiar to children because their "early attempts to imitate writing often have [a] characteristic repetition of...sticks, or circles" (Temple et al., 1988, p. 27). Initially, writing letters in the air and tracing magnetic letters with their fingers can be useful to children, too (Clay, 1991, 2001).

Learning to recognize and write both upper- and lowercase letters so they are recognizable and readable is truly an extraordinary undertaking, and much more difficult than most adults remember. (See "A Different Alphabet" in Appendix E to refresh your memory.) Letter formation becomes readable print because of (1) a child's desire to communicate in writing as he or she independently identifies supportive points of letters by analyzing letters for him- or herself (Clay, 1991, 2001) and (2) many meaningful experiences with written language (McGee & Richgels, 1990).

Spelling Is Developmental

Spelling develops in stages when children are allowed to write in a writing workshop guided by a knowledgeable literacy teacher. It begins with *approximated* efforts that often look like scribbling. Then as kindergartners learn the alphabetic principle, they invent spellings that look like print but usually are not readable at first. As they are allowed to write in a writing workshop, their invented spelling becomes readable print. This invented spelling stage is the major part of developmental spelling. When kindergartners are allowed to practice it every day, it usually ends in conventional spelling somewhere around the middle to the end of third grade (Routman, 1991).

For most beginning kindergartners, spelling is about exploring and experimenting with marker and pen (Calkins, 1994); they draw pictures and write and spell any way they can. Teachers who are knowledgeable about current spelling research promote kindergartners' spelling approximations (scribbling) until these approximations, as seen in their daily writings, become invented spelling and indicate a certain level of development (Bear, Invernizzi, Templeton, & Johnston, 2000; Gentry & Gillet, 1993). Then, certain high-frequency words, word families, and strategies that seem to be needed from observing children's writing can be taught in word study through an inquiry approach (Johnston, 2001; Routman, 2000). Until these observed spelling needs are taught, kindergarten teachers should not expect kindergartners to spell *any* words correctly.

However, some kindergartners expect correct spelling from themselves. These children are afraid to risk being wrong; they know enough about spelling to know there is only one way to spell a word. Being afraid to take risks when the atmosphere in the classroom embraces risk taking is usually due to the temperament of the child and the expectations of his or her parents, former teachers, or both (Temple et al., 1988). This was the case with Jeremy, a student with whom I worked in my role as a literacy coach.

Jeremy entered Mrs. Williams's class near the end of the school year. Although Jeremy was very bright and told wonderful stories, his writing was boring and his spelling was not developing beyond the few words he could already spell. During writing workshop, he wrote, "I love my cat. My cat loves me. I love my cat." Mrs. Williams believed Jeremy's problem was due to his concern for correct spelling, so she discussed this issue with him.

Mrs. W.: Why do you love your cat?

Jeremy: Because she's funny!

Mrs. W.: What funny things does she do?

Jeremy: She fights with the dog, and puts her paw in his eye.

Mrs. W.: Really? Why is that funny to you?

Jeremy: She doesn't have any claws.

Mrs. W.: Your cat fights with the dog. She puts her paw in his eye, but she doesn't have any claws! That is interesting! Let's write that down.

[Mrs. Williams makes a line for each word for both sentences and begins to help Jeremy take risks in spelling as needed. He writes, "My cat," and then he balks.]

Jeremy: I don't know how to spell *fights*.

Mrs. W.: You are only 6 years old. I don't expect you to be able to spell like I do. All I want you to do is try.

[She helps him listen to the sounds as he produces *fits* for *fights*. Then she shows him how close he came to the correct spelling. She explains that she doesn't expect a kindergartner to write letters he can't hear (pointing to *gh*) and she is absolutely thrilled with his effort. Mrs. Williams helps Jeremy finish his first sentence, and after getting him started on his second sentence in a similar fashion, she tells him to finish it as best he can and he does.]

Ultimately, Jeremy becomes less inhibited in writing words he doesn't already know how to spell, and his writing becomes more interesting. Taking risks with spelling is vital to the kindergartner's developing the alphabetic principle and becoming a good speller (Bear et al., 2000; Gentry & Gillet, 1993). Once children realize that they should just try their best to write down their thoughts, and that even adults have to occasionally invent spellings (especially when writing rough drafts), they usually learn to relax and practice using invented spelling.

What Is Invented Spelling?

Research by Read (1975) demonstrates that some young children invent, or make up, the spellings of the words they speak by listening to the individual sounds (phonemes) in words and then attempting to find written letters (graphemes) that represent those phonemes. Connecting sounds to corresponding letters (alphabetic principle) in this manner is called *invented spelling* (Chomsky, 1971). Chomsky encouraged preschool, kindergarten, and first graders to try to write before they read because of the valuable practice they received from translating sound to print, thus developing the alphabetic principle.

Graves (1994) explains the purpose of invented spelling as "[allowing] children to begin to make meaning before they know how to actually spell a word" (p. 257). Invented spelling needs to be embraced for this reason as well as three other important reasons (Temple et al., 1988):

1. Invented spelling helps develop the alphabetic principle.

2. Invented spelling develops into conventional spelling because the child looks for patterns of regularity, rules that enable the standard spelling of thousands of words.

3. Invented spelling aids teachers in analyzing students' reading, writing, and spelling progress so proper guidance can be planned.

Treiman (1993) also studied the merits of invented spelling in English with first graders. At the end of a year of study, her qualitative research produced the following positive results:

• Students often spelled frequently seen words correctly in their writing.

• They demonstrated attempts to hear sounds (phonemic awareness).

• They demonstrated an understanding of the alphabetic principle.

• They used and did not avoid high-frequency function words such as *and* and *of*.

• They were not afraid to take risks and attempted to spell difficult words (e.g., *extinct*, *alligator*, and *armadillo*).

Children are not the only ones to use invented spelling—even adults use it at times. For example, I use it every time I can't spell a word conventionally in my rough drafts so my thought line is not interrupted and when I write out my grocery lists, because no one will read them but me. However, whenever I am going to share my writing with someone as in this book, or in a letter, I care about my spelling because I want my message to be understood.

Students care about spelling for the same reason. Invented spelling is not meant to be read by anyone other than the teacher or the author—unless the reason for the invented spelling is explained, especially to parents

(Routman, 1991). (See Appendix C for a letter to parents explaining developmental spelling.)

Invented spelling should be encouraged in the classroom with one exception: It should not be encouraged when spelling high-frequency words, because these words need to be seen written correctly as often as possible to be learned (Routman, 1991). Therefore, when teachers demonstrate their own writing and spelling in front of children in writing workshop, it is not advisable to demonstrate any high-frequency words in invented spelling. In fact, when I demonstrate spelling a word (other than high-frequency words) with invented spelling, I follow Routman's method. Routman explains that because she can spell correctly, she does not deliberately like to spell words incorrectly. However, because she wants to demonstrate for students how spelling is done, occasionally she asks for the students' help in spelling words with invented spelling. After accepting and praising her students' approximations, she also places the correct spelling within parentheses next to their invented one. This allows her to point out how closely the children came to the correct spelling and also to display the correct spelling. (See Appendix D for a list of high-frequency words that kindergartners and first-grade students can learn and how to teach them.)

Children learn to care about spelling *all* words when they care about communicating in writing. Even high-frequency words that provide little interest to children can be learned when children engage in writing for real purposes and real audiences. According to Graves (1994),

> Students who don't care about their writing or have no idea of what writing can do are the most difficult to help [with spelling].... When the writer's voice is in the piece and the teacher has brought a class to be a good audience, then the author cares more about being respectful of those who will read his work. (p. 265)

Respect for message and audience brings respect for a teacher's spelling guidance. As young writers strive to communicate, they will look to their teacher to help them make progress through the stages of developmental spelling.

Stages of Developmental Spelling

With the guidance of a knowledgeable literacy teacher at students' point of need in meaningful writing, students can construct different strategies of spelling that help them progress through the developmental stages of spelling. It is important for teachers to know and assess these stages for the purposes of providing appropriate instruction.

According to Gentry and Gillet (1993), there are five stages to developmental spelling:

1. Precommunicative
2. Semiphonetic

3. Phonetic

4. Transitional

5. Conventional

Temple and colleagues (1988) and Bear and colleagues (2000) concur with these stages; however, they use different terminology. Table 1 lists the five stages with the differing terminology. Because Gentry and Gillet's stages of spelling are more recognizable to teachers, I use their terms for spelling stages in this book; however, I occasionally refer to Temple and colleagues' (1988) and Bear and colleagues' (2000) terms, too, because these terms help provide readers with a more comprehensive look at information that pertains to spelling. When I use these different terms, I also include Gentry and Gillet's (1993) terms in parentheses.

Kindergarten teachers only need to focus on the first three stages because the last two stages develop in first grade and beyond. However, I discuss all five stages and suggest instructional strategies to give kindergarten teachers a better idea of when and how developmental spelling becomes conventional spelling, and to provide information for primary-grade teachers who may wish to use the book, too.

The Precommunicative Stage

The first stage, the Precommunicative stage, is used to describe spelling that cannot be read by others. In this stage, the young author tries to communicate a message but is the only one who can read it, and he or she often can read it only for a short time after producing it. Throughout most of the Precommunicative stage, children do not understand sound–letter correspondences. Simply writing memorized words like *Mom* or *cat* does not exemplify the alphabetic principle (sound-to-letter relationships) or indicate an understanding of the connection between speech and writing.

In this stage, the use of scribbling, characters, and mock letters (i.e., writing that looks like letters but isn't) decreases and the use of English letters increases. In fact, characteristics of the Precommunicative stage include the following:

- using random strings of symbols, shapes, numbers, and often mixing mock letters with real letters;

- using only a few letters of the alphabet, repeating them frequently (often the letters in their names), or using many different letters of the alphabet—sometimes copying the entire alphabet;

- using some lowercase letters but preferring uppercase letters and using uppercase and lowercase letters indiscriminately;

- using letters that have no relation to the sounds being made, although near the end of this stage making some sound–letter matches;

- possibly understanding the left-to-right progression of print (i.e., directionality); and
- confusing syllables, endings or suffixes, and letters and words—lacking the concept of word but possibly writing some memorized words that are printed or copied.

Figure 2 shows a Precommunicative sample.

Kindergartners should be encouraged to move about the room on their own initiative to copy print. If children voluntarily choose to participate in copying, they will pay attention to the features of letters and learn them

---

Table 1. Differing Terminology for Developmental Spelling Stages

Gentry and Gillet (1993)	Temple, Nathan, Burris, and Temple (1988)	Bear, Invernizzi, Templeton, and Johnston (2000)
Precommunicative	Prephonemic	Emergent
Semiphonetic	Early Phonemic	Letter-Name
Phonetic	Letter-Name	Within Word Pattern
Transitional	Transitional	Syllables and Affixes
Conventional	Conventional	Derivational Relations

Figure 2. Precommunicative Stage Spelling Sample

(Morrow, 1989). When given as external assignments, copying and tracing do not work well; it is the *intent* of the child that is important (Harste et al., 1981, 1983).

This is a time to teach the letters of the alphabet and begin phonemic awareness training. (See chapter 5 for a discussion of Alphabet Time and Phonemic Awareness Time.) Once children can isolate individual sounds in words and they know most of the letter names, they will be able to relate sounds to letters and demonstrate knowledge of the alphabetic principle in their writing (Ball & Blachman, 1991).

Temple and colleagues (1988) state, "Once children begin to experiment with writing, a period of months or years may go by before they know *all* of the upper and lower case letter forms" (p. 32). As children learn to distinguish letters and how to hear individual sounds in words, they begin to realize that writing is somehow related to what is said.

In writing workshops, Precommunicative spellers work hard to distinguish the various features of the letters of the alphabet, especially in names and words that interest them (Temple et al., 1988). Approximated letter formation and spelling are necessary for young children to communicate in the early stages of written language, but they are hard work. A writing workshop approach that incorporates Cambourne's conditions of learning allows students to experience success and thereby provides them with an incentive to continue learning.

Throughout most of the Precommunicative stage, children are not aware that letters represent phonemes or speech sounds (Routman, 1991). Bear and colleagues (2000) state, "The movement from this [Precommunicative] stage to the next hinges on learning the alphabetic principle: letters represent [or stand for certain] sounds and words can be segmented into sounds" (p. 18). Movement to the Semiphonetic stage requires a growing understanding of interrelating Clay's (1991) four emergent reading behaviors, especially concepts of print, phonemic awareness, and visual attention to the graphic cues of print. (See chapter 1, pp. 12–21, for an explanation of the four emergent reading behaviors.)

The Semiphonetic Stage

In the second stage of developmental spelling, the Semiphonetic stage, children recognize that letters can represent sounds. This is a major learning achievement because it represents the emergence of the alphabetic principle (sound-to-letter relationship) and the beginning of reading (Bear et al., 2000). As children develop in this stage and their spelling becomes more complete and accurate, both the child and the teacher usually can read the child's writing (Bear et al., 2000), whereas in the beginning stages the child's writing may be difficult for the teacher to read without the child's input because of less accurate invented spellings.

Some characteristics of the Semiphonetic stage include the following:

• being aware that sounds can correspond to letters (alphabetic principle) and these letter-sounds can be used to construct words;

• writing one or two consonants or only the initial consonant to represent the entire word;

• showing an emerging understanding of the concept of word or word segmentation, which may or may not be observed in their writing but is emerging;

• using the literal name of a letter to write a word with that sound, such as *u* for *you*, *c* for *see*, and *i* for *eye* (Bear and colleagues, 2000, refer to Gentry and Gillet's Semiphonetic stage as the early Letter-Name stage of spelling because of this characteristic);

• having an emerging awareness of left-to-right sequence (directionality) of printed language; and

• becoming more sophisticated in knowledge of the alphabet and sounds of language.

Figure 3 shows a Semiphonetic stage spelling sample.

Semiphonetic spellers often write one or two letters for the entire word (e.g., *B* for *ball*) and then they stop. Or they write one or two letters of a word exemplifying the alphabetic principle, and then finish the word with a random string of letters. Semiphonetic spellers do this because their major problem is a weak concept of word (Bear et al., 2000).

Figure 3. Semiphonetic Stage Spelling Sample

Temple and colleagues (1988) discuss the problem of

> making a word hold still mentally while operating on it: The child must have a very stable image of the word in mind to be able to switch back and forth between the sound of the word, its phonemes, his repertoire of letters, and the motor act of writing each letter. (p. 76)

Temple and colleagues (1988) add that a stable image is difficult to grasp from speech because "[w]e usually attend to the meaning of words rather than to their sounds" (p. 76). Also, words often come to us all run together as in *Gogetmesome*, which causes problems for the young child who is trying to translate speech into writing.

When Semiphonetic spellers attempt to spell a word, they rely on the most prominent sound they have heard. The consonants make the most "noise"; therefore, Semiphonetic spellers usually represent consonants in their writing. Often the sound they represent is at the beginning of a word, but this is not always true as in the case of *hit*, where *t* is the most prominent sound. When Semiphonetic spellers do learn to represent more than just the most prominent sound in a word, they usually do so in the following order: beginning sound, then beginning and ending sounds, and occasionally the middle sound(s) (Bear et al., 2000; Gentry & Gillet, 1993). The middle letters of a word, especially the vowels, are usually omitted in the Semiphonetic stage (Bear et al., 2000). Some middle consonant sounds are more difficult to hear because they do not make as prominent a sound in that position—for example, in the word *sound*, the *n* is very difficult to hear, whereas in the words *net* and *pin*, the sound is more audible. In the case of middle vowel sounds, kindergartners do use vowels occasionally, if they are long or "strong" vowels (i.e., vowels that say their own name)—for example, *I* for *eye*, or *u* for *you* (Bear et al., 2000). Because kindergartners developmentally are not capable of hearing short vowels, they are rarely represented in their work until the end of the year. When they do show up, they are usually represented incorrectly, unless the child is familiar with the word in printed text. Once they know the beginning sounds of words, children have little trouble transferring that knowledge to identifying ending sounds and eventually middle sounds (Bear et al., 2000). As kindergartners learn to use the alphabetic principle, they search for letter names that match (as closely as possible) the prominent sounds they hear in the words they wish to spell; this strategy is called the Letter-Name Strategy (Bear et al., 2000). When using this strategy, sometimes the match between the sound and letter name is found at the beginning of the consonant's name such as *B* /bee/, *K* /Kay/, and *Z* /Zee/. Other consonants have their sounds matched at the end of their name like *F* (eff), *L* (ell), and *S* (es). The following are some examples of this strategy: *see* as *c*, *are* as *r*, and *went* as *yant*. This last example surprises teachers at first, but there is logic to it. Think about the beginning sound in *went*. Does it match the letter name of *W* (pronounced /double-you/) or *Y* (pronounced /wie/) better? Bear and colleagues (2000) explain that "only W (double-you), the consonant Y (wie), and H (aich) have no beginning-sound association when using the [Letter-Name Strategy] and they are often the most difficult to learn" (pp. 104–105). Thus, the Letter-Name Strategy is very useful to spelling progress and should be encouraged.

Temple and colleagues (1988) inform teachers that "Children perceive oddities of pronunciation that adults do not...[because] children [listen more intently and] are not easily taken in" (p. 73). For example, kindergartners often spell *tree* as *chre*. Words like *tree*, *train*, and *trick* are commonly pronounced as if they began with *chr*, but adults are so accustomed to seeing the word *tree* that we tend to forget that we actually say *chree* (Temple et al., 1988). Before I understood this concept, I really questioned what kindergartners were hearing and thinking when they wrote trick-or-treat as *chricrchet* and *train* as *chran*.

Sometimes young Semiphonetic spellers use a subconscious, less desirable strategy that I refer to as the "how sound feels" strategy. Until children grasp the concept of hearing sounds in words (phonemic awareness), they will often rely on how a sound feels as it is produced in the mouth; this really causes problems when it comes to identifying short vowels in the future. However, it also explains some of the rather unusual spellings that children invent, such as *j* for *dr* (e.g., *JP* for *drip*). *Dr* and *j* have similar tongue placement and mouth formation, and young children often omit the letter *r* after the letter *d* or *t* (Bear et al., 2000); the combination of these factors results in the unusual invented spelling of the word *drip*.

When kindergartners correctly represent a short vowel, it is not because they can hear the individual sound; it is usually because they know the letter that represents the short vowel from having seen the word many times. Sometimes they have made a generalization from another word and recognize the sound of the pattern or rime. For example, I observed one kindergartner in a writing workshop spelling the word *sit* correctly. Knowing that developmentally she could not hear the short *i* sound, I asked her with delight how she knew the spelling of the word *sit*. She proudly told me, "*Sit* has an *it* in it." Most kindergartners trying to identify the individual sound /i/ attempt to write *E* for the short *i*, if they attempt the vowel at all (Bear et al., 2000).

Gentry and Gillet (1993) remind teachers that "[c]hildren learn to spell *pattern by pattern not word by word*" (p. 89). Spelling words should be grouped according to sound, visual, and meaning patterns according to students' writing needs and discussed in word study. For younger students, Gentry and Gillet (1993) suggest that words "should be organized around sound, or phonetic features that words share" (p. 90). Because young children develop rhyming ability early and they can hear the "rhyming chunk" or rime in a word family, word families (phonograms) can provide them with strong insights into spelling English words (Johnston, 1999), even though they cannot perceive the individual vowel sounds.

Johnston (1999) states, "Rimes are the basic unit for spelling and reading words by analogy" (p. 66). Gunning (1995), Moustafa (1998), and

Gaskins and colleagues (1997) support this statement. Word families share the same rime (rhyme), although their onsets are different. The onset in any syllable is the consonant or consonants that come before the vowel; the rime is the vowel and the rest of the syllable. For example, the onset of *cat* is *c* and the rime is *at*. There is no onset to the word *at*; there is only rime. (See Appendix D for a list of 37 common rimes from which 500 primary words can be derived.)

When students consistently demonstrate using beginning and ending consonants in their writing (near the end of the Semiphonetic stage) but seldom include a vowel (e.g., *pan* as *PN*, *bug* as *BG*), short vowels should be introduced in the study of word families (phonograms) that share the same short vowel (Johnston, 1999). Although short vowels cannot be heard by themselves in this stage, they can be attended to in the rime or vowel chunk of a word family.

Johnston (1999) suggests beginning with one word family at a time (e.g., *at*). Although there is no particular order to studying word families, the short *a* family is a good place to start because this family is quite prevalent and is the least likely to be confused (Henderson, 1985). As soon as any two word families with the same short vowel (e.g., *at* and *an*) have been studied individually and at length, word sorts that compare and contrast these two families should be introduced. After introducing a couple of word families individually and in depth, the teacher can introduce other word families that *share the same vowel* in sets of two (*ub, ug*), three (*en, ell, est*), or even four families (*ill, in, ing, it*). (See Appendix D for information on teaching word families.)

It is not necessary to study every common word family (phonogram); instead let the children's writing needs direct your choices. (See Appendix D for a list of representative word families.) Once children gain experience with identifying and using "rimes" or "vowel chunks" to read, write, and spell new words, their constructive minds begin to make analogies on an intuitive level (Johnston, 1999; Morris, 1992). What is most important in the study of rimes within word families for young students "is coming to understand that the *rime or vowel chunk is a reliable and generative unit for reading and spelling words* [italics added]" (Johnston, 1999, p. 67).

Once some short vowels have been taught in word families, teachers can hold writing and editing conferences prior to having students publish pieces of writing so they can guide student authors to use what they have learned. For example, if the teacher had introduced the *at* word family and then noticed that a child spelled *bat* like *bt*, Cunningham (2000) suggests responding with "Where's your vowel? Every word needs at least one vowel" (p. 126). Next, the teacher might direct the child's attention to the spelling pattern of the rime *at* highlighted with colored highlighting tape and displayed on the book jacket of *Cat in the Hat* (Dr. Seuss, 1985) or on the name word wall where names students recognize are posted. However, if the vowel has not been taught and the child has made an incorrect attempt at writing it in a word, the teacher should simply acknowledge the good attempt when conferring and make the necessary correction(s) when editing.

Routman (2000) states, "Meaningful pattern making is what the brain does innately...Knowing and applying current brain research helps us teach in a way that makes sense to kids" (p. 423). However, it is not necessary for teachers to be brain research or articulation experts to help kindergartners' Semiphonetic spelling develop. Kindergarten teachers just need to teach patterns of sound when they observe a need in kindergartners' writing, as well as praise kindergartners' attempts to invent spellings, knowing there is probably some good reason for the inventions. Children will construct their knowledge of spelling and develop as spellers with the teacher's guidance.

Teachers new to identifying spelling stages may want to present and give Gentry and Gillet's (1993) developmental spelling test to a few Semiphonetic spellers as a kind of game. Gentry and Gillet advise giving the test for two reasons: (1) It aids the teacher in becoming an expert at recognizing developmental spelling stages in children's writing samples after analyzing only one or two tests, and (2) it aids in the assessment of spelling strategies that children know. The test only consists of 10 words, and it can be used in kindergarten through second grade.

In summary, kindergartners in the Semiphonetic stage demonstrate a basic understanding of the alphabetic principle. During the early part of this stage, students usually record only the beginning sounds (or most prominent consonant sound[s]) of a word; later in the stage they record the first, last, and some middle sounds. It is customary for Semiphonetic spellers to match letter names to the sounds they are trying to write (R for *are*, U for *you*, I for *eye*), also known as the Letter-Name Strategy, which should be encouraged. However, students' movement from this stage to the Phonetic stage hinges on their beginning to use vowels consistently in written syllables (Bear et al., 2000).

The Phonetic Stage

In the third developmental stage of spelling, the Phonetic stage, children represent most of the sounds they hear in a word. Phonetic spellers usually show an awareness of word segmentation by using spaces between words, but initially they may use dots or lines (Bear et al., 2000). Another indicator that concept of word is understood is when children use both beginning and ending consonants of the words they write. An outsider usually can read phonetic spelling; it doesn't look like standard adult spelling, but the spellings are usually quite readable (Bear et al., 2000).

Some characteristics of the Phonetic stage include the following:

- maps most "surface" sounds heard in the word (e.g., in the word *knife*, the surface sounds are *nif*; k and e cannot be heard and, therefore, are not surface sounds);
- spells words based on sound and not conventional English spelling (e.g., *yuts* for *once*, *STOPT* for *stopped*, *traDaD* for *traded*);

- uses vowels, consonants, and *ed* endings;
- represents certain letters consistently, although incorrectly (e.g., *y* for *w*, as in *yant* for *went*);
- inserts incorrect vowel after a correct vowel;
- represents *er* as *r;*
- shows a general awareness of word segmentation but is not consistent;
- uses spellings that are readable to teachers implementing writing workshop.

Figure 4 shows a Phonetic stage spelling sample.

Phonetic spellers literally spell what they hear; they choose letters on the basis of sound with little regard to picturing the correct English spelling of the word. Most young students are not able to hear isolated short-vowel sounds until around the middle or end of first grade; therefore, they often incorrectly represent the short vowel as in the following examples: *but* for *bat, bat* for *bet, bet* for *bit, cit* for *cot,* and *cot* for *cut.*

As Phonetic spellers become more adept at spelling, their spelling choices reflect their developing awareness of systematic thinking about the English spelling system. Temple and colleagues (1988) explain:

> They are just beginning to explore the rules by which letters represent phonemes...but so far their ideas of how phonemes should be spelled sticks closely

Figure 4. Phonetic Stage Spelling Sample

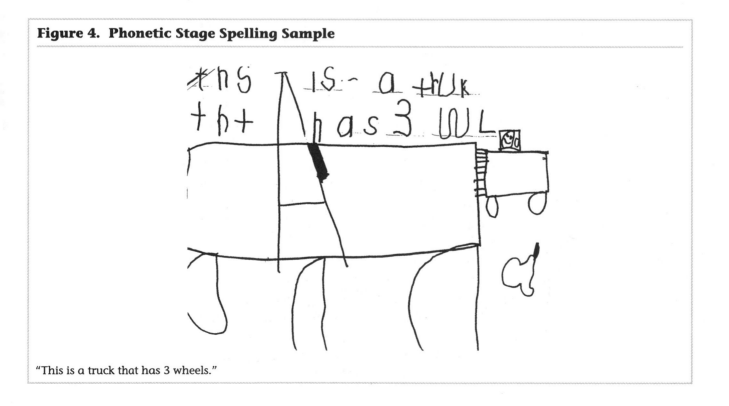

"This is a truck that has 3 wheels."

to the names of letters…. They have not yet realized the complexity that exists in rules for choosing letters to represent words. (p. 112)

If teachers point out too harshly the disparity between their approximated spellings and the standard spellings, they can severely limit children's experimentation and therefore delay their progress into conventional or standard spelling (Temple et al., 1988). The most progress at this stage can be made if children are encouraged to continue to explore and experiment with spelling as they write in a writing workshop (Temple et al., 1988).

When teachers see young children using short vowels but confusing them in their writing (e.g., *pats* for *pets*), they should instruct students to compare word families with different short vowels (e.g., *at, et, it*) by planning both "visual" and "sound" word sorts (Johnston, 1999). Johnston (1999) informs teachers that "The comparison of different [word] families is critical if children are going to do more than temporarily memorize how to read and spell one family" (p. 68). Students need to *actively* make decisions about which rime and vowel define that rime to help them form necessary associations to read and write new words by analogy. Studying word families, then, is about asking children to compare different vowel patterns (rimes or chunks) through word sorts across word families, and not just simply generating lists of word families (Clay, 2001).

Because research has shown that children attempt to use digraphs and blends at the same time they begin to demonstrate using short vowels, they, too, need to be addressed when the need becomes apparent in the children's writing (Invernizzi, 1992). Based on my experience, common consonant digraphs (e.g., *ch, sh, th, wh,* and *ph*) pose real problems to Phonetic spellers. Children usually spell a digraph (i.e., a single sound spelled with two letters) with one letter because it is correctly perceived as one sound. They don't realize it takes two letters to spell the one sound. When children apply the Letter-Name Strategy to digraphs, *ph* sounds like /f/, *sh* sounds like /s/, *wh* sounds like /w/, and although *ch* is a bit tricky, the letter *h* is a good representative (listen to the final sound of /h/). However, *th* poses a real problem using this strategy. Most children represent it as a *t* or a *v*. Although these are both good *approximations,* "there is no clear candidate to represent this digraph" (Temple et al., 1988, p. 61). When *the* is written correctly, it is because children memorize this frequently used word (Temple et al., 1988).

Consonant blends (e.g., *bl, st,* and *scr*) are not too problematic because children can often hear the two or more sounds for the blended letters. However, if the teacher observes that a particular blend is causing several children difficulty in their writing, it should be taught. A good way to present initial consonant digraphs and blends is with tongue twisters and books that concentrate on repetition and alliteration. Teachers can follow this instruction with word hunts and sorts. (See chapter 4 for writing and reading workshop activities.)

Phonetic spellers (until the later part of this stage) spell by sound, and they are not yet aware of silent letters needed to represent most long vowels (Johnston, 1999). Therefore, long-vowel patterns are not introduced until silent vowels begin to appear in children's invented spelling, as in *rane* for *rain* or *lieght* for *light*. These long-vowel patterns are taught within word families. Once students have studied long-vowel patterns (rimes) as word families, they can compare these patterns to short-vowel patterns (rimes) with word sorts. Some long-vowel word families are included in Wylie and Durrell's (1970) word list (see Appendix D), and provide a good start to long-vowel pattern study.

It is not necessary to study every common word family (phonogram). Once children gain experience with identifying rimes, or chunking, and using them to read, write, and spell new words, their constructive minds begin to make analogies on an intuitive level (Johnston, 1999; Morris, 1992). For example, a kindergarten teacher with whom I had worked in my role as a literacy coach relayed an experience she had regarding analogies:

> I was teaching the high-frequency word *saw* in a minilesson near the end of the year in writing workshop, because so many children were having difficulty with it in their writing. After we closely analyzed the sound /s/ and the vowel pattern *aw* in *saw*, I wrote the word on the board. A student raised his hand and said, "Hey, I can make *Sam* out of *saw*." So I asked him to come up and do it. He came up and erased the *w* and put in a *m*. Some other children said they could make words, too; one child made *sad* and another, *sat*. I praised all of their wonderful thinking. Then I continued with my lesson on *saw*, and we were able to make a list of words that had that pattern: *paw, jaw, law, raw*. [Making lists like this familiarizes children with a group of words that have the same pattern, and helps them to be able to spell other unfamiliar words with the same pattern; it also helps them extend this knowledge to other patterns.] Then I thought it might be fun to see what would happen if we changed the *w*'s to *m*'s in all those words, and we got *Pam, jam, lam*(b), and *ram*. We also substituted *t* and *d* for *w*, and along with real words (e.g., *pat, pad*) we got a few nonsense words (e.g., *jat, jad*); so we discussed again that a word needs to mean something to be a word. The children and I had so much fun, and I could see they were making great analogies. They are so bright—I don't think I ever gave them enough credit before. I don't have to tell them everything; they figure a lot out for themselves.

This teacher had taught substitution of sounds in her phonemic awareness activities earlier in the year. Now, in addition to continuing to teach needed high-frequency words, she also taught needed short-vowel patterns within word families in a daily word study. Finding that her children no longer needed alphabet training and phonemic awareness training, she used the "Getting Ready" portion of writing workshop to teach word study. (See Appendix D for information on teaching high-frequency words and word families.)

This teacher found that the pronunciation of vowel patterns is very stable within word families (Johnston, 1999), which is helpful knowledge. Trying to teach vowel patterns in isolation from word families can be confusing because the pronunciation of vowel patterns is not stable across word families (as evidenced in *saw* and *say*), but within their own word family, the pronunciation is consistent.

Johnston (1999) cautions that timing is critical to word family instruction. Instruction should begin when teachers notice children's invented spellings of short vowels indicate a need, and it should continue until children are able to sort word families with little effort and are spelling short vowels correctly for the most part. Then, it is time to move from the study of sound patterns to the study of visual and semantic patterns, which are more inclusive (Gentry & Gillet, 1993; Johnston, 1999).

Routman (2000) explains that as teachers provide links to conventional spelling from observing what children know and need in their invented spelling, teachers should teach "how words work, that most words follow a pattern [and] that the 'tricky' ones just have to be learned," often through mnemonic devices like "Never fry the end of a friend" or "Wed-nes-day" (p. 423). High-frequency words are often tricky, but even half of those words follow a pattern (Cunningham, 2000). Cunningham (2000) suggests putting "a star or sticker [or a helping hand] on word-wall words that children can use to help them spell lots of rhyming words" (p. 64). For example, knowing the high-frequency word *it* and using its pattern can be helpful in spelling *bit, sit, fit, spit,* and so forth.

Sometimes it is difficult to distinguish Semiphonetic spelling from Phonetic spelling in a writing sample. I suggest that kindergarten teachers not waste valuable time deciding which stage children are in when the stages are close enough to cause this problem. I recommend the following common sense approach: If you can read it easily, it's Phonetic. If some of the words prove difficult to read, and you need it transcribed by the author, it's Semiphonetic.

Another important point concerning Semiphonetic and Phonetic spelling is that kindergartners will vacillate between the two stages depending on their experimenting and risk taking with written language. For example, Chase drew a picture of a snowman and wrote *snomn* phonetically (see Figure 5). However, when he wrote a letter to his friend that required extensive writing to communicate his message, he reverted back to Semiphonetic spelling (see Figure 6). The message and use of the new genre (letter writing) were important enough to Chase to risk temporarily making more errors. Weaver (1982) informs teachers that they should welcome errors as signs of growth. Teachers need to know that children will make more errors as they grow in the spelling process, as was the case when Chase wrote his letter and reverted to Semiphonetic spelling. Also, the amount of writing may decrease temporarily when students are struggling with learning new things and trying to get them right, which may have been the case when Chase wrote *snomn* with Phonetic spelling.

Early Letter-Name (Phonetic) spellers may produce Letter-Name spelling before they are able to read. However, the concept of word and the ability to identify phonemes in words are important prerequisites for reading. Thus, when children begin to produce Letter-Name (Phonetic) spellings, they usually begin

Figure 5. Chase's First Spelling Sample

Figure 6. Chase's Second Spelling Sample

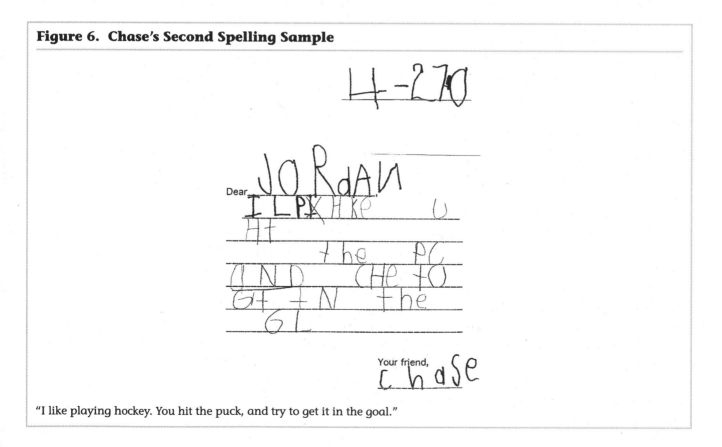

"I like playing hockey. You hit the puck, and try to get it in the goal."

to read soon after (Bear et al., 2000). For a time, they will read words written in standard spelling and write words in Letter-Name [Phonetic] spelling. When children try to read their own writing, they may be confused at first (Temple et al., 1988); however, with continued practice in writing and reading workshops, their active, constructive minds figure it out (Clay, 1991; Temple et al., 1988).

Bear and colleagues (2000) agree that children read in the Phonetic stage: They are early readers. Their reading is dysfluent; that is, they read word by word and often inexpressively. Many kindergartners end the year in the Phonetic stage of spelling when writing workshop is done on a daily basis. Some are still borderline Semiphonetic–Phonetic spellers, and only a few will have progressed to the next stage of developmental spelling, the Transitional stage.

Although it is not difficult to tell the difference between Precommunicative spelling and Semiphonetic spelling, sometimes it is difficult to distinguish Semiphonetic from Phonetic spelling and Phonetic spelling from Transitional spelling, especially if the teacher has had little experience with assessing spelling stages. If this is a concern with one or two students, the teacher may wish to administer Gentry and Gillet's (1993) developmental spelling test.

In summary, Phonetic spellers represent all surface sounds they hear in words but not always correctly. Short vowels pose a great deal of trouble for them. Phonetic spellers literally spell what they hear; they choose letters on the basis of sound, with little regard to picturing the correct English spelling.

It is important to encourage Phonetic spellers to read as much as possible so they will see and become familiar with words that are spelled conventionally in their books. In addition, teachers should read frequently using methods such as a shared book experience where print can be pointed to while reading because movement from the Phonetic stage to the Transitional stage hinges on spelling words they way they look as well as how they sound.

The Transitional Stage

In the fourth developmental stage of spelling, the Transitional stage, the writer realizes that words must be spelled not only on the basis of how they sound (phonetic demand), but also on how they look (visual demand). These spellers notice the disparities between their invented spelling and the standard English spelling (e.g., *brthr* for *brother*), and they attempt to revise their spelling concepts accordingly (Temple et al., 1988). For the first time, words in the Transitional stage look more like English spelling. The Transitional speller is beginning to recognize that spelling requires visual, meaning (semantic), and historical demands as well as phonetic (sound) demands (Gentry & Gillet, 1993). Although words are not always spelled correctly (e.g., *skool* for *school*), more words are spelled correctly than not. Transitional spellers use many features of standard spelling, such as silent letters and short vowels. They also internalize much information about spelling patterns (Routman, 1991).

Some characteristics of the Transitional stage include the following:

- using a vowel in every syllable (i.e., now uses both consonants and vowels);
- beginning to move away from only phonological (sound) spelling to visual spelling (e.g., *eightee* instead of *ate* for *eighty*). Because of this new awareness, they may switch some letters (e.g., *taod* for *toad* and *opne* for *open*);
- using inflectional endings correctly (e.g., *s*, *'s*, *ing*, and *est*);
- beginning to use base words to form new words;
- beginning to use the morphemic (meaning) forms of words (e.g., *happy*, *happier*, *happiest*, *unhappy*, *happiness*, and *happily*);
- using "learned" (correctly spelled) words in greater abundance in their writing.

Figure 7 shows a Transitional stage spelling sample. Although some kindergartners do reach the Transitional stage (as indicated by the sample provided), the majority of students in this stage are in the first through the third grade.

Spelling instruction at the Transitional stage should focus on commonly misspelled words in children's writing within an inquiry-based word study (Johnston, 1999; Routman, 2000). Inquiry is "being able to question independently, seek answers, and modify and extend what you know" (Routman, 2000, p. 466). Both teacher and student should approach spelling with "inquiry" and "wonder" (Routman, 2000, p. 463). Teachers do not need to have all the answers in advance (Johnston, 2001). For example, in a second-grade classroom where I was working as a writing workshop coach, veteran teacher Jill Reiche asked me to address the spelling of *because* in a minilesson. She had observed that most of her children were spelling it incorrectly (even though it had been one of their spelling words in their spelling books). So I

Figure 7. Transitional Stage Spelling Sample

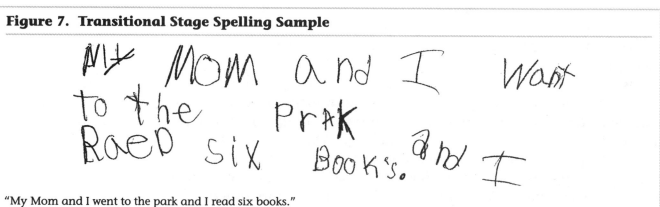

"My Mom and I went to the park and I read six books."

asked permission from a student to "borrow" a sentence from his work that included the misspelling. Then, I presented it to the class, explaining that their teacher had observed that it was a troublesome spelling word for most of them. It was troublesome because the children were only using one of spelling's four demands—the phonetic (sound) demand. They also needed to pay more attention to a second demand of spelling—visual (looks).

I wrote *because* in large letters on the board, and asked the children to take a good *look* at the word to see what the troublesome spots were for them. First, we discussed the meaning (semantics) of the word. Then we noted that *because* was actually two words and it was the word *cause* that proved troublesome to spell. Because the children were familiar with the concepts of *c* replacing *k* and *z* being confused for *s*, and they knew that some words had silent *e* at the end, they dismissed these as troublesome, but the tricky part was remembering *au* instead of *aw*. So we made lists of *au* and *aw* words to see if *one pattern* might be more prevalent than the other, but both patterns seemed to be used fairly equally within words (this chart was added to and posted in the room all year for reference). At this point, I didn't have any more suggestions and I asked the students if anyone could think of some way that we could remember the *au* pattern in *because*. A little voice in the back said, "The little word *use* is in *because*." I happily applauded and thanked him for his brilliant observation.

At the end of the year, Jill informed me that 99% of her students spelled *because* correctly after that day, and they learned a lot about searching spelling words for visual patterns—both word parts and little words.

Writing provides the catalyst for wonder about spelling, and wonder provides the catalyst for inquiry. To further promote inquiry, it is of the utmost importance that the teacher transmits the idea that spelling is not arbitrary; it corresponds to the knowledge children already have about words. Better spelling is the result of an understanding of the relationships between words, not just memorizing individual words letter for letter (Chomsky, 1971; Gentry & Gillet, 1993; Johnston, 2001).

Although English is complex and has some inconsistencies, teachers need to encourage children in the Transitional stage to look for the more commonly occurring spelling regularities (especially long- and short-vowel patterns) that underlie misspelled words (Johnston, 2001). Many words that are irregular when trying to apply phonics rules (e.g., *light, sight, high*) are consistent from a spelling pattern perspective (e.g., *gh* marks the long sound of /i/ and is a very dependable spelling pattern; Venezky & Massaro, 1979).

Routman (2000) suggests adding words like *because* to a class "core word list," a list of words that teachers at a particular grade level work together to develop by concentrating on necessary high-frequency and pattern words that students are using in their writing and need to master by the end of the year. Once "core words" have been studied through an inquiry approach, Sitton (1996) suggests testing students on the words on a weekly "any day, no-excuses" test rather than the traditional Friday spelling test that rarely transfers to real writing. In "any day" testing, students know that one day of every week one of their daily writing samples will be randomly collected by the teacher to assess the correct spelling of "no-excuses" core words. The amount of the writing sample to be assessed is at the teacher's decision for that grade level. It could be a few lines, a paragraph, or more; the area tested in each student's paper is bracketed by the teacher.

A few teachers with whom I have worked have implemented this type of testing. They feel it is especially useful to learning high-frequency words. To prepare their students for "any day" testing, they allot an *extra* 10 minutes for a spell check at the end of every writing workshop. During this time, students check their spelling against their list of studied "no-excuses" core words. Thus, students have a better opportunity to be successful with these words.

After teachers collect and assess writing samples for spelling errors, they return the papers to the students to make corrections. One teacher lightly circles errors; other teachers—in an effort to promote proofreading responsibility—do not mark any errors, but simply tell the students how many errors there are in the bracketed test area of their writing sample. The students are then held *responsible* for not only correcting misspelled words by using their "no excuses" core list but also for finding them, too. Extra credit is given for spelling additional words. (Students can use any spelling reference to make these corrections, along with being encouraged to work with others or even take their papers home so they can work with their parents to correct spellings.) These weekly corrected writing samples are saved as part of students' spelling assessment. Parents appreciate this kind of assessment because they are able to see spelling transfer to real writing, and they also see that invented spelling is only appropriate for those words students are not expected to spell yet.

In summary, the Transitional stage demonstrates a growing ability to represent the features of English orthography (spelling). Transitional spellers come close to the correct spelling of words, but they continue to misspell words with irregular spellings, such as *huose* for *house*, *trubal* for *trouble*, and *egul* for *eagle*. Transitional spellers take a closer look at vowels within syllables, and they begin to examine long-vowel patterns (Henderson, 1990). They begin to realize that patterns do not always have to be consistent with sound, as in the high-frequency words *have*, *come*, and *some*, which do not fit the long-vowel pattern. The movement from this stage to the next stage—Conventional Spelling—depends on the spellers' increasing ability to think more about spoken vocabulary and to reflect on and use abstract patterns of both long- and short-vowel spelling patterns. Teachers need to guide Transitional spellers in this endeavor when need is observed in their writing.

The Conventional, or Standard, Spelling Stage

Conventional or standard spelling is the final stage in which writers spell most of the words in a written piece correctly. Unless they have a visual gift, few conventional spellers spell all words correctly and must occasionally consult dictionaries (Gentry & Gillet, 1993). Correct spelling, especially of words never seen before, is based on perceiving generalizations about the structure of words and not on simply memorizing words (Temple et al., 1988). Conventional spellers have developed an awareness of the English orthographic (spelling) system over years of word study, writing, and reading (Gentry & Gillet, 1993; Temple et al., 1988).

This awareness begins with the Precommunicative stage of spelling. Then as the alphabetic principle is understood, students progress to the Semiphonetic and Phonetic stages, which rely on spelling's phonetic demand. The movement to the Transitional stage occurs when spellers understand that the visual demand of spelling is as important as the phonetic demand (usually around first grade). Finally, as Transitional students begin to think, reflect, and use more abstract patterns (in the middle to end of third or fourth grade), they enter the Conventional stage (Routman, 1991). It is in this stage that formal spelling instruction can begin, which requires an understanding of the third and fourth demands of spelling—semantic (i.e., the meaning unit is spelled consistently from word to word) and etymological (i.e., a word's spelling reflects its history) demands (Gentry & Gillet, 1993).

Some characteristics of the Conventional stage include the following:

- having a working knowledge of the written system of English, including knowledge of prefixes, suffixes, contractions, compound words, and homonyms;

- becoming more accurate in the use of silent letters and doubling consonants when necessary;

- continuing in the development of identifying irregular spellings;

- mastering the use of base words;

- knowing how to proofread and use the dictionary; and

- being able to correctly spell a large body of words.

Children do not reach the Conventional stage of spelling until they are in the third or fourth grade. I included a discussion of this stage in this book so kindergarten and primary-grade teachers can have a better understanding of the entire progression of spelling development—from approximated spelling (scribbling, mock letters, invented spelling) to Conventional spelling.

Instruction at the Conventional level should focus on the morphological structure of language—that is, the study of word formation. This study includes parts of words that have meaning yet cannot stand alone, such as prefixes and suffixes (Temple et al., 1988). Along with affixes, Johnston (1999) recommends studying more difficult consonant and vowel patterns. In addition, Routman (1991, 2000) includes homonyms, contractions, common irregular spellings, possessives, derivations, open and closed syllables, and word endings (e.g., doubling consonants for words ending in *ing, ed, er, est*). Dictionary skills, proofreading, and editing need to be emphasized at the Conventional level, too (Routman, 2000).

Capable readers and spellers respond to phonic *patterns* rather than phonic rules, because these patterns more accurately capture the complexity of English (Adams, 1990). Johnston (2001) suggests students make collections of words and sort them by sound and pattern to discover "what is going on" over studying rules. Although according to Wheat (1932), a few rules for adding suffixes are fairly consistent—like dropping the final *e*, or changing *y* to *i* and doubling final consonants before adding a suffix—Henderson (1990) cautions it is more important to provide meaningful literacy experiences over teaching rules. Children use their active, constructive minds within meaningful literacy experiences that enable them to have a tacit knowledge of words before they are capable of understanding rules. "Literate adults do not use rules; they simply know" (Henderson, 1990, p. 59).

Teachers need to help students become Conventional spellers by guiding them to think about common spelling patterns, high-frequency words, and generalizations observed to be needed in their writing (Routman, 1991). Johnston (2001) favors the activity of word sorting after making and discussing collections of words to transmit the idea that spelling corresponds to the knowledge children already have about words. For example, as a university instructor, I observed one of my students, Elaina, do an excellent job of teaching a spelling minilesson prior to writing workshop in a fifth-grade classroom. First, she explained to the class that *recommend* seemed to be a problem for them because they were often spelling it with two *c*s and one *m*, or two *c*s and two *m*s. One of her students, Gina, a reflective speller, raised her hand and said, "I don't know why it should be a problem. *Re* is a prefix and *commend* is the root (base) word; why would you double the c or take out the m?" Elaina delightedly said, "You know that would be a good way to remember how to spell *recommend*? What does the word *recommend* mean?" Gina replied, "It means you say something good about someone or thing." "Yes," Elaina said, adding, "let's start a list of words that begin with *re* to see what *re* means." The class made a list and discovered that *re* meant "to do again" when used as a prefix in words such as *redo*, *replay*, and *reuse*, but in words such as *reach*, *reap*, and *read*, *re* was part of the root or base word. When they tried to sort their list of *re* words into prefix and base word lists, they decided to put *recommend* in the base word list because they didn't think it meant "to do again." However, they all liked Gina's way of remembering to spell *recommend* and intended to use it.

In another classroom, a fourth-grade classroom, where I was working as a consultant, a student wrote the word *liquid* as *likwid* because she thought it had the same sound as that in "Kwick Trip" (a local gas station and convenience store) and was familiar with this spelling. The students discussed the unusual spelling of *likwid* with lively interest during a spell check following writing workshop. The teacher asked the class to make a list of words they thought began with or had the sound of /qu/. Other than *Kwick*, all their words began with *qu*. They realized that while /k/ and /q/ had similar sounds, they were different; however, /u/ and /w/ had the same sound in *liquid*. Although neither the teacher nor I could explain why they did, the class noted that *u* always seemed to follow *q*; therefore, the class decided *qu* must be a consistent pattern. When the students were asked how they might remember *qu* in *liquid* one student said, "I know how to spell *squid*, and a squid swims in *liquid*." The students also suggested that leaving the chart of *qu* words posted for a reminder would be a good idea. (The teacher told me later in the year that the children did not have any more trouble with the *qu* pattern, and that even though the inquiry approach took time, he felt it was well worth it in spelling that transferred to writing. Plus for the first time, he and his class had really enjoyed spelling!)

Even though these teachers and I did not know all the answers in advance, modeling our own curiosity about words was important to students' learning the prefix *re* and the *qu* pattern within an inquiry approach. However, I must admit it takes a little adjusting from being a "teller of knowledge" in spelling to being a "seeker" with students. Yet this process promotes real thinking.

In summary, students in the Conventional stage demonstrate a growing understanding of the English spelling system and an ability to integrate and process the phonetic, visual, semantic, and historical demands of spelling. More experience with words in meaningful writing and reading, and more formal spelling instruction with words found to be troublesome in these literacy processes, further refine and extend spelling knowledge at this stage. Conventional, or standard, spelling is both the purpose and the consequence of writing and not an entity in itself. However, for Conventional spellers to reach their fullest potential, spelling needs to become a lifelong process. This requires self-direction or an inquiry approach to spelling in the classroom from kindergarten throughout high school.

An inquiry approach is the result of a daily writing workshop. Students learn to care about communicating in writing in these workshops, and this affords teachers an ideal opportunity to invite students to share in the teacher's "spirit of inquiry" when spelling difficulties arise. Activities such as collecting words and word sorting should be planned for the whole class and for small groups around spelling needs with consideration for the students' developmental stage of spelling. This kind of inquiry approach to spelling helps children see that most words fit patterns and encourages them to make sense of the complexities of the English spelling system. This shared "spirit of inquiry" can help inspire students to make the study of words and spelling a lifelong process.

Kindergarten Teachers' Reflections on Spelling Progress

After implementing a writing workshop approach for one year, I asked several kindergarten teachers to reflect on the developmental spelling progress their students had made that year. Mrs. Clark, Ms. Neale, Mrs. Williams, and Mrs. Lentz all felt the most crucial stage was getting the students from the Precommunicative stage to the Semiphonetic stage. I told them that I'd had many kindergarten teachers ask me what they should do to get their students from scribbling and using mock letters to writing with invented spelling. I then asked these teachers to reflect on what they'd done to achieve students' progress from Precommunicative to Semiphonetic spelling. They all agreed the Getting Ready structure (for teaching the alphabet and phonemic awareness) and writing workshop structure (for the individual practice and development of writing and spelling strategies) were necessary to help students progress to invented spelling. (See chapter 5 for explanation of "Getting Ready" and writing workshop.) Of course, immersion in quality literature and exposure to meaningful print were also necessary. They agreed that choice of topic (responsibility) and allowing kindergartners to write it their own way for real purposes and real audiences as they guided their progress on a daily basis were necessary for engagement and development in spelling. They also cautioned that before they encouraged a child to use invented spelling in writing workshop, they checked the child's ability to hear beginning sounds and use the strategy of singing the "Alphabet Song" to find a letter on his or her alphabet strip.

Later in the year, when Mrs. Clark and Mrs. Williams observed most of their children demonstrating the alphabetic principle and a stable concept of word in their writing, they used some of the time from "Getting Ready" and reading workshop to initiate a word study. This study focused on word structures most of their children were using but were confusing in their writing, such as digraphs, short vowels, and high-frequency words. When these words were taught, they were taught within meaningful context. For example, digraphs were taught with tongue twisters and word families and short vowels with word families. (See Appendix D for a description of how to teach word families and a list of high-frequency words and information on how to teach them.) After posting and highlighting targeted words or patterns in meaningful print with playful language, such as nursery rhymes or children's names, when possible, playful activities took place, such as word hunts within the room and word sorts. (For other engaging word study ideas, see chapter 4; "Wordo" in Appendix D; and Gentry and Gillet, 1993, pp. 65–80.)

None of these kindergarten teachers had used Gentry and Gillet's spelling stages (1993) to track their students' spelling progress before. They felt it was an invaluable assessment and evaluation tool. Knowing which spelling stage their students were in aided them in guiding their students to progress to the next stage. (See Appendix C for a simple chart of Gentry's five spelling stages that can be used in assessment.)

These teachers have the following recommendations for other teachers:

- Provide many opportunities and purposes for the student to read and write; make Getting Ready and writing workshop a daily priority.

- Expose students to lots of meaningful print in the room. Once they have been taught these items, highlight high-frequency words and spelling patterns in nursery rhymes, songs, poems, the name word wall, and labels in the room. Read and refer to this print often so it can be used as an aid in the spelling of high-frequency words and recognizing spelling patterns. (See "High-Frequency Word Tent Cards" and "Very Own Words" activity on pp. 129 and 131, respectively, in chapter 4.)

- Encourage students to take risks with their spelling—that is, to use invented spelling.

- Praise attempted spellings but not indiscriminately. Look for the child's reason behind his or her attempt because often it is praiseworthy. Praise how close the student came to the right spelling. This kind of encouragement is essential feedback for spelling development.

- When spelling a word is really important to the child, encourage his or her asking for help from the "resident speller" in the classroom. (Children quickly find out which classmates are good spellers.)

- When children demonstrate the alphabetic principle and concept of word in their writing, initiate word study around their spelling needs.

- When teaching high-frequency words, associate meanings with the words by providing meaningful contexts (e.g., by highlighting within posted nursery rhymes) and meaningful practice through writing and word games like Boggle (see also Wordo in Appendix D).

Summary

As children experiment with and explore print in the attempt to communicate a message in writing, they move from scribbling and using mock letters to learning about phoneme–grapheme (sound-to-letter) correspondences and proper letter formation. They learn the alphabetic principle, they learn the concept of word, and they learn how to represent their oral language in print. As children write and read meaningfully, they refine their knowledge of letter formation, and they continue to grow and learn English spelling (orthography) with their teacher's guidance. This growing spelling knowledge is called developmental spelling.

Kindergarten teachers who use writing workshop and word study help kindergartners progress through several of the five stages of developmental spelling as they become writers. As writers, kindergartners will also progress through several stages of written language. The next chapter provides an explanation of the five stages of written language and also includes instructional techniques and genres appropriate for kindergarten.

CHAPTER 3

Developmental Sequence of Learning Written Language and Understanding Genres

"Kindergarten children begin to write by drawing and naming objects with one-word labels.... By exploring favorite themes in depth, the young writer discovers the need to move from labeling to more complex modes of expression."

—Hiliker (as cited in Newkirk & Atwell, 1988, p. 21)

As writing teachers, we have to remember that children who are beginning to write do not have the same knowledge or skills as adults do. They do not write, speak, read, listen, or think like adults. When young children first begin to write, Graves (1981) reminds us that their writing process resembles "spontaneous play" (p. 7). As the youngest writers write, they talk about what they will write. They also talk through their writing process. It appears that they do this to hear the sounds in words as they decide which letters represent those sounds. As children do more writing, their emphasis seems to shift from talking about ideas as they write to planning their writing. As children develop a sense of audience, they also begin to understand that writing must stand on its own because authors are not always available to explain their writing (Graves, 1981).

Children teach themselves to write in much the same way that they teach themselves to talk and read, experimentally with guidance from literate adults. Morrow (1989) informs teachers that "through personally motivated and directed trial and error—a necessary condition of their literacy development—they try out various aspects of the writing process" (p. 142). Driven by the need to communicate a message, they mix drawing with writing and invent and experiment with letters and words.

Graves explains that kindergartners are egocentric; therefore, they're secure in the fact that they are communicating a message in their writing, and they are eager to share this message. In their writing, as in their talking, young children have a primary impulse to tell and write about the personal experiences in their lives (Morrow, 1989). They need little direct instruction; they just need active models, time to write, supportive guidance, and praise for their efforts (Morrow, 1989).

Children learn about written language long before they enter formal schooling. It is important for teachers to be aware of what children know about writing before school, so teachers can plan appropriate written language instruction in school. Thus, this chapter focuses on the following three areas: (1) the development of written language: what kindergarten children already know and what teachers need to know; (2) the five stages of written language in kindergarten; and (3) appropriate kindergarten written language genres.

Written Language Development: What Kindergartners Know

Young children's introduction to written language begins long before they come to school. Parents, preschool teachers, and other care providers read to the children and model writing, and they provide writing materials with which children can explore and experiment. Some preschoolers are not so fortunate; they are what I refer to as the "literacy poor" children (the opposite of Cunningham and Allington's [1994] term "literacy rich"). Cunningham and Allington (1994) state that these children are 1,000 hours short in literacy learning. It will take them longer to become early readers and writers, but with the proper learning conditions in school they, too, can become literate.

In observing young children as they write, it is obvious that they understand that writing is for communicating a message. They understand the function of writing (i.e., the purpose of writing) before they know how to write in various forms such as labels, lists, and personal letters (Gundlach, McLane, Scott, & McNamee, 1985; Taylor, 1983). For example, I recall an experience with my daughters that illustrates this point. Because my two daughters, who were 4 and 7 at the time, were quarreling, I put them in their separate rooms. I told them they were not to come out until they were ready to play nicely again. A few minutes later, I heard a "pitter-pat" down the hallway, and from a distance, I watched my 4-year-old zing a paper airplane into her older sister's bedroom. Soon, they were playing nicely again. I retrieved the paper airplane, and while I can't remember the invented (or approximated) spelling written on it, I will never forget the message: This is no fun! Let's be friends.

Through experiences in their homes and communities, young children learn about written language. They learn that it carries meaning and is used for a variety of meaningful purposes. They learn that there are many forms or genres of written language, such as newspapers, magazines, personal letters, and menus; they learn that these forms serve different communication functions. However, while reading and writing may be prevalent in one family, they may not be in another. It is important to understand that students from different backgrounds view reading and writing as serving different purposes (Tompkins & Hoskisson, 1995).

Studies by Ferreiro and Teberosky (1982) and Harste and colleagues (1981) found that most children know the difference between drawing and writing when they are 3 years old. Children involved in the study often drew large figures in the center of the page with circular, connected lines and announced they were drawing; whereas their writing (which they defined as writing) was usually off center and linear. If one did not know the child's *intent*, it was difficult to tell which was drawing and which was writing. To the uninformed observer, they both looked like scribbling, but the children knew the difference. (For an illustration of this approximated writing, see the first stage on the chart of Five Stages of Written Language Development in Appendix C.)

Written Language Development: What Teachers Need to Know

Based on the findings of Ferrerio and Teberosky (1982) and Harste and colleagues (1981), children immersed in literature and exposed to a lot of meaningful print in many different ways before they come to kindergarten have richer literacy backgrounds from which to learn to progress as readers and writers.

Immersion in quality literature and exposure to meaningful print needs to continue in kindergarten for *all* children, and most important, *all* children need to individually explore and experiment with their own various hypotheses about writing in a writing workshop approach. Ferreiro and Teberosky (1982) state, "When we keep children from writing (from testing their hypotheses as they produce written texts...), we keep them from learning" (p. 278). Many other theorists agree with this statement (Chomsky, 1979; Clay, 2001; Harste et al., 1981; Read, 1975).

In a classroom where I was serving as a consultant, the teacher, Mrs. Richardson, and I introduced the genre of personal letter writing with a large, plush toy rabbit—Mr. Bunny. The children could write to him at any time, and he would write back and deliver their personally addressed notes to their handmade individual mailboxes. (At first the teacher ran off some copies of a generic message and would sign her name, Love, Mrs. Richardson; later in the year, however, she and I were able to personally respond to the child's readable print.) When Robert wrote his first letter, his writing looked like scribbling. However, he noticed Mr. Bunny wrote back with a different kind of writing. So he tried to emulate Mr. Bunny's writing by doing the best he could in copying an alphabet chart on his own initiative. Soon, his writing changed to make-believe letters (or mock letters). The more he practiced writing to Mr. Bunny, the more he changed his idea of what letters looked like. Because he was immersed and guided in meaningful writing and meaningful print all year, by the end of the year he not only could write readable messages but also read the messages Mr. Bunny wrote to him.

When young children have time to explore and experiment with written language, they construct their own knowledge based on what they already know, and they do this in a similar fashion to the way they learned to talk (Clay, 2001; Teale & Sulzby, 1986). Writing develops through the child's intent (Harste et al., 1981, 1983) and constant invention and reinvention, demonstration, and assistance from literate beings at the child's point of need (Birnbaum, 1982; Dyson, 1986). For the teacher to be able to provide writing assistance to children, the teacher must understand three important points about the development of written language: (1) writing develops as a slow, but steady process; (2) writing develops in the context of meaningful print; and (3) writing requires some risk taking or *approximation* at first (Harste et al., 1981).

Importance of Process, Context, and Risk Taking to Written Language Development

Teachers have not always understood the importance of observing and guiding *process*, providing meaningful *context*, and encouraging children to *take risks* that often result in miscues (or approximations) when they write (and read). Harste, Burke, and Woodward (1981) stress that these three things are crucial for teachers to understand and implement if children are to reach their full literacy potential. Each of these points is addressed separately in the following sections.

Importance of Understanding the Process of Written Language Development

Learning to write, like learning to talk and read, is very complex (Clay, 1991; Holdaway, 1979). It cannot be taught by simply analyzing the finished product. It takes guidance from a knowledgeable literacy teacher at the child's point of need in the process of meaningful writing to help a writer progress, and this takes time. Some teachers wonder if spending one hour in a writing workshop is too much time for young children to stay engaged in the process of writing. However, Harste, Burke, and Woodward (1981) found that children as young as 3 years old spent as much as 25 minutes absorbed in the process of writing. In fact, I have often heard kindergartners beg for more time at the end of their daily writing workshop.

When children participate in the process of writing, their intent is to communicate, even though their written language may not look like it to adult eyes at first (Harste et al., 1981). Murray (1985) describes writing as active thinking: "Meaning is not thought up and then written down. The act of writing is an act of thought" (p. 3). The focus in writing always needs to be on what the young author is thinking (process) as he or she strives to communicate a message; that way, suitable praise and guidance can be given. The following example illustrates the importance of knowing the child's process of thinking as he or she writes (see also "Butterflies" at the beginning of chapter 7).

Mrs. Clark questions Jeremy about the various sized people in his drawing (see Figure 8). He explains that he is trying to show that some people are closer so he drew them bigger, and some are far away so he drew them smaller. Mrs. Clark realizes that she would not have recognized Jeremy's perceptive and praiseworthy thinking about perspective if she had only viewed his final product.

In their second year of implementing writing workshops, Mrs. Clark and Mrs. Williams knew from experience that initially most of the children's meanings were carried by pictures and that the act of drawing and the picture itself both provided a supportive scaffolding within which children could construct their writing and eventually make progress to readable print (Calkins, 1994). Also, these teachers realized the importance of devoting an

Figure 8. People Perspective Sample

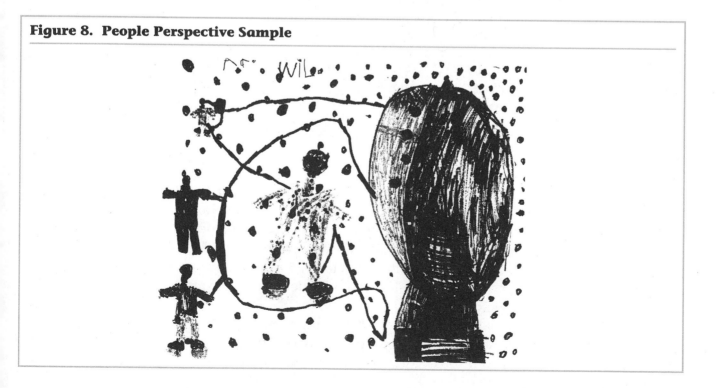

hour a day to approximated meaningful writing, because they had learned to value the importance of process and also context to learning how to write (and read).

Importance of Context to Written Language Development

Learning about written language involves more than just the print itself; it also involves the print setting, or context. Children see print on television, cereal boxes, and road signs; they often learn to read this environmental print with the help of parents or caregivers. For example, when my daughter was 3 years old, whenever we would pass the Kentucky Fried Chicken restaurant sign, she would point to the sign and say, "Shicken!" At that time, she was reacting to the sign and not the print.

Children learn to recognize environmental print—not because this print is less complex, but because it is more familiar. Clay (1991) stresses the importance of familiarity to becoming literate: "Regular contact with familiar material in familiar [or predictable] contexts will suit the slow progress reader [and writer] better than trying to force on him a flexibility on many varied texts which he is not ready to operate" (p. 195). (See Classic Pattern Books, Appendix B.)

Literacy learning requires familiarity with context for the message and its meaning to be understood. Harste and colleagues (1981) advise, "To improve language instruction, the faster we abandon the notion that meaning resides in print, the better. It is not accidental that the word 'text' appears within the word 'context'" (pp. 408–409). For example, as a university instructor, I was talking to one of my student teachers in the hallway of a local elementary school. A second-grade child, not one of my students, was also in the hallway working with some isolated words on flashcards. She came up to us, showed us a flashcard with the word *and* on it, and asked us what the word was. I asked her if she had a little book that she could read. She returned with a book and proceeded to read from it. She read the word *and* in context with no problem. Then I asked her to find a word that looked like the one on her flashcard in the sentence she'd just read. When she found it, she said, "Oh, that's it!"

This situation provided a good learning experience for my student teacher who said, "Now, I understand what you meant about isolated skill and drill not transferring to real reading and writing!"

Print needs to be presented meaningfully in kindergarten in the context of real reading and writing. Although children can learn to identify letters of the alphabet and some sounds (phonemes) that stand for these letters in isolation, they often have great difficulty in applying or transferring this isolated knowledge to the process of writing or reading (McCormick & Mason, 1981). For example, in the beginning of the school year, Mrs. Clark conferred with a kindergartner, Cody, who could parrot the alphabet and provide a sound for each letter as he pointed to his alphabet strip. Cody could find any letter on his ABC strip, too. Mrs. Clark was surprised that the child's knowledge did not transfer to his actual writing. Initially, his writing was just a jumbled concoction of letters, and it showed no sign of understanding the alphabetic principle. She suspected that Cody had been drilled on the alphabet and its sounds, because there was no transference of this isolated knowledge to conventional writing.

After only two months of writing his own meaningful stories in writing workshop, Cody began to realize that letters and sounds are not an entity in themselves. Letters and words were meant to help him put his thoughts (his oral language) into written language in the context of his story. Because Mrs. Clark appreciated and understood the value of approximated spelling, Cody felt comfortable in the risk-free environment she provided. He knew he did not have to spell every word correctly as he tried to communicate his thoughts, and he took risks with spelling. As Cody worked to convey meaning, he was able to test his hypotheses about print and gain an understanding of the alphabetic principle. Eventually, through experimentation like this and guidance from his teacher when he was developmentally ready to understand certain spelling concepts, Cody became a conventional speller near the end of third grade.

Importance of a Risk-Free Environment to Written Language Development

Because some kindergarten teachers do not understand the importance of the condition of risk taking or approximation to the development of writing, they do not always appreciate "scribbling" as an initial stage in written language development. Young children need to use their active, constructive minds to figure out things, which guarantees that some miscues or approximations will be made. (See chapter 1 for a description of approximation.) Approximations should be welcomed and encouraged by the teacher just as they are by parents when their children learned to talk. It is through these approximations that teachers are able to identify students' literacy knowledge and guide their literacy needs.

Risk taking not only needs to be embraced in the classroom but also in the home. I often have heard teachers comment that some children seem to be by nature frightened to take risks. Temple and colleagues (1988) state that a child's personality is indeed a factor in risk taking but so are "the expectations of his parents and the atmosphere of his classroom" (p. 111). Therefore, when teachers promote developmental spelling, which includes invented spelling, they need to enlist parents' understanding and support of its value—in turn, parents will encourage and praise their children's invented spelling (Temple et al., 1988). (See the letter to parents on developmental spelling in Appendix C.)

Teachers should not expect conventional writing, reading, and spelling from emergent writers and readers, especially in the initial stages of written language and spelling (Calkins, 1994, 2001; Clay, 1991, 2001; Gentry & Gillet, 1993; Temple et al., 1988). Creating a risk-free environment promotes approximation, which is a key to becoming literate. Some teachers find it useful to call approximated spelling *kid-writing*; kindergartners seem to enjoy the term because it gives them permission to experiment with written language when they draw and write (Tompkins & Hoskisson, 1995). Permission to take risks with spelling is vital to young children's spelling development and creativity in writing. (See chapter 2, p. 35, for discussion of one student's fear of taking risks and how this fear hindered his creative writing.) In fact, permission to take risks is vital to all learning. The following example illustrates the importance of risk taking with directionality in kindergarten.

When Donald first entered school, he could only print one letter, *D*. However, as he practices his kid-writing, he often prints *D* backward or upside down on his paper. Mrs. Williams encourages Donald's experimentation (risk taking) by pointing out to Donald what is "right" about his letter formation and praising his work as she guides him to compare his *D* to the one on his ABC strip. Mrs. Williams knows Donald is not developmentally ready to understand directionality at this point, but she knows that with time and guidance it will happen, and the evidence of it will show up in his writing. By the second quarter of the year, it does. As the year progresses, Donald not only learns to write the letters of his name correctly, but on his own initiative he can also write a sentence that makes sense and is readable to others.

Progress such as Donald's doesn't happen in a day. The process of learning kid-writing takes experimentation, guidance, and time. Progress must be viewed over time, which is why it is important to keep weekly dated writing samples from each child. For example, Donald's writing sample (Figure 9) shows how he labeled a drawing of his bed early in the kindergarten year; the sample shows directionality of letters but not of line. Later, Donald was able to show directionality of three lines (or sentences) in a story about his turtle.

Simplified Writing Process Guidelines for Kindergartners

When kindergarten teachers implement writing and reading workshops using Calkins's (1994, 2001) approach, they value observing process; immersing students in meaningful writing, which promotes context; and providing a risk-free environment by valuing approximation—all part of

Figure 9. Early Writing Sample

"Bed"

Cambourne's (1988) conditions of language learning. With these conditions serving as the foundation for a writing workshop, kindergartners will be able to make progress in the writing process:

- Prewriting or Rehearsing—Choosing a topic or drawing
- Writing a Rough Draft—Writing about a topic any way possible
- Revising—Adding writing, usually at the end of the piece, and sometimes crossing out
- Editing—Correcting a studied high-frequency word
- Publishing—Informally sharing work with classmates, posting work, or both, and formally sharing writing by creating little books

(See Appendix C for a simple chart of the Five Stages of Written Language Development.)

Prewriting or Rehearsing

Kindergartners use drawing as a rehearsal to help them gather and organize ideas before writing and to keep them on track as they write. Rehearsal does not mean the same thing to young authors as it does to adult authors. Calkins (1994) explains that to 4-, 5-, and 6-year-olds "the act of drawing and the picture itself both provide a supportive scaffolding within which [the student] can construct his piece of writing" (p. 85). As children draw, they do not "plan the direction [their] writing will take" (p. 84). Instead, they arrive at their final product as they draw. For example, kindergarten teachers often hear children saying things like, "This is going to be about my dad and the fish he caught" in the middle of their drawing as they discover their direction or focus. They often talk to their classmates about their topic before beginning to write, too. It is important to note that children need to write on unlined paper during this time because most of their meaning is conveyed through pictures (Calkins, 1994).

Writing a Rough Draft

In the beginning of the school year, kindergartners typically write single-draft compositions. These compositions often begin with a picture and some approximated writing that looks like scribbling or mock letters—there is little or no indication of awareness of the alphabetic principle (Calkins, 1994; Fisher, 1991; Ray & Cleaveland, 2004; Tompkins & Hoskisson, 1995). According to Tompkins and Hoskisson (1995), "The emphasis is on expressing ideas, not on handwriting skills or conventional spelling" (p. 270).

Early in the year, minilessons should convey to students the importance of approximated and, later, invented spelling in a rough draft. It is also very important that kindergarten teachers demonstrate in minilessons that it's acceptable to cross out misspelled words, so children understand that a rough draft doesn't need to have perfect spelling. I have observed many children, including kindergartners, erase words and waste valuable writing time waiting for their teacher to spell a word for them. Perfection should be saved for publishing. Also, implementing handwriting classes to teach proper letter formation slows kindergartners in their process of writing. They become more concerned about how to form a letter perfectly than getting their valuable ideas on paper. (See chapter 2 for guidelines on teaching letter formation.) However, it is important to convey in minilessons that writing should be readable. I tell kindergartners that if a paper is not readable, it cannot be published, which is why Routman (1991) does not like the term "sloppy copy." In a writing workshop, kindergartners learn they can continue to write on the same piece every day; they learn that with their teacher's guidance that they can add to an idea as long as they maintain their focus. As they make progress in the process of writing and spelling, they begin to label their pictures and eventually even make little books of three or four sentences (Calkins, 1994; Fisher, 1991; Tompkins & Hoskisson, 1995).

Revising

Initially, kindergartners' revisions are limited to rereading their text to themselves, to a partner or "writing buddy," or to the teacher to ensure that they've written all that they want to say. Kindergartners make very few changes on their own initiative when they revise, usually limited to adding words or occasionally crossing out words. Later in the year, kindergartners also can be asked to reread for sense because, by that time, the teacher will have taught many minilessons on rereading for sense or focus.

The only exception to the minimal revisions would be if a child and his or her teacher feel that the child's work should be formally published, or made into a little book. Most children want to publish at least one piece (one to three sentences that make sense) by midyear. I have found the following writing conference technique from Dahl and Farnan (1998) useful in helping struggling writers prior to publishing focus and organize their piece for appropriate sequence. This technique can be used for other writers, too, but the condition of *responsibility* must always be kept in mind. Many kindergartners are *responsible* enough to understand focus and sequence from repeated minilesson demonstrations, and they are able to publish papers that don't need this technique. Some children may need to be reminded about steps 1, 2, and 3, but step 4 could be omitted; how the technique is used depends on the individual child's needs.

1. Teacher: What is the one thing [i.e., focus] that your piece is about? [The child answers and reads (or tells) the teacher his or her story as best as he or she can.]

2. The teacher repeats the child's story to the child, highlighting keywords and phrasing sentences so there is good sense (focus) and sequence to them. The teacher may have to ask the child to add words for clarification.

3. Teacher: What things are really important in your story?

   The teacher may have to help the child stick to the point and delete words that are not part of the focus. The teacher writes on separate notecards the few important things that enhance the topic's focus and numbers the cards if necessary.

4. The teacher and the child talk through the story using the cards. Then the child uses the cards independently to write his or her piece. There may be one or two children who cannot do this without further guidance from the teacher; the teacher should help these children get their words onto paper. Then, the teacher edits each piece by pointing out changes to the children, and the pieces can be published.

Editing

Editing is not emphasized in kindergarten, but when it is done, the teacher does most of it. Typically editing is not introduced in kindergarten until a child has a publishable story of three sentences that are readable, but this number depends on the teacher and the child. Editing conferences should occur prior to formal publishing. Editing conferences focus on fixing spelling and mechanical errors with the goal of making the piece readable to an audience other than the author. Grammatical or structure errors, usage errors, or both are corrected by the teacher during editing but should be handled sensitively with young children. As Tompkins and Hoskisson (1995) state, "Some errors should be ignored, especially young children's errors; correcting too many errors teaches students that their language is inferior or inadequate" (pp. 504–505). Correcting only one or two errors in kindergartners' writing by simply saying, "We usually write it this way" can be beneficial because corrections made in writing seem less personal than verbal corrections (Elbow, 1973; Haley-James, 1991).

Editing conferences can provide opportunities for guiding children to use what they have learned about spelling. Children can be asked to take *responsibility* for making spelling corrections for high-frequency words previously discussed and highlighted in context in the room or on the word wall. This is a good introduction to proofreading. For those words spelled incorrectly that have not been discussed in class, the teacher can correct the spelling and acknowledge the good attempt by pointing out how close the child came to the correct spelling. Depending on the teacher's time and the child's level of interest in learning to spell the word being discussed, the teacher can ask the child what the "tricky part" was and perhaps help the child come up with a strategy or mnemonic device for remembering it (Routman, 1991). (See Appendix D for a list of high-frequency words that kindergartners can learn.)

When correcting errors, Calkins (1994) suggests using a blue pen or pencil because the color is less intimidating than red. Calkins also suggests that students can put pieces they want published in a special publishing box after doing the prerequisite editing on their own. This editing might require that the young author follow a checklist decided on by the class, for example, a checklist of writing rules. (See chapter 5, p. 161, for an example of writing rules.) This editing list should change as children become capable of new skills.

Publishing

There are two types of publishing typically used in kindergarten: formal and informal. Formal publishing is used for little books, and informal publishing usually consists of sharing drawings and writings with classmates and posting young authors' work on bulletin boards or in hallways. Some teachers like to use old refrigerator boxes for additional display space or hang blankets in the room for displaying work (see Figure 10). Some teachers use an additional form of informal publishing. Once a week, or less frequently, each kindergartner meets with a fourth- or fifth-grade writing buddy. The kindergartners read their stories to the buddies, and the buddies read a story of their own to the kindergartners. Both tell each other what they liked about their pieces and ask a question or two about things they did not understood or things they'd like to know more about. Then they make

Figure 10. Informal Publishing Display

sure to end the meeting with something they especially liked about the authors' writings. According to Tompkins and Hoskisson (1995), "Through sharing [like this] children develop a concept of audience and learn new ways of writing [from more advanced writers]" (p. 270).

Formal publishing consists of typing a child's rough draft into conventional form and then laminating and binding the page(s) into a booklet (see Figure 11). Published pieces are often kept in the classroom library for classmates to read. Kindergartners should not be expected to recopy their work—unless it's so messy that it is unreadable and the child is capable of neater work. Copying takes the joy out of writing. Sometimes teachers take papers home and type them or they use parent volunteers to type papers. It is best to type papers with the young author at the teacher's side so corrections can be explained to the child, but teachers know that the ideal isn't always possible.

Observing students taking part in and comprehending the writing process provides more evidence of student learning than simply viewing a finished product. However, it is important to note that the different parts of the writing process—rehearsing, drafting, revising, editing, and publishing— are not done in an orderly, step-by-step manner. Graves (1994) states, "I've found some teachers have misunderstood the writing process. They deliberately take children through the phases of making a choice, rehearsing, composing, and then rewriting" (p. 82). Even when writers intend to publish a piece, the writing process is recursive. Writing is "untidy"

Figure 11. Formal Publishing Display

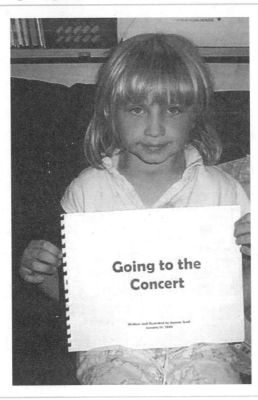

Going to the
Concert

because "a new topic may emerge while writers are in the midst of writing about another" (p. 82). Writers should not be expected to stick with every piece they begin and take it through the writing process step by step; this is especially true for kindergartners. Instead, writers should be encouraged to tell their stories with "voice," so they will voluntarily engage in the process and progress in the five stages of written language development.

Five Stages of Written Language in Kindergarten

The five stages of written language described in this section were developed by Kathleen Buss (unpublished material) and are based on Woodward's (1981) research study that uses the Language Experience Approach (i.e., children dictate a story or experiences, and the teacher records their dictation) to understand the young child's concept of story.

1. Stage One: Picture Writing
2. Stage Two: Picture and Label Writing
3. Stage Three: Taking Inventory
4. Stage Four: Taking Inventory and Adding Description

5. Stage Five: Acquiring and Developing Textual Features of Nonfiction and Fiction

Most kindergartners' written language develops and progresses through the first four of the five stages of written language development. The fifth and last stage, acquiring and developing textual features of nonfiction and fiction, is not evidenced often in kindergarten; however, by implementing writing and reading workshops based on Cambourne's (1988) conditions of language learning, it may well be seen more frequently in the future. Having knowledge of these stages is especially helpful to kindergarten teachers, so they can track and assist each student to make good progress in written language development.

When kindergartners begin to write in a writing workshop, they usually add some scribbles, or mock letters, as well as some real letters to their pictures. It is not unusual for these pictures to focus on cartoon or video characters. Kindergarten teachers should try to encourage children to tell their own personal stories, because this will help develop each kindergartner's voice, which promotes engagement with writing. Once they are engaged, kindergartners will be more capable of making progress in the five stages of written language. The following sections provide more detailed descriptions of the five stages and corresponding student samples.

Stage One: Picture Writing

Very young children usually begin to communicate ideas by drawing a picture, or using Picture Writing. Children's drawings are often about things they are interested in or things that are happening or have happened in their lives. At around 3 years old, children know the difference between their drawing and their writing. However, most adults would find it difficult to determine the difference between the two without knowing the child's intent because children's drawing and writing often resemble one big scribble. If it is important to know what the child has written, ask the child, "Where is your drawing?" "Where is your writing?" and "What did you write about?" The child's answer to these questions will help to identify his or her intent to communicate a message.

Encouraging picture writing is important because the act of drawing and the drawing itself provide support to children so they can attempt to construct a piece of writing (Calkins, 1994). Testing their theories about writing and trying to figure out the alphabetic principle is difficult for children and it takes time; children's pictures provide them with direction and serve as a starting point for teachers to help them determine what each child knows and needs to know about print (see Figure 12).

To encourage picture writing,

1. Ask the student to tell you about his or her drawing.

Figure 12. Picture Writing Sample

2. Entice the student into a deeper discussion about the drawing. Ask, "What else would you like to add to your drawing?" or "Can you tell me more about your drawing?"

3. Praise the student's effort while conferring in the one-on-one student and teacher conference. If you see something noteworthy, or if the child needs an extra boost in self-esteem, quickly show his or her picture to the classmates at the table and point out something you like in a "Quick Share" (Fisher, 1991). Be honest in your praise. (There is always something praiseworthy in every child's picture, even if it is simply the beautiful colors the child chose to work with. Teachers need to focus on what the child knows or can do, rather than what the child cannot do. New learning must be built on what is already known—this is the very nature of developmental learning.)

Stage Two: Picture and Label Writing

During the Picture and Label Writing stage, children start to incorporate mock letters and words, and sometimes real letters and words, within their pictures to communicate their messages. For example, they might incorporate labels into their pictures to represent their messages more accurately. These pictures tend to be about their likes, their families, or their experiences. The emphasis in this stage is on children's emerging awareness that writing communicates a message.

In addition to writing about their personal experiences, teachers might occasionally demonstrate picturing and labeling to students by drawing some related objects in a picture and then labeling them. I often like to draw my family, including my cat and dog, because children often enjoy writing about their families and can relate to this topic. Then I label the people and animals in my drawing and tell the students something about each one.

Figure 13 shows Olivia's writing sample from the Picture and Label Writing stage. In conferring with Olivia, I wanted to encourage the development of her voice to help her progress to the next stage of writing. Graves (1994) explains voice:

> The writing process has a driving force called voice... Voice is the imprint of ourselves on our writing.... Take voice away and there is no writing, just word after boring word.... When voice is strong, writing improves, along with the skills that help to improve writing. (p. 81)

In order to encourage her voice, while conferring with Olivia, I followed Calkins's (1994) recommendation: I became genuinely interested in her writing and pursued one line of thought. For example, I said, "Olivia, I notice you've written five names in your picture. Can you tell me about these people?" After Olivia told me the people were her family, I singled out Anna. "What can you tell me about Anna?" I asked. Olivia replied that Anna was her sister; she was 9 and she played with and helped Olivia. I wanted to see some excitement in Olivia, what I refer to as the "fire" in her eyes, so I asked

Figure 13. Picture and Label Writing Sample

Olivia, "What do you play with Anna?" Olivia responded, "We pretend to be cheetahs and we fight each other." As I saw her excitement and heard her voice emerging, I told her to write that down, and I repeated to her what she just said, praising the idea and *any* written approximations.

Thus, when children are in the Picture and Label Writing stage, they often repeat the same theme, especially when it concerns their family, friends, and pets, because these people have great significance to them. However, kindergarten teacher Judith Hiliker (as cited in Newkirk & Atwell, 1988) explains why progress is made from this stage to the next: "With each repetition the associations that the child makes with the drawing/text become more complex and differentiated. Once the one-word label is no longer capable of bearing the weight of accumulated association [and a writer's voice emerges] word sequences become necessary [and the child moves forward]" (p. 21).

Stage Three: Taking Inventory

Buss defines Taking Inventory as a child's way to use written language to list his or her thoughts, or to communicate his or her experiences or likes and dislikes. In this stage of writing development, children tend to make lists, or inventories, of what they know (e.g., thoughts and experiences) and of what they have drawn in their pictures. They write these lists in sentence form, but they do not elaborate (see Figure 14). The sentences are very simple (e.g., *I*

Figure 14. Taking Inventory Writing Sample

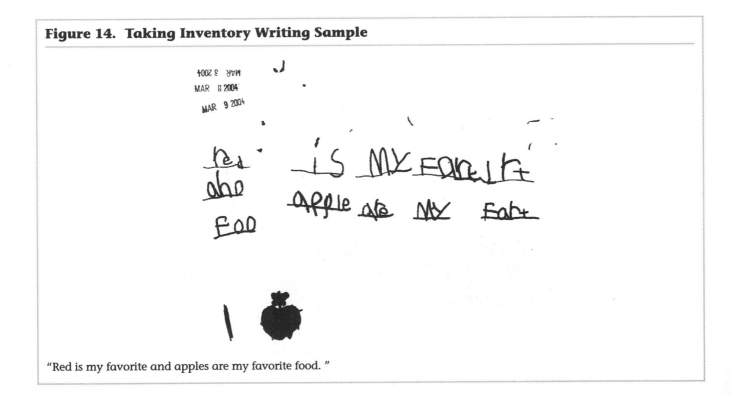

"Red is my favorite and apples are my favorite food."

like dogs; This is my house; My mom went shopping; I saw a monster). Still, at this stage, children use print to describe what is in their pictures (Harste et al., 1981), and they write their messages under the pictures, rather than in the pictures as they did in the Picture and Label Writing stage. This change indicates that children are noticing a separation between picture and print.

In all stages of writing, children should be encouraged to tell you more about the things they've chosen to write about. This is especially true in this stage so students can progress to the next stage.

Stage Four: Taking Inventory and Adding Description

In the next stage of writing development, students take inventory of what is in their pictures and they add some elaboration beyond what is in the pictures. This elaboration sometimes includes an explanation of why they like something. Young authors in this stage usually write a sentence and develop it more with description (see Figure 15). These sentences usually have something to do with describing an action and expanding personal thoughts. For example, the sentence *I like dogs* (simple inventorying) becomes *I like dogs because they wag their tails*.

To extend children's writing development, teachers should demonstrate in writing retelling their own personal experiences. When teachers demonstrate their own writing, Cudd and Roberts (1994) advise using the sentence expansion technique to teach more complex sentences, because

Figure 15. Taking Inventory and Adding Description Writing Sample

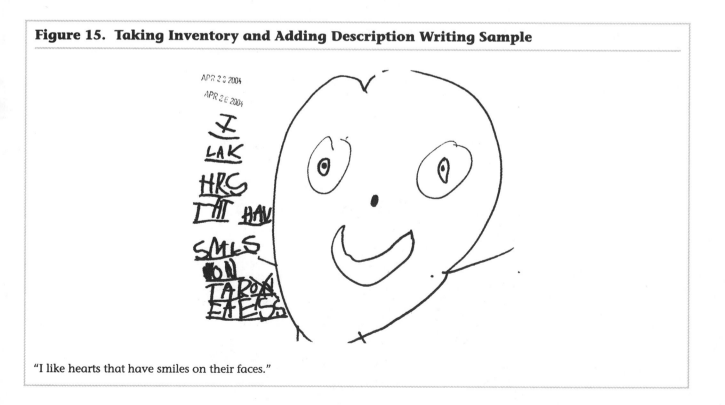

"I like hearts that have smiles on their faces."

they found it to be the most useful of sentence manipulation activities. Once teachers have demonstrated their own personal sentence expansion, Cudd and Roberts suggest demonstrating the procedure by writing a simple sentence stem that has been personalized by adding children's names and familiar events, people, and places—in other words, by drawing on children's common experiences as much as possible. For example, the teacher can use the sentence stem *Jimmy likes frogs* and then discuss why Jimmy likes frogs. The stem might be expanded to, *Jimmy likes frogs because they jump and make funny noises.* Other questions that enhance sentence expansion might include the following: "What kind of frog?" "How high did it jump?" "Where did you see it?" or "Where did it jump?" However, questions that focus on asking why are the most important.

Asking students "Why?" in a manner that shows you appreciate their work also proves helpful to sentence expansion. For example, when I conferred with one student, Cody, I said, "I've noticed you draw a lot of dinosaurs and you're very good at it. I'm just wondering why you draw so many dinosaurs?" Cody said, "I like dinosaurs because they are humongous!" "What a wonderful word!" I responded, referring to his use of *humongous.* "Would you please add that to your sentence?" He successfully wrote the sentence using *humongous.*

Demonstrating, listening, praising, and questioning can develop children's use of simple inventory into their use of inventory and description. I believe the best way to help children develop and progress through these stages of written language development is to encourage each child to draw and write about the personal experiences in his or her life so his or her voice emerges "as a unique personality on paper" (Fletcher, 1993, p. 77).

As kindergartners attempt to convey information in writing beyond the simple labeling and listing used in the previous four stages, their written language begins to take on more sophistication. They begin to acquire and develop the textual features of nonfiction and fiction in their writing.

Stage Five: Acquiring and Developing Textual Features of Nonfiction and Fiction

According to Graves (1994), fiction is the genre or form of written language that is enjoyed most by children; it is also the most demanding. On the other hand, writing personal narratives or personal recounts is one of the easiest genres for young children to write, and it is a good way for them to begin writing and employing the features of nonfiction text.

Further, the writing that comes most naturally to children is the "expressive" mode, more commonly referred to as personal narrative (Britton, 1970; Morrow, 1989). The author puts him- or herself directly into the piece and rarely thinks about the reader. Often the purpose of the piece seems to be to express likes and dislikes (Britton, 1970). Temple and colleagues (1988) characterize it as "a free flow of ideas and feelings" (p. 131), and Morrow

(1989) defines it as a "primary impulse" (p. 145). Buss and Karnowski (2002) prefer the name *personal recount* to *personal narrative* because "narrative" has a strong connection to fiction and story. In a personal recount, Buss and Karnowski explain that "an author writes a retelling or interpretation of an event or series of events that are memorable in his or her life" (p. 6). However, because the term *story* is familiar to kindergartners, it is often used in the classroom rather than personal recount. (See Figure 16 for an example of a personal recount.)

In addition to teaching personal recounts, teachers should include other genres of nonfiction writing, too. Exposure to nonfiction genres is very important because it enables children to learn how to present their thoughts and opinions in writing, and know an area particularly well (Graves, 1994). Teachers should increase their reading of nonfiction texts to students during the day to provide frequent models for this kind of writing (Calkins, 1994).

Moving away from personal recounts to other forms of nonfiction depends on students' ability to develop a sense of audience, which may take some time (Temple et al., 1988). Temple and colleagues (1988) advise teachers that until students have demonstrated an awareness of audience, they should not approach other nonfiction writing that involves giving information, instructions, and attempting to advise others, or writing that is to be admired as a whole, like poetry and fictional stories (Temple et al., 1988). Once students demonstrate this awareness, they can begin to consider the structural requirements of these different genres of written language. Although I have never taught the structure of poetry in

---

Figure 16. Nonfiction Textual Feature Sample: Personal Recount

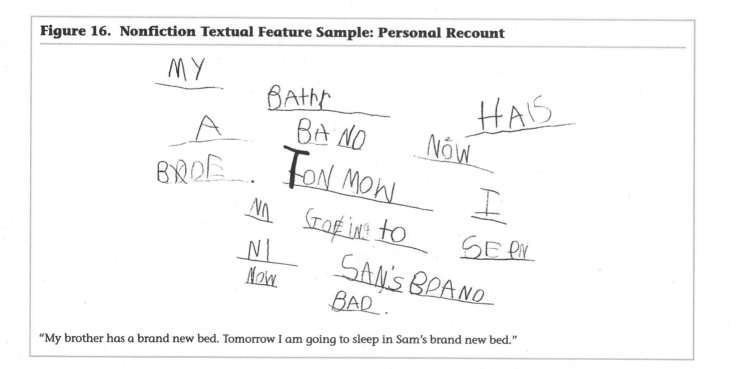

"My brother has a brand new bed. Tomorrow I am going to sleep in Sam's brand new bed."

kindergarten, I have observed that poetic language comes naturally to children, so kindergarten teachers might want to help children put their poetry into a proper structure—mostly free verse—and publish it. For example, a kindergartner wrote the following: "I see white butterflies, I see yellow butterflies, I see 'pokey-dotted' butterflies. I love butterflies."

Although children are capable of writing all these genres, according to Temple and colleagues (1988) and Graves (1994), it is really quite difficult for kindergartners to write fictional stories (see Figure 17) unless they come from a literate home where they have been immersed in fiction. Writing fictional stories requires kindergartners to resist putting in their own egocentric concerns and to stay with the focus of the story (which is asking a lot). Although I do not recommend teaching fictional story writing to kindergartners, I do recommend immersing them in such stories so they can develop a sense of story and an understanding of story structure.

Once children start to show expansion in their written language, teachers can start to expand knowledge of different forms and functions of writing. Until that time, children should write any way they can, but they should be encouraged to use their own *voice* as they recount their personal experiences. Also, teachers can enrich and expand children's lives by incorporating an array of literature into the classroom.

Figure 17. Fiction Textual Feature Sample: Fairy Tale

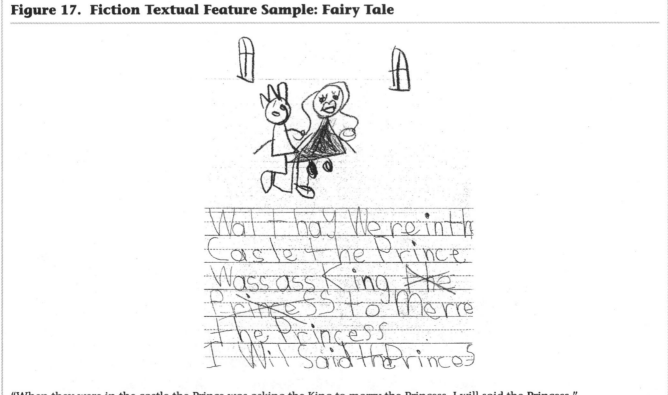

"When they were in the castle the Prince was asking the King to marry the Princess. I will said the Princess."

Genres Appropriate for Kindergarten

The last section of this chapter further delineates the fifth stage of written language, Acquiring and Developing Textual Features, and outlines some nonfiction forms that kindergartners are capable of writing. To better understand this stage, it is important that teachers be aware of the genres of literature appropriate for kindergarten. Written language genres are simply different forms of writing that serve different functions (Routman, 1991). Children show that they can use a variety of genres in their early writing in school, especially lists, labels, and signs, as well as rudimentary stories (Chapman, 1995). Some kindergartners like a little variety in writing, even though most enjoy recounting personal experiences and episodes from their lives. Students' growth in understanding the features of text continues into adulthood as they master the genres of written language.

In most cases, when teachers introduce a new genre for the children to try, teachers demonstrate the genre in their writing in minilessons prior to writing workshop and read several books during read-aloud illustrating the genre, and perhaps in reading workshop. If the book is a quick read, it might even be used in the minilesson section of writing workshop. Calkins (1994) recommends that all genre studies should begin with examples that "knock [your] socks off" (p. 364). With each of the following genres, I list some examples of appropriate literature to use in the classroom. (These books as well as additional books also can be found in Appendix B under Children's Books by Genre.)

When teachers read books to stimulate students' interest and help them understand a new genre, teachers should discuss

- the purpose of the genre,
- how children might want to use this genre, and
- how its structure is different from other genres.

Most lessons that I use to introduce a genre last a few days to a week. I encourage all children to attempt to write in the genre once. Some form of publishing for the child is usually enough incentive to try. Once a genre has been introduced and a sample has been published in some way (formal or informal), the choice of genre and topic during writing becomes the young author's again. The genre I model and encourage most often is the retelling of the personal experiences or recounts in my life, which is a type of nonfiction.

Nonfiction

Within the genre of nonfiction, there are many choices of text structure that are dictated by the author's purpose. For example, an author who writes an ABC book will organize the text very differently from an author who writes a personal letter. Deciding which genres to teach and when can often be determined by the genre you see your students attempting, but the key to this decision is to observe and identify which writing stage students are in and choose genres appropriate to their writing abilities.

With kindergarten students, it is best to begin writing instruction with nonfiction because most students' initial attempts to write are nonfiction. Extending their knowledge of nonfiction includes the following genres: ABC books, number books, labels, lists, notes, letters, and informal reports.

ABC Books

ABC books are the first genre that I recommend to kindergarten teachers because these books can be used with kindergartners when the school year begins. Obviously, ABC books help kindergartners learn the letters of the alphabet, and I recommend both showing published ABC books to kindergartners and having them make their own ABC books. Some books that can be used to introduce making an alphabet book include *Animal Babies ABC: An Alphabet Book of Animal Offspring* (Knox, 2003b) and *ABC Under the Sea: An Ocean Life Alphabet Book* (Knox, 2003a; see Appendix B for more ABC books).

Clay (1993b) explains the value of having children make their own ABC books: "The child has a feel for the size of the task" (p. 26). By making their own alphabet books, they know how far they have come and what they still need to learn. It is important to praise all letters known and newly learned letters. Also, let children know that they are not *expected* to know the entire alphabet yet, and they will learn it during the kindergarten year.

Clay (1993b) recommends the following method of making an ABC book. Teachers with whom I have worked have found the method to be more useful than published books in helping children develop the alphabetic principle so they can engage in written language.

Children make a paper book with 26 pages, or a page for each letter. When the child knows some letters (Clay suggests 10, but the amount can be less), write these letters in his or her alphabet book, leaving blank pages or gaps for letters yet to be learned. The alphabet should be printed in sequence, with a drawing for each letter that the child knows. Use a key picture that the child already identifies with that letter. Teachers should use the form of the letter that the child already knows (uppercase, lowercase, or both). The book should be an ongoing project until all letters are learned. (See Figure 18A and B for a sample of an ABC book, and Appendix C for a letter to parents introducing the purpose of this project and how to make the book.)

Some kindergarten teachers like to do this project with parents on parents' night in the fall, making it a family project. Mrs. Clark introduced making this book on the first day of school to parents and kindergartners as they came for orientation. The children began the books at school but finished them at home with the parents' guidance. Then they brought them to school to share in Author's Chair. This is an excellent activity for extending children's knowledge of the alphabet, and it provides the teacher with the knowledge of the letters each child knows.

Figure 18. ABC Book Sample

My ABC Book
By _HY HArLet_

A

Ff   Farm

B

Number Books

Kindergarten children need to learn numbers as well as letters, and some entering kindergartners cannot distinguish between numbers and letters. Therefore, many kindergarten teachers like to have children make their own book of numbers in addition to making ABC books. The book of numbers is made in a similar manner to the ABC book, beginning only with the numbers from 1 to 10 that the child knows. As the year progresses and the student learns more numbers, more pages can be added. Number books that kindergarten teachers have enjoyed using include *1, 2, 3* (Hoban, 1985) and *1, 2, 3 to the Zoo* (Carle, 1968).

Some kindergartners confuse numbers with letters. The number book and the ABC book are helpful in resolving this confusion. As teachers teach children to understand the difference between letters and numbers and help them develop the alphabetic principle, children begin to demonstrate more sophisticated writing. When this happens, the kindergarten teachers with whom I have worked like to provide some variety in written language, and they have introduced the following genres: labels, lists, note writing, letters, and informal reports.

Labels

Newkirk (1987) believes that young children's writing begins with labels and lists, and not as speech written down. He discovered that young children's lists and labels are related to the sorting and display of information. Children are very familiar with labels. Teachers label the children's desks and coat hooks and other items in the classroom. Labeling shows children that print makes messages in a very elementary manner (Clay, 1975).

Around the beginning of November, many kindergarten teachers observe that most of their kindergartners are beginning to do some simple labeling of their pictures. This is a good time to introduce labels in writing workshop. First, teachers should read several books about labeling during their daily read-aloud. An excellent book about labeling to share during read-aloud is *Carlo Likes Reading* (Spanyol, 2001). This book is about a giraffe who labels things all over the house for a child. Although the book is fictional, I highly recommend it for labeling because it provides a good model of labeling in children's homes and at school, and children enjoy it. Another book I recommend for labeling is *Clifford's Word Book* (Bridwell, 1990).

To stimulate interest in labeling, the teacher can bring into the classroom a can of beans or soup and perhaps a milk carton and a cereal box. The teacher can ask the children what they think is in each container and discuss what the print might say. During this activity, students can listen for beginning sounds (phonemic awareness). Have students identify the letter that stands for the sound, and have them try to find that letter on the container. Teachers can even show the children a can that has no label to make the point of a label's importance. Then, ask the children where else they have seen labeling. For example, putting their names on coats and crayon boxes is labeling. Labeled objects should remain labeled and visible throughout the school year for continued learning.

Mrs. Williams and Mrs. Clark ask their children to label the room on the second day of working with labeling. These teachers label their desks with a complete sentence to serve as a model (e.g., *This is Mrs. Williams's desk.*). Then, the children choose one thing to label (see Figure 19).

Figure 19. Labeling Sample

Labeling is especially beneficial to English-language learners because it allows them to see and learn the meaning of the relation between the object and the print in a graphic and simple way.

Lists

Around October, teachers may notice that the children have produced some lists of words. Often these lists consist of the names of students' family members and friends or letters of the alphabet—or even a list of red things in the classroom (see Figure 20).

Mrs. Clark has observed that most of these lists that students produce do not indicate knowledge of the alphabetic principle; rather, they are simply a result of the children copying print in the classroom.

Similar to the process used to introduce labels, the teacher should read aloud some books about making lists. As a literacy coach, I have found it difficult to find interesting nonfiction models for making lists. However, the models I have used, although they are fiction, have helped students learn the purpose of making lists. For example, Bottner and Kruglik have written a book about making lists called *Wallace's Lists* (2004). Wallace is a mouse who can do anything as long as he has a list. In addition, teachers also can use the short story "A List" in *Frog and Toad Together* (Lobel, 1971). Finally, *Don't Forget the Bacon* (Hutchins, 1976) is a good lead-in for writing a grocery list for a recipe that a kindergarten class might make, perhaps for an Author's Party. (See chapter 7, pp. 265–267, for a description of an Author's Party.)

Teachers also can model creating a list to encourage prediction; this strategy requires the use of the concept book *Is It Red? Is It Yellow? Is It Blue? An*

Figure 20. List Sample

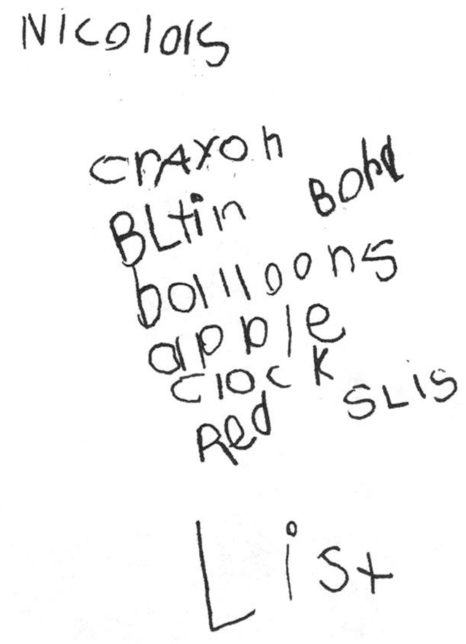

Adventure in Color (Hoban, 1978). Before reading the book, the teacher should ask the children to predict and make a list of what things might be pictured to represent these different colors. Then, after reading the book, the teacher and children can compare the children's list with the author's or artist's choices.

When children's knowledge of print has grown beyond the simplistic forms of labeling and making lists, note writing and friendly letter writing become a good follow-up, especially because real audiences who can respond are involved. Karelitz (1993) asserts that the lessons learned in note writing carry over to other forms of writing.

Notes

January is a good time to introduce note writing. From the beginning of the school year, the teacher should call attention to the notes he or she writes in the classroom. Also, the teacher should instruct children to write notes for him or her as reminders. With this background knowledge, a book like *The Jolly Postman, or, Other People's Letters* (Ahlberg & Ahlberg, 1986) can serve as a good lead-in to note writing, even though it's fiction. Other good books to serve as models for note writing are suggested in the next section on letters.

To encourage note writing, teachers can have children make small, individual mailboxes. For example, students can make mailboxes in art class from milk cartons or some other material. Children can then put notes in each other's mailboxes whenever they wish. (See Bryce's note to his friend Kayden in Figure 21.)

Teachers can ask parents to donate old notecards, old postcards, and junk mail for the children to reuse in note writing activities, or perhaps some new cards, envelopes, and stationery.

Note writing can easily be developed into letter writing and a thematic study of the post office. For example, some teachers set up a post office and

---

Figure 21. Note Writing Sample

"Kayden C. We are going to a wedding, so you can't call me. Love, Bryce."

students can "mail" notes and letters. Children can take turns doing the various jobs needed in the post office such as sorting and delivering mail. A field trip to the post office is a great way to initiate this thematic study. Using the language experience approach (in which the children dictate their experiences and the teacher organizes and records the information into a readable format) to write about the trip is good follow-up, and writing a group thank-you to the post office is a good lead-in to letter writing.

Letters

Next, teachers can introduce writing friendly letters. "The Letter" in *Frog and Toad Are Friends* (Lobel, 1975), *Dear Tooth Fairy* (Edwards, 2003), and *Arthur's Pen Pal* (Hoban, 1976) can serve as models for writing letters. After reading aloud some of the suggested books, teachers should discuss with students the different parts of a letter: greeting, body, and closing. I show kindergartners a letter that I have written on a special letter form. (See Appendix E for the Friendly Letter Forms, one with labels and one without labels.) I point out the greeting, body, and closing that I've written on the form. Then, I give a blank form to each child and direct children in filling out the date and signing their names after the closing. These forms can be reused the next day as children learn how to begin writing the body of the letter.

Before children begin to write their letters, they need to have someone in mind to write to. This unit is much more meaningful for students when it is purposeful. I often send a letter home to the children's parents to see if there is someone in the family that the child could write to and receive mail from. I also ask parents to send to school with their child a stamped, addressed envelope to that person. Many teachers also find pen pals for their children from other schools if parents or caregivers are unavailable. (Of course, children can always write to other classmates or another kindergarten or classroom in the school, too.)

Before I do my demonstration of writing a letter the next day, I show the children the first two steps in the simple list in Table 2 that helps me write my letter.

I show the children the Friendly Letter Form with labels that has my greeting written on it. Then, I demonstrate "telling" something on my form—for example, "My family took a walk in the woods yesterday, and I showed them how to make a snow angel." Next, we discuss what telling something means, and the children give some examples and tell something about themselves on their copies of the Friendly Letter Form.

On the third day, I show the children the next two steps on the list in Table 2. We discuss what asking means, and the children give some examples. Then I demonstrate asking in my letter. For example, I write, "My family took a walk in the woods and I showed them how to make a snow angel. Have you ever made a snow angel?" Then, I invite students to try adding an "asking" part to the body of their letter and to reread the closing (see Figure 22).

Teachers also can choose to discuss addressing envelopes, but many teachers address envelopes for the children or give them a sample to copy when first beginning a letter writing unit.

Initially, I tried to teach letter writing in two days, but as most teachers know, covering the material is not the same as teaching it. Because I was so busy, I forgot that minilessons are about *one* thing, but teachers are allowed approximation, too! The kindergarten teachers and I found it worked best to break down letter writing into three days with a strong introduction as described.

For recipients of friendly letters (such as friends and relatives) who are uninformed about approximated writing, it is a good idea to follow Tompkins and Hoskisson's (1995) suggestion of using the writing process of prewriting, drafting, revising for sense or clarity, editing for conventional spelling, and publishing (by rewriting, if necessary) before mailing. Parents might be enlisted to help their children in this meaningful homework, especially in the revising, editing, and publishing stages.

Table 2. What Makes a Good Letter?

1. Write the **date and a greeting**.
2. **Tell** something about yourself.
3. *Ask* something about the person you're writing to.
4. When finished, **sign your name** next to the closing.

Figure 22. Letter Sample

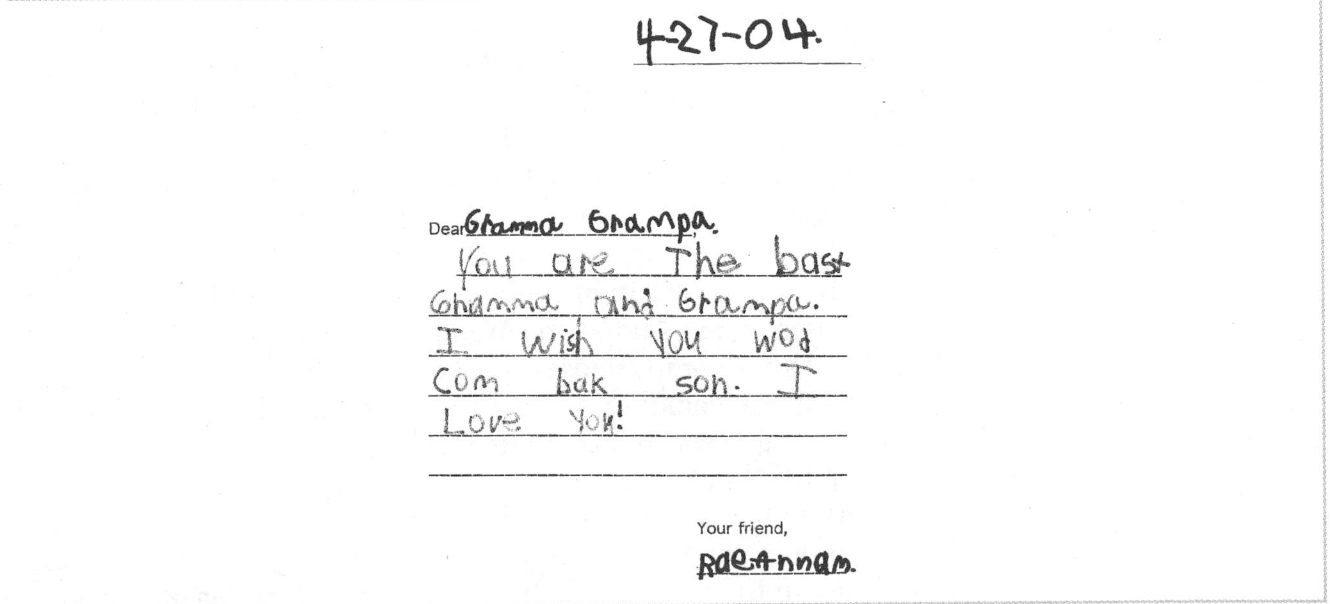

4-27-04.

Dear Gramma Grampa.
You are The bast
Ghamma and Grampa.
I wish you wod
Com bak son. I
Love you!

Your friend,

RaeAnnan.

Note writing and letter writing are two very useful forms (genres) of writing. They not only provide an opportunity for kindergartners to sharpen their writing skills but also to increase their awareness of audience (Tompkins & Hoskisson, 1995). Note writing and letter writing can help negotiate relationships, settle arguments, show gratitude, report, and question things. Of the two forms, notes are easier for children, especially boys, who have difficulty sustaining narrative to write (Karelitz as cited in Newkirk & Atwell, 1988). Children become increasingly successful in using note writing to control their own behavior and to influence others, plus the benefits carry over to other forms of writing such as the informal reports (Karelitz as cited in Newkirk & Atwell, 1988).

Informal Reports

When students question things, there is no better way to find answers than searching for information and writing about it in an informal report. Toward the end of the school year (late March or April), teachers can introduce informal report writing. It is a good idea to tie informal report writing in with other content areas, because there often is not much time for these areas in a busy kindergarten schedule. Science is a good area to begin with, because children have a natural curiosity about living things and know a lot about them. Students' curiosity and desire for knowledge are very important when first writing an informal report if children are to understand the reason for writing a report (Graves, 1994).

When interest in a subject is high, children will often use information books beyond their abilities to conventionally read to find answers to their questions, especially if the book contains many useful pictures and diagrams (Huck, Hepler, Hickman, & Kiefer, 1997).

Many children's librarians, like Mrs. Zielinski, recommend teachers become informed about good authors and good series of books as an excellent way to find quality information books.

She specifically recommends the following series: Eye Witness Juniors (Knopf Publishers), Eye Wonder (Darling Kindersley Publishers), and All Aboard (Grosset and Dunlap). Also, Crabtree Publishers' life cycle series includes butterflies, sea turtles, lions, frogs, whales, spiders, wolves, birds, trees, and koalas. Scholastic has a good selection of nonfiction books for grades K–2, too. (See Appendix B for individual listings of nonfiction information books.)

In an activity that used informational books, Mrs. Clark's and Mrs. Williams's kindergartners studied the broad area of animals. The teachers asked each kindergartner to choose an animal that he or she knew something about but would like to know more about. I demonstrated to the children and their teachers how a writer might choose an animal to write about. First, I told them I chose a bat, and then I told them why: When I was a little girl, I picked a plum off a tree in our yard. I saw something that looked like a mouse with wings hanging upside down from the tree. I was very curious about this strange-looking animal that slept during the day.

My older sister said it was a bat, and I began to wonder about bats. I especially wanted to know where they slept in the winter. That was my "big question." Having my story as an example, the children had one week to make their choice of animal and another week to try to find some good books about their animal. The teachers also found books through the help of librarians at the school and the public library.

On the first day of writing their information reports, the children brought to school the live animals they chose, if it was possible to transport them in a cage or bowl, and if not, they brought in a photograph or a picture of the animal from a magazine. For example, children brought in tadpoles, toads, frogs, snails, slugs, spiders, and so forth.

I began my writing workshop demonstration by showing the children the toy stuffed [bat] *Stella Luna* from the fiction book of the same name (Cannon, 1993). (Teachers can choose to contrast this book with other nonfiction books on bats during read-aloud time, such as *Bats: Creatures of the Night*, Milton, 1993, part of the All Aboard Series.) Looking at my stuffed bat and a picture of a real bat in my book, I drew a picture of a bat. As I did this, I thought aloud about two or three things that I observed and found interesting about bats. I jotted these things down in a list beneath my picture. For example, *Bat's wings have bones that look like fingers in them!* As I did this, I showed the children a list of items that make a good report (see Table 3), and I *only* showed them the first two steps of report writing. (I told them we would do the third step the next day.)

The next day some children had finished their pictures and lists, and others were still working on them. I told the children they would have time to finish, but I wanted them to think about one more thing. Then I asked them to think about something they really wanted to know about their animal—a "big question." As I said this, I referred them to step 3 of Table 3.

Next, I demonstrated how they were to write their big question on a separate piece of paper and give it to their teacher. I told them they would be looking in books to find their answers. When they found their answers, they would record them under their questions. (Teachers should make two copies of these questions. One is for the school or public librarian and the other is for themselves. The original should be given back to the child.)

Table 3. What Makes a Good Report?

1. Draw a picture of your animal. Use detail.
2. List two or three interesting things beneath picture.
3. Identify your BIG QUESTION.
4. Go to the library.
5. Share.

Adapted from Graves, D. (1994). *A fresh look at writing.* Portsmouth, NH: Heinemann.

After the children completed the first three steps, they went to the school library (step 4). The librarian referred them to a section she'd set up with picture books that had facts about their animals.

As the librarian and the teachers conferred individually and in small groups with the children, they showed the children how to examine books for pictures and diagrams of their animals, and how to look at the big print (captions) under pictures to see if their answers might be in that particular book. Children were also encouraged to go to the public library with their parents. The teachers wrote a letter to the parents explaining the project, and most parents really enjoyed helping in this manner. (See Appendix C for a letter to parents about writing nonfiction reports.)

When the children were ready to write the answers to their big questions, I demonstrated how by writing an answer to my big question. I reviewed how I had looked at books and talked to others about my question to find my answer, and now I was going to put my books aside and write my answer in my own words.

Once the children finished their reports, they shared their work in Author's Chair, and each one was interviewed as an expert on his or her animal (step 5).

Figure 23A and B shows an information report in which the student has completed these steps.

Figure 23. Informal Report Sample

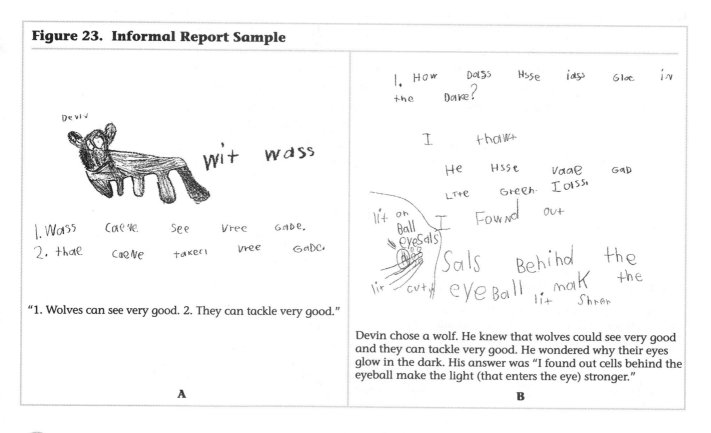

"1. Wolves can see very good. 2. They can tackle very good."

Devin chose a wolf. He knew that wolves could see very good and they can tackle very good. He wondered why their eyes glow in the dark. His answer was "I found out cells behind the eyeball make the light (that enters the eye) stronger."

A   B

Devin even drew a diagram with his answer. This was partly because his mother had drawn one to explain the answer, which was found in a difficult text. However, once Devin understood the answer, he wrote his own answer in his own words and drew his own diagram.

Notice that Devin even added his own hypothesis about why wolves' eyes glow in the dark before he answered his question. The making of a true scientist!

Before students experience formal report writing, it is important that they first experience informal report writing in kindergarten and the lower grades. Thus, teachers should have a good selection of books and magazines in science and social studies available for children to browse through in the classroom to promote further interest in report writing and to help provide answers when they come up with questions.

In addition to personal recounts, kindergartners enjoy writing in the other various nonfiction genres that have been described, and they build an understanding of a sense of audience. With a sense of audience and a lot of exposure and immersion to fictional stories, some kindergartners can attempt writing a fictional story.

Fiction or Narrative Text

The second type of written language that uses textual features is fiction. Unlike nonfiction, fiction follows one basic story structure. This structure includes the setting, character(s), initiating event, subsequent events, and final event. When working with kindergartners, teachers should refer to the initiating event as the "beginning," subsequent events as the "middle," and final events as the "ending."

Although the genres of fiction have a basic story structure, the literary elements of the various genres differ. For example, although folk tales and mysteries are organized using story structure, there are differences between the types of characters within the structure. Flat or undeveloped characters are found in folk tales, and round or fully developed characters are found in mysteries (Buss & Karnowski, 2000).

According to Tompkins and Hoskisson (1995), fiction includes three types of stories:

1. Traditional literature, which includes fables, folk tales and fairy tales, myths, and legends;
2. Fantasies, which include modern literary tales, fantastic stories, science fiction, and high fantasy; and
3. Realistic stories that include contemporary fiction and historical fiction. (pp. 45–46)

Although I do not recommend formally teaching fictional genres in kindergarten, I do recommend exposing children to story structure in fiction and the language of storybooks. Children often incorporate familiar story language in their personal recounts. A classic example is adding "The End" or "Happily ever after" to their stories (see Figure 24).

Figure 24. Story Ending Sample

"Me and Karter are playing happily ever after."

To further promote an understanding of story structure, teachers should retell some of the classic folk tales using one of the following art forms: flannel board (to make characters, photocopy them, laminate them, and add sandpaper to their backs), puppetry, artwork (children could draw a picture of the *beginning* and the *end* of the story), and creative dramatics.

Research supports creative dramatics as the most meaningful postreading activity (McCaslin, 1990). Creative dramatics requires no props or dialogue. The teacher simply rereads or retells the story and the whole class reenacts it in their own personal ways. This can be done with individuals or as groups of animals or characters. See, for example, the groups of bears and the multiple Goldilocks characters in Figure 25A and B creatively dramatizing Goldilocks and the Three Bears.

With immersion, exposure, and retelling, a few children may develop a sense of story and attempt to emulate the structure of a story on their own initiative (as Maggie did in Figure 18A and B on p. 84). With this goal in mind, it is best to read stories that have an obvious story structure and are familiar. Most stories that are familiar to children come from the traditional category of fiction. Therefore, the remainder of this chapter highlights nursery rhymes and folk tales.

Nursery Rhymes

Nursery rhymes by Mother Goose are as beloved today as they were hundreds of years ago. Children love the musical quality of the patterned words and phrases, the rhythm, rhyme, and alliteration. All these things are key ingredients to developing writing and reading skills. Young children love

Figure 25. Goldilocks and the Three Bears

A   B

the sound of the words in rhymes; rhymes satisfy their preoccupation with language as they strive to develop their language abilities (Huck et al., 1997). Young children also love to reenact nursery rhymes with creative dramatics, and this is a good way to teach the meaning of some of the words in the rhymes. *My Very First Mother Goose* (Opie, 1996) and *The Arnold Lobel Book of Mother Goose* (Lobel, 1997) are good collections of nursery rhymes. (See Appendix B for a more detailed list of books.)

For example, Mrs. Lentz, a veteran kindergarten teacher, noticed the importance of nursery rhymes and song in children's literacy development. On the first day of school, after she read an old favorite story and a nursery rhyme during the teacher demonstration of reading in reading workshop, she gave each child a simple spiral notebook and a copy of the rhyme she had read. Then, during the time when children are to *approximate* reading on their own and the teacher confers with them, they read the rhyme and colored the illustration she had provided. (Although Mrs. Lentz had considered allowing the children to draw their own illustrations, the main purpose of this book was to provide reading material, and the picture had to be recognizable. In some kindergartens, children may be able to draw illustrations that are recognizable.) These notebooks became filled with rhymes, songs, and poems as the year progressed, and they provided wonderful books for children to read when they left kindergarten.

Folk Tales

Folk tales include all forms of written and oral narratives that have been passed down from one generation to the next. Epics, ballads, legends, and folk songs, as well as myths and fables, belong to this classification (Huck et al., 1997). Folk tales are often classified as cumulative, beast, and wonder tales. Many of these tales have become favorite stories. (See Appendix B for suggestions of folk tales to use with kindergartners.)

Folk tales have plot structures that are simple and direct, and the characters are shown in flat dimensions. Folk tales offer children many opportunities to hear rich language and a wide variety of language patterns. However, the basic purpose of folk tales is to tell a story that presents an important theme (Huck et al., 1997).

Because folk tales are often transferred through storytelling, it is difficult to know which version of a tale is correct. Because every telling is thought to be correct by the storyteller, a great deal of variation is acceptable in print versions of oral folk tales. However, if the story originated in Africa, for example, it should include references to the country (Huck et al., 1997).

Cumulative tales are stories in which a pattern or phrase is repeated and often becomes more involved with each incident, as found in *Rosie's Walk* (Hutchins, 1968), *The Great Big Enormous Turnip* (Tolstoy, 1968), and *The Very Hungry Caterpillar* (Carle, 1987).

Beast tales are stories in which beasts act and talk like human beings; they are probably the favorite type of folk tale for young children. Classic examples include *The Three Little Pigs* (Murdock, 1985), *Three Billy Goats Gruff* (Dewan, 1994), *The Little Red Hen* (Schmidt, 1984), and *The Three Bears and 15 Other Stories* (Rockwell, 1975). There are many versions of beast tales, and kindergartners find it fun to compare the different versions. For example, students can compare *The Little Red Hen* by Schmidt with Galdone's (1985) version.

Wonder tales are stories of magic and the supernatural, for example, stories about giants, goblins, elves, witches, demons, and dragons. Fairy tales (which originally referred to stories about fairies and fairy godmothers) are included in this category. Classic examples of wonder tales include *Little Red Riding Hood* (Hyman, 1983), *Rumpelstiltskin* (Zelinsky, 1997), *Hansel and Gretel* (Ross, 1994), and *Grimm's Fairy Tales* (Nemerson, 1997).

Although I focused on nursery rhymes and familiar folk tales in this section, it is also appropriate to read fantasy and realistic fiction to kindergartners. Huck and colleagues (1997) explain, "Although young children need books that mirror their own feelings and experiences, they also need books to take them beyond those experiences and to help their imaginations soar" (p. 173). Thus, promoting immersion, exposure, and retelling of familiar stories to teach story structure is imperative if teachers wish to have children "soar" on their own and try writing a fictional piece as Maggie did.

Summary

As kindergartners learn about and experiment with written language in writing workshop, their teachers provide encouragement, guidance, and praise for their approximations and listen attentively. With positive guidance, kindergartners' written language develops according to the five stages: (1) Picture Writing, (2) Picture and Label Writing, (3) Taking Inventory, (4) Taking Inventory and Adding Description, and (5) Acquiring and Developing Textual Features of Nonfiction and Fiction.

As kindergartners progress through these five stages, they tend to rely on nonfiction writing as they recount the personal experiences in their lives and develop voice. However, children should also be exposed to fiction. There are several fiction genres that kindergarten children can learn about through quality literature, even though they might not actively write in these genres. The teacher's primary purpose in introducing genres is to extend kindergartners' knowledge of how writers write in different forms. Different genres also provide interest and variety to a writing workshop.

Chapter 4 highlights some useful approaches and activities to further aid kindergartners' development in written language. To ensure that all aspects of literacy receive appropriate emphasis, chapter 4 also presents and explains a possible kindergarten schedule to aid in planning a comprehensive literacy program.

Planning a Comprehensive Literacy Program

You may have tangible wealth untold:
Caskets of jewels and coffers of gold,
Richer than I you can never be—
I had a Mother who read to me.

—"The Reading Mother" by Strickland Gillilan (1869–1954)

Young children's ability to read and write is greatly influenced by their parents or caregivers and their home's literacy environment from the time they are born (Morrow, 1989). I can personally attest to the value of a literacy-rich home from the perspectives of both a young child and a mother. My three siblings and I were early readers, and both of my children were early readers. My mother knew the value of reading to her children, and we were read to every night before bedtime and often before our naps. I repeated my mother's reading behavior with my own children, and they, too, read before they entered kindergarten.

When they were only months old, both my children interacted with books as I read to them. Soon they began to look at books on their own. My husband and I still smile when we remember seeing Robyn, our oldest child, poring over her books when she was only 1 year old. We remember specifically how she would look through the pages of her beloved book of farm animals and kiss the pictures of favorite animals. Robyn, in turn, has transferred my reading behavior to her own daughter. (Figures 26 and 27 show Robyn and her husband, Randy, reading to their 4-month-old daughter, Hanah, and Hanah looking at books alone.) Yet, I have seen children from literacy-poor homes not know the back of a book from the front.

Researchers have noted and studied the importance of a literacy-rich home to the child's becoming literate (Clark, 1976; Durkin, 1966; Ferreiro & Teberosky, 1982; Heath, 1983; Holdaway, 1979; Mason & McCormick, 1983; Nineo & Bruner, 1978; Snow, 1977; Sulzby, 1985; Taylor, 1983; Teale, 1982). A primary finding among the researchers was that parents and caregivers in these homes immersed their children in and exposed their children to meaningful print because they prized literacy. The parents and caregivers not only read themselves but also read and immersed their children in

Figure 26. Robyn and Randy Reading to Hanah

Figure 27. Hanah Looking at Books Independently

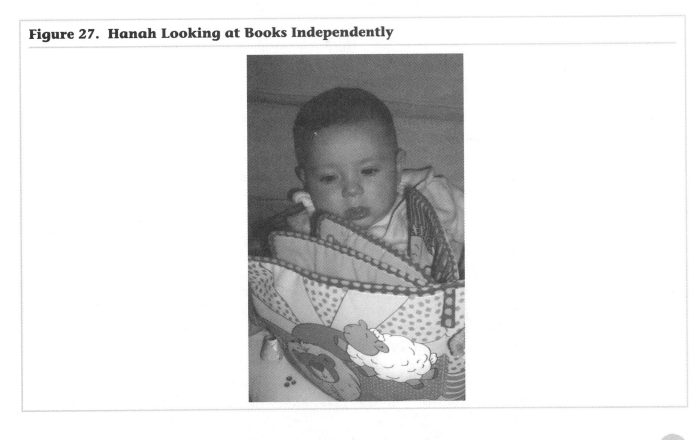

quality literature, especially classic stories such as The Three Little Pigs, Dr. Seuss books, and nursery rhymes. They answered their children's questions about print and engaged them in it, often pointing to words and asking children to make predictions as they read. They made the books they read to their children available to them, so children could puzzle over them and practice "pretend" reading. When their children attempted pretend reading or writing, they encouraged it, often praising the child's efforts (Calkins, 1994, 2001; Clark, 1976; Durkin, 1987; Morrow, 1989).

Literate parents and caregivers also modeled the act of writing in many forms and provided books, pencils, crayons, markers, and unlimited supplies of different kinds of paper for their children to experiment and explore with on their own. For example, a friend of mine who knows the importance of encouraging experimentation with writing used green slate board for wainscoting on the lower three feet of her kitchen walls, and attached a chalk tray as a divider between slate and wallpaper. She remembered the joy of writing on the blackboard (and sometimes the walls, until reprimanded) as a child and wanted to allow her children to explore in this way.

I did not understand writing's value to reading as a young mother, but I did provide writing materials. My children were always drawing and writing on things. Because I provided a literacy-rich home and read to my children on a daily basis, they became interested in print. I remember my youngest daughter, Stacey, copying letters on her own initiative from her ABC books when she was 3 and 4 years old. She would often make the letters incorrectly in her experimenting and her exploring of print (her dad and I still smile at the memory of her "hairy Es"), but eventually she got it right. Yet, I have seen many kindergartners from literacy-poor homes who do not know any letters of the alphabet, not even the first letter of their first name. Some children do not have a concept of letters and cannot distinguish letters from numbers. Temple and colleagues (1988) describe these children as "high-risk" (p. 48). They suggest that preschools and kindergartens provide print-rich exposure to all children, including those who are considered "high-risk," by reading to them and providing reading and writing workshops of approximation. Thus, "high-risk children can then be spared the often impossible task of learning what print is all about at the same time the first-grade program is trying to teach them to read" (p. 48).

Many of the successful findings, conditions, and experiences that help immerse children in and expose children to meaningful print as found in literate homes have been adapted by research educators like Holdaway (1979) and Calkins (1994) and transferred to school literacy programs. Kindergarten teachers need to be aware of and understand what is successful in the home environment so they can explain to parents, administrators, policymakers, and other teachers that emergent reading programs based on study of literate homes are developmentally appropriate and not just an adaptation of the first-grade curriculum; indeed, the emergent reading and writing programs discussed in this book support successful literacy preschool practices (Calkins, 2001; Cambourne, 1988; Clay, 2001; Durkin, 1966; Holdaway, 1979; Morrow, 1989).

Past practices such as teaching letters and sounds in isolation (e.g., letter or sound of the week) and teaching words in isolation (e.g., using flashcards, dittos, and workbooks) downplayed the need to work at understanding messages in real reading and writing and made it more difficult for the literacy poor to learn, although it didn't seem to impede the progress of literacy-rich children (Clay, 2001). However, Clay (2001) states that attempting to teach "standardized sequences of learning may confuse the low achievers and hold back proficient children" (p. 94). Sampson (1986) adds, "The young child's reading and writing abilities mutually reinforce each other, developing concurrently and interrelatedly rather than sequentially" (p. 5). Teaching letters, sounds, words, and isolated skills first undermines the purpose and the processes of learning to read and write (Clay, 1991, 2001). Understanding and communicating message is the reason for both reading and writing, and reading for message, which involves specific skills, needs to be learned *during* the process of learning to write and read, not sequentially (Clay, 1991, 2001).

As a reading teacher, a fifth-grade teacher asked me to assess a fifth-grade student's reading problem. The student was quite intelligent and had good language abilities, but she read so slowly, she could not understand the message—the whole purpose for reading. As I observed her reading, I noticed she read one word at a time, and then she would pause before going on to the next word. I asked her about her pauses, and she said she was "rechecking" the letters and the sounds to make sure she had them right. I told her that wasn't necessary and showed her how to read for message by using Holdaway's (1979) cloze procedure, an enjoyable and useful prediction strategy. First, I covered up a fairly predictable word (with a small piece of sticky paper) in the next sentence of the text she was reading. Then I asked her to read the sentence. When she came to the covered word, I gave her the initial consonant of the word and asked her to predict the word from the meaning of the sentence using these two cues. Once she gave me her prediction, I asked her to confirm it by checking the rest of the letters in the word under the sticky. She was amazed that she had predicted correctly, and she said, "I didn't know you read for message!"

This student had a limited view of reading; she only knew to "sound out" letter by letter. However, because a writing workshop had just been introduced in this student's classroom, the prediction strategy also was reinforced when she predicted what she would write. By the end of the school year, the student developed into a fluent reader and writer because of the emphasis on predicting message in both these literacy processes.

It has been my experience, as it had been Clay's (2001), that isolated practices of the past that did not deal with meaningful reading and writing failed the literacy-poor child and probably did little for the literacy rich. Thus, young children, especially the 20% who are failing at reading, will benefit from literacy practices that emulate the same literacy conditions found and adapted from literacy-rich homes. These practices will not only aid the literacy poor in school but also aid the literacy rich to become more proficient readers and writers. In the case of literacy development, what is good for the rich is good for the poor (Clay, 2001).

Through experimenting with meaningful print and receiving guidance from a proficient language user at their point of need, young children can construct their understanding of written language and how to write and read it. Children draw on their oral language as they learn to compose during reading and writing. What on the surface appears to be word-by-word reading or writing involves the children linking many things from many sources (refer to chapter 1 for information on the four cues of early and fluent reading). Children learn to talk by talking, and they need to learn to read and write by reading and writing (Calkins, 1994; Clay, 1991; Gentry & Gillet, 1993; Graves, 1994; Sampson, 1986; Tompkins & Hoskisson, 1995). Reading and writing can only be learned in the "process" of "doing" them (Clay, 1991, 2001). When teachers try to isolate parts of this process and teach them in isolation, the parts may be learned but often the process is not. Literacy is more than just decoding and encoding; it is about communicating a message. There are several instructional approaches that can be effective in teaching reading and writing to young children.

Which Instructional Approaches Should Be Priorities in Literacy Instruction?

Clay (2001) asserts that the reciprocity of early reading and writing has been neglected by some theorists and some educators. However, when we write we must attend to every feature of every letter in correct sequence to compose the words of our texts. We do the same thing with reading, although we do not write the words (Clay, 2001). Writing and reading reinforce each other, especially in the first 18 months of formal schooling if children's reading and writing approximations are encouraged and valued, which they are in writing workshop and reading workshop (Calkins, 1994, 2001; Clay, 2001; Robinson, 1973).

Other approaches that value approximation such as shared reading, language experience approach, shared writing, interactive writing, learning logs, and "signing-in" also can be used to promote the reciprocity between reading and writing.

Because read-aloud time and writing and reading workshops must be priorities for children every day, a separate time slot needs to be set aside each day for these activities. As children read and write across the curriculum, the teacher can use any of the other literacy approaches when appropriate.

Writing Workshop and Reading Workshop

Writing workshop and reading workshop (which includes guided reading) are designed around supporting children as active constructors of their own literacy learning. These workshops provide self-initiated practice time with teacher guidance at the student's point of need; therefore, the workshops need to be priorities in all elementary classrooms. They are especially important to kindergartners' becoming literate because they encourage and support independent approximated writing and reading (Calkins, 1994, 2001). Furthermore, they provide many opportunities for socialization and they promote self-esteem as I have seen no other approach do.

Reading Aloud

Reading aloud needs to be a separate entity in kindergartners' daily schedules; however, it also may be used as a teaching approach during the day in areas of learning across the curriculum. Informational books as well as rhymes, poems, and stories should be shared orally with students to help them develop an appreciation of literature, especially literature students are not capable of reading independently. Tompkins and Hoskisson (1995) explain that reading aloud will encourage interest in reading, provide ideas for writing by expanding background experiences, expand vocabulary and sentence patterns, and create a community of learners in the classroom.

Calkins (2001) states that reading aloud allows children "to lose themselves in the story" and "become passionately engaged in the world of the story" (p. 50). She also adds that reading aloud is so important that she has often proposed that student teachers not be placed in the classroom of a teacher who doesn't read aloud each day. In *Becoming a Nation of Readers: The Report of the Commission on Reading*, Anderson, Hiebert, Scott, and Wilkinson (1985) support reading aloud and state, "The single most important activity for building the knowledge required for eventual success in reading is reading aloud to children" (p. 23). This report also claims that reading aloud should be done in all classrooms, and not just for children who can't read for themselves. Calkins (2001) reminds teachers that reading aloud doesn't need to take a lot of time, it might be only five minutes; the important thing is to "Let kids feel and think. Teach your children to be moved" (p. 53).

Shared Reading

Teachers often share fiction and nonfiction with children by reading aloud as the children follow along in a Big Book—a book with enlarged text that everyone can see—on charts or in individual books. This approach is called shared reading or shared book experience by Holdaway (1979). Holdaway developed this approach by creating Big Books so the classroom teacher could emulate parents who immersed their children in and exposed their children to print as they read aloud to them at home. The shared book experience should be used often during read-alouds and during reading demonstrations in reading workshop and writing workshop.

Trachtenburg and Ferruggia's (1989) research concerning the use of shared reading from Big Books with first graders shows that making and reading Big Books dramatically improves children's reading scores on standardized achievement tests. The teachers involved in the study reported that children's self-concepts as readers improved as well.

Holdaway (1979) strongly advises pointing to the words as the book is read to involve children with print because there is little instructional value to reading aloud if "the print cannot be seen, shared and discussed" (p. 64). In addition to pointing to the words as they are read, parents often call their children's attention to caption words and interesting print like *huff* and *puff* or an animal sound such as an owl's hoot—*Whoooo*. Through shared reading of a big picture book placed on an easel, a teacher can point to print, call attention to interesting words, and demonstrate how print works.

Holdaway also recommends using masking devices as another technique to call attention to print and to isolate certain graphic cues during shared reading. Teachers in Holdaway's study used a set of various sized masks to put around or isolate a particular concept of print such as a letter or word to locate positions like first, last, and middle. Making and using various sized masks, however, took a lot of teachers' valuable time, so a sliding mask was devised. A large rectangular cut is made in a cardboard card, and a sliding piece of cardboard long enough and just wide enough to cover the hole is placed on the back of the card (see Figure 28). Using a sliding mask allows the teacher to focus on a letter, word, phrase, or

Figure 28. Student Using Red Masking Card

sentence within a Big Book using only one mask. Many kindergarten teachers also use their hands in a cupping motion around certain print they wish to isolate or focus on.

Although calling attention to print is necessary, reading is about message or meaning. The use of the prediction strategy is essential to the success of emergent reading and reading comprehension (Holdaway, 1979). To understand this concept, Holdaway strongly advises teaching the strategy of prediction when using Big Books using oral cloze technique. The following example illustrates this point.

As a kindergarten teacher reads the Big Book version of The Three Little Pigs, she occasionally pauses (when a highly predictable word appears on the page), leaving an oral gap in the flow of her reading. She asks the children to fill in the gap, "The wolf huffed and _____ and blew the house down!" Once the gap has been filled, the teacher accepts the children's predictions with "Could be" or "Yes it might be" and then leads the children to confirm their predictions by looking at the printed word in the text and saying, "Well, if it is *puffed* (or some other approximation the children might have made), what would the first letter be? Let's check our word in the book. Is that the letter?" (If necessary, the teacher and children can continue in this manner by checking the last and middle letters, too [Holdaway, 1979].)

During shared reading teachers also should ask children to predict what will happen in the book *before* and *as* they read it, thereby providing opportunities for students to use the prediction strategy (Holdaway, 1979). Predictable texts that concentrate on repetition, rhyme, alliteration, cumulative lines, and rhythm are preferred reading material for young children because they provide support to the challenge of reading (Weaver, 1988). (For a list of predictable books, see Appendix B.) After reading, teachers can ask the children which predictions came true; they also can ask children to discuss their favorite parts of the story or retell the story with a flannel board or creative drama to provide closure.

All of these activities increase children's confidence in their ability to read. For the most part, these are the same reading activities that literate parents did and do in the home.

The Language Experience Approach

The language experience approach is based on children's language and experiences (Lee & Allen, 1963; Stauffer, 1970). In a language experience approach, children (usually the whole class) dictate sentences about their experiences, and the teacher records their dictation in enlarged print.

Because the language and the experiences come from the children, children are usually able to read the text. A text like this provides children with the experience of learning that their oral language can be written down and read. The skills of reading and writing are connected as students actively read what they have written (Tompkins & Hoskisson, 1995). For example, this approach is often used after field trips to not only learn more about recording oral language in print but also to condense and confirm any new knowledge gained in the excursion.

Shared Writing

In the shared writing approach, developed from the language experience approach (McKenzie, 1985), the teacher still acts as a scribe but places more emphasis on the composing process and on making the text readable later on than he or she does with the language experience approach in which children's exact words are written down. Children (either the whole class or in small groups) and their teacher both work at this composing task, but the teacher plays a more dominant role in that he or she helps children to develop and organize their ideas. The dual goal is to teach good writing and make the writing easier for students to read (McCarrier, Pinnell, & Fountas, 2000).

Routman (1991) advises teachers to use language that is positive and encouraging so children will want to participate in the collaborative effort of writing such a text. Rather than saying, "I don't think that works," the teacher should ask the children, "What do you think about...? Does it fit?" (p. 60) or "Let's reread it to see if it makes sense."

In shared writing, children and their teacher plan the text together (McCarrier et al., 2000). Shared writing often develops naturally as a response to shared reading in that young students create their own innovations of a story read-aloud with guidance from their teacher. On occasion, innovations on text could be done during the sharing time of reading workshop. Author Jon Scieszka (1996) provides an example of a most successful innovation on the Three Little Pigs in his best-selling book, *The True Story of The Three Little Pigs! as told by A. Wolf.*

Interactive Writing

Interactive writing is an extension of shared writing. McCarrier, Pinnell, and Fountas (2000) describe it as "the teacher and children 'sharing the pen' at strategic points in the construction of the text" (p. 26). The teacher decides when to write or let the children write as he or she tries to encourage children in the writing process and draw attention to the specific conventions of written language. At the teacher's discretion, children may come to the easel on which a large tablet of paper stands; take the pen; and add a certain letter, word, or perhaps some punctuation to the proposed composition (McCarrier et al., 2000). This technique can be used during any time of the day that a class or group of children might write the following: a list of class rules, a shopping list, recordings of observations from a field trip, a new version of a familiar text, or a list of questions for a classroom visitor (Bear et al., 2000).

For interactive writing to be most effective, Routman (2001) recommends that this technique be used in small groups, one on one, or sparingly with the full class:

> When children are gathered in a large group, their switching places at the easel and their often slow, laborious letter formations can disrupt the group's attention and engagement [and]…stress is placed on conventional spelling and overall correctness, which many students may not be developmentally ready for. (p. 44)

Mrs. Clark and Mrs. Williams use interactive writing sparingly with the whole class, and when they do, they like to have the children show them what they will write on their dry erase boards before children write it in the text. Then, students can have a trial run and can discuss the text beforehand. The teachers explain this approach by saying, "Children, charts are like your published books. They need to have correct spelling and punctuation so you can read them easily and don't learn something incorrectly."

Learning Logs

Students use learning logs (Routman, 1991), or journals, to describe their learning processes—that is, to record or react to what they have learned or are learning in math, science, social studies, or other content areas. Learning logs are based on the idea of "writing to learn" (p. 229). Routman describes writing to learn as one of the "most powerful techniques available for developing critical thinking" because knowledge is clarified and extended through writing (p. 67). (I can personally attest to the truth of this statement in writing this book.) Routman states, "I learned what I knew, what I didn't know, and what I needed to learn" (p. 68).

Thus, this type of writing activates critical thinking skills; encourages learning of content information; and develops students' writing (and reading) fluency, strategies, and skills (Gere, 1985). For example, Mrs. Poirier, a veteran kindergarten teacher, wants to emphasize writing in math, so she plans to use a math journal where students can draw a picture and write about what they learned in math class each day.

Routman (1991) also strongly supports literature response learning logs as a part of guided reading. (See "Reading Workshop and Guided Reading," p. 133, to better understand when to use these logs.) Kindergarten teachers can use these logs throughout the year as part of guided reading. Only one teacher question and therefore only one student response should be required a day. Teachers need to demonstrate how to answer the questions they might ask in the minilesson portion of reading workshop.

In the beginning of the year, when children are not conventionally reading, they can be asked to draw a picture in response to an open-ended question after they do their "pretend" *approximated* reading—for example, the teacher might ask children to do any of the following items: Draw a picture of the main character (and be ready to tell us what you think of this main character in sharing time); Draw a picture of your favorite part of the story (and be ready to tell us why it is your favorite part); Draw the setting of the story (and be ready to describe it).

When kindergartners gain the alphabetic principle (which can be observed in their daily writing) and they begin to read conventionally, Routman (1991) suggests the teacher ask questions that require responses in invented spelling such as the following:

What do you think is the most important part of what you just read?

Was there anything about what you just read that surprised you?

What do you think the author is trying to tell us about...?

What do you think it means when...?

What would happen if...?

Were you reminded of something in your own life as you were reading?"

What questions came to your mind as you were reading?

Children also can be asked to copy any unknown vocabulary, which can then be discussed in sharing time (Routman, 1991).

All of the previously described instructional approaches aid teachers in immersing kindergartners in and exposing them to reading and writing throughout the day. The question most kindergarten teachers have is, How do you design a comprehensive literacy program using these approaches?

Designing a Comprehensive Literacy Program

Scheduling is one of the most difficult things for kindergarten teachers to do because it usually requires incorporating time for specialists. Kindergarten teachers need the support of their administrators in scheduling so literacy workshops can be scheduled in the morning when children typically are able to focus and think more clearly. Also, kindergarten teachers need to think more about incorporating required instruction and instructional devices into their schedules, where appropriate. Mrs. Williams and Mrs. Clark did this with the incorporation of computer time into math and occasionally science (see Table 4 for a sample kindergarten daily schedule).

In 2003, Mrs. Clark and Mrs. Williams added a writing workshop to their daily schedule and were amazed at the way their children learned the alphabetic principle. And although they had used guided reading in the past, in 2004 they added a reading workshop in addition to their writing

Table 4. Kindergarten Daily Schedule

7:45–8:15
Opening Activities: Attendance with "sign-in," lunch count, assigning room helper jobs, reading morning message and schedule (Students read schedule by themselves later in the year.)

8:15–8:45
Centers (When children finish signing-in, they can go to their centers until the morning message is read. Some teachers occasionally incorporate computer orientation into the science center by using Sammy's Science House, 1994.)

8:45–9:45
Writing Workshop (This activity might not use the whole hour at first.)

9:45–10:15
Snack and Recess

10:15–11:00
Reading Workshop and Guided Reading

11:00–12:00
Lunch

12:00–12:30
Math (Once a week for 20 minutes, computer time is incorporated into the math session by using Millie's Math House, 1992.)

12:30–1:00
Read-Aloud (Library time replaces read-aloud time on Tuesdays; during library time, the librarian reads aloud to the children and then they find and check out books.)

1:00–1:30
Rest Time

1:30–2:15
Specials (Music Tuesdays and Thursdays and Physical Education Mondays, Wednesdays, and Fridays.)

2:15–2:30
Recess (An art session of approximately 20 minutes replaces this recess every Tuesday, and a guidance session of approximately 15 minutes replaces this recess every other week on Monday.)

2:30–2:45
Class Newspaper and Friendship Circle

2:45–3:00
Prepare to leave/line up for bus

Note that this schedule is based on a full-day kindergarten program. Teachers in half-day kindergarten programs should adapt this schedule as needed.

workshop as recommended by Calkins (2001). They were even more amazed: most of their children became early readers by the end of kindergarten. Upon follow-up this year, they discovered that all of their children had become early readers in first grade. These teachers plan to anchor their literacy programs again with writing and reading workshops and reading aloud.

Mrs. Williams and Mrs. Clark had to work hard to overcome traditional mindsets about literacy acquisition, and they had to revise their old schedules to make writing and reading workshops a priority in their rooms. However, once they saw the results of these approaches in their kindergartners' literacy development, they realized their impact.

Thus, kindergarten teachers should share appropriate research (see chapter 1), writing samples, and writing tests (see chapter 7) with principals to help achieve the scheduling they desire.

The daily schedule that Mrs. Williams and Mrs. Clark plan to implement in their kindergartens this year follows. Note that in the beginning of the year, reading and writing workshops often do not take the allotted hours that this schedule provides. Kindergarten teachers often increase center time in the beginning of the year when reading and writing workshops take less time, and decrease it to the half hour shown in the schedule as the year progresses and reading and writing workshops expand to their full allotment of one hour each.

To open each day, Mrs. Clark and Mrs. Williams begin with opening activities that include the following: attendance, by having the children "sign-in" (Harste et al., 1981); lunch count; assigning weekly room helper jobs; and reading morning message, often incorporating "showing what you know" (Routman, 2000) and reading the daily schedule.

Opening Activities

Mrs. Clark, Mrs. Williams, Mrs. Poirier, and Ms. Neuenfeldt are kindergarten teachers who believe in putting responsibility on children as soon as they are ready for it. Based on their experiences (and my own), responsibility aids children in becoming self-sufficient. These teachers introduce *responsibility* on the first day of school when they ask children to "sign" their names to some form of attendance sheet and to the lunch count sheet. In addition to giving children some responsibility, this practice that continues throughout the year enables students to write their names, which is fundamental to both reading and writing in kindergarten (Clay, 2001; Temple et al., 1988).

Sign-In

Teachers can place a large piece of manila paper (9" by 18") marked with the day's date at the top on a table for all kindergartners to write their names on, the best that they can, when they come to school. The teacher should sign in, too. Then, this sheet can be used to take attendance. If a student cannot write his or her name, the teacher should work with the student during center time so the student can soon participate in the activity (Fisher, 1991; Harste et al., 1984).

Ms. Neuenfeldt, a novice kindergarten teacher, uses attendance sign-in in the following manner: She writes the children's first names in enlarged print on laminated sheets of chart paper (four names on a chart) and asks the children to find and sign their names under the printed version that she provides. (This is a good way to begin daily sign-in for those students who still can't write their names.) After all the children can write their names, Mrs. Neuenfeldt replaces this chart with one blank sheet of paper for signing in (see Figure 29).

Mrs. Clark, a veteran kindergarten teacher, uses two-pocket charts for signing in because she has many children who can't write readable names at the beginning of the school year. When students are capable of writing their names, she replaces this device with a sign-in attendance sheet. She labels one pocket "Home" and the other pocket "School." She places each of her children's names on a laminated 3" by 5" index card and puts them in the "Home" pocket. Then, as the children come into the classroom, they find their name cards, attempt to sign their names beneath the one Mrs. Clark

Figure 29. Student Signing In

has printed on the card, and then put the card in the "School" pocket. (Children who are absent cannot make this transfer, so it is easy to see who is absent.) Mrs. Clark assigns a room helper (who can read the name cards) to record absentees whose name cards remain in the "Home" pocket chart.

Mrs. Clark also provides two cans of popsicle sticks: one can of blue sticks for indicating the choice of a cold lunch and one can of red sticks for indicating the choice of a hot lunch. The children choose the appropriately colored stick and place it with their name in the pocket chart labeled "School." Mrs. Clark assigns another room helper (who can count) to record the number of hot lunches needed by counting the red popsicle sticks in the "School" chart (see Figure 30).

Morning Message and Schedule

Near the end of the opening activities, Mrs. Clark and Mrs. Williams ask the children to come to the community circle to read the morning message. A community circle is a gathering place for the entire class. (Some teachers assign spots in the circle by writing children's names on masking tape and placing them on the floor.) Then, they read the daily schedule that often includes explanatory rebus print—that is, a representative picture of a printed word (e.g., a piece of paper with some writing on it might represent the words *writing workshop*, or an open book might represent the words *reading workshop*). This kind of print can enable young readers to read before they fully understand the alphabetic principle and decoding. Both teachers realized that too much valuable time was being used on discussing the

Figure 30. Student Using Pocket Charts

calendar and the weather, but they did not want to give up this activity entirely. Instead, they incorporated this information into the morning message as follows: "Good morning. Today is _____ and the weather is _____. We are going to mail our letters at the post office today."

Teachers often record the most exciting thing that will happen on a given day in this morning message. In addition, they can help children develop various concepts of print and explore questions about meaning during the morning message. For example, they can discuss the meaning of certain words (Morrow, 1989). High-frequency words, digraphs, and word families, once taught, can be found by a volunteer and pointed out using a masking device or by cupping your hands.

Many teachers find shared writing and interactive writing useful during the morning message. Mrs. Clark uses shared writing when the room helper in charge of the calendar and the weather gives his or her report. Mrs. Clark records the child's name and what he or she said with shared writing, and then she uses interactive writing (also known as "sharing the pen," McCarrier et al., 2000) to teach punctuation and sound-to-letter correspondences. On one such occasion, Mrs. Clark—using shared writing— wrote the following: Dylan said, "Today is Monday, January 24, 2005, and the weather is cloudy and cold." Then, using interactive writing, Mrs. Clark asked Dylan to put quotation marks around the words he actually said. Mrs. Clark also pointed out the importance of the word *said* in relation to the quotation marks.

If the teacher feels it's appropriate, he or she may add more to the morning message by using shared writing. As a consultant, I remember an occasion when the children in a kindergarten class read their morning message, which stated that a trip to an apple orchard was being planned. The students began to wonder about various things, but a predominant thought seemed to be, would they get to taste the apples? The teacher added their question to her original morning message, and in this way, the teacher *and* the children wrote this *shared* morning message. This morning message also offers a good opportunity to use interactive writing to help teach the use of the question mark. For example, the teacher might point out what a question is and how it is different from a statement and then ask if anyone can make a question mark. The volunteer can be allowed to "share the pen" with the teacher, and place the question mark at the end of the sentence. (The primary purpose in teaching punctuation in kindergarten is not that children will use the marks appropriately—because they are often not able to at this age—but that they will understand their meaning.)

Mrs. Poirier likes to use interactive writing to reinforce the spelling of high-frequency words such as *the*, *a*, and *to* when she sees her students using these words in their daily writing. When one of these words is included in Mrs. Poirier's morning message, she offers the pen to a volunteer to try to write the word within the morning message. If she knows the child understands the alphabetic principle, she asks the child to help her write a word that is not a high-frequency word in her morning message, too. As the child writes, using invented spelling, either the child or Mrs. Poirier explains what he or she is doing. Then, Mrs. Poirier writes the correct spelling of the word in parentheses right behind the child's approximated one, praising how close the child's approximation is to the real spelling.

Showing What You Know

Reading a morning message as a class also can provide a good opportunity for reviewing learning, which Routman (2000) refers to as "Showing What You Know" (p. 490). The teacher asks students to identify letters, words, punctuation, or anything that they can read in a morning message by asking them to "Show us what you know." It also is a good idea to ask, "How did you know that?" such as in the following exchange because it solidifies the child's thinking and may serve as a learning strategy for other students.

Morning
message: *We are going to mail our letters at the post office today.*

Teacher: Do you see anything that you know or can read in our message this morning?

Student: I see *the*.

Teacher: Can you come up and draw a line under the word *the*? How did you know that word?

Student:	It's in *Jack and Jill* on the door.
Teacher:	You remembered it from reading *Jack and Jill*. That's great!
Teacher:	Can anyone tell me something else that they know?
Student:	I know *today*.
Teacher:	Come up and underline *today*. How did you know that?
Student:	I know *to* and *day* and I put them together.
Teacher:	Wonderful, that's really thinking!

Showing What You Know only takes a few minutes and can be incorporated after any writing approach at the teacher's discretion. Thus, literacy and responsibility can be interwoven into opening activities so these activities become more of a learning time and not just a time to get organized for the day. The kindergarten teachers with whom I have worked have found it useful to follow opening activities with center time, so if they have some last-minute organizing to do, they can accomplish it as the children work independently in their centers.

Center Time

Schwartz and Pollishuke (1991) describe the child-centered classroom as one that challenges and encourages children to discover, create, decide, share, and take risks as they actively learn to participate in meaningful experiences. The atmosphere is fostering, stimulating, and liberating, and the teacher is a facilitator who moves around the various areas or centers and chats, encourages, and guides. Effective learning centers allow children opportunities to interact, share, and cooperate with each other. Because centers are usually made up of only four children, they encourage risk taking. The goal is for children to do their best for their own benefit and for the benefit of the small group.

Well-designed centers can shape the cognitive and social growth of children through the use of readily available materials and easily followed directions. Too often, centers end up being "busy work"; teachers must plan carefully for facilitating both mental and social development when they set up their centers (Schwartz & Pollishuke, 1991). All centers should have paper and pencils and some appropriate books placed within them. Mrs. Poirier is an advocate of incorporating some reading and writing activities in all her centers. This promotes immersion in and exposure to meaningful print and invites children to participate in reading and writing in any way they can. Table 5 shows a list of centers suggested by Mrs. Clark, Mrs. Williams, Ms. Neuenfeldt, and Mrs. Poirier.

Tompkins and Hoskisson (1995) describe centers as areas where the functions of reading and writing are utilized by the children in their dramatic play. For example, as children play with blocks, they often label buildings or print warning signs. As they pretend to be teachers, they read to

Table 5. Possible Centers for the Kindergarten Classroom

- Science and environmental play center, which could include at different times the following: sand table, water table, magnets, plants, and/or fish tank
- Social science center, which could include globes, United States map and individual state map, and picture books about the world
- Listening center, which should include taped books, tape recorder, and earphones
- ABC center
- Dramatic play center, which can include house, post office, and general store
- Flannel board and puppet center
- Blocks center
- Workbench and building center
- Library center
- Writing center
- Music center
- Art and finger-painting center

dolls and stuffed animals, or they write on a chalkboard in an effort to impart some knowledge. Through dramatic play, kindergartners re-enact everyday activities and practice literacy for a variety of functions.

A housekeeping center is probably the most common dramatic play center in the kindergarten. By changing props, it and other centers can, on occasion, be transformed into different places such as a hair salon, office, restaurant, veterinarian clinic, bank, grocery store, medical center, or post office. Teachers often transform a center to coordinate with units and themes. For example, many kindergarten teachers include a unit or theme about the post office as they teach the genres of note and letter writing. The children make mailboxes in art class so notes can be delivered to them in their own personal mailboxes. Teachers often write brief notes to their students, too, and put them in students' mailboxes to offer a compliment, ask a question, present birthday wishes, or thank the child for doing a favor (see Figure 31). Mailboxes are often kept in the permanent writing center; therefore, the center serves as the writing center and the post office.

A writing center is necessary in every kindergarten classroom. In addition to providing a variety of paper and writing tools, a writing center needs to house publishing materials: a stapler, staples, and staple remover ("jaws"); art supplies for making books; rulers; scissors; tape; a computer; picture dictionaries; and a date stamper. Also, upper- and lowercase letters need to be displayed on an alphabet chart or laminated alphabet strips taped low on the table's surface. Morrow (1989) recommends the following setup for the writing center: a table, chairs, a rug for children to lie on as they write papers on the floor, and a bulletin board for displaying children's work. Cunningham (2000) recommends a "word wall" of kindergartners' names and other needed spelling words such as high-frequency and pattern words.

Some of the centers listed in Table 5 are free choice and are used primarily for playful exploring, while other centers would have certain

Figure 31. Note to Student

Dear Kara,
  I liked the note you wrote for me at home. It was very funny.

            Love,
            Mrs. Clark

requirements. Some centers should be focused and purposeful, and the level of difficulty in these centers should change throughout the year. For example, Mrs. Poirier's ABC center is available all year long. Center activities begin with manipulating the alphabet with props such as ABC puzzles, magnetic and sponge letters, stamp pads and alphabet stamps, and various ABC books. Next, activities progress to matching a child's name letter for letter with magnetic letters, building names with letter tiles, or cutting names out of play dough. Then, activities progress to copying words from around the room and eventually matching sounds with appropriate letters and writing with a purpose.

Specific examples of jobs that Mrs. Poirier lists for the ABC center include the following:

- Find a color word (posted in the room) that begins with the letter *p* or *o* and copy that word. Use a crayon of the same color to write the color name or color a little next to the word with that color. Then read your words to a friend.

- Find a number word (numbers 1 to 10 are posted in the room) that begins with the letter *t* or *o* and copy that word. Read it to a friend.

- Stamp the letters of the alphabet; stamp the lowercase letter to match the uppercase letter or vice versa.

- Stamp a friend's name, and show it to your friend.

Mrs. Poirier gives each student a job and writes it on a piece of construction paper (which serves as meaningful print) and places in the center. When the children finish their specific ABC center jobs, they can manipulate things in the center in any way they wish, or they can choose some ABC games or toys to play with from a nearby shelf. Mrs. Poirier also uses this time to begin teaching those who finish first how to operate a computer, a skill that is mandated in the state in which Mrs. Poirier teaches. (Mrs. Poirier incorporates computer time into her schedule as often as possible.)

Another focused and purposeful center activity that Mrs. Poirier recommends to promote story structure and practice *approximated* reading is set up within the listening center. After reading aloud a story (see Appendix B for a list of Classic Pattern Books), Mrs. Poirier puts the corresponding audiotape and book in her listening center. In the beginning of the year, Mrs. Poirier requests that the children illustrate a favorite part of the story after listening to the taped reading. Before they take their illustrations home, students retell their stories to a friend. Later in the year, the children add a title for their stories to their illustrations and include one thing they want to tell their parent about the story. At the end of the year, Mrs. Poirier and the children work on identifying the main character, the main topic, the setting, and any interesting words in these stories.

How centers are handled is at the kindergarten teacher's discretion based on time limitations and what he or she feels students' needs are. Many kindergarten teachers allow students free choice or "exploring time" of some centers but require that all children visit certain centers, such as the science center or the ABC center, one time during the week. Some teachers like to assign a time for students to work in each center. For example, Mrs. Poirier assigns one half hour of purposeful structured centers at one time of the day and provides free choice of centers for one half hour at another time during the day. (Note that Mrs. Poirier teaches in a different school district, so her timetable is different from that in Table 4 on p. 109; she uses an adaptation of this schedule.)

While students complete center activities, teachers can incorporate interactive and shared writing, especially in the science and social studies centers. Because science and social studies often do not have a special time set aside for their study in kindergarten other than center time, the kindergarten teacher often "mans" these purposeful centers when particular tasks are required. For example, while studying magnets, the teacher and students can make a large interactive chart to provide the results of "What things magnets will pick up and what they won't." The chart should have two columns, and the teacher and the kindergartners work together to print a heading for each column. Then the teacher can place the chart (with a line dividing the two columns) on a table, and students can place the tested objects in the appropriate column. Later in the school year, students can print what is in the column using invented spelling. This chart provides verification for work done in the center (McCarrier et al., 2000).

In addition, when using the water table in the science center, children can study things that float and things that sink. A similar chart to the one made with magnets can be made. Children place (and later, record) on the chart what sinks and what floats.

Shared and interactive writing charts are useful in exposing children to meaningful print and teaching them to use expository writing as they write information reports. (See chapter 3 for a discussion of information reports.) As the children learn to make these charts interactively, they will eventually be able to write texts independently for their science inquiries and experiments (Vygotsky, 1934/1986).

As children progress in writing and spelling development, they record their own observations as real scientists do. For example, as they study snails or the life cycle of the butterfly, they can record their observations on a sheet of paper (e.g., "Facts About Snails" or "Facts About Butterflies"). These fact sheets can be posted in the classroom or in a learning log. Kindergartners also can make and record a list of the steps in a process such as making apple juice after visiting and seeing it done at an apple orchard. Before visiting the orchard, children can write questions about the orchard. After visiting the orchard, they can fill in the answers. This writing can be done as a group in the writing center or individually (when children seem ready developmentally). As previously mentioned, this kind of writing is referred to as "writing to learn" by Routman (1991).

Centers provide many interesting and varied opportunities for children to use their active, constructive minds in the pursuit of knowledge as they "do" things. Centers also provide the teacher with an opportunity to focus on science and social studies units. This is important, because most of the scheduled part of the kindergarten day is taken up with literacy approaches and *needs* to be if children are to reach their full literacy potential. Kindergarten teachers must remember there is nothing more important than teaching literacy, and teaching it "right" requires time, which is why writing in a writing workshop needs to be a priority. When children are allowed to learn the process of writing in writing workshop, they learn the alphabetic principle as they learn to write (or encode) their messages, and reread (or decode) their messages to check to see if they make sense.

Writing Workshop

In this section, I provide a brief overview of writing workshop to enable you to understand how the following activities might be used within these structures. However, I discuss how to prepare for writing workshop, or "Getting Ready," and writing workshop itself in more detail in chapter 5. Getting Ready consists of two things: (1) teaching children to identify the alphabet on an alphabet chart so an alphabet chart can be used to identify and find letters they wish to write during the workshop, and (2) teaching phonemic awareness activities—that is, teaching children to identify individual sounds in words so they can attempt to find corresponding letters for the sounds they wish to write in writing workshop. Writing workshop has three parts: (1) teacher demonstration of his or her own writing, which may or may not include a specific minilesson (when included, this minilesson is dependent on the students' writing need that the teacher has observed); (2) children independently writing for an extended period of time with the teacher guiding their writing according to their development in spelling and written language stages; (3) children sharing their writings or portions of their writings with the entire class and the teacher in Author's Chair.

Teachers should schedule writing workshop as soon as possible in the morning because, as previously mentioned, students are usually able to think more clearly at this time of day. Many teachers schedule it before center time, but afterward is a good choice, too, because centers often provide good ideas for writing.

Some of the activities that follow are activities that only require the teacher's time and can be done any time before, after, or during school hours that the teacher finds time to do them. Other activities require the children to participate, and these activities can be done during the day when appropriate or during "Getting Ready" (or later on in Word Study when it replaces Getting Ready), and some can be done as minilessons, too, in the first part of a writing workshop—teacher demonstration of his or her own writing and minilesson part.

Once teachers implement a writing workshop (again, chapter 5 tells how) and are able to determine their students' spelling and written language development stages, they will be able to determine when and where these activities are best used. For the purposes of this chapter, I list the various activities with their appropriate spelling and written language developmental stages. (For a brief review of these stages, see Appendix C.)

Precommunicative Stage and Picture Writing Stage

Most kindergarten children enter school in the Precommunicative spelling stage and the Picture Writing stage of written language development. The goals at this stage are to introduce to children the concept that writing is a means of communicating a message and to provide them with practice in interrelating Clay's (1991) four emergent reading behaviors through writing (see chapter 1 for more information on these behaviors). Therefore, the following activities demonstrate the importance of writing and invite children to hear sounds and explore and experiment with the letters of the alphabet and are appropriate in the beginning of the school year.

Using Words in Context: First, use simple statements and questions to label the classroom environment, such as "Have you signed in yet today?" "The date stamp is kept here," or "Please wash your hands in the sink after using the toilet." Teachers can label much of the classroom in this manner before school begins; however, labels must be read and pointed out to the children often at point of need. One kindergarten teacher said she had made the mistake of labeling things in the classroom one year without discussing the labels with the children, and the labels did little good.

Second, post nursery rhymes in enlarged print around the room and read them often. Later, when introduced and studied, high-frequency words within the rhymes can be highlighted by the teacher. (See Appendix D for a list of high-frequency words appropriate for kindergartners.) Many kindergarten teachers like to post *Jack and Jill* on the door. Then, it can be read or sung often as children line up for recess or lunch. Based on my experience, singing nursery rhymes is even better than reading them for retention of sight words and high-frequency words.

Third, write notes to students. Fisher (1991) likes to write notes to children that require them to read and sign-in. She posts a piece of paper that asks a question, and the children must sign in under the appropriate answer. For example, the question might be "What kind of lunch do you want?" and students write their names under hot lunch or cold lunch, or the question might be "What do you want to eat at the Halloween party?" and students write their names under cookies and milk or punch and a snack.

Finally, expose children to environmental print in the classroom. A stop sign (that says "Go" on the back) might be useful by the entry door or bathroom door. Children also should be encouraged to bring in environmental print like cereal boxes, toothpaste tubes, ketchup bottles, and so forth to place in the housekeeping center. Discuss this print during the alphabet portion of "Getting Ready," especially the beginning letters of the words. Teachers might even ask children if they can match a beginning letter on a box to the beginning letter in a classmate's name on the name wall. Students should listen to the beginning sound, too, to see if the sound in the name and the environmental print match. If you decide to leave a container that has environmental print on it near the word wall, leave the container intact for the first few months; don't cut the word out. Children need to see the meaningful context to identify the word at first. For example, the word *Cheerios* by itself would not be identifiable to most children unless it is in the context of the box of Cheerios.

Using the Name or Word Wall: Names are the first *words* that kindergartners want to write. Posting all kindergartners' names in alphabetical order on a large bulletin board or area of a wall in the classroom is the way many kindergarten teachers begin their word walls (Wagstaff, 1998). Teachers often write students' names boldly on different colors of construction paper, or they cut out letters of a child's name from one color of paper and paste them onto another color to add configuration (i.e., the shape of the letter) as a clue. Photographs can be placed next to the children's names, too, thus providing rebus print.

Word walls should be placed low on the wall so names and words are accessible to kindergartners. For this reason, writing centers are an ideal place for posting word walls (see Figure 32).

Figure 32. Name (Word) Wall in Writing Center

Over the course of the year, teachers often add to the word wall the repeatedly misspelled high-frequency words they've observed in children's writing. (See Appendix D for a list of 24 high-frequency words for kindergartners.) These words are added to the wall as well as words beginning with digraphs (e.g., *sh, ch, th, wh,* and *ph*) and some short-vowel patterns or word families (e.g., *at, an,* and *ug*). Commonly used and needed words and "word chunks" (digraphs and word families) are added slowly to the word wall and presented and posted meaningfully in context, often within nursery rhymes or on book jackets.

The purpose of the word wall is to encourage kindergartners to use it as a ready reference during their independent writing time and during editing. Although initially the word wall holds classmates' names and students should be encouraged to copy these names to learn letters (Morrow, 1989), Gentry and Gillet (1993) recommend that students also use the word wall to practice writing the high-frequency words they've been taught, using the "Look, Cover, Write, Check" strategy (p. 78), rather than simply copying these words. This strategy helps students learn to visually spell a new word by practicing its spelling in the following manner: First, the student *looks* at the word and says it softly. Next, the student *covers* the word and tries to see it in his or her mind. Then, the student tries to *write* the word from memory. Last, the student *checks* his or her word against the correct spelling of the word on the word wall (Routman, 1991).

For struggling writers and readers, Cunningham (2000) informs teachers that "having a word wall is not sufficient; you have to **do** a word wall" (p. 60). This includes

- choosing only really common words that are necessary to children's writing such as high-frequency words,
- adding no more than a word a day,
- making words accessible so they are seen easily by all students,
- chanting and writing words often and doing review activities to provide practice so words are read and spelled instantly, and
- ensuring that word wall words are spelled correctly in any writing students do.

If kindergartners request help with a posted word, refer them to the word wall and remind them to *try* to use the Look-Cover-Write-Check strategy for the high-frequency words they have been taught. If they need help in finding the word on the wall, advise them to ask a friend for help.

Listening for Same and Different Sounds: The teacher can give half the class a red card with *Same* written on it to signify words that rhyme, and the other half a blue card with *Different* written on it to signify words that don't rhyme. Next, the teacher pronounces some words in pairs or threes; some of these words rhyme, and some don't. The children raise their cards at the same time to indicate whether or not the words rhyme. (Watch for those children who are slow to raise their cards; they may need extra help in phonological awareness of identifying rhyming words.) These same cards can be used later when children begin to develop phonemic awareness (a subset of phonological awareness) to test students' discrimination of beginning sounds in words. (This activity could be used for checking discrimination of ending sounds, too.) Teachers also should watch for any children who might have to look at someone else's card before they hold up their own. Those few students who are having difficulty may need extra help with phonemic awareness, and the next activity, Elkonin Sound Boxes, helps address this area.

Using Elkonin Sound Boxes: Using Elkonin Sound Boxes is a Reading Recovery technique (Clay, 1993b) that I typically use with struggling students. Elkonin (1973), a Russian psychologist, strongly believed that children should hear the sounds in words in correct order (i.e., phonemic awareness) before being exposed to letters. He designed a training method to accommodate his belief that uses what he called "sound boxes." To illustrate his method using the word *boat*, the teacher should first show students a picture card of a boat. Next, the teacher should draw three adjoining squares, one for each sound segment in the word *boat*. As the teacher slowly articulates the word *boat* and its three sounds /b/, /o/, /t/, he or she pushes one counter (any small item like cereal, checkers, or pennies—whatever is in abundance and small enough to fit into the squares) for each sound into the appropriate squares. Next, the children should try pushing

Figure 33. Students Using Elkonin Sound Boxes

the counters for the sounds in the word *boat* into the appropriate squares just as their teacher did (see Figure 33). After practice with this word and other words of no more than three phonemes, so children are not overwhelmed as they learn the concept, the teacher can introduce the term "beginning sound" and demonstrate its position in a word.

Lining Up by Sounds: As children line up for an activity, the teacher can use the beginning phonemes of their names to have students practice phonemic awareness. For example, the teacher could say, "Everyone whose name begins with /j/ can line up now," and Joe, Jane, and Jimmy would get in line.

Promoting Writing's Usefulness (Temple et al., 1988): When teachers write, they should take every opportunity to point out to their students how they are using written language. For example, when writing a note to the lunchroom telling the number of children that want hot lunch, the teacher should show the note briefly to the children and explain it. The central message is that writing is important, it helps people communicate, and it is a worthy use of time.

"Be" the Alphabet (Cunningham, 2000): As children line up, the teacher can hand out laminated alphabet cards—one to each child—with the teacher keeping the leftovers. Then, the teacher should sing the "Alphabet Song" slowly as each child takes his or her place in line.

Taking an Alphabet Walk: When going to and from the classroom and to other areas in the school, teachers should ask their students to read the letters they know as they go on an alphabet walk. Teachers might even lead a game of letter "I spy," in which they give students hints about a certain letter in the area. Later in the school year, this activity could be changed to a word hunt.

Manipulating the ABCs: Many kindergarten teachers place magnetic letters on the side of a filing cabinet for their children to explore and experiment with at will. Teachers also can choose to read *Chicka Chicka Boom Boom* (Martin & Archambault, 1989), a favorite ABC book of kindergartners, and place the book and a coconut tree on the side of the filing cabinet to add more excitement to playing with the magnetic letters. The children can follow the story line of the book and place letters on the tree, too. This idea could be used during the alphabet portion of "Getting Ready," in an ABC center, or whenever children have a little free time.

Semiphonetic Spelling and Picture and Label Writing Stage (With Progression to Taking Inventory Stage)

When children progress to the *beginning* stages of the Semiphonetic spelling stage and Picture and Label Writing stage of written language development, most of the following activities can be introduced; however, the activities that focus on directionality, writing notes, and introducing word families with the same short vowel should be introduced when children progress to the *later* stages of Semiphonetic spelling stage and Taking Inventory stage.

Using Name Sorts (Gentry & Gillet, 1993): The teacher prints each child's first name on a large index card and gives each child the card with his or her name on it. Next, the teacher prints the alphabet horizontally on the chalkboard. Beginning with A, the teacher has all children whose names begin with that letter come up and place their name cards on the chalkboard tray under that letter. The teacher and students then discuss which letters have more than one name under them, which ones have none, and which letters are most common. For each letter that begins a name, the teacher brainstorms with the children other words or names that begin with the same letter. Students also can sort the name cards by the number of letters in each first name, the number of syllables in each name, and so forth.

Making a List of Class Names (Calkins, 2001): The teacher gives students a list of the names of all the children in the class (possibly with their class portraits) to be kept in their writing folders. Children love to copy classmates' names, and they often use the names as references when spelling words. Many kindergarten teachers can attest that it is commonplace to hear a child proclaim something like, "Oh, I know how *turtle* starts; it starts like *Tommy*!"

Shared Labeling: Shared labeling, in which the teacher and students share thought processes, can be done during the phonemic awareness time of Getting Ready. Each day the children can choose one item in the room (e.g., clock, flag) to label. The teacher labels the item in front of the children by placing it in a simple sentence like "This is Mrs. Williams's *desk*." Then, as the teacher writes the word *desk*, he or she may want to enlist the help of the children in hearing its initial sound. For example, the teacher could ask the children, "What sound do you hear at the beginning of the word *desk*?" (The teacher should emphasize the sound of the *d* in the word.) If the children give the wrong sound, like /p/, the teacher should practice iteration (i.e., repetition of sound) as follows: "Listen children, /p/, /p/, /p/. Does that sound the same as /d/, /d/, /d/?" These sounds really need to be emphasized both in speech and facial movements to highlight the way they are produced. Next, the teacher demonstrates how he or she finds the correct letter on the alphabet chart by using the strategy of singing the "ABC Song" to find the *d*. (In subsequent labeling, the children can be asked to do this part with interactive writing.) The teacher then continues to spell the rest of the word without the children's help.

Children should be encouraged to label things that belong to them, such as "John's markers." In addition, labeling can be very useful in other content areas such as science—for example, by labeling the various parts of a pumpkin plant (real is best). Then, literacy is promoted as well as the specific content.

Using Elkonin Sound Boxes to Make Words: Once children have developed some phonemic awareness, have demonstrated that they can push counters into sound boxes to represent sounds, and have learned to recognize some letters of the alphabet, they can push letter cards or magnetic letters (of the letters they know) into the sound boxes. (Later in the year when children are in the Phonetic stage of spelling, this device also can be used to practice spelling certain high-frequency words or words containing word families like *at*. For example, the teacher might give the children the letters *m, b, s, t,* and *a* and then ask the children to spell words such as *sat, bat,* and *mat* [Cunningham, 2000; Gentry & Gillet, 1993]).

Developing the Concept of Directionality of Print: Teachers should draw attention to directionality of print when modeling writing to the class until all students understand it. As some teachers model writing, they put a green arrow on the left-hand side of the page pointing to the right to remind the children where to begin and which way to arrange their writing (Clay, 1975). In addition, some teachers find it very helpful to ask questions such as, "Where do I start writing my story?" When the teacher reaches the end of one line, he or she could ask, "Where do I go now?" or "What do I do now?"

Because this is a whole-class lesson, there are usually students who are able to answer these questions, and the other students learn from these responses.

Developing a Concept of Letter and Word Directionality: When teachers observe that kindergartners can write their own names and perhaps a few of their classmates' names, they should begin teaching students an awareness of the concept of letter and word directionality. During Getting Ready, I put the magnetic letters of a child's name on a cookie sheet or other magnetic surface. Next, I put the initial letter of the child's name upside down and ask the child if his or her name looks right that way. I also ask the child to fix the letter so it is right and then read his or her name. Finally, I remind students again how letters in names have to be placed just right from left to right and also have to be placed right side up. Once children understand this concept with their names (*known*), we branch out into other words (*unknown*), especially words that contain letters that are easily confused with other letters because of directionality like *b*, *p*, and *d*, or *w* and *m*.

Differentiating Between Concept of Letter and Concept of Word: To differentiate between concept of letter and concept of word, I scramble the letters of a name on my cookie sheet and ask the students if I have a name anymore. Children usually answer that I have "just a bunch of letters" or the "ABCs," and I agree. (Mrs. Poirier's students love to describe this as "mumble-jumble" in emulation of their teacher's description.) Next, I put the letters back together into the child's name, explaining that when I put these letters together in this special way (pointing out directionality), they are not just a bunch of letters anymore. Now they mean something because they form a child's name. I tell the students that a name is a word, and a name is a very special word. That's why we capitalize the first letter of the name. After doing one name as an example, I invite children to choose a name and we do the process again.

This activity is repeated in many different sessions of alphabet time of Getting Ready (see chapter 5) as all the kindergartners' names are eventually targeted. If the teacher wishes, he or she can target high-frequency words after names, emphasizing the known (i.e., the name) to the unknown (i.e., the word).

Understanding Concept of Word: Once most of the children can write their first names and understand that names are words, I broaden the experience by using magnetic letters to spell one kindergartner's name twice on the cookie sheet, leaving no spaces between the two names. Next, I ask each child to separate his or her name from the other name until each child understands. This activity can be done with the whole class during alphabet time of Getting Ready.

The next activity, also a concept of word activity, can be done with the whole class at first for demonstration purposes, and then on an individual basis if the teacher so chooses. The teacher writes a child's name three times on a strip of paper without leaving any spaces between the names. Next the child is asked to help separate the names. The child spells his or her name first, pointing to each letter. When the child comes to the end of one spelling, he or she cuts the name apart from the one that follows. When the child has cut the names apart, he or she may paste them on another piece of paper, leaving spaces between them (Temple et al., 1988). This can be done during alphabet time of Getting Ready or students could use it in a center once it has been demonstrated by the teacher.

Understanding Directionality on the Page: Directionality in writing is often a matter of the best use of space available on a page. It is very common to see a child run out of space at the bottom of his paper and begin to write the words up the side of the paper. To avoid this practice, kindergarten teachers like to demonstrate folding a paper in half to leave a crease separating the top from the bottom of the page. Some teachers even demonstrate drawing a line between the top and the bottom of the page. Then, teachers demonstrate drawing a picture on either the top or bottom part of the paper and writing on the opposite half, which helps children learn directionality on the page (Clay, 1975). This could be presented as a minilesson in writing workshop.

Drawing Lines for Words to Demonstrate Concept of Word: Drawing horizontal lines for the number of words in a sentence helps the child focus on his or her message and the concepts of word and directionality and the concept that oral language can become written language. This activity can be presented as a minilesson. For example, Amy had been running all the letters of her words together with no spacing as in *Imhobabn*. However, when the teacher asked Amy to read what she had written during a one-on-one writing conference, the teacher noticed that Amy had most of the initial and final letters of her words, which is a strong indicator that Amy understood the concept of word, but just doesn't know how to show it with spacing. Because Amy's teacher believed she understood the concept of word, she showed her how to put in spaces by drawing lines for words and leaving spaces. First, the teacher asked Amy to read the sentence she had written: *I am holding a balloon*. Next, the teacher and Amy counted the words in Amy's sentence on their fingers, and then the teacher drew on a piece of paper five lines of appropriate length for Amy's words. Then, Amy carefully listened to the sounds in her words again as the teacher pronounced them. She wrote on the lines, "I m hob a bn" (see Figure 34). If other children in the class are having a similar problem, this same example could be used in a minilesson in front of the class, with Amy's permission of course. (It also is a good idea to photocopy samples such as Amy's to use for future minilessons. I like to keep a folder of writing samples that I can use in minilessons in future years.)

Many children have developed the concept of word, but it is not always seen as spacing between words. It may be observed as dots or lines between the children's words, or there may be no demarcation between their words, but both initial and final letters of most of their words are demonstrated, as

Figure 34. Drawing Lines for Words Sample

"I am holding a balloon."

in Amy's case. When teachers observe dots and lines between words or initial and final letters of most words being used but no spacing, they can introduce this concept to teach spacing between words. (This device also can be useful for teaching directionality and the concept that oral language can be written down in the initial stages of writing.)

Writing Notes: It is important for students to communicate through print as well as speech throughout the day whenever the opportunity arises. Parents in literate homes often communicate with their children and family by writing and leaving notes. Teachers can write notes to the children and they can ask children to write notes back. Mrs. Clark and Mrs. Williams often ask their children to write a note for them (in any way they can) when the children or the teachers want to remember something special. For example, Kyle wrote a reminder to Mrs. Williams (see Figure 35).

Modeling Articulation: As teachers confer with students, they may notice that a few Semiphonetic and Phonetic spellers hear and represent more sounds than the teacher might hear, but that is because they stretch the word out too slowly and listen so intensely that they hear more then they need to. Teachers should try to explain and demonstrate how they hear the sounds in a word. Teachers should be careful not to draw out the word too much, just slow enough to hear the sounds that are there. For example, if the letter *T* is drawn out too slowly, you will hear the sounds /t/ and /e/. I

Figure 35. Writing Notes Sample

MRS WilliAMS We Hf
bRT MilK

FEB 17 2005

Kyle

"Mrs. Williams, we have to read *Milk* [a guided reading book]. Kyle"

have seen a third-grade child's writing that was unreadable because she had
two and three letters written for each sound (phoneme). Using Elkonin
Sound Boxes aids this problem also (see p. 122).

Introducing Word Families With the Same Short Vowel: Johnston (1999)
suggests beginning word family study when children are consistently
representing initial and final consonants in their writing, usually near the
end of the Semiphonetic stage. Johnston also recommends beginning this
study with word families that contain the same vowel. The *at* family is often
chosen first because it is so prevalent. Students can hunt for *at* in books like
The Cat on the Mat (Wildsmith, 1983), and eventually do *at* word sorts with
other word families that have been introduced and share the same vowel;
for example, the *an*, *ap*, and *ag* word families. (See Appendix D for more
detailed instructions on using word families.)

Phonetic Stage and Taking Inventory and Adding Description Stage
When most children progress to the Phonetic spelling stage and the Taking
Inventory and Adding Description stage of written language development,
their concept of word is beginning to stabilize. The goals at this stage are (a)
to develop children's descriptive writing abilities; (b) to allow them to further
explore the rules by which letters represent phonemes; (c) to extend their
sight word vocabulary; and (d) to teach digraphs and different short vowels,
when the need is evidenced in children's writing.

High-Frequency Word Tent Cards: Teachers should introduce "tent cards"
to children who frequently struggle with spelling any high-frequency words.

In order for students to learn high-frequency words, they need to be seen and used often in meaningful print. For example, children often have difficulty with the words *me*, *my*, and *you*. To make a tent card, the teacher takes a large index card and folds it in half so it looks like a tent. Using interactive writing, the teacher and student write a sentence on both sides of the card, targeting the highlighted word. The reason for writing the sentence on both sides of the tent cards is so other children at the table can see the word, too. Then, the teacher should place the tent card in front of the child to use for reference as long as he or she needs it (see Figure 36). Children can keep tent cards on their desks permanently, or they can store them in their writing folders for daily use at writing time.

Wordo: Once they are studied, high-frequency words need to be practiced in meaningful print to become words recognized on sight (i.e., sight vocabulary); however, some high-frequency words that need to be learned do not receive equal practice in all young children's approximated readings and writings. Dickerson (1982) found that some games such as Sight Word Bingo worked well in practicing high-frequency words in an engaging manner. Cunningham (2000) adapted Bingo to "Wordo" for practicing needed high-frequency words in the classroom. Many teachers have found this a very useful game to play on "bad weather days" during recess and lunchtime. (See Appendix D for Wordo directions and Appendix E for Wordo form.)

Figure 36. Tent Card Sample

Building a Sight Word Vocabulary: Ashton-Warner (1963) describes a method to build sight vocabulary that she used successfully in New Zealand. By printing words that her students had requested on note cards (one word per card) and then giving the cards to the children to keep, she was able to teach her students an initial sight word vocabulary that proved useful to their reading and writing. Because these requested words (e.g., *spider, Mum, blood, skeleton*) were so special to the children, they were rarely forgotten. Morrow (1989) referred to this method as "Very Own Words." Temple and colleagues (1988) and Bear and colleagues (2000) recommend a similar activity that they describe as word banks. Many kindergarten teachers and I have found "Very Own Words" to be useful in engaging kindergartners with letters and words, especially if the words are names of their family, friends, and pets. Most teachers put these words on shower rings with a laminated card on the front that might include a title such as "Jamie's Very Own Words." (These cards can be kept in children's writing folders and may be transferred to a box if the folders get too bulky.) This method can be used when children request special words during independent writing and conferring time.

Reviewing Sight Words: Holdaway (1979) suggests reviewing children's sight words in the following manner: Once a week, the special words that students have collected as their "Very Own Words" or words collected in word banks are laid out on the floor. Each child locates his own and reads them. Cards that are not claimed—typically because a child does not remember the word—can be destroyed, simply because they no longer fulfill any function. Most teachers have found this activity works best with partners and in small groups, rather than large groups.

Pointing Out Reversals and Adding Visual Reminders: Reversing letters, especially *b*s and *d*s, is common for children. Teachers can point out reversals in the Phonetic Spelling stage, but only after praising approximated messages. When conferring with a child, the teacher should draw attention to a reversal by asking the child to say the name of the letter and then find it on his or her ABC strip. Usually the child will fix the miscue or error and say, "Oops, I got it backwards." Some children who habitually reverse *b* and *d* can be instructed to think of the word *bed* and make fists with their thumbs up and then rotate their fists to form a bed to visualize the letters *b* and *d* (see Figure 37).

Working With Initial Consonant Digraphs: Tongue twisters, rhymes, and books that concentrate on an initial consonant digraph (e.g., *ch, sh, th,* and *wh*) can be taught in the minilesson portion of writing workshop. Some useful tongue twister books include *Six Sick Sheep: 101 Tongue Twisters* (Cole, 1993), *Faint Frogs Feeling Feverish and Other Terrifically Tantalizing Tongue Twisters* (Obligado, 1987), and *Busy Buzzing Bumblebees and Other Tongue*

Figure 37. Visual Reminder

Twisters (Schwartz & Abrams, 1992). Also, if a child in the room has a name that begins with the targeted digraph, it is important to highlight it in the child's name on the name word wall and refer to it often. Any digraphs not represented in a child's name can be highlighted in the context of a tongue twister and posted on the word wall. For example, one teacher posted the book jacket of *Sheep on a Ship* (Shaw, 1989) on her word wall and highlighted the digraph *sh* with a removable and transparent colored tape made for this purpose.

Introducing Word Families With Different Short Vowels: When children attempt to represent short vowels but confuse them, Bear and colleagues (2000) recommend introducing word family study that compares the rimes or patterns with different short vowels (e.g., *at, et, it, ot,* and *ut*). This is done in the same manner as teaching word families with the same short vowel. (See Appendix D for a more detailed description.) This study should be followed by word sorting.

Using Rebus Print for Posting Word Families: When teachers introduce a word family (see Appendix D), they can post a representative picture (with the rime written on the picture) to act as a header for the ensuing list and to provide context. For example, a picture of a cat can be used as a header for the *at* family and a picture of a van could be the header for the *an* family. Children can help choose the representative picture, too. If children have trouble thinking of rhyming words, the teacher should read several rhymes (e.g., nursery, jump rope, or other types of rhymes) for inspiration.

All of the activities addressed within this section enhance writing in a writing workshop, and what enhances writing also enhances spelling and reading. Therefore, following writing workshop with reading workshop is beneficial for students—after they have had a snack and recess so they can refresh themselves.

Reading Workshop and Guided Reading

In this section, I provide a brief overview of a reading workshop because my focus is writing workshop. (A quality reading workshop based on Cambourne's conditions [1988] is thoroughly discussed in Calkins's *The Art of Teaching Reading*, 2001; for a complete description, see her chapter 13.) The structure of a reading workshop, which also includes guided reading, has three parts just like a writing workshop: (1) teacher demonstrates reading and teaches minilessons, (2) children read and teacher guides reading, and (3) children share.

Teacher Demonstrates Reading and Teaches Minilessons (5–15 minutes): When beginning reading workshop, children gather in a community circle for a teacher demonstration of reading from Big Books (or enlarged print of nursery rhymes and poems), which includes a minilesson based on the children's reading needs—that is, their pretend or approximated reading. At first, minilessons should be based on book knowledge, "reading the pictures," directionality, and so forth. However, as children demonstrate knowledge of the alphabetic principle in their writing, teachers can introduce conventional guided reading in small groups (usually around December), and then teach minilessons to address reading needs that the teacher has observed and that require immediate attention. Teachers can look for evidence of need in students' writing but should remember that when these areas are studied depends on students' spelling and writing stages.

Children Read and Teacher Guides Reading (10–30 minutes): Guided reading, as defined by Routman (2000), is "any reading instruction in which the teacher guides one or more students through any aspect of the reading process: choosing books, making sense of text, decoding and defining words, reading fluently and so on" (p. 140). As previously mentioned, when children first begin to read they approximate or "pretend" read. If children cannot do this, they need guidance because approximated reading provides a predictive base for conventional reading. Once children have acquired the alphabetic principle, which is learned and is observable in their writing, teachers can begin traditional, guided conventional reading, which typically is small-group reading where the teacher helps students with any problems they may be having in the conventional reading process.

However, until that time, it is necessary for teachers to be observant and aware of students' spelling and written language stages, so only reading needs that are appropriate within that stage are addressed. For example, when children are in the Precommunicative spelling stage or Picture Writing stage of written language development, it is appropriate to focus on aspects of directionality such as how to turn the pages in a book or how to read the pictures and approximate a story, but it is not appropriate to expect them to decode words. As Calkins (2001) explains, "If children aren't yet labeling their own drawings [Picture and Label Writing stage], they won't tend to notice the double b's in rabbit!" (p. 267) There is little point in beginning independent, conventional guided reading until children have had the opportunity to approximate writing and reading and demonstrate knowledge of the alphabetic principle in their writings, usually around midyear (Calkins, 2001; Routman, 2001). Until that time, reading workshops should consist of what the child is able to do, working from the known to the unknown. A description of an early-in-the-year reading workshop follows:

After the teacher demonstrates in a minilesson (5 to 15 minutes) how she looks at pictures and predicts the story by looking at the pictures in a book, she has the children go to their desks (or teachers can have students go to a special reading spot in the room) to "pretend" read for 15 to 20 minutes (this time can be extended to 30 minutes later in the year). The books they are reading have been pulled from a special book box or bags. (Mrs. Clark was lucky enough to find a mother who sewed book bags for all her students—one per child.) They contain a few well-known books. (For example, Mrs. Clark includes two or three familiar nursery rhymes and one or two classic pattern books; see Appendix B for a list of these books). As the children pretend read, the teacher walks around the room aiding and guiding them in book knowledge and picture reading within individual one-on-one conferences.

After independent reading time, the children return to the community circle to share (for 15 minutes) with the class and the teacher some insights they discovered from their approximated reading. (Mrs. Clark and Mrs. Williams often ask students to share their favorite part of a rhyme or a story. It is a good idea to suggest this idea and demonstrate how it is done in the minilesson portion of reading workshop first. For more good prereading suggestions, see Routman's suggestions for using learning logs, p. 107.)

"Pretend" reading continues for the next couple of months. During this time and all year long, the teacher exposes students to high-frequency words in the context of posted nursery rhymes and little poems and songs that are read and sung often as the teacher points to the words. When certain high-frequency words appear in the children's writings, the teacher addresses and teaches them (see Appendix D for a list of high-frequency words and information on how to teach them).

Once they are taught, the teacher highlights these words in their contexts within the room. Children participate in this highlighting by doing a "word hunt" in the room to find a newly introduced high-frequency word, and then the teacher highlights it. (Children also enjoy doing "word hunts" in Big Books; it is almost like a game of "I Spy" to them.)

Quite often, teachers think children have comprehension problems when the problem is insufficient sight vocabulary, especially high-frequency words or function words. Meaningful practice is necessary for fluent reading (Clay, 1991, 2001; Routman, 1991; Temple et al., 1988). Fluent reading requires relatively no time lapse between a reader's seeing and identifying words (Durkin, 1966). Although practice is necessary, it should not be done in isolation with flashcards (Clay, 1991, 2001; Harste et al., 1981). To encourage children to use these words in their writing and recognize them in their reading in the beginning of the year, it is a good idea to play "Read the Room." The teacher or the child can point to the words in a posted rhyme or other print in the room that is in context, and the class can read it. Then, the teacher can ask a student to find a specific high-frequency word in that rhyme by masking it, or pointing to it, and reading it in context again. This is also a useful center idea when done in pairs until children are actually using these words in their writing (and then it's still a good idea).

High-frequency words must become a part of the child's sight vocabulary as soon as possible to anchor a child's reading; however, they must be introduced slowly, one at a time in context of meaningful reading and writing.

Usually a couple of months into the school year, the teacher can introduce reading centers. Calkins (2001) describes these centers for kindergarten as a partnership of two students of the same reading ability. For two weeks, children meet with partners to read and respond to texts that are part of a whole-class theme. The first theme studied is usually wordless books and then the second theme is pattern books. (See Appendix B for booklists.) The centers are similar to a book club or literature circle where the teacher confers and assists approximations.

When kindergartners understand that print represents their oral language and they demonstrate the alphabetic principle in their writing (around December), the teacher can begin teaching conventional reading strategy lessons in small, guided reading groups of similar ability. Guided reading books need to be chosen carefully and should be at the child's *instructional* reading level, which means approximately 9 out of 10 words are familiar to the child (Calkins, 2001). This is important so the child can comprehend the message and use the meaning of the message to support the challenge of decoding a word with which he or she is not familiar in its printed form. If too many words are unknown in their printed forms, the child will become frustrated with the task of decoding them, and while he or she might be able to do it, the child will pronounce these words so slowly that all message will be lost—the very purpose for reading (Calkins, 2001; Clay, 1991, 1979). Trying to work on text like this is too difficult and considered to be at the child's *frustrational* reading level. Text that is too easy for the child to read independently is said to be at the child's *independent* reading level; the child makes very few errors in independent reading perhaps 1 error in 20 words (as cited in Calkins).

Some teachers with whom I have worked prefer the PM Collection of little books (Starters and Story Books) for guided reading because these books have engaging titles and are carefully leveled. (See Appendix B for complete reference of recommended literature and resources.)

Routman (2000) highly recommends the PM Collection, too, and also suggests Books for Young Learners as "a wonderful addition to any classroom" (p. 86b). Two other series Routman (2000) recommends include Oxford Reading Tree, interesting, real-life stories with eight wordless titles; and Discovery Links, an outstanding nonfiction series. (Again, see Appendix B for booklists.)

In the past, beginning readers have been forced to read books at their frustrational reading level. Clay (1991) alerts teachers to the necessity of providing familiar and predictable (i.e., involving repetition, rhyme, and rhythm) picture books to beginning or emergent readers, especially struggling emergent readers, so they can read at their independent reading level when reading alone and the instructional reading level in guided reading.

Choosing the appropriate "just right" book for each student requires that books be graded according to their readability level (Calkins, 2001, p. 121). Calkins (2001) asserts that most teachers should level about a third of the books in their classroom libraries, so children are able to find books at their independent reading level. Calkins also advises using dots to represent a book's level; she suggests selecting a few representative books from each level to be assessment books for that level. Mrs. Clark and Mrs. Williams like to color-code their books. For example, students might say, "I need a yellow book" or "I need a red book." Teachers must consider the features of books and anticipate the reading work children tend to do in order to choose a book that is just right for them (Calkins, 2001). Rog and Burton (2002) suggest teachers focus on the following five categories when considering the difficulty of a book: (1) vocabulary, (2) size and layout of print, (3) predictability, (4) illustration support, and (5) complexity of concepts. With these categories in mind, Rog and Burton developed a fairly simple 10-step leveling system that can be used for beginning reading instruction:

- Level 1 books have one or two words per page to label illustrations of familiar concepts, like a ball or the moon. The font is large and clear and located in the same place on every page.

- Level 2 books describe the illustration of familiar objects, but they also contain repeated phrases or simple sentences. There is usually a pattern repeated such as "Here is a horse," "Here is a dog," "Here is a house," and so forth. The first and last sentence of the book may be slightly altered.

- Level 3 books contain a few more words per page, usually in complete sentences. Sometimes there are two sentences on a page and there may be two pattern changes such as "At my party I ate some cake," or "At my party I opened some presents." Illustrations support the text.

- Level 4 books maintain a strong language pattern, often with two word changes in the pattern or a changing prepositional phrase such as, The dog jumped over the fence, The fish swam in the lake, or The birds flew in the sky. There is no more text on each page than in previous levels but it is simple and familiar, with many high-frequency words and concept words matching the illustrations. There usually is no story line at this level. There often is a distinct space between lines.

- Level 5 books allow for "reading work" to begin. Students must rely on more than just looking at pictures or reciting patterns; they must know a lot of high-frequency words and have some decoding skills. There usually is a predictable story line, which requires the reader to pay attention to meaning or message. Increasing sentence length requires an understanding of syntax, and there may be dialogue among characters. Although the text structure follows a pattern, it usually changes distinctly on the last page.

- Level 6 books move away from reliance on repetition on every page, but some repeated language patterns may appear throughout the text. A simple, predictable story line is evident with strong support from the illustrations. Sentences are short and choppy, but there is more print on every page. Print is large and consistently placed on each page. High-frequency words and decodable words predominate.

- Level 7 books have some literary language and structure emerging. There may be more than one event in the story and more detail in the story line. Sentences are still simple and, in general, the language still tends to be choppy. If sentence patterns are used, there may be several in the text. When new vocabulary is introduced, it is repeated several times. High-frequency words and decodable words still dominate. Illustrations may represent ideas rather than specific words.

- Level 8 books are longer with noticeably more text on each page—however, the text is enlarged. There are more new words, often repeated, and most vocabulary is high frequency, phonetically regular, or accessible from context. There is a more sophisticated story line with multiple events or a single event continuing over several pages. Illustrations are more detailed and support the story concept. Repetitive language patterns may be used but do not continue throughout the book.

- Level 9 books begin to take on the characteristics of a real story with occasional use of literacy language. The story line is predictable but is more sophisticated such as including a surprise ending. The books are longer and have many compound sentences in them. There may be four or five lines of text on each page, dominated by high-frequency words. More new vocabulary also is introduced.

- Level 10 books contain more unfamiliar words. There may be a full page of text, in enlarged print. There are more compound sentences. Illustrations are more subtle and detailed, enhancing the story line rather than providing cues to the text. The concepts in these books are familiar to children, like going to school or playing with friends. Shorter books with poetic language, expository text, or sophisticated concepts may be found at this level.

For teachers not experienced with leveling or working with the developing early reader, I suggest using preleveled books at first like the PM Collection or using the examples of leveled reading books from various publishers and authors that Calkins (2001) suggests (see pp. 543—546 of her book). Using preleveled books while observing the suitability of these books to developing readers' abilities makes it fairly easy to incorporate Rog and Burton's 10-step leveling system in the future. Most teachers level their books in the summer months because it is a time-consuming job; they often do it with another teacher(s) or with the help of the school's reading teacher. Mrs. Clark and Mrs. Williams leveled about one half of the books in their classrooms. Because they like to give children the *responsibility* to pick out some books on their own, one half of their books are not leveled.

Mrs. Clark and Mrs. Williams usually begin guided reading around December; however, sometimes they find it works best to wait until after the holiday break to begin. When they implement conventional guided reading, they form small groups of readers (approximately four students per group so there are two sets of reading partners in each group) who are able to read similar texts with some support.

They only work with one guided reading group a day for approximately 10 to 15 minutes, which gives them some time every day to devote to those students who struggle; if they can, they instruct aids or other volunteers to tutor these children, too.

To begin a guided reading session, they give a brief introduction (3 to 4 minutes) that includes a summary of the book in a few sentences, discussion of key concepts, new vocabulary words, and a walk through the tricky parts. Then they observe and guide readers as they read the text.

Calkins (2001) recommends using coaching statements and questions:

If the reader needs help with one-to-one matching

- Read it with your finger and make sure it matches.

- What letter did it start with?

- Did it match? Did you have any words left over? Was it enough words? Try again.

- Back up, try it again, and get your mouth ready.

- Does it sound right? Check it.

- Do you know any part of the word? OK, let's back up and try again.

- You almost got it right, but not quite. Can you go back and try again?

- I notice you are unsure. What are you noticing? (praise the observation)

If the reader isn't thinking about the text or story

- Let's think about the story—discuss it. OK, now back up and read it again.

- Check the picture. Does it make sense with your words?

If these questions and statements don't work, the teacher could ask, "Could it be...?" and then provide the correct word (Calkins, 2001, p. 76). Calkins also suggests that the following two questions to stimulate fluency:

- Can you put your words together; say it quickly?

- Can you say it as if you are talking?

Repeated reading of the text is a useful strategy to stimulate fluency, too. In addition, when children are in the early reading stage and are able to decode quite well but are still reading too deliberately to reach the fluent stage, I recommend using "progressive exposure" (Holdaway, 1979, p. 121) to aid the flow. With this technique, the teacher covers the text with an index card and then at a steady rate uncovers the text as he or she reads it. Then, the teacher allows the child to try reading the text as he or she uncovers the words at a fluent rate. (An overhead projector is a good device to do this technique with, too, when a whole class is involved.) It also is a good idea to explain this technique to parents if their children are struggling with fluency, because it prevents letter-by-letter and word-by-word reading.

Because there is little discussion during guided reading, guided reading ends with a brief book talk and practice strategies. The story is discussed briefly and the "tricky parts" are revisited. If the teacher notices a particular problem area, he or she can guide students to look at it and discuss strategies that might aid in their decoding or comprehension of the word(s). Calkins (2001) suggests having a white board handy so the word(s) can be pulled from the text, discussed in isolation, and then put back in the text to be read in a meaningful context.

When the teacher is conducting guided reading sessions, Calkins (2001) recommends the rest of the class read independently or with partners. (Some teachers allow students to find a nice nook in the room; others prefer students stay at their desks.) Reading like this employs Cambourne's (1988) conditions of learning literacy—that is, children are immersed in meaningful print as they use a large block of time to practice new learning (approximations) on their own initiative (responsibility). Children know what to practice because the teacher has provided demonstrations and has given positive and appropriate responses to guide each student's approximations. Therefore, both the child and the teacher expect the child to become literate.

Children Share (5–15 minutes): The whole class gathers for sharing. Initially, sharing can be done with some form of retelling (e.g., classic, or "old favorite," stories or nursery rhymes). Some teachers provide puppets or cutouts for a flannel board of some main characters in more popular rhymes and stories for retelling. Most teachers prefer to use creative drama or simply talk about the book. Later in the year, when children become early readers, children might use sticky notes to bookmark parts they especially liked or a "tricky part" they had difficulty with. Teachers can also use this time to point out any good "reading work" they have seen. They might even ask children to demonstrate the good reading work they have observed.

For example, as a literacy coach, I remember listening to Mrs. Clark's students early in the year share favorite parts of nursery rhymes after their independent approximated reading of rhymes. One student said, "I really like the words 'Twinkle, twinkle,' 'cause that's what stars do."

Both Mrs. Clark and Mrs. Williams like to employ creative drama for sharing in the beginning of the year at least once a week. In addition to retelling classic stories as a class (see chapter 3, pp. 93–95, for a description and visual), children are encouraged to retell a nursery rhyme by reenacting it.

Activities that support reading workshop need to be implemented when children demonstrate certain levels of spelling and writing development. Most of the activities that follow can be taught during a reading workshop minilesson, and later on, when word study is initiated.

Precommunicative Stage and Picture Writing Stage

The goals at this stage are to introduce to children the concept that a message is conveyed in what they are reading, to point out print to them, and to further extend their phonological and phonemic awareness. At this stage, children are emergent readers.

Using the Cloze Technique for Group Prediction: Teachers should use the shared book experience (Holdaway, 1979) to invite gap-filling predictive responses while reading a story. At appropriate places, the teacher should stop and ask the children, "What do you think will happen next?" This technique is especially effective when using a pattern book and often the appropriate place is at the turn of a page. In this way, teachers can teach problem-solving techniques without a lot of explaining or providing rules that kindergartners can't understand.

Clapping Syllables: The teacher can demonstrate and have students practice clapping the syllables in spoken words. The teacher should begin with children's names. The teacher should say each name in a natural way and then repeat it, emphasizing each syllable as he or she and the children chant it and clap once for each syllable in the name. The teacher can then repeat this procedure with other words that children find interesting like *chicken*: chick-en (with two claps) and *butterfly*: but-ter-fly (with three claps). The teacher should let students take the teacher's role and lead the class in clapping as soon at they are ready (Gentry & Gillet, 1993).

Making Innovations to Nursery Rhyme Text: The teacher can choose to change the words to nursery rhymes to provide more engagement for the children. For example, the lyrics to the song "Do You Know the Muffin Man?" (i.e., "Do you know the muffin man/the muffin man/the muffin man?/Do you know the muffin man/who lives on Drury Lane?") can be changed to "Do you know Kara Jones who lives at 1105 Grand Drive?" (as cited in Fisher, 1991). Other rhymes can be changed in a similar fashion.

Semiphonetic Spelling and Picture and Label Writing Stage (With Progression to Taking Inventory Stage)

The goals at this stage are to further extend the idea of reading for a message and to expect children to begin to demonstrate one-to-one correspondence between print and a message. In the early stages of Semiphonetic spelling and Picture and Label Writing, children are still emergent readers but as they progress to the later stages of Semiphonetic spelling and Taking Inventory, they become early readers.

Finger Pointing: Mrs. Clark and Mrs. Lentz often teach concept of word when they do word work or word study during the minilesson of their teacher demonstrations during reading workshop. They monitor the children's developing concept of word as children begin with vague left-to-right sweeps and progress to self-corrected, careful matching of speech to print as they point to words in short poems or songs that they have memorized like "Jack and Jill" and "There Was a Little Turtle" (Vachel, 1986). Teachers can make smaller copies of these rhymes and photocopy them so each child can finger point for him- or herself (Bear et al., 2000; Temple et al., 1988). Teachers should have children finger point when reading their own writing, too; even if it is just approximated pointing, it eventually proves useful to pointing in early reading.

Providing Remediation for Individual Pointing: Temple and colleagues (1988) suggest reading one on one a little rhyme or song with children who are having difficulty pointing to words as they read. The teacher and student point to each word together as they read it aloud. Then the teacher points to a single word and asks the child what it is. The child usually recites the line to him- or herself and guesses what the word is, which enables the student to think about words as units of writing and practice matching a word in his or her head with one in print.

Walk the Words: "Walk the Words" is another technique kindergarten teachers like to use to develop the concept of word. Teachers take a sentence from a short, familiar song or rhyme (e.g., "Jack and Jill went up the hill") and write each word of the sentence on a 5" by 8" index card. Then, teachers lay these cards on the floor and exaggerate the spaces between the words. They should ask the children to step on each word and read it as they walk. (Kindergarten teachers often laminate these words for this purpose.)

This same technique can be done in pairs of children. Teachers can copy the sentence onto an index card and have the pairs cut it into words. Then, the pairs can match the words to the sentence in the Big Book or on the posted nursery rhyme.

Phonetic Stage and Taking Inventory and Adding Description Stage

The goal at this stage is to continue to immerse children in meaningful print in order to extend their concept of reading for a message, widen their sight word vocabulary, and stabilize their concept of word. At this stage, children are early readers.

Reconstructing Sentences: To develop concept of word, Gentry and Gillet (1993) suggest reconstructing sentences from familiar Big Books, rhymes, or songs. The teacher prints the first sentence from such a text on a long piece of tagboard. While the children watch, the teacher uses scissors to cut between each word and then randomly hands each individual word card to a child. Next, the teacher demonstrates how he or she would match a word card to the word in the sentence. For example, the teacher might say, "What letter would you expect to see at the beginning of Jack if the first sentence from 'Jack and Jill' was being reconstructed?" Then the teacher asks the children to match their word to the correct word in the text. Once children get the idea, these cut-up words can be put in a plastic bag and stored with the corresponding book, rhyme, or song for future use. (The teacher should ensure that the cards are mixed up before being put in the bag.) This also makes a good center idea. Working in pairs, children can lay all the words in correct order on the floor. When matching becomes easy, children can try to reconstruct the sentence without matching the text but from reading the cards. Then the text could be used to confirm their work.

Matching Words in Print: The teacher asks children to match high-frequency words within a nursery rhyme, too. The teacher gives each student an index card with a high-frequency word that is found in the chosen rhyme and then has each student match his or her word to the one in the rhyme.

Hide a Word (Gentry & Gillet, 1993): The teacher places the word cards that make up one of the sentences in a well-known nursery rhyme in their correct order in a pocket chart. After reading the sentence chorally, the teacher tells the children to cover their eyes. Next, the teacher turns over one of the word cards to hide it. At the teacher's signal, the children uncover their eyes and try to figure out which word is hidden. Then, the teacher can choose a child to be the "word hider" and have him or her choose the next player. If one sentence is too easy, the teacher can use two, or even three, sentences in proper order from the rhyme or song.

Word Hunts: The teacher asks students to do a word hunt or find certain targeted words the teacher has chosen within the room. First, the teacher tells the children the word, and then volunteers point to the word in the room. Children can also do word hunts in text.

Using the Cloze Technique for Individual Prediction: Holdaway (1979) suggests using the cloze technique to get children to predict a word using the message of the text. When a child is reading and is stumped by a word (be sure to allow "wait time" first—that is, an opportunity for the child to try), the teacher covers the word and rereads or reads as much of the text that is necessary for him or her to make a good guess or prediction for a substitute. When the child makes a prediction, the teacher asks him or her what letter the word would have to begin with. (The teacher may have to go beyond the first letter if the words begins with a blend or digraph.) Then, the child learns that reading involves predicting a message and confirming it using graphemes (written letters). As a reading teacher, I have found this technique to be very useful to teach reading as understanding a message and not just applying phonics.

Read-Aloud

In the early afternoon, Mrs. Clark's and Mrs. Williams's students rest for half an hour. Mrs. Clark and Mrs. Williams like to read to the children prior to rest time to emulate a bedtime story routine. Every kindergarten teacher with whom I have ever worked has implemented a read-aloud in his or her classroom. Routman (2000) reports that experts as well as research have validated reading aloud as a critical factor in a child's becoming a successful reader. Routman states that reading aloud

- helps a child enjoy reading;
- helps develop a sense of how written language works;
- helps build a rich vocabulary; and
- helps a child learn to predict, a necessary strategy in reading.

Young children who seldom are read to are deprived of exposure to the complex syntax that is found in written language (Purcell-Gates, 1989). These children are at a disadvantage, both in understanding writers' syntactic constructions and in choosing appropriate constructions in their own writing. It is important to read books above the child's independent reading level because this builds comprehension by increasing the child's exposure to new forms of language and rich language (Calkins, 2001; Routman, 1991).

Children who do not come from literacy-rich homes need this kind of reading exposure if there is any chance of them catching up to their literacy-rich classmates (Clay, 2001).

Reading a variety of text is important, too. Holdaway (1979) suggests reading poems, nursery rhymes, songs, and stories every day. Many kindergarten teachers develop a file of poetry that ties in with a favorite book, and they keep the poems in the book. (See *Read-Aloud Rhymes for the Very Young*, Prelutsky, 1986, for examples of poems to use.) Any time is a good time to read a poem, but capitalizing on the first day of snow or a fight on the playground can be an especially good time to share feelings through poetry. When children request rereading of certain favorite stories, teachers should be sure to accommodate their requests in future read-alouds. Nonfiction books should be included, too, because children find them enjoyable and informative, and they provide a good model for children's own written language, which is mostly nonfiction.

Mrs. Clark and Mrs. Williams explain the value of reading aloud to the parents of their kindergartners. They show parents how to read to their children at the first parent–teacher night at school. They explain the value of pictures as cueing devices and the value of pointing to the words as they read so children will visually attend to the print. They also explain the value of children predicting the text prior to and during the reading, and discussing the reading with the children during and after to promote comprehension. In addition, they provide parents with a list of books that they have found to be favorites of kindergarten children. (See the list of pattern books in Appendix B.) Many schools promote family reading programs and find them to be effective. For example, one school asks parents to unplug their televisions for at least one night a week and read to their children. See *The New Read-Aloud Handbook* (Trelease, 1982) for information on how to plan such a program.

Class Newspaper

Often when parents ask their children what they did in school, they reply, "Nothing." A class newspaper is a good daily culminating activity to refresh students' minds about exciting learning from the school day or the best part of a day. It's an excellent way to provide closure each day and keep parents informed of daily happenings. Fisher (1991) recommends dividing a sheet of paper into six boxes: one box for each day of the week and one box for general notices. Mrs. Clark and Mrs. Williams simply use large chart paper and draw heavy lines between each day's entries. They usually write only one sentence of something that was learned or exciting on any given day, for example, acting out *Rosie's Walk* (Hutchins, 1968) in reading workshop, taking a field trip to the post office, or even reporting the children's findings of what magnets will and will not pick up. The class newspaper is a good place to use shared writing or interactive writing. At the end of the week, teachers type the final rendition, make a copy for each child, and send it home.

Friendship Circle

In the late 1980s when I began my educational search for how to teach reading to the beginning reader in the best way possible, I began by asking teachers who they thought of as outstanding teachers in their districts. One such teacher was Maggie Pempeck of the Wausau School District. (She is currently a literacy leader in the district.) I observed her classroom and learned so much. One of the things I admired was the way she ended her day with the children because it promoted kindness and self-esteem; she referred to it as a "friendship circle." The entire class stood up and formed a big circle in the front of the room. Ms. Pempeck began the procedure by saying, "I noticed that Mary helped Sammy tie his shoes today. Did anyone else notice something nice that one of you did for another classmate today?" Then each child had a chance to mention something nice that someone else did. This is, in fact, a simple and wonderful way to promote kindness and self-esteem, and it's a lovely way to end the school day.

Summary

Learning to write and read must be a priority in kindergarten as well as in first grade. Literacy is a priceless gift that teachers can help their children achieve if they understand the conditions necessary to promote literacy (see chapter 1) and use the best field-tested literacy approaches and strategies based on these conditions. With this foundation, a comprehensive literacy program is capable of evolving.

This chapter explains and provides many examples of how over 60 kindergarten teachers have used these approaches and strategies and how two teachers in particular have incorporated these approaches and strategies into their daily schedule, which is the model I provide. All these instructional strategies are child-centered and duplicate the influence of a literacy-rich home. They are constructive and purposeful and provide engagement for egocentric, curious, and playful kindergartners. However, some deserve priority in the daily schedule such as writing workshop and reading workshop.

Daily writing and reading workshops that are 45 to 60 minutes long must be a priority in kindergarten because they enable *all* students to become literate. They provide the proper literacy conditions to help literacy-rich students and students who struggle more frequently, often students from literacy-poor homes, to reach their fullest literacy potential. Chapter 5 explains how to implement a writing workshop so teachers can prompt reciprocity of writing to reading and aid all their kindergartners to become writers and readers.

CHAPTER 5

Getting Ready and Writing Workshop

"Children view writing...[as] exploration with marker and pen.... [They] learn the power of their gestures by our response to them."

—Calkins (1994, p. 59)

Most young children enter kindergarten believing they can write. In addition to responding positively to each child's written language approximations, Calkins (1994) advises teachers to follow the child's lead, ask questions that teach and challenge, and absolutely resist taking over the child's writing and making it the teacher's writing.

To enable kindergartners to write readable messages, Clay (1991) suggests that kindergarten teachers (a) provide the proper conditions of learning language (Cambourne, 1988) so children will want to write (see chapter 1 for an explanation of these seven conditions) and (b) keep focused on both the dominant goal of guiding young writers to communicate messages and the secondary goal of using Clay's (1991) four behaviors of emergent literacy (see chapter 1 for an explanation of these behaviors).

As a literacy coach, I have found that the best way to guide teachers in providing these conditions and fulfilling these goals is to demonstrate a writing workshop in their classrooms, followed by a discussion with the teachers.

I would like to note that while it may seem as if things always go perfectly in these lessons, this is far from the truth. I am presenting a composite of my best work to serve as a model. When I first attempted to do a writing workshop, I was armed only with my books as resources, the schedule I've presented in this chapter, and the knowledge that a conference should be a "simple conversation" based on students' interests with the goal of helping writers think for themselves as they learn to put their thoughts in writing (Graves, 1994, p. 49). As problems came up, I looked to the research to help me, especially the books of Calkins (1994) and Graves (1994). I read and reread my copy of Calkins's (1994) book until it literally fell apart. I made—and continue to make—mistakes, but I've found kindergartners (and most young students) to be very kind and tolerant of my teacher approximations. Learning is a process, and approximation (trying) is a part of the process. It is necessary for all learning, even teachers' learning.

As teachers implement a writing workshop, they should concentrate on kindergartner's primary impulse to want to tell the personal experiences in their lives. This will provide the engagement required for students to do the laborious task of interrelating Clay's (1991) four emergent reading behaviors as they learn to write with invented spelling in a writing workshop.

I usually begin demonstrations the second or third week after school has started to allow time for teachers to get students accustomed to routines and to observe students' reactions to print. During this time, teachers also begin laying the groundwork for developing phonemic awareness by teaching or reviewing phonological awareness of rhyme using nursery rhymes, Dr. Seuss books, and songs. They also work on syllables (beats) by clapping the parts heard in their students' names (Cunningham, 2000).

Structure of "Getting Ready" and Writing Workshop

After I demonstrate the structure of "Getting Ready" and writing workshop to kindergarten teachers, they use these same two structures every day for approximately an hour in their daily schedules. (See Table 6 for a brief explanation and outline of these structures.)

Teachers can record their daily lesson plans on an outline that incorporates these structures (see Appendix E). For example, although the "Alphabet Song" is presented daily in the alphabet time of Getting Ready, teachers may wish to record an additional alphabet activity for the day. Also, although most teachers begin phonemic awareness time with the "Name Song," they should also record any other phonemic awareness activity that they plan to do. The same is true for writing workshop. The teacher can note new minilessons for the day and possible reminders to review previously taught material that needs additional attention under "Teacher Demonstration and Minilesson" and "Teacher Confers as Students Write."

And, on occasion, the teacher may wish to advise the children before they share their work in Author's Chair of something that the teacher has

---

Table 6. Sample Schedule for Getting Ready and Writing Workshop

Getting Ready for Writing Workshop (15 minutes)
• Alphabet Time: Teach the alphabet and "Alphabet Song" (5 minutes)
• Phonemic Awareness Time: Teaching phonemic awareness with playful language (10 minutes)

Writing Workshop (45 to 60 minutes)
• Teacher Demonstration and Minilesson: Demonstration of drawing and writing and minilesson based on need (10–15 minutes)
• Teacher Confers as Students Write: Teacher confers, guides, and celebrates while students draw and write (10–15 minutes at first; later on, 30 minutes)
• Sharing in Author's Chair: Teacher chooses a few student authors to share their work in Author's Chair (15 minutes)

observed needs to be corrected—for example, phrasing questions politely by saying, "I wonder why you did..." rather than saying "Why did you do...?" (As previously mentioned, Author's Chair refers to the time that a few student authors selected by the teacher share their work with the class.)

The first day lesson plans for Getting Ready and writing workshop are presented in two parts: (1) the outline for the lesson plan and (2) the written implementation of the lesson plan. I begin by providing the lesson plan for the first day of Getting Ready, and then the implementation. (Readers may wish to bookmark these plans and refer to them while reading the chapter.)

Getting Ready

Many beginning kindergartners do not know the letters of the alphabet well enough to write them at will, and most kindergartners do not know how to isolate individual sounds in words (i.e., phonemic awareness). These things need to be taught within meaningful playful language, the purpose of Getting Ready. Following is the outline for Getting Ready.

Lesson Plan Outline for First Day of Getting Ready (15 minutes)
Alphabet Time: Teaching the Alphabet and "Alphabet Song" (5 minutes)
Using a large, colorful ABC chart, *point* to the letters as you sing the "Alphabet Song." Sing it a few times to familiarize all students with the song (see Figure 38).

Phonemic Awareness Time: Teaching Phonemic Awareness With Playful Language (10 minutes)
Using a chart with the "Name Song" (see Appendix A, p. 279) printed on it, point to the words and sing it a few times until students are familiar with the song.

Figure 38. Student Pointing to Letters

Using the first day lesson plan outline for Getting Ready as a basis, I present an in-depth description and discussion of the implementation of Getting Ready's Alphabet Time and Phonemic Awareness Time. Although this implementation, which I refer to as a written demonstration, may appear lengthy, the actual time it takes to enact in the classroom is only 15 minutes. (Note times given throughout chapter.)

When I explain my written demonstrations in the remainder of this section on Getting Ready and the next section on writing workshop, I outline them as follows:

- Aim
- Classroom Setup and Materials
- Procedures
- Discussion

The discussion section focuses on questions that kindergarten teachers have asked me after demonstrations.

Demonstration of First Day Lesson Plan for Getting Ready

Alphabet Time: Teaching the Alphabet and "Alphabet Song" (5 minutes)

Alphabet Time Aim

To promote visual scanning of the alphabet by familiarizing kindergartners with the "Alphabet Song" so it can become a tool (or strategy) to help them find and copy letters of the alphabet from their individual alphabet strips as needed in their writing.

Alphabet Time Classroom Setup and Materials

Kindergartners are seated in the community circle. The teacher has access to a pointer and a large colorful alphabet chart that includes both upper- and lowercase letters. The words of the "Alphabet Song" should be added to the bottom of the chart: "Now, I know my ABCs, next time won't you sing with me?" (first verse) and "Now, I know my ABCs, tell me what you think of me" (second verse). Providing the words gives students exposure to meaningful print and enhances their sight vocabulary.

Alphabet Time Procedures

1. Point to the alphabet on a chart and ask the kindergartners if they can tell you what it is. Usually they know; however, if not, tell them it's the alphabet. Then tell students that they are going to learn all these letters by singing and pointing to them every day as they sing the "Alphabet Song." (This song will be sung daily throughout the year, once or twice,

until all children can use the alphabet as a strategy to find any letter of their choosing.)

2. Point to the letters as you sing the first verse of the song. Try to watch the students' eyes, especially those who do not know how to write their names. It is imperative that kindergartners look at the letters as the song is sung so they can become familiar with the various shapes of the letters and will be able to find any letter through the use of the song. For example, Ms. Neuenfeldt asks her students to look up by saying, "Let's see if I can see all your beautiful eyes looking up here." (In the same kindly manner, single out any child not looking.)

3. Select a kindergarten volunteer to be the teacher as you sing the second verse of the song and instruct the volunteer to point to the letters of the alphabet. If the volunteer has difficulty pointing to the letters as you sing the song, point to the letters with your finger from above as the volunteer points with the pointer from below. Remind all students to keep pace with the volunteer's pointing; letters *only* should be sung when pointed to.

Familiarizing kindergartners with the "Alphabet Song" and learning to point to and scan the letters as the song is sung a couple of times is all that is necessary for the first day. However, on subsequent days I add the following steps:

4. Have students find the first letter of their names, and eventually any letter that you target. If they have difficulty finding a letter, the class can help the child sing the "Alphabet Song" and find the letter by saying, "Stop!" when the targeted letter is sung.

5. Have students write the first letter of their names and, later in the year, any letter that you target. Also ask the children to write letters in different ways such as in the air with their fingers; on each other's backs; on individual dry-erase boards, or "magic slates," and miniature chalkboards; or with their bodies.

Alphabet Time Discussion

Being able to name the letters of the alphabet is a good predictor of beginning reading achievement, even though knowing the names of the letters does not have direct impact on a child's ability to read (Adams, 1990). Simply teaching children to name the letters without accompanying writing and reading experiences will not promote reading (literacy).

Learning the "Alphabet Song" is a meaningful activity, and by learning to point to the letters as they are sung, students learn how to use the song as a tool (strategy) to find any letter of their choosing as they try to write it (Cunningham, 2000). Pointing to letters of the alphabet as the song is sung is mandatory so children can find any letter and eventually learn to associate that letter with its graphic representation (Holdaway, 1979). (See chapter 2 for a discussion of developmental letter formation.)

When teaching the "Alphabet Song" as a strategy to find letters of the alphabet, it is important to stick to the *same* melody. Using other melodies will only cause confusion and will probably obstruct the song's usefulness, especially to the literacy-poor child.

Although using the same song every day may seem boring to the teacher, students depend on its familiarity to guide them in finding unknown letters. On occasion a child or two might object. If this happens, check to see if the child can find a particular letter, and then demonstrate the song's purpose, as Mrs. Clark did with Danny (and Betty) when they both said, "I already know that song!"

Mrs. Clark: Danny, will you find the letter *v* on this chart?

[Danny is unable to locate the letter, but when the class sings the song and he and Mrs. Clark point to the letters, he is able to.]

Mrs. Clark: Class, remember I said you need to know this song so well that you can find any letter with it.

[Next, it is Betty's turn to find letters, and Betty is able to find every letter Mrs. Clark targets.]

Mrs. Clark: Betty, I am so pleased for you; you really do know all these letters! In fact, you know them so well, I would like you to help me teach them. Would you like to do that?

[Betty beams and answers "yes" with enthusiasm. Then Mrs. Clark lets Betty point to the letters as Betty leads the class in singing the song.]

Mrs. Clark: Class, whenever any of you learn your letters as well as Betty knows them, you can become a teacher, too. When you know something as important as this, you need to help the other children to learn it, just like I do.

When students point to, find, and write letters, they need a risk-free atmosphere that supports approximation. Students need to be encouraged to try, and if they have difficulty, they need kind, nurturing support to complete the task. Often, this support can be provided by classmates as well as the teacher by saying, "Stop!" when the targeted letter is identified. Another alternative if a student gets stuck is to ask the student to call on a fellow classmate to whisper the answer in his or her ear. Students should not be afraid to try; mistakes can be pathways to learning with proper guidance.

Phonemic Awareness Aim

To introduce kindergartners to phonemic awareness (the ability to hear individual sounds in words) through the use of the "Name Song" and sound matching of initial consonant sounds, the least difficult of phonemic awareness activities.

Phonemic Awareness Classroom Setup and Materials

Students are seated in the community circle. The teacher has access to a pointer and the "Name Song." (The words should be printed on chart paper in enlarged print; see Appendix A.)

Phonemic Awareness Procedures

Because kindergartners love to work and play with their names, I like to begin each category of phonemic awareness activities (i.e., matching, isolating, substituting, blending, and segmenting) with the "Name Song." (See Appendix A for phonemic awareness activities.) When first introducing the "Name Song," I use only those student names that begin with single consonant sounds because they are the easiest to hear. (Names beginning with long vowels, digraphs, and short vowels are addressed last, when they become familiar to students.)

1. Direct the students' eyes to the words of the "Name Song" with the pointer (see Appendix A, p. 279, for lyrics).

2. Sing the song (sung to the tune of "Skip to My Lou") once to familiarize the students with it.

3. Choose a phoneme (a beginning consonant sound of a child's name) to insert in the first verse of the song (e.g., "Who has a name that starts with /m/?"). Repeat this line three times. Then in the second verse of the song, supply the answer to the question by inserting a name that corresponds with the phoneme that you chose in the first verse (e.g., "Mary has a name that starts with /m/"). Repeat this line three times. As you sing the song, ask the student whose name you are using to stand up. For example, if Mary is the only one whose name begins with /m/ in the room, she is the only one to stand up. If other students in the class have a name that begins with /m/ like Marvin or Marilyn, they would stand up, too. It is helpful to repeat the song with these students' names in it. Children also love to hear their names used like this.

4. Sing the first line of the song again and insert a new phoneme, "Who has a name that starts with /j/?" When I ask students to listen for a sound, I usually give a gentle tug on my ear lobe. Again, all the children who have a name that begins with /j/ are to stand up. If a child does not recognize the sound of /j/ as the beginning of his or her name, the child will soon with this kind of practice. For now, simply ask the child to stand.

    If some children say a name that does not begin with the appropriate phoneme, practice "iteration" (Yopp, 1992). (Iteration is a Reading Recovery technique similar to slow stuttering, that I typically only need to use in the beginning of the school year and have found to be extremely useful.) For example, if someone answers that Billy is a name that starts with /j/, I say, "Now listen closely: /b/-/b/-/b/-/b/ Billy, does the /b/ sound the same as /j/-/j/-/j/-/j/, Joey?" I really emphasize the beginning phoneme in both names.

5. As students become more familiar with names, target all the students' names, even those beginning with long vowels, digraphs (e.g., *sh*, *th*, *ph*, and *ch*), and short vowels.

Kindergartners understand that digraphs represent one sound; however, they do not know that a digraph is one sound spelled with two letters. The following example provides an introduction to digraphs and illustrates how a child's name became an important teaching tool for the digraph *sh*.

[Mrs. Clark introduces Shane's name in the "Name Song," and Shane stands up.]

Mrs. Clark: Class, what letter do you think stands for the sound /sh/ in Shane's name?

Children: *S.*

Mrs. Clark: Shane, will you write your name on the board for us, please?

[Shane writes his name.]

Mrs. Clark: [pointing to Shane's name] Class, did you notice that Shane begins with an *s* just as you said, but it also has an *h* following it? Listen closely now as I say /sh/, /sh/, /sh/. Does it sound different than /s/, /s/, /s/?

[The children agree it does.]

Mrs. Clark: That's because whenever *h* follows *s*, it makes this *one* sound, but this one sound is spelled with these *two* letters, *s*, and *h*. So, whenever you hear that /sh/ sound, I want you to think of Shane's name, and how he spells it with an *s* and an *h*.

[Mrs. Clark walks over to the word wall and circles the *s* and the *h* in Shane's name so the children have a ready reference to this teaching strategy.]

After all the children's names that begin with single consonants, long vowels, and digraphs have been introduced, Mrs. Clark can introduce any remaining names that begin with short vowels. By this time, the class will have become somewhat accustomed to the sounds at the beginning of these children's names. However, she would not introduce any other words beginning with short vowels because short vowels prove much more troublesome for kindergartners and beginning first graders than digraphs or long vowels. Routman (1991) states, "Most kindergarten children and beginning first graders are...not yet developmentally ready [to hear and perceive isolated] short vowels" (p. 154); they are not ready to apply short vowels correctly in their reading and writing until the end of the first grade. Additional research supports this point (Bear et al., 2000; Gentry & Gillet, 1993; Johnston, 1999; Temple et al., 1988). For example, I remember a first-grade teacher in the beginning of the year attempting to coax a child into identifying the isolated short vowel /i/ while trying to spell the word *bit*. The child was almost in tears as she tried various incorrect responses. Interjecting, I asked her if she knew the word *it*. She did, and her knowledge of the word family *it* solved the problem. As the first-grade teacher and I discussed this situation later, I explained that my thinking had been the same as hers until I read the research on the timing of teaching short vowels developmentally in kindergarten and first grade. (For more on teaching short vowels in word families, see "37 Common Rimes" in Appendix D.)

After the beginning sounds of all the kindergartners' names have been targeted and the children understand the idea of sound matching through the use of the "Name Song," other sound matching activities can be included in this time frame. Most kindergartners understand the concept of sound matching within two to four weeks, and then sound isolation can be introduced. (See Appendix A for phonemic awareness activities and a suggested progression for teaching them.)

Once most kindergartners can hear the beginning sounds in names and words and know how to use the "Alphabet Song" to find a letter of the alphabet, they can be asked to find and write the targeted letter during this time.

Some teachers, especially novice teachers, have found it easier to initially use the "Word Song" (Yopp, 1992; see Appendix A, p. 279, for lyrics) instead of the "Name Song," because it gives them total control of which beginning sounds to choose. However, they eventually include the "Name Song" because children love it.

Phonemic Awareness Discussion

Teachers need to encourage students' *hearing* of individual sounds first, before asking students to write letters that stand for those sounds. Kindergartners who have not been exposed to letters of the alphabet and the use of written letters (graphemes) may be distracted if asked to write letters before they have developed the concept of phonemic awareness (Chomsky, 1979; Clay, 2001; Elkonin, 1973; Yopp, 1992).

Using the terminology *starts with* when discussing letters that stand for initial sounds can be confusing to some students. Normally, I do not have a problem with this terminology when using the "Name Song"; however, when I was a literacy coach working with mostly English-language learners, I did. I used the "Word Song" as an introduction to my phonemic awareness activities because I was unsure of my pronunciation of the children's names. The children appeared to be totally lost when I asked them "Who has a /b/ word to share with us?" However, I was able to resolve the problem by using Elkonin Sound Boxes (see chapter 4, p. 122).

When I first started working with the "Name Song" and phonemic awareness activities, I directed the students to listen for and match only beginning sounds in words because, initially, matching sounds is the easiest of phonemic activities, and hearing beginning sounds is easier than hearing ending sounds and far easier than hearing middle sounds (Clay, 1991). Children, on their own initiative, can transfer their knowledge of beginning sounds fairly easily to ending sounds, and eventually to middle sounds (Bear et al., 2000).

Because students should not be encouraged to write a letter that stands for a targeted sound until they have developed some phonemic awareness and either know the letter or know how to find the letter through the use of the "Alphabet Song" and their ABC strip (Elkonin, 1973; Yopp, 1992), teachers must be observant as to what individual students know. Kindergartners need to work diligently on hearing individual sounds in words and on learning to use the "Alphabet Song" as a tool because research has shown that relating visual letters to the sounds heard in words by children who knew their letters provides greater gains in phonemic awareness than when letters are not related to spoken sounds (Ball & Blachman, 1991).

Developmentally, it is much easier for children to go from sounds (which they are familiar with from learning to talk) to letters (which they are just learning) than vice versa (Clay, 1991).

To avoid confusion when talking to students about letters and their corresponding sounds, Holdaway (1979) suggests referring to letters as "standing for sounds," rather than asking for the sound a letter makes or the sound of a letter (p. 117). For example, if I ask a classmate of Catherine's to write the letter that makes the /k/ sound in Catherine's name, the student might write a K. Because the question was phrased as it was, his answer would be technically correct. However, if I ask a classmate to write the letter that stands for the sound of /k/ in Catherine's name, a C could be the only correct answer. Normally, approximations are allowed when a student writes independently, but in the case of classmates' names, kindergartners will not allow approximations. Their names are precious to them and should be.

In the kindergarten classrooms where I have worked as a consultant in implementing writing workshop, most kindergartners demonstrate some knowledge of the alphabetic principle by writing with invented spelling at the end of October or November because their teachers also were committed to reading and understanding the research on reading (see chapters 1 through 3). However, in the handful of kindergartens and first-grade classrooms where I first worked as a consultant solely implementing literacy-rich reading experiences but not Getting Ready and writing workshop, it was not unusual for me to find at least 20% of the class to have little to no knowledge of phonemic awareness or the alphabetic principle at the end of kindergarten. I knew this to be true from having observed their one-day-a-week writing samples in writing centers throughout the year, and because I administered Clay's Dictation Test at the end of the year. Needless to say, I felt terrible about the results of this test (but they made me really think about the possible value of writing to reading). I also learned that these children (the 20% who had trouble with Clay's Dictation Test), have continued to struggle with reading and school—and some have even dropped out of school. Based on my experiences, the findings from a study by Lundberg, Frost, and Peterson (1988) are accurate: Poor readers entering first grade without phonemic awareness remain poor readers with little understanding of the alphabetic principle at the end of fourth grade if they still lack phonemic awareness training.

Of course, there are individuals who write using letters of the alphabet from the first day of school because they come from literacy-rich backgrounds. These children should be encouraged to continue writing letters, but they should use their alphabet strips as they form the letters to learn proper letter formation.

Ultimately, teachers need to be observant of children's stages of written language development and spelling to guide students' learning. (See chapters 2 and 3 for descriptions of these stages.)

Getting Ready provides the training or teaching for students to learn two of Clay's (1991) important emergent reading behaviors: (1) phonemic awareness and (2) visual attention to the graphic cues of the letters of the alphabet. It is important for teachers to understand the research presented in this book (see chapters 1 and 2) so they are able to teach the alphabet and phonemic awareness activities in a developmentally appropriate manner within meaningful, playful activities that follow a developmental progression (see Appendix A for phonemic awareness activities and a developmental progression). Although it is necessary to teach children how to recognize the letters of the alphabet by singing the "Alphabet Song" and pointing to the letters as the song is sung, it is not necessary for them to learn all the letter formations before they begin to practice approximated writing. They can learn from trial and error as they attempt to communicate their thoughts in written language with the use of the "Alphabet Song" and their ABC strip in a writing workshop.

Writing Workshop

While Getting Ready focuses on *teaching* phonemic awareness and the alphabet, writing workshop provides *practice* in these areas. Practice is essential, but it must be practice that children initiate themselves as they actively use their constructive minds to figure out what they need to know based on what they already know about written language. The teacher's challenge is to find out what each child knows and what his or her needs are as they attempt to figure out the alphabetic principle and put their thoughts in written language. As the teacher makes these ongoing observations, he or she provides guidance to the child's search for understanding written language. This practice is best done within the process of meaningful writing in a writing workshop that is based on Cambourne's (1988) conditions of learning language.

This section begins with an outline of the first day lesson plan for writing workshop, just like the first section of this chapter began with an outline of the first day lesson plan for Getting Ready, and then provides the implementation, or written demonstration.

First Day Lesson Plan Outline for Writing Workshop

Teacher Demonstration and Minilesson (10–15 minutes)
The teacher demonstrates his or her own writing while presenting and incorporating writing rules within the minilesson.

Teacher Confers as Students Write (10–30 minutes)
The teacher hands out unlined paper. (Unlined paper is the preferred writing material to begin with because the young child's manuscript evolves from his or her drawing. The child needs to be unencumbered by lines to draw freely [Calkins, 1994; Fisher, 1991; Morrow, 1989]. However, providing an assortment of paper as the year progresses is encouraged so the children can have choices; these choices often act as a catalyst for more writing [Calkins, 1994; Fisher, 1991].) Students can use the paper horizontally or vertically, and they can use their choice of markers or crayons to draw, write, or both. The teacher circles the room nudging and encouraging students to draw and write. The teacher helps students write their names and stamp the date on all papers, if necessary (see Figure 39).

Figure 39. Teacher Conferring With Student

Sharing in Author's Chair (15 minutes)
The teacher chooses two or three students who have done exemplary drawing and some form of writing to share their work with the class in Author's Chair (see Figure 40). It is important to choose good role models when beginning writing workshop, and eventually all students can have an opportunity to share.

Using this outline as a basis, I present an in-depth description and discussion of the implementation of writing workshop. Although this written demonstration may appear lengthy, the actual time it takes to conduct is usually no more than one hour. (Please note times given.)

The procedure for each part of the writing workshop (i.e., demonstration, conferring, and sharing in Author's Chair) is broken down into the following sections:

- Introduction
- Examples
- Conclusion

Figure 40. Student Sharing in Author's Chair

Demonstration of First Day Lesson Plan for Writing Workshop

Demonstration Aim

Demonstration is a powerful way to learn and teach (Graves, 1994). Holdaway (1979) asserts that the easiest way to learn something is to watch someone who is good at it demonstrate how to do it.

Demonstration Classroom Setup and Materials

Students are seated in the community circle. The teacher is seated near a large tablet of chart paper and has access to markers of various colors.

Demonstration Procedure

Introduction

Introduce writing workshop by showing kindergartners a book that you've read and discussed with them earlier. For example, I begin as follows:

> Boys and girls, what do I have in my hand? [I show a book that I've read earlier.] Do you remember what we called the person who wrote the words [point to some words] in this book? [The children respond, "Author."] Does anyone remember what we call the person who drew the pictures [point to a picture]? [The children respond, "Illustrator."]
>
> Kindergartners, you are all going to be given the chance to be authors and illustrators every day at this time. I'd like to show you some kindergarten authors' and illustrators' work from last year.

If you have some kindergarten writing samples from the first day of the previous school year, show a few and perhaps read one. You also can use samples from published materials. (See samples throughout this chapter.)

Example

> Now I'm going to show you how these authors and I know how to write.
> We followed the rules on this chart.

Display a chart with the writing rules (see Figure 41). Then decide what topic to write about, and as you write about it, demonstrate your thinking aloud. Point to the chart (when relevant) to show how it helps you write. The following example illustrates my thinking aloud:

Step 1: Name and date

> Once my picture and writing are finished, I will want everyone to know that I was the author, so I want to write my name on my paper first so I don't forget. I am going to write it on the back of my paper, so it doesn't get in the way of my picture or writing. [I write my name.] I will stamp the date on the back of my paper, too. [As I use the date stamper, I inform the children that I will stamp the date on their papers, too.]

Figure 41. Writing Rules

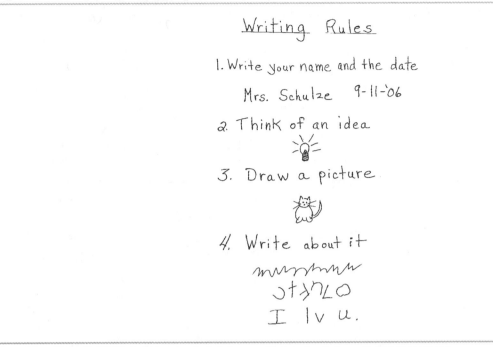

Adapted from Fisher, B. (1991). *Joyful learning: A whole language kindergarten.* Portsmouth, NH: Heinemann.

Step 2: Think of an idea

Now, I must think of an idea. [Pointing to my chart] I drew a light bulb [i.e., rebus print] for thinking on my chart because when I get an idea it's like a little light goes on in my head. Actually, a little light went on in my head yesterday about an idea, and I'm going to write about it now.

Step 3: Draw a picture

Next, I must draw a picture of my idea. [I proceed to draw a picture of my cat, explaining what I am thinking about as I work.]

Step 4: Write any way you can

Now I must write something about my picture. [I point to the fourth step on my writing rules chart where I have various kinds of writing demonstrated; I adapted this idea of demonstrating writing from Routman, 1991.] Then, I point to the personal cursive [scribbling]. How many children write like this?

[Several hands go up, and I congratulate them on being writers. Then I point to a random stream of letters including mock and real letters.]

How many of you write like this?

[Again, many hands go up and again I congratulate them on being writers. However, I do not take this count too seriously because I notice that several children have raised their hands twice. Finally, I point to some invented spelling.]

Can anyone read what I have written?

[Usually a few children can read the writing. I explain that some children write letters for sounds they hear when they write, and I slowly stretch out the sounds in the words.]

This is a special kind of "kid writing" that I will help you all learn to do before you leave kindergarten.

[Before printing the words to my story in conventional spelling, I tell students the following.]

Children, I am a teacher who has gone to school for many years, so I write like this now. When you are older you will, too.

[As I print the words to my story, I read them out loud.]

My cat likes to sleep on my dog's head. It doesn't bother him because he really likes the cat and he's so big!

[After I finish writing my teacher demonstration, the children and I read what I have written, and we discuss my story briefly. After one or two stories about students' pets, I usually wind down the discussion.]

Children, you have the most wonderful stories to tell, and I want to hear them all. Do you know how we could do that? Save those stories in your head, because you are going to get to write them in just a few minutes, and then we can all hear them.

Conclusion

After I have finished my teacher demonstration, I explain to the class that now it is their turn to be authors and illustrators. Ask them to raise their hands if they have an idea to write about. As the children respond with the *one* thing that they will write about, send them to their tables to draw and write. (Mrs. Richardson, a veteran kindergarten teacher, suggests that on another day, before the children go to their seats, the teacher should say, "Children, please turn to the person sitting next to you and tell him or her what you are writing about.")

I like to ask the entire class what they will write about as a brainstorming technique on the first day of my writing workshop demonstration. Hearing what classmates are writing about helps stir students' creative juices. However, on this first day I usually find one or two students who need additional nudging to think of an idea. A question I often use to initiate a simple conversation is, "What did you do last night when you came home from school?" When students mention something that they seem interested in, I ask them to draw and write about it. Talking about students' pets and families also provides good writing material. It is very important to know your students, especially their favorite activities or hobbies.

Demonstration Discussion

This first session of writing workshop may take a little longer than 10–15 minutes because you are establishing the guidelines for writing. It is helpful to display these guidelines or writing rules in the classroom so students can refer to them briefly as needed. In fact, many teachers leave this chart up all year.

In the beginning of the year, I present demonstrations with conventional spelling. However, as I see more and more kindergartners writing with developmental or invented spelling (around November), I ask the students to help me use invented spelling to spell one or two words that are fairly easy to sound out during my writing demonstrations. I do not use invented spelling to demonstrate spelling high-frequency words because there is a danger that children may learn these words incorrectly (Routman, 1991). Sometimes I teach a high-frequency word in a minilesson if several children are using but confusing it. (See Appendix D for a list of high-frequency words for kindergartners.)

Minilessons that are based on the observed needs of the students should be brief and about only one thing. One minilesson will usually not suffice. I've found it works well to teach one new "needed" thing in a minilesson and briefly review something already taught in a previous demonstration. For example, if I've noticed that students are not referring to their ABC strips when they need to know how to form a letter, I will hesitate as I make a letter in my demonstration and ask the children where I can look to get help. They usually respond, "Look at your ABC strip!" I look, and then I make the letter. This takes less than a minute and serves as an effective review of a minilesson already taught. (For other minilessons for writing workshop, see chapter 6.)

When the teacher confers with the children, the teacher can expect them to demonstrate what they learned in procedural minilessons, such as writing rules, and certain strategy minilessons, such as using the "Alphabet Song" and ABC strip to find letters of the alphabet. However, this is not true for every minilesson taught—for example, a minilesson on titles may not be appropriate for a child to use that day during writing and conferring time because titles are usually written when children feel invested in their work and want to publish it. During conferences, the teacher needs to observe each child's needs according to his or her developmental stage in the process of writing (see chapters 2 and 3 for a description of these stages). These needs also should be addressed using what the child already knows about written language as a foundation.

Conferring Aim

The first and foremost concern in a writing conference is to get the children talking and then really listen to them so teachers can help guide their attempts to communicate their thoughts in written language. As a byproduct of their desire to communicate in writing, kindergartners learn to interrelate Clay's (1991) four behaviors of emergent reading.

Conferring Classroom Setup and Materials

Student Materials

Kindergartners should be seated at their tables and will need the following items:

- One unlined sheet of white or manila paper, approximately 8" by 11", and access to more, if needed.

- One laminated name card for each child (many teachers like to use a tent card for this purpose) and an ABC strip with the letters of the alphabet printed on it as well as representative pictures of animals. Each ABC strip should be affixed as low as possible on the child's table or desk so it can be referred to as needed (see Figure 42); the strip should be kept in good condition or replaced if necessary because it is used throughout the school year.
- One set of thin colored markers per child.

Thin markers are the preferred writing utensil in the beginning of the year because kindergartners like them, they are easy to handle, and students do not need to erase (Calkins, 1994). Many young students spend too much valuable writing time erasing their good efforts when using pencils; therefore, thin markers are preferred initially until students understand the purpose of erasing. Also, students' writings show much of what the children know about print, so the teacher should see all their attempts (Clay, 1991). Because approximation is an important condition of learning, young students need to feel free to "explore with markers" and not be frightened of making mistakes (Calkins, 1994, p. 59). Later in the year, regular-sized pencils and pens can be introduced as writing utensils to provide more choice. Research indicates that beginner "fat" pencils are no better than regular-sized pencils for young children (Lamme & Ayris, 1983).

Figure 42. Student Using Alphabet Strip

Teacher Materials

Teachers need the following items as they circulate around the room holding conferences with individual students:

- A clipboard with a Weekly Conference and Instructional Guidesheet form (WCIG; see chapter 7 for a detailed explanation and Appendix E for a template). The teacher uses this form to determine who to confer with on any given day. It is also used to record any immediate instruction from a previous conference that is necessary.

- A three-column chart, known as a CID form, to record observations, assessments, and evaluations. The three columns feature what the Child knows, what I know, and what I will Do (see chapter 7 for a detailed explanation and Appendix E for the CID template). One form is used per child conferred with on any given day.

- A small writing tablet or dry-erase board for demonstration purposes. I like to use a tablet when I model drawing something or printing a letter. I model only those letters that I see children struggling with; these are usually letters in children's names.

- Some sticky notes for recording in conventional print what the child has written in approximated print. Some teachers also like to use sticky notes for taking assessment notes. Then, these sticky notes can be transferred to the CID form later on.

- A stool with wheels to sit on while conferring. The stool is important because it helps teachers get down to the kindergartner's level as in a real conversation, and it is also very beneficial to teachers' backs and knees.

Conferring Procedure

Because conferring is the heart of writing workshop, this section is quite detailed.

Introduction

1. Encourage and guide children to write about topics from everyday moments of their lives. These are moments children know best. They often burst into the classroom every morning and tell the teacher about such moments with comments like "My tooth fell out," "I went to a wedding," or "Our cat had kittens." Once the children have each chosen a topic, the conference becomes a time to have them show you what they know about topic and print, and what they will do next (Graves, 1994).

   During conferences, use the following questions, recommended by Graves (1994), to guide students:

   - What is the picture or story about?
   - Where did the idea come from?
   - What will the student do next?

2. It is best to give the students a few minutes to start working before beginning conferences. Survey the room quickly to ensure that all students are engaged and working. After you observe that all students are working, you can begin conferences. If some students are not working, approach them, find out the problem, and try to guide them so they are more capable of handling the problem independently in the future. It is important for students to learn to be responsible (Calkins & Oxenhorn, 2003).

   Usually there are a few students in the room who need a quick conference to help them remember what to do. I specifically tell these students to ask their neighbors for help, and I instruct their neighbors to be helpful. It is important to have some children who are strong writing models at each table to offer support (Routman, 1991). Soon after (usually one or two days), I teach a minilesson on "Adding Writing Teachers" (see Procedural Minilessons in chapter 6, p. 191).

3. On the first day, stamp the date on everyone's paper. (This is something the children can do in the future, and this activity will be addressed with a future minilesson. See Procedure Minilessons in chapter 6.)

4. Once all the students are engaged in their work, concentrate on a few students for the day. For example, I divide the number of students in the class (20) by the number of school days in a week (5). The answer (4) becomes the number of students that I work with in a day. I am able to confer with each student in a week's time using this formula. I fill out my WCIG form according to this formula.

   For the children who struggle with writing, I may find I have time during conference time to provide some extra help. However, I do not want to deprive those who are more proficient of their conference time. If necessary, I provide extra time for struggling writers during lunch break or recess. If possible, I also train an aid (if available) or older student to help in this capacity during writing workshop.

5. Conferring with students should only take a few minutes per student (Graves, 1994). A "focused vision" is the key to conferring (Stiggens, 2001, p. 65). This focus requires setting teaching goals. The two goals that I target to guide my conference (as well as my assessments) are the following: First, guide the student to communicate a message. This is the key to engagement. The student's language abilities, attitude, and ability to follow procedures will affect his or her ability to communicate a message. Second, once the student has an idea to communicate and is talking freely about it, help him or her develop the alphabetic principle so the student's writing will communicate a message on its own. To develop the alphabetic principle, the student will need to learn how to interrelate the other three of Clay's (1991) four emergent behaviors—which are phonemic awareness, visually attending to graphic cues, and concepts of print—with his or her language abilities.

6. When conducting conferences, I have found the following comments and advice helpful (Calkins, 1994; Graves, 1994):

- "Tell me about your picture or drawing." The young child rehearses for writing by drawing; initially the drawing is far more important than the writing.

- "Where did you get such a good idea?" Ask this question, then listen to and show interest in the student's topic, and get the student to talk more about the topic so he or she becomes really interested in it, too. The first entry point into writing is a simple conversation, with the child leading the conversation (Graves, 1994).

- Repeat students' words to them. This is a good way of showing interest, enhancing your correct understanding of what was said, and also reinforcing the proper pronunciation of words to the student in a positive way.

- If there is something you don't understand in the child's picture or writing, ask the child about it. For example, I remember an occasion when I thought a child had no writing on his paper because all I saw was a drawing, so I asked him if he could show me his writing. He flipped his paper over and showed me his writing on the other side. I also learned to ask, "Can you tell me about your picture?" rather than guess what the picture is about, because many times I have guessed incorrectly and this has created a negative note to the conference. In addition, if children have no writing on their papers, it is important to ask them about their pictures. Often their responses lead the teacher to see a relationship between the objects that were drawn and a possible story that they can encourage the child to write about. Teachers need to encourage children to be excited about telling the stories in their lives in print so they will work hard and be engaged in the laborious task of learning to encode.

- "What are you going to do next?" When the child tells you, respond with delight and interest and say, "I'll be back to see what you've done later." This comment has allowed me more time to confer without interruption. Teachers do not need to watch children do all their work. Teachers can discuss students' incomplete work and come back to check their completed work later.

7. Do not be unduly concerned about taking anecdotal records this first day or week, other than recording what the child tells you he or she wrote if you cannot read the writing. (I record this transcription on a sticky note after the conference. When I photocopy the student's writing sample later in the day, I also photocopy the sticky note on the back side of the sample.)

Once conference routines and procedures have been established and children understand them, concentrate on taking observational or anecdotal records between conferences directly on the children's CID forms. Also, if several children are struggling with the same problem, make a note of the problem on your WCIG form for a possible minilesson.

Examples

Focus on what children can do (strengths) to teach their needs (weaknesses) based on the two goals previously described. The following examples illustrate first-day conferences and brief observations and assessments. (See chapter 7 for more information on assessment and evaluation.)

Billy's Conference:

Billy appeared to be busy at the beginning of the workshop, but when I first came to confer with him, he had nothing on his paper.

Me: Billy, will you tell me everything that happened from the time you left school until you went to bed yesterday?

Billy: I got off the bus at my house. Me and Buddy played for awhile.

Me: Who is Buddy?

Billy: He belongs next door; he's a dog.

Me: What do you and Buddy do when you play?

Billy: We roughhouse.

Me: Would you like to draw and write about the dog and roughhousing?

Billy: Yes.

[After five minutes, Billy's paper is still blank.]

Me: Billy, why is your paper blank?

Billy: I don't know how to draw a dog.

Me: Close your eyes and try to picture Buddy.

Billy: I can't.

Me: Look around the room for a picture of a dog. [I attempt to put the *responsibility* on him.]

[Billy sees a picture of a dog, but he says he still can't do it. I take note of the words *try* and *praise* to record on Billy's CID form later.]

Me: Billy, we can always try to draw a dog. You know, I don't think I've ever drawn a dog either, but I'm going to try right now.

[I demonstrate drawing a quick, rough sketch of a dog by using mostly circles and loops on my tablet. Next, I ask Billy to try. Hesitantly, he puts his marker to his paper and begins to draw, and I praise his effort as an interesting dog begins to appear. Then I tell Billy that I will check with him later to see his finished dog. When I return, Billy has finished his dog, but a student next to Billy says that Billy's dog doesn't look like a dog.]

Me: I think Billy has a great-looking dog. See, it has four legs, a head, ears, eyes, and a tail, and to tell you the truth, I like it better than mine [showing my drawing next to Billy's].

[I do not allow other students to criticize attempts at drawing and writing; in fact, I do not allow negativism of any kind. Every attempt is precious and a beginning to something better. As Calkins (1994) says, "Teachers must delight in what youngsters do and...respond in real ways to what they are trying to do" (p. 70).]

[Billy smiles shyly. Billy continues to work on his picture the next day, adding a pheasant and more detail. I ask him about the pheasant and he tells me, "Me and Buddy walk the corn fields and chase pheasants." I respond by saying, "That is a really interesting thing to add, Billy." Then, I guide him to hear the /b/ sound at the beginning of his name and form the letter *B*. (We make plans to work on the other letters in his name later; *B* is a good start.)]

By the end of the year, Billy can draw dogs better than anyone in the room. Because his interest in dogs was encouraged and his efforts praised, Billy became interested in writing and became a writer and a reader. (See Figure 43.)

Billy's Assessment:
Billy had great difficulty coming up with a topic; I think he was afraid to try. After leaving Billy, I briefly recorded on Billy's CID form the following: *Try*, *Work on topic choice*, and *Needs lots of encouragement and praise.* Concerning

Figure 43. Billy's Sample

the alphabetic principle, I recorded, "Can't hear sounds or write letters, not even in name. Help him form a *B* & do some form of writing tomorrow." I translate these brief notations later in the day to complete statements on Billy's CID form.

When I confer with Billy in the future, I will help him expand on his drawing and written language, and I will spend a little of the conference time helping him hear individual beginning consonant sounds through sound matching. For example, I may slowly say *pheasant* and then say that *pheasant* has the /f/ sound in the beginning. Then, I would ask Billy if he could hear that same sound in the beginning of different words such as *farm*, *phone*, and *dog*. (I also use iteration, if necessary, to help students with responses.) When Billy can hear isolated beginning single consonants, and when he gains the ability to use his ABC strip to find letters of the alphabet, I will ask him to write letters. Now it is too soon, although we will work on writing his first name. I have expectations of Billy and I know with my guidance and Billy's self-directed search, they will be met.

Kara's Conference:

Kara has drawn a picture of her sister and herself playing on a swing set, but she has no writing. After talking to Kara about her drawing, I say, "While I'm here, I'd like you to put some writing down, Kara. What do you want to say?" (I thought Kara could write with invented spelling because of my observations of her in the classroom and during Getting Ready.)

Kara: Me and my sister and my dog went to the park and we went on the swings and we had fun.

[In the future, I plan to guide Kara in writing a sentence or two; however, because of my prior observations of Kara, I feel this might be too difficult initially. First I respond with interest to what Kara has said.]

Me: That would be a lot to write Kara. If you could write only one thing about your picture, what would that one thing be? [It is important for teachers to remember to use the words *one thing* rather than *one word*. Most kindergartners do not understand the concept of word in the beginning of the year.]

Kara: Swing set.

Me: Swing...set. [I say it slowly repeating her words drawing them out like pulling taffy or bubble gum.]

Me: [handing her a marker] Try writing it.

[She writes *C t*.]

[I would accept whatever she writes, but I am thrilled with this close approximation. I believe Kara thinks of swing set as one word, so she wrote the beginning and ending sounds that she heard in *swing set*. The spaces between words in print do not correspond to actual pauses in oral language (Ferreiro & Teberosky, 1982). This example should remind us all as teachers to always look for the logic in a child's approximations because there is usually logic to it.]

Me: [in a delighted manner] How did you know how to make both those letters?

Kara: 'Cause I know my ABCs. [This makes sense when you compare the initial sound of /c/ and the initial sound of *swing*. Teachers should accept such attempts, which is a condition of approximation. At Kara's young age, guessing a *c* for an *s* is an excellent try.]

As the year progresses, with more visual knowledge of words through immersion and exposure to meaningful print in our classroom, Kara will come to understand that some letters have more than one sound and that spelling requires visualizing the word as well as listening to its sounds. (See Figure 44 for this sample of Kara's work.)

Kara's Assessment:

I did not need to write on a sticky to remind me of what Kara said. Her writing of *C t* and her picture were enough. I did record on her CID form the following: *talkative, needs focus as far as communicating message, said she knows her ABCs,* and *can hear sounds*. After Author's Chair (see p. 173 for a description), I also recorded on my WC IG form what Kara had said she was going to add to her piece tomorrow: *I'm gonna write about running home in the rain.*

Figure 44. Kara's Sample

Conclusion

At the end of the writing session, students are asked to hand in their work. Make sure all students have their names written on their work; I write the names of those children who can't write their names. Normally, I only photocopy and save the work of student I conferred with on any given day. However, on the first day of writing workshop, I make a photocopy of *all* the children's dated writing samples and save them in my evaluation file portfolio to demonstrate writing progress from day one to the end of the year. Also, whenever you make any future observations outside of writing workshop that pertain to students' writing strengths or needs, record such information on a sticky note and place it in the student's file.

Conferring Discussion

On this first day of writing workshop, my main concern is that everyone is working and understands the procedures. Students should do some form of writing as well as drawing. Accept whatever they put down. Have students refer to the various forms of writing displayed on the writing rules chart to remind them they are all writers. Congratulate them on being writers no matter what form they use, and when they have written something, ask them to read their approximated writing with their fingers.

After a conference, you probably will have observed and recorded several "needs" (mostly procedural) on your WCIG form under possible minilessons that you will have to address within the next few days (e.g., students stamping dates on papers, encouraging students to help each other, trying, handling interruptions, finding a more expedient way for students to get their paper to write on). Most of these minilessons deal with handling procedures with responsibility (see chapter 6 for minilessons on procedures).

In addition to procedures, content usually needs to be addressed, too. As I confer with individual students, my main goal is to encourage them to compose and communicate a message in writing in "whatever way they can" at first. Children can compose before they learn to write (Temple et al., 1988). Composing is thinking and creating, and kindergartners do it all the time (Temple et al., 1988). I try to guide them to tell me their thoughts about their personal experiences to develop their "voice," which is the driving force behind writing (Graves, 1994).

Kindergarten teachers are sometimes surprised that some children who initially knew a lot about print do not necessarily write easily (Clay, 2001). Writing is complex; there is a lot to learn. It is also laborious. All writers need to receive positive response for their retellings of experiences to develop voice and be engaged in writing.

Also, all writers struggle with trying to keep their focus—that is, trying to stay on the one topic they've chosen to write about without wandering to secondary topics. When conferring with young writers you should work with them to ensure that their pieces are about one thing so they make sense, which explains why it is useful to ask each child to tell you about the one thing that his or her picture or story is about (Calkins, 1994).

As I guide kindergartners in composing and communicating a message in print, I work toward my second goal of encouraging each child to practice interrelating Clay's (1991) four emergent literacy behaviors. When children can isolate the individual sounds in their oral language and know how to use their ABC strips to try to find representative letters, I guide them to use the alphabetic principle. In their desire to record their thoughts, students learn to write readable print.

As I confer with students, I keep these two goals in mind. I usually do not write anything during a conference, but I take a few minutes between conferences to record any pertinent information that applies to these two goals—or anything else that I think is important. (I do not rely on the photocopied sample of the child's work to be enough to refresh my memory.) In the beginning of the year, this usually includes recording what the child stated that his or her approximated writing said.

In the spirit of appreciating the developmental writing process, the teacher needs to applaud approximated intent as a written message. This will help kindergartners move to a point where they talk about print in the same manner that they talk about their drawing, and they will then come to the realization that print represents their oral language (Clay, 2001; Temple et al., 1988).

Without an encouraging audience, there is little reason for writers to try to develop their abilities to communicate in written language. Writers need readers.

Guidelines on conducting an Author's Chair, which teaches children how to listen to and look at text include the following:

- Classmates should be asked to listen carefully as authors describe their pictures and tell their stories so classmates can tell the author what they *remember*. Also, encourage classmates to remember as many of the actual words the author used as possible.

- Classmates should *comment* on what strikes them in a piece. Encourage classmates to talk about anything they particularly liked and why they liked it.

- Classmates can ask *questions* to learn more about the author's work and possibly extend it. These questions should always be put in a "positive light"; the teacher must often help the questioner to do this. (Graves, 1994, p. 134)

Author's Chair Aim

To celebrate, praise, and help extend young authors' attempts to tell about the personal experiences and episodes in their lives.

Author's Chair Classroom Setup and Materials

Students should be seated in the community circle. Select two or three authors for the day to bring their writing to the circle to share with the class. These students should be seated in a special chair labeled "Author's Chair." The teacher should hold their papers until and after they share in the first sessions of Author's Chair. However, as the year progresses, children can be taught to be responsible for holding their own papers.

Author's Chair Procedure

Introduction

1. Ask three students with whom you have conferred that day to share their work at the end of writing workshop. Authors must give their permission to share. Sometimes kindergartners do say no in the beginning of the year, but once they understand the procedure, they all want to share.

2. Before the first author takes his or her seat in the Author's Chair, model or role-play the sharing procedure. Read something you have written. Prior to reading, tell the group the one thing that your piece is about to reinforce the idea of focus, or main idea (Graves, 1994). After reading, ask the group, "What was the one thing that my piece was about?" (If an answer is incorrect, refer to your piece and reestablish its focus.)

3. After teacher modeling, the first author can sit in the Author's Chair, show his or her picture, tell what the piece is about, and talk about it. The teacher sits next to the author and usually holds the author's picture (so it is high enough for all students to see) as the author points out and describes objects in it. The teacher should help to help students identify relationships between objects to help develop a sense of story.

    The author should also be guided to point out any writing on his or her paper, and the teacher should laud the author's efforts. Praising these first attempts at writing by young authors helps generate more writing by the rest of the class.

4. After discussing focus, the author gets to choose classmates who raise their hands to tell him or her what they remembered and then what they liked about the piece. If classmates wonder about something in the picture, they can ask questions about it, but this questioning must be handled in a positive manner. (I usually remind authors that what their classmates remember is what they especially liked.)

    Although the teacher sits next to the author and helps out as needed, the teacher becomes part of the audience. As part of the audience, the teacher should raise his or her hand and wait to be called on by the author in order to serve as a role model in remembering, commenting, and questioning in a positive, celebratory manner.

Example

Following is an example of Kara's first day in Author's Chair.

> [Kara sat in the Author's Chair and I sat next to her, holding her paper high enough for all to see.]

> Me: Kara, will you tell the class the *one thing* that your writing is about?

> Kara: It's about me and my sister swinging.

> Me: What made you think about swinging?

> Kara: I saw some kids swinging on the swings this morning.

> Me: Class, it will be your job to listen very carefully to everything Kara tells us about her picture and her writing. When she is finished, we are going to tell her what we remember about her story.

> Kara: This is the swing set in the park, and this is me and my sister swinging. This is my dog, and this is the grass, and this is the sun. And this is some clouds.

> [Kara does not point out her writing, so I do.]

> Me: Kara, can you read what you wrote here?

> [I notice she has added another word on her own (*Me*) since I conferred with her. Kara points to her words (*ME Ct*) and reads "My swing set." If Kara had been unable to read her words, I would have helped her.]

> Me: Kara, that is so wonderful that you were able to write this word all by yourself [pointing at the word *me* on the board to indicate *my*]! And class, look at Kara's beautiful letters, don't they look like the letters on our ABC chart?

The class all agrees the letters are good. (If a child in the class happens to know the correct spelling of the word *my* and points this out, I would favorably compared Kara's close approximation of *me* letter by letter to *my*. However, this would be highly unusual, because this kind of approximation [i.e., *me* for *my*] is quite common in the beginning of kindergarten. Therefore, I just praise the good approximation as if it were the real word.)

> Me: Kara, will you ask the class what your piece is about? [She does.] All right Kara, you can be the teacher and call on the children whose hands are raised?

> [After establishing the focus, the class tells Kara what they remember about her story. Some children repeat what others say.]

> Me: Class, I want you to listen very closely to what your classmates are saying to Kara. It isn't very interesting for Kara or any of us to hear the same thing said again.

[Kara calls on Timmy.]

Timmy: I like the swing set.

Me: We usually remember things that we like about the author's picture or story. Tell, me Jimmy, why do you like the swing set? [I ask Timmy to tell us why he likes the swing set to encourage making connections. Also, "I like" becomes meaningless and trivial when a reason does not accompany it.]

Timmy: I got a swing set at home, and my Dad swings me on it.

[Kara calls on Andrew next.]

Andrew: I like your dog. I drew a dog in my picture, too.

Amy: I like your letters. They look good.

If a child had not said this, I would have. Teachers must give positive praise to get children to do the laborious job of hearing individual sounds and then searching for the appropriate letters on their ABC strips.

After the children had done a good job of remembering what Kara had told them and made comments that revealed their connections to her piece, I tell students they can ask Kara some questions.

Me: Class, if there is anything about Kara's picture or writing that you would like to know more about or don't understand, you can raise your hand now and Kara will call on you. [Kindergartners often do not understand the meaning of the question at first, but with modeling by the teacher and time, they eventually get the idea.]

Cody: Why do you have a dog in your picture?

Me: You'd like to know more about Kara's dog? [I rephrase this question more positively to prompt Kara to add description to her writing.]

Kara: That's my dog, and he likes to go to the park with me.

[After raising my hand like the other kindergartners, Kara calls on me.]

Me: Kara, I noticed that you drew some interesting puffy black clouds in your picture. Can you tell me why they are black?

Kara: It started to rain when we were at the park. The clouds got black and we had to run home.

[I repeat to Kara all that she said in Author's Chair in an effort to scaffold and build her story.]

Me: So, you, your sister, and your dog went to the park. You and your sister swung on the swing set, but it started to rain. And you all had to run home. My, that was quite an experience, and it makes a very interesting story! Kara, would you like to write some more tomorrow about this story?

Kara: Yes.

Me: What will you write? [It is important to establish what students intend to write so they have a better chance of remembering.]

Kara: I'm gonna write about running home in the rain.

Me: I think that would make your story even more interesting Kara. Class, do you think this would make Kara's story even more interesting?

They all agree it would. Kindergartners are very susceptible to their teacher's suggestions. This knowledge can be used to influence kindly behavior.

I record Kara's addition idea to her story on my WCIG form so I will remember to remind Kara about this addition tomorrow. However, if she doesn't wish to follow through on her idea, it will be her choice.

Many teachers have asked me if they should have the children clap after an author has shared. I think clapping is acceptable if Author's Chair has been handled in the way I described. However, if children simply get up, show their picture and describe what's in it with no interaction from the class and the teacher—that is, no remembering, commenting, or questioning to help writers grow—clapping can become a meaningless ritual.

Conclusion

First, it is a good idea for teachers to ask the child what the one thing their story is about to establish focus, and then ask children where they got their idea for their choice of topic, as I did when I asked Kara, "What made you think about swinging?" A question like this helps other children to understand how they can get ideas for their writing. Graves (1994) suggests that "other children may be better sources than the teacher for thinking of entry points into writing" (p. 275). Next, asking about relationships between objects in a picture or simply mentioning objects in the picture, as I did when I told Kara I had noticed she had drawn some black clouds in her picture, can sometimes extend the story. Last, but most important, praising any print is a good way to get more.

Author's Chair could go on all day. Time limits are important. Many teachers set time limits for each author in discussing his or her writing; five minutes per author is customary. Some authors spend too much time choosing a classmate to ask them a question or tell them something they remembered. If this is the case, students are not using their responsibility well, and the teacher may have to intercede with a comment such as, "I will count to three, if you haven't chosen someone by then, I will have to."

Because everyone wants to share and usually teachers only have time to allow three authors the privilege on any given day, the teacher can hold up some writing samples from children who did not get the opportunity to sit in Author's Chair, and these children—or the teacher—can quickly tell one or two important things about their work. Routman (2000) also promotes a Quick Share; she likes to use it when minilessons and conferring run over the allotted time for those students "who have worked hard, done something well, or tried something new" (p. 256).

Mrs. Clark used a Quick Share when she wanted to highlight Jeremy's creative use of perspective in his drawing (see Figure 8, p. 64). She asked Jeremy to show his picture as she pointed out how he had tried to show perspective in his picture by drawing those things that were close as larger and those things that were far away as smaller.

Calkins (1994) suggests that in addition to sharing and supporting a finished work in Author's Chair, the teacher can teach the class how to help an author who is puzzled or stuck in the writing process during Author's Chair, too. To do this, the teacher should role-play helping the author get ideas with his or her writing as the class watches. (The class can give input, too.)

Authors who have already shared can sign their names on a chart entitled "Authors Who Have Shared." When the chart shows everyone's name, a new chart can be started, or teachers can choose to laminate the chart so it can be erased and used again. Thus, the chart serves as meaningful print and helps the teacher and classmates keep track of who has shared so far. Teachers also can keep a record of who has shared on their WCIG forms.

Author's Chair Discussion

Author's Chair is a time to celebrate the things the author has done well and to require students to listen carefully to the author's piece. Share sessions can become boring and formulaic if children do not think long enough to understand the text before they ask questions. That is why Graves (1994) suggests that children work through the "remembers" (p. 134) and comments before the teacher allows questions. The young audience tends to get "remembers" and "reminders" mixed up. Because they are egocentric, kindergartners tend to tell about their own experiences that were stimulated by the author's experience. Graves (1994) tells of how a young author solved this problem; after he'd finished reading his text, he said, "Okay, remembers, reminders, then questions....and only two reminders" (p. 134).

Teachers do have to help out with reminders. When children give lengthy reminders, tell those children that they can write about those ideas tomorrow, and then steer them back to the author's piece. Eventually, with guidance, lengthy reminders will surface in independent writing time rather than in Author's Chair.

Graves (1983) lauds questions that teach. Graves defines good questions as "those that provide surprises for both child and teacher" (p. 107). When teachers model asking good questions, students understand that only questions that help the audience learn more about the author's picture, and eventually the author's story, are worthwhile.

For example, as a literacy coach, I remember asking such a question of Austin, a young author. He had written about catching a fish, but his writing lacked voice. I asked, "How did you go about catching that fish?"

Austin said, "I casted in my line and said 'Come to Papa.'" The entire classroom erupted into laughter.

I asked Austin to put those words down, just as he had said them to us right then, so he wouldn't lose them. He did, and the next day Austin added those words to his piece. Later he shared this revised version in Author's Chair. The children laughed almost as hard as they did the first time they heard it, and Austin beamed proudly.

Temple and colleagues (1988) suggest that when children ask questions of the author,

> They are participating in a most important part of the composing process. By answering the questions, children are forced to sustain their topics, to tell more, and yet more. With encouragement and regular opportunities for asking and answering questions, children will eventually be able to ask (themselves) their own (questions) as they write. (p. 217)

As a literacy coach, I have heard many kindergarten children say, "I know they [classmates] will ask me this," as they add on to their piece. They have learned a very important question to help guide their writing that good authors usually depend on: "What more will my reader want to know?"

Classmates' questions need to be handled carefully; the teacher must strive to make questioning positive. There are children who will ask insensitive questions. Sometimes young authors handle these questions well; however, if the young author falters, the teacher should provide a response. Author's Chair is about building self-esteem as a writer and person.

Author's Chair, along with guidance from the teacher, can help children develop a sense of self-esteem and good social skills that are often hard to develop in the classroom context. For example, one girl, who was new to the school, wrote that she didn't have any friends and she felt sad. Her classmates responded with wonderful comments that made her feel better, and one student gave the best comment of all. She said, "I'll be your friend."

Another girl had written about her grandfather dying and how much she missed him. The children were very sympathetic and shared similar stories, and the girl felt better. One child asked, "Did you feel bad?" When the girl said she did, the child responded, "I feel bad, too."

It is important for teachers to ensure that all comments are appropriate. This is an excellent time to teach children how to be kind and helpful to one another. Appropriate questions, comments, and remembering what the author said are all ways for the young author to get response or feedback during Author's Chair, a necessary condition to learning literacy. The teacher is instrumental in making this response or feedback appropriate and positive. It is this kind of response that encourages young authors to want to communicate the happenings in their lives through writing while practicing Clay's four behaviors of emergent literacy, which enable authors to become early writers and readers.

Summary

This chapter has outlined and provided in-depth descriptions and demonstrations of a first day lesson plan within the two structures of "Getting Ready" and writing workshop. Getting Ready focuses on teaching children the alphabet and phonemic awareness; writing workshop allows children the time to practice hearing the sounds in words and writing the graphic cues of the letters of the alphabet, while interrelating them with Clay's (1991) other two emergent reading behaviors—language abilities and concepts of print—in the process of learning to write. An important point to remember from Getting Ready is that children should not be expected to write in invented spelling until they have a basic ability to hear individual beginning sounds in words (i.e., phonemic awareness) and can use the "ABC Song" and alphabet strip to find most letters of their choosing. Important points to remember from writing workshop include the following: (1) Teacher demonstrations of her/his own writing are essential to the young child's process of writing; (2) while conferring, teachers should observe each child's writing needs and teach these needs from the foundation of what each child knows; (3) teachers and classmates must learn to appreciate and praise approximations; and (4) while Author's Chair is a place to celebrate what the author has done, it is also a place to teach the young writer to grow. Chapter 6 provides additional ideas on how to teach the young author to grow through minilessons.

Minilessons for Writing Workshop

"I've always been afraid to demonstrate my own writing to kindergartners because they always copy what I've written."

This is an observation many kindergarten teachers have made. However, Morrow (1989) explains that copying in the beginning stages of writing can be beneficial if children do it on their own initiative. In addition, when teachers demonstrate their own writing in a daily writing workshop based on Cambourne's (1988) conditions of learning language, children's primary impulse to communicate their own message emerges and copying ceases (Graves, 1994; Morrow, 1989). Finally, and most important, the best way to teach children that their oral language can be written down and how to do it is to show them (Graves, 1994). It is through watching demonstrations of writing that children come to understand the organizational patterns or structures involved in written language and what they should make of them (Harste, Burke, & Woodward, 1984). Teacher demonstrations of how to write teach writing in the best possible way (Atwell, 1987; Avery, 1993; Calkins, 1994; Fisher; 1991; Graves, 1994; Harwayne, 2001; Holdaway, 1979; Morrow, 1989; Ray & Cleaveland, 2004).

The Importance of Teacher Demonstration Minilessons

Many teachers who are new to writing workshop wonder what specific writing demonstrations they should do. I often tell new writing teachers if they are at a loss at what to teach at first to simply demonstrate their own writing and talk out loud about what they are thinking about as they write. This is the best demonstration possible until teachers learn to identify children's developmental writing needs.

Young students tend to bond easily to their teacher; they care deeply about what he or she thinks, does, and writes. This bond is a powerful influence on students' classroom performance (Graves, 1994). When teachers happily demonstrate their own writing, they show children how they choose topics; work for meaning by rereading for sense; choose a more appropriate word over another; and how and why they use conventions such as spelling, spacing, directionality, and punctuation. These kinds of demonstrations make powerful statements to their young students, especially when teachers are able to identify a student's writing needs and demonstrate strategies directed at those needs. By using writing demonstrations, children's copying soon gives way to independent thinking and originality.

Graves (1994) states, "You, the teacher, are the most important factor in creating a learning environment in your room" (p. 109). "Demonstrating a mood of discovery and experimentation" helps establish this environment (p. 110). When Mrs. Williams and Mrs. Clark demonstrate their own writing, they often reread sentences and ask themselves questions aloud, such as, "Does that make sense?" "I wonder if I could say it better?" "Maybe, I could use a more interesting word to say it?" Kindergartners can be extremely helpful in giving advice to improve a piece of writing.

Many kindergarten teachers also are concerned about what topics to write about and providing a good writing model. I believe these concerns are a byproduct of the way these teachers (including myself) were taught to write. Finished pieces were "red penned" beyond recognition. Previously, teachers' main concern seemed to be "What might help this writing?" rather than "What might help this writer?" (Calkins, 1994, p. 228.) They did not demonstrate strategies while students were in the process of writing. Students were taught to be totally dependent on teachers' writing assessments and advice, which dealt mainly with mechanics. Ultimately, this led many students to feel defeated as writers, and many students learned to hate writing. Graves (1994) and Calkins (1994) have changed educators' thinking regarding writing as a process. Until I read Graves and Calkins, I tried to avoid writing; now I find it hard work, but I've discovered my "voice" and its driving force. I completely understand author Dorothy Parker's statement, "I hate writing, but I love having written" (as cited in Graves, 1994, p. 31). Writing is about the joy of communicating a message you care deeply about. It doesn't have to be perfect the first time. It can be an approximation at first; you can always revise and improve it later. (This is true even for teacher demonstrations.) In his book *Time for Meaning: Crafting Literate Lives in Middle and High School* (1995), author Randy Bomer discusses the importance of urgency in getting down initial thoughts quickly. He explains that all the problems of a finished piece do not have to be solved in the first rough draft—even the sequence of events does not have to be addressed then. In fact, the first draft should leave an author unsatisfied, so he or she *wants* to make changes.

Harwayne (2001) suggests that as teachers reflect on the quality of their writing demonstrations, they can strive to improve as writers. Teachers can enhance, or "jazz up," their writing through reading about how to improve writing quality. I recommend *A Writer Teaches Writing* (Murray, 1985); *Crafting a Life in Essay, Story, Poem* (Murray, 1996); and *On Writing Well: The Classic Guide to Writing Nonfiction* (Zinsser, 1998).

In the past, teachers rarely showed their students how they struggled to get the message just right. Students often believed that the goal of writing was to "get it right the first time," which referred to the prioritizing of mechanics, especially spelling, over content. Yet content is what draws the reader in and keeps the reader's attention. Who ever bought a John Grisham novel for its spelling or mechanics?

When concentrating on content, Graves (1994) suggests "a writer's first act is to listen and observe the details of living" (p. 36). Teachers need to write about the interesting things or the special moments in their daily lives. Then, teachers should share their feelings about these events with their students through their writing. When teachers allow students to hear their "voices," their students will follow suit.

Calkins and Oxenhorn (2003) also advise teachers to focus on the "small moments" in their lives as a useful writing strategy (p. 1). For example, rather than writing about everything that happened at your birthday party, focus on one part that was really important to you, such as anticipating and then receiving a present you've always wanted, like a new bicycle. Then on subsequent days, you could demonstrate how to stretch a small moment like this into a longer story by adding more detail. Calkins and Oxenhorn refer to this as taking a "bare-bones" piece and showing how details can fill it out (p. 62).

Graves (1994) advises writers to be in a "constant state of composition" (p. 104). Many of the kindergarten teachers with whom I've worked follow this advice and have found it invaluable. They are never at a loss for writing ideas because they are always thinking about possible topics as they go about their daily lives. Some even carry little notebooks and jot down writing ideas throughout the day.

There are stories everywhere. We just have to open our eyes to them. We all have interesting moments in our lives that we can't wait to tell our friends about; share some of these with your students in your writing demonstrations. Students will soon relish sharing their written stories with you and the class. How teachers demonstrate values and show the meaning of writing as a craft will have a profound effect on their students' written language development (Bear et al., 2000; Clay, 2001; Gentry & Gillet, 1993; Graves, 1994; Temple et al., 1988).

The Purpose of Minilessons

During the writing and conference time of writing workshop, teachers are able to observe children closely and identify areas of learning that need immediate attention. Teachers can address these areas of concern or needs with minilessons, which focus on a brief demonstration of one needed aspect of writing or the management of writing. To determine the specific area of concern, Calkins (1994) advises teachers to ask themselves, "What is the *one thing* I can suggest or demonstrate that might help [students] most?" (p. 194).

A minilesson is defined by Calkins (1994) as "a forum for making a suggestion to the whole class—raising a concern, exploring an issue, modeling a technique, reinforcing a strategy [that the class has demonstrated a need of in their writing]" (p. 193). Because minilessons are based on students' writing needs and improvement objectives, students are usually interested in learning them. In addition, minilessons are brief—usually 5 to 15 minutes. Thus, the brevity and focus of minilessons prove quite helpful to students learning to write. Calkins suggests that minilessons are especially helpful to kindergartners because minilessons help them "understand the functions and power of print [through demonstration, not just words]" (p. 200). Avery (1993) also supports the power of demonstration to teach and describes a minilesson as more about "showing than telling" (p. 121).

Repeating and Reinforcing Minilessons

Calkins (1994) describes minilessons as "a way of adding information to the class pot" (p. 200). However, the "pot" often needs stirring. Simply showing a child how to do something in a minilesson does not mean that he or she will do it independently. Some minilessons need to be repeated or reinforced primarily for two reasons: (1) All students are not developmentally in the same place at the same time, and (2) kindergartners often need reminders as they work things out for themselves and attempt to fit new information into the context of what they know.

Once they are presented, some minilessons prove to be very useful timesavers to teachers because they can be quickly referred to if things go amiss. The following example illustrates the how minilessons can be referred to throughout the year:

In the beginning of the year, Mrs. Clark and Mrs. Williams teach minilessons on what being responsible means in the kindergarten classroom (i.e., following classroom procedures and helping each other). As a visible reminder of these lessons, Mrs. Clark chooses to wear a scarf (see Figure 45), and Mrs. Williams wears a string of beads. Pointing to these items often is all it takes to change improper behavior to proper behavior.

During a minilesson, Mrs. Williams shows her children where extra writing paper is and she makes a point of telling them, "From now on, if you need extra paper, I expect that you will be able to find it for yourself." When a child tries to interrupt a writing conference to ask where he can get more paper, Mrs. Williams simply points to her "responsibility beads." The child realizes he should know the answer, and he asks a classmate for help.

Figure 45. Teacher Wearing Scarf to Reinforce Minilesson

Promoting responsibility is especially important in writing workshop because children need to learn to work on their own. Teaching responsibility like this also makes for more attentive listening. The children should not be continually asking the teacher for help, especially when their questions relate to procedures already discussed.

Other kindergarten teachers wear similar items, such as a hat with the words *Be Responsible* printed on it. The word *responsible* needs to be discussed with kindergartners and used often throughout the year in many situations. Children need to be taught how to conduct themselves, to learn the right way from the wrong way, and to take responsibility for their actions. Teaching responsibility may take some time initially, but it is well worth the effort.

Considering Developmental Stages

If a minilesson is not successful, it is usually because the teacher has not considered students' developmental spelling and writing stages or levels. (See chapter 2 for more about developmental learning stages in spelling and chapter 3 for more about developmental learning stages in written language.) The lesson was probably beyond students' instructional level.

For example, teachers often notice that children do not leave spaces between words for quite some time. Until children are in the Phonetic stage, or third level, of spelling, they often do not have the concept of word firmly in mind. (See chapter 2 for the developmental stages of spelling.) Trying to teach spacing before children have a concept of word proves to be frustrating and fruitless for the teacher and students.

Also, teachers should not expect kindergartners to write beneath their pictures when they are in stage one (Picture Writing) and stage two (Picture and Label Writing) of written language. (See chapter 3 for descriptions of these stages.) When they are in the third stage, the Taking Inventory stage of written language, it is developmentally appropriate to demonstrate a minilesson of drawing on the top half of a sheet of paper and writing on the bottom.

Explaining the Need When Presenting Minilessons

Most writing needs can be addressed with minilessons, especially if teachers incorporate them into writing demonstrations. When teachers present minilessons to the class, they should explain the reason for addressing the issue. Calkins (1994) likes to begin minilessons by saying, "Last night, I was looking through your writing and realized that many of you are struggling with something that is difficult for me as well" (p. 189). If the minilesson is needed by all writers, they should spend some time that day, or even right then and there, implementing the lesson (Calkins, 1994). (For an example of this, see "Using the ABC Strip," p. 215.)

Some minilessons do not require immediate application by all students. It is important to realize that all students may not be in a place in their writing where they can use a particular minilesson. Often a minilesson only pertains to what several children are doing on any given day (Calkins, 1994). For example, if the teacher introduced a minilesson on creating a good title, some children may not be at the point in their writing where they have need for a title. Calkins (1994) suggests teachers end a minilesson by talking about how children *might* go about using what has been taught.

Using Whole-Class and Small-Group Minilessons

In addition to teaching whole-class minilessons, teachers may decide to teach small-group minilessons. All children may not need the repetition of a particular lesson. In addition, some children might not be ready developmentally to learn something that other children in the class are ready for. For example, Mrs. Williams had a few proficient writers who needed a more advanced minilesson on using descriptive words. She called these children together in a small group right before conferring. Then, following Calkins's (1994) example, she said, "I want to read something I found that is lovely. The words make pictures in my head. I'd like you to close your eyes as I read, and pay close attention to the pictures the words make in your heads." During the silence after she read, she said, "Let's go quietly back to our tables, and begin to write." This same technique can be used by the whole class when the students are in or near the Taking Inventory and Adding Description stage of written language development.

Another day, Mrs. Richardson was conferring with a child who had drawn a picture of his family and wanted to add a drawing of his cat, but he didn't want to try making a cat for the first time on the same paper. Mrs. Richardson provided some extra paper and put it in the center of the table declaring it "Help Paper." Because it only took a minute and most of the children at the table were already aware of what was happening, Mrs. Richardson explained to all the students at the table how to use the help paper. On another day, she introduced this idea in a whole-class minilesson.

Sometimes previously taught minilessons need reinforcement for only a few students—for example, using proper pencil grip. The teacher should reinforce the most common, comfortable position when teaching pencil grip (Graves, 1994). Also, if possible, the teacher should group "lefties" together and request (if not left handed) a left-handed teacher come to the class for a brief period to help instruct them. Minilessons on pencil grip and pressure also can be reinforced when the teacher demonstrates using a marker correctly in writing demonstrations and when he or she confers individually with students, too.

The majority of the time, teachers can teach whole-group minilessons. Teachers should teach small groups when (a) the opportunity presents itself (as in the case of the on-the-spot minilesson concerning help paper), (b) a small group is developmentally ready to learn something new (e.g., using descriptive words), or (c) a few students need more help in learning previously taught minilessons.

Dealing With Specific Problems in Minilessons

Writing About the Same Topic

Some kindergarten teachers have asked me how to design a minilesson to address the issue of children who write on the same topic every day. However, I do not recommend teaching minilessons on this unless it is truly a need; writing on the same topic can be desirable. Many good authors write about the same topic; authors need to write about what they know. This is especially true for kindergartners as kindergarten teacher Judith Hilliker observed:

> Certain representations or themes have significance for the child and are repeated many times. With each repetition the associations that the child makes with the drawing/text become more complex and differentiated. Next year I won't be discouraged by the repetition I find in my kindergartner's writing. Instead of asking them to draw something different, I'll ask them to tell me more about their pictures. (as cited in Newkirk & Atwell, 1988, p. 21)

Routman (2000) concurs with this advice and states, "students have to care about their writing [topic] to write well" (p. 213). However, teachers need to observe students' progress closely. Graves (1994) advises the following question be used as a determinant: Is the child "growing as a writer" (p. 274)?

To determine if the child is progressing, Graves (1994) advises teachers to "Ask the child to put four or five samples on the same topic in order from first to last" (p. 274). Together, the teacher and student should look through the samples to see if there are any changes from the first piece to the last piece. Graves recommends asking the child, "What were you trying that was new for you in each of these?" (p. 274). Of course, the child might not know, but this is a good teaching question for him or her to ponder in the future.

The following example illustrates a kindergarten teacher using Graves's suggestion to determine if a student writing on the same topic is progressing.

....

In the beginning of the school year, Timmy draws and writes about Thomas the Tank Engine every day. Mrs. Hawley is concerned that Timmy's writing seems to be the same every day. So Mrs. Hawley and Timmy sit down and examine his pictures from the past two weeks. Mrs. Hawley asks Timmy if he can tell her how these pictures changed. Timmy looks at them very carefully and says, "See, in this picture there's smoke 'cause Thomas has to climb a hill. I made the smoke really black because it was a mountain. And in this picture, Thomas says 'Choo, choo'" (represented by little o's coming out of Thomas's smoke stack). Timmy continues to point out different details he has added to his pictures from day to day. Also, in his later pictures he tried to print the words *Thomas the train*.

....

If students who are writing about the same topic are not improving (usually because they are writing about Thomas the Tank Engine, Scooby Doo, Pokémon, and so forth), teachers should provide some alternative suggestions. In this scenario, Graves (1994) advises teachers say to the child, "You keep on writing about the same topic. I'm curious about why you do that. Tell me about it" (p. 274). Then Graves explains that he may give the child a nudge to try something new. This requires brainstorming topics the child is interested in. It is helpful if the teacher has prior knowledge of the child's interests. For example, Mrs. Clark seriously began to doubt that Jacob had many interests outside of Pokémon. Jacob wrote about Pokémon every day, and his writing was not advancing. He was so wrapped up in Pokémon, he talked of nothing else. She called Jacob's parents and discussed the situation with them. They decided to limit Jacob's time with his computer games to increase his active playtime. At Mrs. Clark's suggestion, they also began to read bedtime stories to Jacob as often as possible. Soon, Jacob was able to find his own "voice" and produce some interesting and creative writing.

If parents are not responsive to suggestions, the teacher may have to give children with such difficulties additional help as needed to prompt their topic choices. Teachers can talk about stories in read-alouds and guide children to make connections between the stories and their lives.

Drawing for Too Long

Some children like to draw so much that they have little or no time left to write. Many kindergarten teachers do a minilesson or two using a "Quick

Draw" (Fisher, 1991). Basically the teacher shows children how to do a quick sketch, rather than draw an intricate picture. Calkins and Oxenhorn (2003) advise teachers to explain the difference between sketching and drawing. Also, teachers should emphasize that sketching is more appropriate for writing activities so that there is enough time to write. If the child decides to publish his or her piece, more intricate drawing can be done then.

Using Topics Not Appropriate for School

Sometimes teachers need to deal with students writing about topics that are not appropriate for school, such as topics containing violence. Children see violence on television and in movies and video games, and they try to emulate this in their writing. If a child's writing is filled with violence, it should be addressed sensitively and not be allowed. The child should be informed that this kind of writing is not appropriate for school. Then, the teacher should have a discussion about kindness with the child, especially how it feels when you are not treated kindly. Also, dependent on how prevalent this writing is for any particular author, teachers might call parents in for a discussion. (Communicating with parents is important in attempting to solve such problems.)

In addition, reading quality literature during read-alouds—followed by discussions—can be very useful in teaching kindness. Aesop's fables can be helpful in this endeavor, too, because these fables are meant to teach lessons. Creatively dramatizing fables can be helpful to discussing these lessons—and the children find it fun, too.

Minilesson Formats

Minilessons in kindergarten usually are presented in the following six formats:

1. teacher demonstrating content, strategy, or skill with his or her own writing;

2. teacher using student writing samples (with permission);

3. teacher using a piece of quality literature;

4. teacher using role-playing;

5. teacher using brief experimentation with a strategy or skill (i.e., telling students to try it for a moment); and

6. teacher leading class discussion of a problem.

Using the formats of role-playing, class discussion, and teacher writing demonstrations provides a variety of presentations when a minilesson needs to be retaught. For example, I taught a minilesson on rereading my work as I wrote to ensure that my writing made sense. The minilesson then was easily retaught and reviewed as I wrote on new topics in the future. Because

I always have to reread to ensure that I am making sense, I simply point this out. Near the end of the year, I have overheard kindergartners saying, "I gotta read this again; it's gotta make sense."

Minilesson Categories

When kindergarten teachers address students' needs using the six formats presented, they find these needs can be categorized generally into four types of minilessons: procedures, content, strategies, and skills (Avery, 1993).

1. Procedures: Procedural needs have to do with classroom management—of students and materials. In the beginning of the year, it takes a while for students to become familiar with the various writing workshop procedures, so most minilessons during that time deal with management issues.

2. Content: The primary purpose of teaching writing is to communicate messages that make sense (i.e., focus), which requires proper order (i.e., sequence). In a writing workshop, the teacher moves to minilessons on improving the quality of writing as the primary focus once procedures are going smoothly.

3. Strategies: A strategy helps the child to use a skill and know if he or she is using it correctly (Holdaway, 1979). To enable kindergartners to be able to improve the quality of their writing, teachers teach strategies that help the child be responsible about his or her own learning.

4. Skills or Conventions: Skills include knowing how to use letters of the alphabet, directionality, spacing, punctuation, and correct spelling. Graves (1994) states that skills, or conventions, are like "little sign posts" that aid the reader in understanding the message (pp. 191–192). Although skills are important, they should never overshadow the focus on content, and they are best taught within a strategy.

In the next section, I discuss the minilesson formats and categories in-depth within models of actual written demonstrations that have been presented in kindergarten classrooms.

Written Demonstrations of Minilessons

The following written demonstrations of minilessons are those that have been requested most often by kindergarten teachers with whom I have worked. Because most teachers have had little prior knowledge of these minilessons, I've found demonstrations to be instrumental in helping teachers understand the concept. Once understood, teachers have been able to easily design their own minilessons.

The following sampling of minilessons demonstrates the various minilesson formats and minilesson categories previously discussed. These minilessons are not provided as prescriptions but simply as demonstrations of how a minilesson might be designed. They are not presented in any specific order. The developmental writing and spelling needs of a particular class will determine the timing and type of minilesson the teacher will need to provide.

Each written minilesson demonstration includes the following:

- Objectives

- Introduction of Purpose

- Description of Presentation

- Assessment

- Suggestions

Unless otherwise indicated, the following minilessons were taught at the beginning of writing workshop, while the students were gathered in the community circle prior to their independent writing time. (A list of additional minilesson topics can be found in Appendix A.)

Procedural Minilessons

Kindergarten teachers find the management of a writing workshop to be the most important issue to address first. Once the structure of a writing workshop is in place (see chapter 5), the most difficult area to manage is the independent writing and conferring time. Procedural minilessons on managing the students, classroom materials, and classroom are kindergarten teachers' initial priorities.

Date Stamper

Objective
To encourage the students to take responsibility for certain tasks and to reduce the amount of the teacher's time spent on stamping the date on students' papers.

Introduction of Purpose
Mrs. Clark says, "Children, I am very pleased with how responsible you have become in helping in each other, and I wonder if you could help me, too. When I have to stamp the date on all your papers, I do not have the time to talk to you about your writing that I would like to have. What do you think we could do about stamping the date on your papers?"

Description of Presentation

Mrs. Clark discusses solutions with her class. (She has one in mind, too.) Her class decides to add the job of "Date Stamper" to the "Room Helper Weekly Chart."

Assessment

I've seen some teachers in the valid effort of teaching responsibility deliberately use some suggestions that were not workable. For example, one class tried to have each child stamp the date on his or her paper. The next day was mass confusion because all the children converged on the date stamper at once. A minilesson was done "on the spot" via a class discussion. The children came to the conclusion that only one person should be responsible for stamping dates for the week. (On occasion the experience of trying out something that doesn't work can be very valuable to devising one that does.) However, later in the year, when the children were more responsible, they were able to date their own papers. In some classrooms, no date stamper is used; children become responsible for copying and writing the date themselves.

Suggestions

If the children's suggestions do not work out, the problem should be discussed with the children again in future and on-the-spot minilessons.

"I'm Working On" Folders

Objective

To convey to students the idea that they do not have to finish a writing sample every day; they can continue writing on a sample the next day, and even the third day, if they desire and if their work is productive.

Introduction of Purpose

The teacher says, "Today at the end of the writing time, I want you to make a big decision. I want you to decide if you would like to keep writing on your same story tomorrow."

Description of Presentation

The teacher demonstrates his or her own writing and says, "I am running out of time and I want to work on this more tomorrow, so I think I'll put this in my writing folder." (Some teachers prefer to have children hand in "I'm Working On" papers at first and then introduce the folder idea in a later minilesson.) The teacher holds up a colored folder and shows the children where his or her name and the words "I'm Working On" have been printed. Each child is then given a colored folder to take to take to his or her writing table. (Some teachers ask children ahead of time what their favorite color is and give them a folder of that color.)

At the end of the independent writing and conferring session, the teacher reminds each child about making that big decision. If the author wants to keep working on a sample, he or she should put the sample in the colored folder marked "I'm Working On." The teacher collects all the colored folders, and children put finished samples in the "I'm Finished" basket as usual. (The "I'm Finished" basket was introduced in a prior minilesson similar to this one.)

Assessment

This minilesson proves to be very effective when the timing is right. Timing is an important factor when it comes to encouraging students to be responsible. Although students should be encouraged to take on responsibility for certain tasks, it should not be meted out before children are ready developmentally.

Suggestions

Until most procedures are running smoothly, the teacher should collect the "I'm Working On" papers. It is normal to have one or two children have difficulty with this minilesson, but the teacher can easily address this problem by assigning a helper to aid children in doing this filing until they can do it independently. (If writing teacher-partners have already been established, this duty would be assigned to that child; see "Adding Writing Teachers," p. 195.)

Writing Folders

Objective

To encourage students to take on the responsibility of filing independently. (Most teachers do not address this issue until all procedures are running fairly smoothly and they feel their children are ready. Some teachers prefer to hand out and collect "I'm Working On" folders on a daily basis and use "I'm Finished" baskets all year long.)

Introduction of Purpose

The teacher says, "Boys and girls, you have become so responsible. I am very proud of you, and I think you are responsible enough to do another big teacher job. Let me show you how."

Description of Presentation

(Prior to the demonstration, the teacher prepares a file box for each group of four children at a table by placing these children's colored folders in a file box and printing their respective names on the outside of the box.) For the minilesson, the teacher chooses one of the file boxes from one of the tables in the room. Then she asks the four children whose names are on the box to each demonstrate pulling their colored folder from the box and then putting it back again.

Assessment

At the end of the workshop, repeat a quick review of this procedure, so each child can practice filing. It should be evident if children understand how to complete this procedure.

Suggestions

If there is a problem with all four children descending on the file box at once, do a minilesson on the spot. Ask the class for help in solving the problem. Some suggestions other classes have made include the following: The teacher could appoint one child in each group of four to hand the files to the other three, or the teacher could give each child a number so the children approach the file box in numerical order. These suggestions suffice until the children gain the responsibility to do it for themselves.

Once children learn how to file their unfinished work in their colored "I'm Working On" folders, the teacher demonstrates another similar minilesson that helps in the filing of finished work. The teacher shows the children a manila folder with the words "I'm Finished" printed on it. Next she shows the children some writing she finished, and she places this writing in the manila folder. Then she places the manila folder and its contents inside the colored folder. Last, she places the colored folder in the file box. The teacher can ask a couple of children to demonstrate this procedure, too. At the end of the writing session, the teacher "walks" all the children through this procedure again.

Both folders (manila within colored) would be taken out of the file box each day, and children would attend to the contents in the colored file if they are still working on a piece, or they could start a new piece. At the end of the first few sessions of using file box and folders, the teacher should demonstrate and direct the proper filing of papers (see Figure 46).

"I'm Finished" folders get too full if they are not cleaned out on a weekly basis. Once a weekly best work is chosen to be saved (see "Choosing My Best Work," p. 218), the rest of the papers can be sent home or saved by the teacher in special files or boxes (see "Getting New Ideas From Old Ideas," p. 221). Most beginning writing teachers do not like to be too encumbered with papers, and so the papers not chosen are sent home. However, I have noticed that as teachers become more

Figure 46. Working With Writing Folders

comfortable with a writing workshop, they tend to save all papers. Teachers explain to students and parents that reviewing these papers can be a useful strategy for generating more writing (Graves, 1994), and these papers will be returned to students at the end of the year.

Adding "Writing Teachers"

(Adapted from Calkins & Oxenhorn, 2003, pp. 21–27.)

Objectives
To encourage students to use one another as resources when the teacher is conferring with a student. (When this problem arises, it should be addressed with an on-the-spot minilesson.)

Introduction of Purpose
Mrs. Clark instructs the students, "Tomorrow we will talk about children coming up to me during writing time while I am trying to work with someone. For the rest of today's writing workshop, I want you to talk to your teacher-neighbor if you need something. You are not to come to me unless you are sick or hurt."

Teachers must stand firm once this rule is made. Children appreciate knowing their boundaries and want the security of knowing their teacher means—and will provide support for—what he or she says.

When the children come to school the next day, they are excited to find their seats have been changed. Mrs. Clark explains, "Remember how

I told all of you yesterday that you were not to come to me during writing time unless you were sick or hurt? [They nod yes.] From now on, as soon as writing time begins, I am going to put my 'Be Responsible' scarf on as a reminder to you that you should not come up to me."

Then Mrs. Clark asks the children, "Who did I say you should ask for help?"

Most of the children know they should ask their neighbor. Mrs. Clark says, "All writers need someone to listen to their work and help them sometimes. So I have given each of you your own 'writing teacher.'" (In assigning partners, consider compatibility with regard to friendships, behavior issues, and ability levels, and don't be hesitant about redoing certain partnerships if they are not working. If you need to establish a group of three, choose three responsible, cooperative children.)

Next, Mrs. Clark explains that the person seated next to each child—and whose name is on the colored piece of paper in front of them—is their "writing teacher." Each name has the number one or two by it, indicating which teacher will be partner number one and which one will be partner number two. The children ask about the numbers. Mrs. Clark simply explains, "One of you will be teacher number one and one will be number two. Try to remember which number you are."

Before the children come to the community circle for the writing minilesson, Mrs. Clark reminds the children that they should look at the paper again to see who is teacher one and who is teacher two. Students should take the hand of their writing teacher and come up together.

Description of Presentation

Mrs. Clark says, "Boys and girls, Olivia [kindergartner chosen prior to workshop] and I are going to pretend that we are writing teacher–partners. We are going to show you how to give and get help from one another. I was teacher number two on our paper, and Olivia was number one, so Olivia will talk about her story first and I will ask her questions."

Mrs. Clark: Olivia, are you done with your story from yesterday, or are you going to write a new story?

Olivia: I'm going to write a new story about my new bike!

[If Olivia had said she was going to add on to yesterday's story, she would be asked to tell what she wrote yesterday and what exactly she planned to say today.]

Mrs. Clark: How will your story go? [This question is intended to get the child to say exactly what he or she is going to write. Then Mrs. Clark turns to the class.] Now, I am going to listen with both ears to Olivia's answer.

Olivia: I got a brand-new red bike, and I can ride it without training wheels!

Mrs. Clark: Wow! That is interesting. I know I couldn't do that when I was five! Now, it is Olivia's turn to ask me the same questions. [The teacher then plays the part of the author who is going to add to her story, and she says the exact words that she is going to add.]

Mrs. Clark then has two classmates role-play as writing teachers following the teacher–student-led demonstration. Basically the questions they ask revolve around the topic and sequence and whether or not the child is finished (i.e., "What are you going to write today?" "How will your story go?" "Are you done?" "What are you going to add?"). The main concern here is not repetition of these questions; they are only given as initial guidelines. What is important is young authors really listening to each other's writings and needs, and doing their best to help.

After role-playing, Mrs. Clark tells the children to go to their seats and get out their writing folders. Then she says, "Look in your 'I'm Working On' folders. Do you have any work there that you want to finish today? If you do, take it out. Now, everyone who is teacher number one raise their hands. You can talk about your writing first; then it'll be teacher number two's turn. Remember to talk in your 'quiet voices.'" Mrs. Clark walks around the room helping out where needed.

Assessment

Establishing long-term partnerships takes time. This lesson took 15 minutes, but it will take students time to develop partnerships. Teachers should observe partnerships to ensure that they are progressing.

Suggestions

This minilesson will need to be repeated. Once partnerships are established, they should be used often, and the teacher should carefully observe students for any problems and address them one by one in future minilessons similar to the minilesson described.

In support of writing teacher–partners, Calkins and Oxenhorn (2003) suggest the following ideas also could be presented in separate minilessons:

When young authors share with their partners, they need to be encouraged to point to their writing as they read (see Figure 40, p. 159), which helps establish a good habit. So eventually when real words appear, the partner is able to help the author reread his or her text for any missing words that are needed to make the meaning clear. Pointing should be encouraged whenever the kindergartner reads, even though it is just approximated at first.

When the teacher conferences with one partner, the other partner should listen, too. The following example illustrates how a writing teacher–partner aids the writer in carrying out the teacher's suggestion.

[Collin tells Mrs. Fry and Tom about a story that he plans to write.]

Mrs. Fry: [to Collin's writing partner] Tom, I'm not too sure I understand what happened in Collin's story. He had several things happening, but they didn't seem to be in the right order. [to Collin] Collin, Tom and I are going to listen to your story again, and we're going to try to figure out what happened first [she touches one finger], then what happened next [she touches a second finger], and then what happened last [she touches a third finger]. Collin, could you tell us your story again?

[As Collin tells the story, Mrs. Fry and Tom help him organize his story so the three parts in his story follow each other. Collin retells his story, and then Mrs. Fry puts a little booklet with several blank pages in front of him.]

Mrs. Fry: Will you touch each page, and say what you will write on it?

[Collin retells his story in proper sequence easily with this booklet.]

Mrs. Fry uses an adaptation of this strategy for children who really struggle with sequencing. Mrs. Fry writes a representative word (or sometimes she uses rebus print) for each part of the story. Then she asks the student to place the cards on the proper page (or in the proper order on the table if not using the booklet) to use as a guide when writing the story, with assistance from the writing teacher–partner when needed.

In addition to providing order, these techniques can be helpful in aiding the writing teacher–partner to help the writer to record his or her thoughts (especially if the story is only a verbal rendition as Collin's was). The partner should be encouraged to help the writer get some words down, too—in any form possible. Some useful suggestions are "As a reader, I'd love to hear more about that" and "Let me help you get some words down" (Calkins & Oxenhorn, 2003, p. 25).

Furthermore, Calkins and Oxenhorn (2003) suggest that partners should sit next to each other throughout all three parts of writing workshop so partners can do brief "turn-and-talk" sessions during any part of writing workshop. Once these seating plans have been established, they suggest partnerships can be used in the following ways:

- Following a minilesson on choosing topics, the teacher might ask the young authors to tell their partners about the "one thing" they will write about.

- At the end of writing and conferring time, the teacher might request that partners ensure that each person has some writing along with his or her drawing.

- On infrequent occasions when the teacher does not have much time left for the remainder of the lesson, the teacher might request that the partners share their work with each other in place of doing Author's Chair.

Although the following suggestion follows this particular procedural minilesson, it can be used for any lesson where the child seems to need special one-on-one instruction. When a child persists in coming to the teacher for help after minilessons, it usually is because he or she is in real need of help. Many teachers have an aid or parent who can help during writing workshop time, and many teachers seek aid from fourth- and fifth-grade students, too (especially if these students are in writing workshop classes themselves). For example, Mrs. Kropland (a former reading teacher and current classroom teacher) had a student who loved to tell about his personal experiences but had great difficulty with writing due to problems with muscle skill development. Mrs. Kropland trained a volunteer eighth grader to work with this student on his writing every day. The eighth grader could not meet with the student at writing workshop time, but because Mrs. Kropland understood the value of writing to literacy and literacy to education in general, she allowed her student to miss instruction in one content area in favor of learning to write. Mrs. Lentz only has an aid for one half hour a day, but because she knows the value of writing, she chooses to use her aid during the individual writing time of writing workshop.

If no other help is available, the teacher will need to train a fellow classmate to be the child's writing scribe and teacher. A writing scribe records some of the information and shares the pen whenever possible. The children chosen as scribes need to be literate and enjoy coaching. Also, these children have to be properly trained by the teacher. Most teachers who have used student scribes appoint more than one scribe, so the scribes get to do their own writing as well as help others. The teacher should also arrange to work with the child who struggles during recess, lunch, or after school, if necessary.

"I'm Done" Writing

Objective

To encourage students to continue writing after they have written and drawn on one piece of paper.

Introduction of Purpose

Some children think they are "done" writing before the time of writing and conferring is up, and they announce, "I'm done!" Mrs. Clark does an "on-the-spot" minilesson and asks her children, "How do you know you are done writing?" (Graves, 1994). Some students answer that they have followed the writing rules; others say they have filled up their paper. Mrs. Clark says she is pleased if they have followed the writing rules, and if they haven't followed them, they should. Then she says in a quiet, serious tone, "Boys and girls, I have something very important to tell you. Good writers are never done writing. If you've followed your writing rules and you really think you are done with one story, then start another story. If you need more paper, it is right here in the writing center. Just get up and get it."

The next day Mrs. Clark says, "Yesterday, I asked you a question, How do you know you are done writing?" Some children mention having followed the writing rules, and Mrs. Clark agrees that is one way. As she directs their attention to the posted Writing Rules Chart, she reminds them that if they really think they are finished, they can always start another story. (She often refers to a favorite author like Dr. Seuss or Joy Cowley, noting all the books they wrote.) Then she says, "I would like to read a story to you, and I want you to tell me if this story is done yet."

Description of Presentation

Mrs. Clark says, "This story is written by a young boy like you [shows picture on back of book]. His name is Dennis Vollmer. When I stop reading, I want you to tell me if you think Dennis was really done writing." Mrs. Clark reads part of the book *Joshua Disobeys* (Vollmer, 1988). (An interesting side note to share with your children is that Dennis became a reader from writing this book.) Mrs. Clark stops her reading at an interesting part and says, "Oh dear, there is no more. Wait a minute, it says the author said he was done at this part, and stopped writing. What do you think of that, class?"

The children ask questions such as, "What happened to the boy?" "What happened to the whale?" "How did the story end?" Mrs. Clark writes their questions on the board, and then she says, "Writers write for readers, so writers need to answer their readers' questions. Let's read the rest of the book and see if Dennis answers your questions." After reading, it is noted that Dennis did answer all the children's questions. Then Mrs. Clark says, "Today, near the end of your writing time, I will ask you to read your story to your writing teacher to see if he or she has any questions that you might want to answer. This will help you decide if you are really done."

Assessment

It takes a great deal of practice for children to ask good questions and for authors to respond to them in writing. At the end of this writing session, many teachers substitute writing teacher–partners sharing their work with each other in place of Author's Chair. The teacher should walk around the room, helping students and making note of any other needs and possible minilessons that may need to be addressed based on his or her observations.

Suggestions

Some teachers post a big sign in the room that asks, "What does your reader want to know?" This is the crucial question for writers. This sign can be introduced and explained in a separate minilesson. (It can serve the dual purpose of providing a quick referral if children say they're done; and the question mark can be taught, highlighted, and referred to when children begin to use question marks or show a need of them in their writing.)

When the teacher employs Cambourne's conditions of learning language within his or her writing workshop, it does not take long before children do not want to be "done" with their writing. However, in the beginning of the year, kindergarten teachers will hear this comment. The minilessons just presented can be referred to quickly by pointing to Vollmer's book, or later on by pointing to the posted sign that reads, "What does your reader want to know?"

Making a Book

Objective
To gather students' writing about one topic and use it to make a book.

Introduction of Purpose
Mrs. Williams says, "Kindergartners, I have noticed that some of you are writing about the same idea from one day to the next, just like I have been writing about my husband's birthday. I'd like to show you what could be done with pages that are all about one idea."

Description of Presentation
Mrs. Williams demonstrates making a book from her writing demonstrations of the past three days. She takes the three pages she had written and staples them together. The pages consist of the following:

Page 1:   Two simple pictures that were on the two birthday cards Mrs. Williams had purchased for her husband.

Text: Today is my husband's birthday. When I left for school, I put two cards on the counter for him. I hope he likes them.

Page 2:   A picture of a birthday cake with many candles.

Text: When I got home from school, I made a chocolate birthday cake with fudge frosting. We ate the cake after my husband blew out all his candles. It was delicious!

Page 3:   Mrs. Williams's husband lying on a massage table.

Text: My husband got a massage for a birthday gift. He liked it; he'd never had one before. I was happy that I thought of a gift that he liked.

Once procedures are in place and running smoothly, teachers can concentrate on the real purpose of writing workshop—writing to communicate a message and creating writing that is readable. This requires that certain elements related to content be addressed, including focus, sequence, and voice.

Content Minilessons

Kindergartners care about content when they get to choose their own topics and share their work with their classmates and teacher. Because of their engagement with communicating their own messages, they want to learn strategies and skills to become better writers. Content is everything to a writer and to his or her reader.

Titles That Hook the Reader

and says, "I need to give my book a name just like all these other books have names." (She points to a few other recently read books and their titles.) She asks if anyone knows what a name on the book is called. Several of the children know the word is *title*. She says she is going to show the children how she thinks of a title.

Description of Presentation

Mrs. Williams explains that some people like to write a title when they begin writing a story, and some people like to wait until the story is finished. Mrs. Williams explains that if she had put a title on her story right away she would have called it "My Husband's Birthday," but after thinking about it, she doesn't think that title is very interesting anymore. She thinks she can write a better title. She says that books need interesting titles so readers will want to read them. A good title should "hook" a reader. She and the children brainstorm a possible list of titles. Then she asks the children which title makes them want to read her story. They choose the title "A Strange Birthday Present."

Assessment

Teachers will need to provide several minilessons on how to write a title because one minilesson will not be sufficient. Although several minilessons are necessary, children will eventually be able to write titles effectively.

Suggestions

Additional minilesson ideas include the following:

- Look at several good books with intriguing titles. Discuss why a title is interesting and what makes it good. Children also can bring books to school with interesting titles, which can be displayed in the classroom.

- Show and discuss good titles that students write.

- With a student's permission, the teacher and class could help a young author think of a title for her or his piece as the teacher did in this minilesson.

Developing Voice

Objective

To engage students in their writing so they can develop their "voices" and ultimately progress beyond ideas students see on television or in the movies. Students need to be more engaged in their writing. (When voice is strong, readers feels like someone is talking to them, and they are able to identify with the author's feelings [Graves, 1994].)

Introduction of Purpose

Mrs. Williams says, "Kindergartners, you all have interesting things that happen to you in your lives. Maggie told me how she put her head under water and blew bubbles in her bath water; Earl told me how he lost his tooth last night; and Sara told me she has so much snow at her house that it has covered the mailbox. I love to hear your stories. I would like to see you write about these things. Now, I am going to write about something that happened last night in my life."

Description of Presentation

Mrs. Williams says, "You know my kitty, Cyrus, always tries to run out the door when I come home. I am going to write about something that he did last night that made me laugh." Mrs. Williams writes, "Cyrus ran out the door and slid right into a snow bank. 'Meooooooooow,' he screeched! Then he made a beeline back to the house. Cyrus looked like a flying snowball! My husband and I laughed so hard, tears came to our eyes."

Mrs. Williams asks the children if her writing gave them a good picture of what happened. She asks them to close their eyes as she reads her story again. Then she asks them to describe what they see, hear, and feel. She tells the children that writing about what they see, hear, and feel helps the reader to see, hear, and feel, too. To do this well, students need to write about things that really happen in their lives.

Assessment

This minilesson will need to be repeated many times; however, it is necessary because as Murray (1996) states, "Voice is the single most important element in attracting and holding a reader's interest" (p. 39). Teachers should be able to identify voice easily; typically the teacher will feel as if the student or author is talking to him or her and is able to identify the author's feelings.

Suggestions

The best way to teach voice is for teachers to demonstrate it every day with their personal recounts. Graves (1994) reinforces this concept by explaining that children won't use voice unless their teachers demonstrate it. Routman (2000) explains how teachers can demonstrate their own voices—they should let their students "see and feel the passion" they have for a topic that is personally important to them (p. 212). Routman adds that as teachers write about a topic they care deeply about, they should allow "detail, description, and emotion to permeate [their] entire writing" (p. 212). Adding dialogue can be very helpful to giving writing voice, too.

Discussing "seeing, hearing, and feeling" after reading quality literature in a read-aloud is a good way to reinforce voice, too. Also, if the teacher sees voice in one of the student's papers, the teacher should ask permission to share it in class so the children can discuss the "seeing, hearing, and feeling" in the piece. The class can question the author about how he or she chose the words.

Finally, Mrs. Wagoner provides an idea for a bulletin board she calls "Kindergarten Voices." She posts copies of the children's papers that illustrate voice on this board. She highlights the part that showed voice. This bulletin board serves as a good model for the other children in her class. (It is also a form of informal publishing, and publishing, either informal or formal, promotes more writing.)

Once children are attempting to write about their personal experiences, Karelitz (1993) recommends changing passive pieces into "feeling" pieces. Teachers can ask young authors questions such as "How did it feel?" or "What did it feel like?" The following example took place in a one-on-one writing conference with a student. With the student's permission, the teacher might do a reenactment of such a situation in a minilesson:

[The young author had written *I went skiing. I went over a jump.*]

Teacher: What did it feel like when you went over the jump?

Author: I fell down.

Teacher: How did that feel?

Author: It was scary, but it was cool!

Teacher: Could we add that?

[The young author agrees, and the final result reads as follows: *I went skiing. I went over a jump and fell down. It was scary, but it was cool!*]

In addition to Karelitz's suggestion, Routman (2000) suggests the following for developing voice:

- As you read aloud to students, note passages that show voice. Discuss the words that let the reader know what the author thinks and feels.

- Compare pieces of writing with voice and without. Discuss the difference. For example, compare what Mrs. Williams wrote about Cyrus (which had voice) with the following example (which lacks voice): *Cyrus ran outside last night. He didn't like the snow and came back in.* Notice the lack of emotion, description, detail, and dialogue in the "voiceless" piece.

- Save samples of student writing with strong voice (past and present) and show them to your students. Discuss the lines or words that show voice. Note how and what the author said and did.

Some samples of kindergarten "voices" follow:

On Monday I'm going to pick sunflowers. I tried to pull the sunflowers out. I could not get them. I tried to catch butterflies, but I could not get them. I was sad. (Sandra's voice)

The horse is yellow, and then when I went to look at the horse, it had poop on its face, and it was scared. (Brandon's voice)

I went to the pet store. I got a big Saint Bernard. I got real excited. I said, "Yeah!" My mom said, "I know you are excited, but you don't have to get that excited!" (Clark's voice)

I went to my Grampa's. I was sad, because he died. Everybody gave him flowers. It was getting dark, so we went home. (Olivia's voice)

Although voice is hard to describe, it is easy to recognize and demonstrate (Routman, 2001). The first year Mrs. Williams implemented a writing workshop, she did not know that much about writing workshops, but she did know the value of demonstrating her own writing and showing her "voice." She believes this was the major contribution to her children's amazing progress as seen in their writing samples over the course of the year and on Clay's Dictation Test. Mrs. Williams also requests that students who have used good voice share their pieces in a minilesson format. After the child reads the piece, she asks the students the parts they liked the best and why. Invariably, they are the parts that help the reader see, hear, and especially feel the writer's voice.

Focus

(Adapted from Calkins & Oxenhorn, 2003, pp. 83–91.)

Objective
To encourage students to write retellings or recounts of personal experiences that are about "one thing" (Graves, 1994), or are more focused. (Calkins and Oxenhorn [2003] explain focus for kindergartners as "limiting the size—the scope—of a subject" [p. 83].)

Introduction of Purpose
Mrs. Williams found that the students' writings retell two or three different unrelated experiences in one recount; these writings do not have focus.

Mrs. Williams says, "A photographer can look at our whole room, or he can zoom in and take a picture of our hamster cage. Today, I'm going to show you how to zoom in on the most important part of your writing just like a photographer does when he takes a picture."

Description of Presentation

Mrs. Williams says, "First I am going to think about what happened yesterday. Let's see, I wanted to see my friend who lives in another town. I got in my car and then I had to get gas. I decided to get some coffee, too. Then, I pulled out of the gas station and started driving to my friend's house. Then I saw a beautiful field of daisies. I love daisies. I thought about stopping and picking some for my friend, but I was running late. Then I saw something really interesting—a hot air balloon up in the sky. I wondered what it would feel like to ride in a balloon like that. Finally, I arrived at my friend's house. We had fun. We went shopping. Then I came home and went to bed."

Mrs. Williams asks the children what they think of her story so far. They respond that it sounds like the daily schedule. She agrees that it does sound like a big, long list of things. She needs to zoom in on one of these things and only write about that. As Mrs. Williams shows with her hands how she will zoom in from a big topic to the most important part of her memory, she says, "I'll zoom in and write about the one most important part to me. My story will sound like this: 'Yesterday, I saw a hot air balloon high up in the air. It was every color of the rainbow. What would it feel like to ride way up in the sky? Would it be scary? Would it be a thrill to look down at the world below? I'll bet it would be fun. Someday I'd like to take a ride.'"

Following this demonstration, Mrs. Williams asks the children to go to their desks and open their writing folders and reread their most recent story. She asks students, "Is it too big? Or is it zoomed in and about one thing? If it is big, tell your partner how you could zoom in to one thing. Maybe your partner can help you zoom in." Mrs. Clark walks around the room, listening to some of the conversations, helping, and taking notes for future minilessons.

On subsequent writing workshop days, Mrs. Williams reminds the children to zoom in on the one most important part of a memory.

Assessment

Focus takes years to develop, so many minilessons will be necessary. However, teachers will be able to see evidence that students' focus is developing by observing a narrowed focus in students' work—that is, their writing is about "one thing."

Suggestions

Every writer battles with focus. Graves (1994) suggests that demonstrations of the teacher's writing are the best way to introduce younger children to narrowing their focus and choosing one thing or element to write about. He also suggests follow-up minilessons of a similar nature.

Graves (1994) states, "Deciding what your piece is about is the most basic step in learning to focus" (p. 216). A good question teachers can ask young writers during writing conferences is, "When you wrote this, what did you want your piece to be about?" (p. 216). Sometimes, children don't know, and teachers have to help them identify their focus.

Teachers can look for a sentence or words that tells what the piece is about. They can look for supporting sentences for that main idea or focus. Those sentences that do not add support to the main idea can be crossed out when publishing. Again, the guiding question in crossing out or adding on is, "What will the reader want or need to know?"

Graves (1994) gives some additional advice on practicing focus with the following suggestions:

- When a child reads his or her text in Author's Chair, the child should say, "This is what my piece or book is about" before reading it.

- After a child has shared his or her writing, the teacher asks the group, "What is Margaret's piece about?" Then after the group responds, the teacher turns to Margaret and asks, "What do you think about what we said?"

- During individual writing conferences, the teacher should ask the child, "What's the one thing that your writing is about?" (Graves begins every writing conference this way.)

- When a child is reading a book, poem, or short selection, the teacher should ask, "What is the one thing that your reading is about?" (pp. 215–216)

Interesting Conclusions

(Adapted from Calkins & Oxenhorn, 2003, pp. 101–107.)

Objective
To have students add creativity to their retelling or recount endings.

Introduction of Purpose
Ms. Finnegan tells her children that she loves hearing and reading their stories because they are so interesting. As she explains to her students that their stories are really great, she holds up her hands as high as she can, as if their stories were really tall. Then she let her hands fall in her lap as she says, "But then they go like that!"

After a few seconds of silence for impact, Ms. Finnegan reads an example of such a story (saved from a previous year for this purpose) to the class: "Our class went to the pumpkin patch to buy a pumpkin. We saw a mouse run out of the pumpkin. The pumpkin man said, 'That mouse probably lived in the pumpkin.' [Then Ms. Finnegan's intonation changes to suggest that everything fell apart as she reads the ending.] Then we went home."

After a brief silence, Ms. Finnegan says, "What a letdown! Children, today you are going to learn how to write good endings to your wonderful stories!"

Description of Presentation

Ms. Finnegan explains to her children that when they write endings like the one they just heard, the endings "jump away" from the important part of the story.

Ms. Finnegan:	What is the important part of the story?
Children:	The mouse living in the pumpkin. [If the children didn't know, Ms. Finnegan would have told them what it was and why it was important.]
Ms. Finnegan:	When stories end with "then we went home," the ending "jumps away" from the important part—the mouse living in the pumpkin—and it goes to a whole different place. Your endings should "stay close" to the important part. As we read the story again, let's try to think of an ending for our story that stays close to the mouse living in the pumpkin. One way to end a story is to remember the last thing that happened in the story when you stopped writing about the important part—and then stop. Let's see that was— The pumpkin man said, "That mouse probably lived in the pumpkin." Could that be our ending?
Children:	Yes, it could.
Ms. Finnegan:	If you are going to write an ending for one of your stories today, let's say that you are not allowed to end your piece with "and then I went home" or "and then I went to sleep." Remember how we ended our story today? We stayed close to the important part of the story—the mouse living in the pumpkin; we didn't jump away to a whole different time—going home. When we wanted to stop writing about the mouse, we reread the last thing that happened concerning the mouse, and we stopped.

Assessment

Teachers cannot expect children to write good conclusions after only one minilesson on endings. This will take many teacher demonstrations and a lot of practice on the part of the children.

Suggestions

When conferring with kindergartners who are attempting to write endings, Calkins and Oxenhorn (2003) suggest that teachers read aloud what they've written as if it were the greatest piece of literature in the world, and then pause and leave a space for the ending. Often this is enough for the child to think of an interesting conclusion. If this doesn't happen, the teacher should show the writer how he or she comes up with conclusions. First, the teacher should show the child how he or she would reread the text (or at least the last part) to get a running start at producing a conclusion. Then, the teacher should try out a poor conclusion and think aloud about whether he or she likes it or not. If the teacher doesn't like it, the teacher should show the child how one must reread the end of the text again to produce another possible ending. After demonstrating this, the teacher should tell the child to "try it" and guide the child to do the same thing.

When Ms. Finnegan saw many children following the advice this minilesson offered by not writing "we went home" or "I went to sleep" at the end of their stories and trying to stay close to the important part, she taught another way to end their writing.

Ms. Finnegan:	Today, we are going to learn another way to end a story that might make it more interesting than just stopping. First we will need to reread our story. [Ms. Finnegan uses the same story about the pumpkin and the mouse because it is familiar.] Now, let's reread the last part again, and after we've read it, I want you to tell me what you were thinking about or what you were feeling.
Ms. Finnegan [after rereading the last part of the story]:	What did you think or feel when the man showed everyone the mouse hole in the pumpkin?
Gary:	I thought the mouse's house was smaller than mine.
Christine:	I wondered if the mouse lived all alone in the pumpkin.

Ms. Finnegan congratulates all the children and records their answers on the board. Then she and the class try some of the "new endings" by rereading the story and adding them. As they do this, they discuss how these endings stay close to the important part of the story and don't jump away. They also discuss how the children's additions add an interesting thought to the ending.

The children like their new endings and think they are more interesting. Then, before they go to their seats to write, Ms. Finnegan reminds them that if they are writing an ending to their story, they should try to use one of the two ways she showed them.

Ms. Finnegan: First, decide on the important part of your story, and then stay close to it—don't jump away from it. Or, if you want to add more interest, reread your ending, and add anything that it makes you think of, or maybe feel.

Ms. Finnegan also records these things on a chart and displays the chart on a bulletin board for the remainder of the year. Periodically she adds kindergartners' writings to this board around the chart as exemplary samples of good endings.

Calkins and Oxenhorn (2003) also recommend the following follow-up minilesson:

1. Tell the class that you need help to write an ending to a story based on a shared experience (already written on large chart paper).
2. Read aloud the piece.
3. Tell the students to turn to their "writing teachers or buddies" and talk about whether this story has a good ending. Could they improve it?
4. After a few minutes, ask the class about their suggestions.
5. Reread the piece and use one of the suggestions.

Other "conclusion" minilessons Calkins and Oxenhorn (2003) suggest include the following:

• Celebrate a child's good story ending. Ask the children to explain how the ending stays close to the important part of the story.

• With a child's permission, show and discuss how he or she might have changed an ending that jumped away from the important part of the story to one that stayed nice and close.

• Read a picture book and explain that the author probably tried 10 different endings before deciding on the one chosen. Discuss how this ending stays close and why the children like it. Give an example of another ending that stays close and perhaps one that doesn't. Discuss.

• Help young writers begin to realize that there are a few predictable ways authors end their stories. This would be accomplished best with teacher demonstrations of writing and by pointing out types of endings in stories read in class.

Interesting conclusions are difficult to write. However, similar to Calkins and Oxenhorn's (2003) advice on writing good conclusions, Zinsser (1980) states, "When instinct tells you its time to stop...send the reader on his way quickly and with a provocative thought to take along" (p. 73). This is a thought teachers might try to remember as they write endings to their teacher demonstrations of written language. They should also remember when teaching elements of content to young authors that it's important to let them write about topics of their own choosing—topics about which they care deeply.

Teachers need to find out what students are really interested in and encourage them to "tell me more" if the quality of their writing is going to improve. Further, students need to know writing strategies so they know how to improve their writing.

Strategy Minilessons

Routman (1991) explains a strategy as "knowing how and when to apply a skill; that is what elevates the skill to the strategy level" (p. 135). Holdaway (1979) notes, "The major difference, then, between 'skills teaching' and 'strategy teaching' concerns the presence or absence of self-direction on the part of the learner" (p. 136). Children learn strategies best when they are demonstrated by the teacher as he or she writes and when the teacher explains the purpose for using the strategy. Children need to practice using different strategies as the need arises in their writing.

Choosing Topics

Objective
To encourage students to think of writing topics. (This minilesson could be done in a small group because usually there are only one or two children who have this problem, but it can also be done as a whole-class lesson because it is useful for everyone.)

Introduction of Purpose
Mrs. Williams says, "Boys and girls, when I first started writing, I sometimes had trouble thinking of things to write about. Now, I am always ready to write. I'd like to talk to you about what I do."

Description of Presentation
The teacher says, "Every day, wherever I am, when I see something that is interesting to me, I say to myself, 'Oh, that would be so interesting to

write about in writing workshop; I must remember it.' Sometimes I even write it down in a little notebook that I carry with me. [She shows the children her notebook.] Last weekend, something that meant a lot to me happened, and I am going to write about it now."

First, Mrs. Williams draws an airplane. Then, she writes about the airplane beneath it: *I took Mr. Williams to the airport. I watched his plane take off and felt sad.*

Assessment

Kindergartners rarely have problems with topic choice once they realize that they can write every day. Topic choice is mainly a problem in the beginning of the year because children are not used to the luxury of having daily time to write or are not used to seeing demonstrations of writing by their teacher (Graves, 1994; Temple et al., 1988). However, there can be one or two children who persist in needing help with topic choice. This is usually because these children need help in everything. (See the follow-up suggestion on p. 197 under "Adding 'Writing Teachers.'")

All writers, especially kindergartners, need to write about what they know. Graves (1994) explains that the "objective is to help writers listen to themselves" (p. 57). There is no better way to show this than the teacher demonstrating what he or she does to think of topics (Graves, 1994). Other children can be called on to discuss what they do, too, or the teacher may wish to have a student do a minilesson on topic choice. Children who usually have topic choices in mind might be asked to share their knowledge in a student-led minilesson.

Suggestions

There are many minilessons concerning choosing topics that could be used as a follow-up to this lesson, such as brainstorming a list; looking through your writing folder to stimulate an idea for writing; discussing where classmates get their ideas; discussing what to do when you're stuck; role-playing a suggestion that was given in Author's Chair the day before; and, of course, using quality literature to get an idea.

Using the Names on the Word (Name) Wall

Objective

To encourage students to copy words from around the room so they can learn the letters of the alphabet. (This should be done during the Picture Writing stage and the Precommunicative stage.)

Introduction of Purpose

Mrs. Clark says, "Yesterday, I noticed Danny was using the word wall to copy Cody's name. I thought that was a wonderful idea."

Description of Presentation

Mrs. Clark asks, "Danny, would you please show your paper to the class?" (She had already asked Danny's permission.) Danny shows his paper, and the teacher and children praise his very readable printing. "Danny, would you please show us what you did when you wanted to copy Cody's name?" Mrs. Clark prompts.

Danny walks over to the word (name) wall, takes Cody's name off the board where it is attached with an adhesive, copies it, and puts it back on the wall when he is done. (Because the children initially are very excited about this, the teacher may have to set some boundaries such as allowing only one or two students at the word [name] wall at any one time.)

Assessment

This minilesson is usually very effective because children naturally like to copy print in the room, especially their classmates' names. Follow-up lessons are usually not needed, but the teacher should observe students to ensure that they are copying print from the room correctly.

Suggestions

To promote this activity, when the teacher sees other children copying the alphabet or copying names, he or she should briefly bring this to the attention of the other students. This is a good time to do a "Quick Share"—simply hold up the student's writing at a table or stand up and show the whole room the interesting writing that the student is doing.

In my work as a consultant, many kindergarten teachers ask me if it is appropriate for children to copy print that is in the classroom. Many of these teachers were taught that tracing, copying, and drilling does not transfer to real writing. This is true if the activity is given as an external assignment; however, when children voluntarily decide to copy or trace a letter it can contribute to their learning the letter (Morrow, 1989). (See "Letter Formation Is Developmental" in chapter 2 for more information on this topic.)

When teachers observe that most children are in the Semiphonetic stage of spelling, they can begin teaching high-frequency words (see Appendix D for a list of high-frequency words and how to teach them). Once a word has been taught and placed on the word (name) wall, the teacher can include a minilesson on copying these words using Gentry and Gillet's (1993) "Look, Cover, Write, Check" strategy (p. 78). Merely copying these words will not help children remember them. However, by looking carefully at all the letters in the word, covering the word, trying to write it from memory, and checking it, children can learn to spell the word (Gentry & Gillet, 1993).

Objective

To ensure that students write the letters of the alphabet correctly. (This is done during the Semiphonetic stage.)

Introduction of Purpose

Miss Neale says, "Kindergartners, I have noticed that many of you are writing letters now. That is wonderful. But I've also noticed that some of you are forgetting to use the 'Alphabet Song' and ABC strip on your table when you write the letters. Let me show you what I mean."

Description of Presentation

Miss Neale begins by drawing a hawk flying in the air. As she begins to write *The* she says, "Hmm, I want to write *hawk*. I know the first sound is /h/, and I know *h* is the letter, but I can't remember how to make it. What can I do?"

Several children remind Miss Neale to use her ABC strip and she does. She and the class sing the "Alphabet Song" until they get to the *h*, and then everyone yells, "Stop." Miss Neale copies the letter *h*.

Assessment

After the minilesson, the teacher can ask students to go to their seats and then find a specific letter by using the strategy. For example, the teacher can say, "I would like you to sing the 'Alphabet Song' and find the letter *f*." Then, the teacher should walk around the room and ensure that all children can find the letter. The teacher can use this same method after any minilesson and during one-on-one writing conferences.

Suggestions

The teacher can review how to find a letter by demonstrating this strategy using the alphabet chart.

Identifying Good Writing Traits

Objective

To encourage students to know and understand the criteria for good writing so they can incorporate these qualities in their writing.

Introduction of Purpose

Mrs. Clark says, "Kindergartners, you are all becoming wonderful writers, but a writer always wants to get better and better. So today we will discuss what good writing is before you go to your seats to write. We will make a chart of what we consider good writing, and we will add to it every week. Let's begin our chart."

Description of Presentation

The children list the qualities they think are important to good writing as the teacher records them on a large sheet of tagboard. See Table 7 for a list of qualities created at the beginning of the year.

Mrs. Clark demonstrates using this chart to ensure that each quality is featured in her writing during and after her demonstration of writing. Then she asks the children to keep the chart in mind as they write.

Assessment

In the beginning of the year, this chart will look more like a writing rules chart, but as good qualities (e.g., focus, sequence, voice, details, titles, and so forth) are taught, the children will add these to the chart. See Table 8, a compilation of Mrs. Williams's and Mrs. Clark's end-of-the-year good writing charts.

When teachers confer with students one-on-one, they can check for these qualities, and they can reteach them within individual writing

---

Table 7. Good Writing Chart: Beginning of the Year

What Is Good Writing?
• My **name** is on my paper.
• The **date** is on my paper.
• I have drawn a **picture**.
• I have some **writing**.

Table 8. Good Writing Chart: End of the Year

What Is Good Writing?
• My name and date are on my paper.
• My writing is readable, not messy.
• My story has spaces and punctuation.
• My story has colorful illustrations.
• My picture and writing tell the same story.
• My story is my own.
• My story is about one thing.
• My story doesn't go "hippety-hop"; it makes sense.
• My story is about an interesting thing.
• My story has some big and interesting words.
• My story has our "over and over" words (i.e., any of the 25 high-frequency words) spelled right.
• My story has lots of details.
• My story has a title that fits my story.
• My story has a good ending.

conferences (as Mrs. Fry did when she taught Collin a strategy to help him with sequencing; see p. 198).

At the end of the week, the teacher can guide authors and their writing teacher–partners to decide on which paper to choose that exemplifies these qualities.

Suggestions

At the end of each week, it is a good idea to review with the children any good qualities of writing they may have learned during the week. These qualities should be added to the good writing chart.

Teachers can use the following questions and ideas during writing conferences (and minilessons) to help young children develop good writing. These questions and ideas focus on the three most important qualities of good writing: (1) focus (i.e., making sense; sticking to one idea), (2) sequence or order of events in the story, and (3) voice.

- To establish focus, Graves (1994) suggests asking the children, "When you first wrote this, what did you want your piece to be about?" (p. 216) or as Calkins (1994) suggests, "Can you tell me the 'one thing' that this story is about?" (p. 64). In addition, ask, "Do you think everything that you have in this story is about that one thing?" (If something isn't, ask the child what he or she could do about it, and then suggest crossing it out.) Or, perhaps in the case of a writer who is in the Taking Inventory and Adding Description stage of written language but has one important part missing from a good story, the teacher can show the student how to add it. Usually the addition can be put at the end of the sample, but if it needs to be inserted in the text, it can be numbered (e.g., 1, 2, 3, and so forth) and then the number can be placed in the text where this addition should go.

- Ask the student, "When you read this story, ask yourself, 'Did it really happen this way?'" (Calkins, 1994, p. 238). "What do I want to tell first?" "What do I want to tell second?" and so on. If the child has difficulty with this, Calkins suggests that the teacher disassemble the work by cutting it apart sentence by sentence and then reassemble the sentences into the proper order (this can be a useful minilesson, too).

- Ask the student, "Do you hear yourself talking to your reader in this story?" "Can you show me some interesting details that only you—and not your writing partner—would know about this story?" "Can you show me a part that lets me know how you feel?" "How you see?" "How you hear?" (Each of these questions should be asked separately; Routman, 2000, p. 248.)

Another useful technique that I have seen Mrs. Scaffidi use successfully is to take a book that illustrates voice to use as an example during conferences. She reads a part from the book with voice to illustrate certain points like details, and then she reads the sentence again, taking the details out. (This is an excellent minilesson.) Finally, children can be asked to share any book titles with the class that might have influenced their writing.

Further, when conducting minilessons or conferring with students one on one, the teacher can ask the children what they have done to become better writers (Calkins, 1994).

Choosing My Best Writing

Objective
To encourage students to analyze their work for the qualities of good writing so they can become better writers.

Introduction of Purpose
Mrs. Clark says, "Boys and girls, remember how we made this chart about good writing last week? Well, today we're going to use it to pick our best writing for the week."

Demonstration of Presentation
Mrs. Clark says, "Before we begin, I wonder if we should add anything to this chart. Did we learn anything this week about good writing that you think should be added to this chart?"

Mrs. Clark then guides the children to think about the minilessons taught that week. (Teachers can quickly flip through teacher demonstrations and minilessons for possible additions to the chart and add them.)

Mrs. Clark says, "Class, I asked Ethan if we could use his work today to show you how he would use this chart to choose his best work, and he has agreed." Ethan sits next to Mrs. Clark. He has his manila file of "I'm Finished" papers with him.

Then Mrs. Clark says, "Ethan has already chosen two papers he really likes. Now we are going to use our chart to help Ethan choose his best writing sample. The writing he chooses will be saved in my teacher file, so when Ethan's parents come to school, I can show them what a good writer Ethan is becoming."

The class helps Ethan make a choice using the criteria on the chart. First, Ethan reads his two stories and their titles. In the first story, Ethan tries to kiss his painted turtle, but the turtle bites him on the lip and won't let go. Ethan has to go to the doctor to get the turtle off his lip. But he still loves his turtle. In the second story, Ethan goes to the circus and sees a clown named

Chico twirl a lot of plates on sticks. He throws them up in the air, and he has to twirl them really fast so they won't crash on the ground.

Then the class assesses each story according to the list of qualities they have on their good writing chart (see Table 7, p. 216). Ethan, the teacher, and the class check off the qualities one by one. They decide that Ethan's story about the turtle is the best because it has more of the qualities of good writing than the second story. Also, the children had difficulty understanding Ethan's second story. The children help Ethan add voice to the story by asking him what he said when the turtle bit him. Ethan replies that he said, "Ouch!" so he adds that part to the story right after the turtle bit him. When the teacher asks Ethan why he chose these two stories he says that he likes to write about his turtle and it was really exciting to see Chico keep all those plates in the air.

Children often try to write about exciting things they've seen—movies, television stories, and so forth. They think others will feel the excitement they felt, too. However, because the story is not about them, they don't understand it well enough to get all the details in the proper order in the story to make it interesting or understandable to others. The class had to ask Ethan many questions before the children really understood his "Chico story."

Ethan then puts his turtle story in Mrs. Clark's special basket marked "My Best Writing." (Mrs. Clark puts this basket on her desk every Friday and the children put their choices in it.)

Assessment

Children may experience difficulties with this lesson on the first day, especially children who are not as responsible as others. Therefore, the whole writing session on this first day is often spent carrying out this minilesson. The teacher needs to walk around the room supervising and guiding students. Also, students should be able to demonstrate with two writing selections how they chose their best writing.

Suggestions

Many kindergarten teachers like to precede this minilesson with a minilesson that helps students narrow the five or more papers from the week to two; otherwise, picking one paper out of five might be overwhelming at first for students. Calkins (1994) describes this lesson as follows:

> When you read over your work [for the week], how do you feel about it? If you were to lay out all your finished drafts [writings] from this week and then sort them into piles of "very best," "good" and "less good," which pile would this be in? Why? (p. 226)

Most kindergarten teachers with whom I have worked prefer sorting writing into two piles: "good" and "not so good." In this preliminary lesson, children do not need to think about the qualities as deeply as they do in the minilesson revolving around Ethan. Later in the year, as children become more adept at choosing their best work, it may not be necessary for them to use this narrowing step.

When using this minilesson, teachers should choose a student who is a good model of writing and has at least one paper that fits most of the criteria on the good writing chart.

Many teachers have found that this is a good time to incorporate writing teacher–partners. Partners can help each other apply the chart's criteria to the two papers chosen by the author. When children are finished with their task, they put their samples in the "My Best Writing" basket and continue to write.

Initially, the child's manila "I'm Finished" folder holds two weeks' worth of papers, unless the teacher allows the children to take papers home the first week, which is advisable because children might have difficulty choosing their best work if they have too many papers in their folders. Most of the time, this file only includes one week's worth of papers, which makes assessment easier for the child.

Each week, children improve in their ability to analyze their writing. In fact, in one classroom, analyzing went relatively smoothly the second time it was tried because the teacher reminded the children every day that they would be using the chart to choose their best piece of writing at the end of the week. Then, most of the children were able to make their choices quite easily.

Students' chosen samples should be photocopied; the photocopy and the original go in the teacher's assessment file. After the original is discussed at conference time, it is sent home to the parents.

A minilesson that reinforces this one consists of showing children how they can list "Things I Can Do" on their writing folders to show how they are becoming good writers. Whenever students feel they have control over something on this list or something they just feel is important to their writing (e.g., "I can spell *Hershey*"), they can be encouraged to record it. Sharing these lists occasionally in Author's Chair is important to promote self-esteem and provide good examples for other children to follow.

It is also helpful to show, discuss, and post pieces of quality writing that students produce. Observing and discussing the good features in an exemplary piece of writing enables kindergartners to become astute evaluators of their own and others' writings (Dahl & Farnan, 1998).

Routman (2000) recommends that teachers label some exemplary samples of various good writing traits with the words, "Here is where the writer has done such and such" and post these samples in the room to help children become better at self-assessment (p. 574). She also recommends routinely looking at samples of average and poor work. (Samples can be saved from previous years and names can be omitted;

also, other teachers can provide samples or the teacher can create some.) By looking at samples of differing quality, students can begin to identify when certain qualities are missing in one piece but are present in another. This helps students recognize what they need to change or add to their own writing to become better writers.

Getting New Ideas From Old Ideas

Objective

To stimulate students' writing ideas with their previous writing selections.

Introduction of Purpose

Mrs. Williams says, "Children, many of you have asked to take some of your papers home, and I have asked you to keep them here. There is a reason for that and I'd like to show you why."

Description of Presentation

Mrs. Williams pretends to think about what to write in her teacher demonstration. Then she says, "Boys and girls, I'm really having trouble thinking of something to write about. What can I do?" (The children give some suggestions.)

Then Mrs. Williams's face brightens, and she says, "I've got an idea! I'm going to look through my writing to see if there is something I've already written about that might give me a new idea." She pages through her teacher demonstration writing samples until she comes to one about getting a gift of jelly beans from a friend. "Oh, I know something that I want to tell you about now." She draws a picture of herself sitting in a dentist's chair and then writes, *I had to go to the dentist to get a new tooth. A piece of my tooth broke off when I ate a jellybean.*

Mrs. Williams and the children discuss the usefulness of saving writing samples. Then Mrs. Williams says, "Tomorrow, I will show you how we will save all your writing."

Assessment

Teachers can determine whether or not students are generating new ideas by observing students during their daily writing and observing their students choosing their best work at the end of the week.

Suggestions

The next day's minilesson should show children how all their writing can be saved so they can be revisited to help the children generate new ideas for writing.

Mrs. Williams says, "Boys and girls, on Fridays you always choose your 'Best Writing' for the week. I save that writing to show your parents what you are learning in school. But it would be a good idea if we saved all or at least some of your other writings, too. At the end of the year, you will get all your papers back. Remember how I used some of my old writings to think of something to write about yesterday? Well, you should have your old writings to look over just like I did. You have become so responsible about making decisions that I am going to let you decide which papers you might want to save here at school to get more ideas about writing, and which papers you will take home. The papers you wish to save will be put in this drawer in my file cabinet labeled 'Kindergarten Writing 2004–2005.' Each of you will have a folder with your name on it in this drawer. You will save your writing in folders like this [showing folder], and they will be kept in this file. At the end of each week, you will decide what stays at school and what goes home. Amy is going to help me show you how this works."

As Mrs. Williams explains the procedure, Amy demonstrates it. Mrs. Williams says, "Amy wants some papers to be saved, so she gets her folder from the drawer, puts the papers she wants to save in the folder, and then puts the folder in this basket here on the chair by the filing cabinet. Then I will put them back in this drawer. [The teacher repeats this procedure with other children until they all understand.] Then, any time you want to look at your papers to get 'new' ideas, you can take your folder out of this drawer and look at them." (Other student volunteers can demonstrate doing this, too.)

Graves (1994) states that all writing samples should be saved so they can be revisited later to generate ideas. Some veteran kindergarten writing workshop teachers attempt to save all students' writing, except the sample that needs to be saved as a best work for the week and any samples that kindergartners insist on taking home. At the end of every week, these teachers distribute individual file folders to all the children to place all their weekly samples in (minus the exceptions mentioned). Then, either the teacher files these folders or she shows some children how to do it. When this "Kindergarten Writing" file gets full, the teacher begins another file box and labels it appropriately (usually by the month). These kindergarten files should be available for the children to look through at any time.

By learning the strategies presented in this section, young authors can become self-directed in their writing. These strategies are tools that help writers know how to choose new writing topics from looking at old topics, how to analyze their writing so they can choose the best one, and know when and how to use certain skills.

Skill Minilessons

When skills are taught in predetermined sequences and practiced in isolation, they rarely transfer to real writing or reading. Application of a skill in writing and reading is far more likely to occur when the skill has been taught in a meaningful context (Routman, 1991).

Teaching minilessons that focus on skills depends on the needs of the students and an understanding of their developmental spelling stage and written language stage. Developmental stages (see chapters 2 and 3) are especially important to consider when teaching skills. Usually the skills addressed in writing workshop include punctuation, spelling, and mechanics of writing. The main reason to teach skills, or conventions, is so children will understand what they mean when they see these items in text (Graves, 1994). Graves (1994) prefers using the term *conventions* rather than *skills* and explains that conventions are tools that help the author show the reader what the author wants the reader to do as his or her work is read: perhaps slow down, by using commas; or to stop for a bit, by using periods. The word *skills* often denotes predetermined sequences and isolated practice of the mechanics of writing, especially punctuation and spelling, apart from the meaningful process of writing.

It is not essential that kindergarten children demonstrate proficiency using conventions; however, approximated practice will lead to children having a better understanding of conventions (Angelillo, 2002; Graves, 1994).

Endings Need Punctuation ("Listen to the Stops")

Objective

To help students understand the purpose for using periods in their writing. (This minilesson is appropriate for students who are in the Taking Inventory stage of written language.)

Introduction of Purpose

Mrs. Williams says, "Boys and girls, I've noticed that some of you are using little dots like this in your writing, but you need to know why we use them." Mrs. Williams points to a period in a Big Book and tells the children, "This little dot is called a period. It's like a little stop sign. It helps you read the story the way the author wants you to. When you use a dot like this it means your voice should stop for a little bit. Let me show you what would happen if there were no periods in this story."

Description of Presentation

Mrs. Williams begins to read the story in the Big Book without using the periods. She overacts and becomes very winded, and she finally collapses in her chair. The children enjoy the dramatization, and they get the idea. Mrs. Williams straightens up and says, "I wonder, though, can we put periods anywhere we want to?" Next, Mrs. Willliams reads some of the text, pausing for a period between each word. Then her slow reading is discussed by the class.

(This minilesson could be divided into two parts. This first part, just described, could be done during the minilesson time of reading workshop, and the second part, which follows, could be done in writing workshop.)

Mrs. Williams says, "Kindergartners, remember how we talked about periods being like little stop signs when you are reading? Well, now I'm going to show you how to put in periods when you are writing. I'm going to write something I've been thinking about, and when I come to the end of that thought, my voice is going to stop. I want you to listen for that stop."

Then Mrs. Williams reads as she writes, "I saw a car in the ditch this morning." After reading her sentence, she asks the children if they noticed how her voice stopped at the end of her thought. They say they did. Then she says, "When your voice stops like this, you need to put a little black dot—a period—there. Remember, it means you can take a little breath."

Mrs. Williams then tells the children that she is going to write some more; they should listen to where her voice stops and tell her where the period should go. She writes, *The snow made the road very slippery this morning.*

Mrs. Williams exaggerates the stop with her voice, and the children have no trouble deciding that a period should come after the word *morning.* (Having the children place the period is a good use of interactive writing.)

Assessment

Ending punctuation should not be addressed in minilessons until most of the children are using it in the Inventorying stage of writing, and the latter stages of Semiphonetic or Phonetic spelling. It is essential, especially in the area of skills, that minilessons are geared to developmental levels of writing and spelling for some measure of success, but teachers should not expect students of this age to use punctuation and skills correctly.

When children first learn about a new skill, they tend to overgeneralize its use; they apply it everywhere. Children love punctuation marks and want to use them immediately, even if they don't grasp the concept or correct usage. Gradually, with repeated exposure— such as through more demonstration minilessons like the one provided— they begin to realize the purpose of punctuation marks and have some idea of where to use them.

For example, one kindergarten teacher, Mrs. Buska, observed a student's development concerning the use of periods over the course of the school year. She was fascinated by the progression she noticed: At first, the child put periods around the top and bottom of his paper; around midyear, he put them between his words; then a month or two later, he put some at the end of each line; and finally, near the end of the year, he often put them at the ends of his sentences.

Using periods in the correct place is a very difficult concept for young children to grasp. Most of the teachers with whom I have worked find that explaining that periods go where the voice stops at the end of a thought is the most effective strategy to teach students until they figure out this concept for themselves through approximated use of periods. This process takes time. When Cordeiro (1988) analyzed and compared first graders' use of periods to third graders' she observed development of punctuation. However, she also observed that as sentences grew more complex, students encountered more difficulty with punctuation.

Suggestions

Teachers need to reinforce punctuation minilessons often with teacher demonstrations serving as a quick review. After a shared reading of a Big Book or other enlarged print, teachers also can point out or have children point out periods and other punctuation marks and discuss why they are used. (Calling attention to isolated parts of a text for tutoring purposes should occur only after an enjoyable reading of the text, though.)

Question marks and exclamation points (or "excited" marks) can be introduced in the same manner if teachers see a need for them. However, a minilesson should only be about one thing, so each of these marks should be introduced independently and on separate days.

Using Speech Bubbles or Quotation Marks ("Talking Marks")

Objective
To introduce and discuss with students the purpose of quotation marks.

Introduction of Purpose
Mrs. Williams shows the class some of the children's work that includes speech bubbles. She praises the idea of representing "talk" in this manner. Then she says, "Children, do you know there is another way to show that people are talking? I'm going to show you how to do that today."

Description of Presentation
Mrs. Williams writes, *Last night my cat was chewing on one of my favorite plants. I had to tell him, "Cyrus, you stop that!"*

When Mrs. Williams gets to the part in her demonstration where she would use quotation marks, she stops writing and turns to the children. She says, "Now I want to show you the exact words that I said. I could put them in a speech bubble, but speech bubbles are normally used within pictures. [She shows the class some cartoons with speech bubbles.] When writers want to show the exact words in their stories, they do it with talking marks like this." (She points to the quotation marks in her text.)

Assessment

Just like other punctuation marks, children overgeneralize the use of quotation marks at first. However, quotation marks are introduced so children will know what they are when they see them in text, not so they will use them correctly. Indeed, whether the children use these marks or not is up to the children.

Suggestions

On subsequent days, Mrs. Williams shows the children books with "talking marks" and comic strips with speech bubbles. The children gradually get the idea of the appropriate place to use quotation marks (i.e., in text) and speech bubbles (i.e., with drawings). Also, they begin to understand that certain words and phrases like *she said* must precede the quotation marks in text.

Some teachers introduce the term "quotation marks" in the initial minilesson or in a subsequent minilesson. Some kindergarten teachers do not introduce the term at all, content with calling quotes "talking marks." I usually introduce the term and break it down into syllables. I explain that the term means that someone is talking. I tell children that they may use this term or the term "talking marks." Some children enjoy using "grown-up" terms such as quotation marks from time to time.

Temple and colleagues (1988) as well as Calkins (1994) inform teachers that it is common for kindergartners to put dialogue in their writing. When teachers observed that students are incorporating dialogue in their writing, they should introduce quotation marks.

Using Kid Spelling

Objective

To encourage all students to use invented spelling when many children are demonstrating it in their writing. (This minilesson should take place when most of the students are in the Semiphonetic spelling or Phonetic spelling stages.)

Introduction of Purpose

"Kindergartners, I see many of you making up spellings of words you can't spell, and I am so pleased. When you make up spellings like these [shows some samples of work observed], I call it 'kid spelling.' Kid spelling is wonderful because it allows you to get all your precious ideas down on paper, and it will help you become a good speller."

Description of Presentation

Ms. Neuenfeldt says, "Did you know that grownups and teachers can't spell all words correctly? When they can't spell a word and want to keep writing, they use kid spelling, too. The words I am going to use today in my writing I can spell, but I am going to let you help me spell a word with kid spelling."

Ms. Neuenfeldt writes, *I saw some trees with blue bags on their trunks. Someone must be making (maple) syrup.*

When Ms. Neuenfeldt comes to the word *maple*, she asks her students to help her spell it. First she says, "Let's stretch the word out like a piece of bubblegum." She says the word slowly and asks the children what they hear. Often, this is all that is required for students to identify the beginning sound. However, if they have trouble, Ms. Neuenfeldt is more direct and asks, "What sound do we hear at the beginning of *maple*?" (*Maple* is a good word to have the children spell because its long-vowel sound and surface consonants are heard easily.) The children answer /m/. (Teachers should use the answer from the majority of the class.)

Next, Ms. Neuenfeldt asks what letter stands for /m/ in *maple*.

At this point, Ms. Neuenfeldt uses interactive writing and asks if someone can write the *m*. If children seem hesitant to print the letter, she asks them to find the *m* on their ABC strips to refresh their memories. (Most children will not have trouble finding the letter on the ABC strip at this point, but if a student does have difficulty, the teacher should have the student ask a friend to help him or her, which encourages a risk-free learning atmosphere.)

Ms. Neuenfeldt continues through the word in a similar manner. If the children happen to say an incorrect letter (which is rarely the case by the middle of the school year), she writes the letter anyway and praises the approximation.

Next, Ms. Neuenfeldt asks the children if they hear anything else in the word. (If the children do not say a sound or letter in order, the teacher places it in the correct order. For example, if students choose the sound or consonant /l/ next, the teacher should say, "Yes, an *l* belongs at the end of the word" and then place it there. Then the teacher can ask for other sounds that the children hear, discuss both the letters that would stand for those sounds and their placement, and place them accordingly.)

Ultimately, the children spell *maple* as *mapl*. Their approximation is put in parentheses next to Ms. Neuenfeldt's correct version of *maple*. Ms. Neuenfeldt then shows the children how close they came to the correct spelling of *maple* and praises them for their wonderful effort. She also congratulates them on how much they learned from the beginning of the year—when they couldn't hear sounds or write many letters.

Assessment

"Getting Ready" teaches children how to isolate sounds and how to find letters of the alphabet, and writing workshop provides practice, so most children are ready for kid spelling around the end of November or December. This is an ability that the teacher wants all children to acquire, so through practicing writing, as well as repeating minilessons such as this one, all children can be expected to use kid spelling by the end of the year.

Suggestions

In the beginning of the year, when Ms. Neuenfeldt demonstrated her own writing, she spelled all the words correctly. However, as students begin to use invented spelling, Ms. Neuenfeldt begins to include a few words using invented spelling in her teacher demonstrations, with the exception of high-frequency words. The teacher should always spell high-frequency words correctly to prevent children from learning them incorrectly.

Using the term *kid spelling* gives hesitant children a better feeling about making approximations. It sends children the message that it's OK to take risks with spelling. Parents like the term, too, because it helps them realize that their children will not always spell this way—the stage is only temporary.

Later in the year, the teacher can add another strategy to spelling. In addition to the children listening to sounds to write letters as they spell, the teacher can ask children to close their eyes and try to picture the word, too.

Forgetting the Spaces

Objective

To help children understand the importance of leaving spaces between their words. (This minilesson is appropriate for students in the Phonetic stage who indicate a knowledge of word separation.)

Introduction of Purpose

Mrs. Poirier says, "I've noticed that you are writing some great stories, but I am having trouble reading them because there are no spaces between the words." (She points to spaces between words in a Big Book as she says this.)

Description of Presentation

Mrs. Poirier demonstrates her writing but leaves no spaces between her words. Children make note of this immediately by saying, "Mrs. Poirier, we can't read your words because they're all 'smooshed' together."

Mrs. Poirier then proceeds to make slashes for the spaces, and she and the children count the words in her sentence as Mrs. Poirier holds up a finger for each word counted. Next, she and the children count the total number of fingers (or words). Then, she repeats her sentence, and starting at the beginning of the sentence, she makes a line for each word with a generous space between it and the next word. Finally, she completes each line she made with the appropriate words of her sentence. To reinforce what she's done, she repeats the steps she used:

1. Count the number of words in your sentence.
2. Make a line for each word, and leave a space between lines.
3. Write your words on the lines.

Assessment

Until teachers observe that students are in the Phonetic stage (see chapter 2) or Taking Inventory stage (see chapter 3), they are not ready developmentally to understand or use spaces in their written language.

Suggestions

When Mrs. Williams observes that many of her children are in the Phonetic stage of spelling and their concept of word segmentation is emerging, she demonstrates forgetting spaces at least once in her daily writing demonstrations. When Mrs. Williams "goofs" and forgets a space, the children delight in reminding her of what she has to do. She finds this type of "teacher reminding demonstration" to be most effective. Spacing is a difficult concept to learn, and it should not be taught until children are developmentally ready for it.

Kindergarten teachers should not be overly concerned about spacing. It is a developmental process and will happen within writing and reading workshops (Calkins, 1994, 2001).

Summary

It may seem that utilizing these minilessons takes forever to teach anything, especially when we, as teachers, are so used to thinking that "telling" solves problems. Telling sometimes makes a problem go away temporarily, but it is still lurking under the surface. Minilessons of the nature just described not only help solve writing problems in the classroom but also enable students to solve their own writing problems throughout their education and possibly even their lives. These minilessons epitomize a saying by Chinese philosopher Confucius that I have come to fully appreciate: "I hear and I forget. I see and I remember. I do and I understand."

Minilessons can be done in several ways, but the most powerful minilesson of all is a teacher demonstrating her or his own writing. When I first started working with kindergarten teachers, many of them were concerned about which minilessons to teach. I reminded them that demonstrations of their own writing are minilessons in themselves. Once kindergarten teachers have implemented a writing workshop for a few months and have read the appropriate research (provided in chapters 1, 2, 3, and 7), they begin to see the many needs children have. Then they say, "I don't know why I asked for a list of minilessons because everything's a minilesson!"

When teachers keep children's developmental level of spelling and writing in mind, writing needs concerning procedures, content, strategy, and skills can be taught with minilessons. Teachers must constantly assess the success of the minilessons they've taught to guide future instruction. Chapter 7 provides more information on assessment leading instruction.

Assessment, Evaluation, and Reporting

The grandmother plaited her granddaughter's hair and then she said, "Get your lunch. Put it in your bag. Get your apple. You come straight back after school, straight home here. Listen to the teacher," she said. "Do what she say."

Her grandfather was out on the step. He walked down the path with her and out to the footpath. He said to a neighbor, "Our granddaughter goes to school. She lives with us now."

"She's fine," the neighbor said. "She's terrific with her two plaits in her hair."

"And clever," the grandfather said. "Writes every day in her book."

"She's fine," the neighbor said.

The grandfather waited with his granddaughter by the crossing and then he said, "Go to school. Listen to the teacher. Do what she say."

When the granddaughter came home from school her grandfather was hoeing around the cabbages.

Her grandmother was picking beans. They stopped their work.

"You bring your book home?" the grandmother asked.

"Yes"

"You write your story?"

"Yes"

"What's your story?"

"About butterflies"

"Get your book, then. Read your story."

The granddaughter took her book from her school bag and opened it.

"I killed all the butterflies," she read. "This is me and this is all the butterflies."

"And your teacher like your story, did she?"

"I don't know."

"She said butterflies are beautiful creatures. They hatch out and fly in the sun. The butterflies visit all the pretty flowers, she said. They lay their eggs and then they die. You don't kill butterflies, that's what she said."

The grandmother and grandfather were quiet for a long time, and their granddaughter, holding her book, stood quite still in the warm garden.

"Because you see," the grandfather said, "your teacher she buys all her cabbages from the supermarket and that's why."

From Grace, P. (1988). Butterflies. In *Electric City*, p. 15. New York: Penguin.

When I first read "Butterflies," I got angry. I could not understand why the teacher hadn't asked the girl why she killed all the butterflies (actually moths). Even though my assessment of literacy at the time did not include observing or inquiring about process, my beliefs about literacy education did. My beliefs were ahead of my knowledge base of literacy.

When I recall my previous means of assessment in the primary grades, I remember judging product without observing process most of the time as I made red slashes on my students' papers. Worse yet, I often assessed workbooks and worksheets as if they were important to the reading process, when in truth they were mostly "busy work" consisting of isolated skills that rarely transferred to reading (Chomsky, 1975; Clay, 1991; Ferreiro, 1981; Harste et al., 1981; Holdaway, 1979; Krashen, 1996). Even though my observations of my students' reading progress made me doubt they were learning anything from these papers and books, I felt accountable using them; I knew other teachers, parents, and administrators embraced them.

Once I gained teaching experience and confidence, I replaced reading workbooks and worksheets with a classroom library of age-appropriate, recommended literature that included many books I'd loved as a child. I wanted my students to experience a love of reading books as I did. I allowed students a choice of reading material and a large block of time for reading, and I moved around the classroom guiding students in their process of reading. The basals my students had been forced to read before my transition now became optional, and they didn't fare well. Although some of these basals contained classic stories, my students preferred the rich language in the original texts that was missing in the basals so the basals could provide easier vocabulary.

Every Friday, I held a share session. Children could present their book reviews in more than 100 ways, which served as enticement for other children to read the books their classmates shared, and it was an entertaining form of assessment as well. Roller movies (i.e., presentation of story scenes on a large roll of paper, which is unrolled scene by scene), flannel board stories, and plays (sometimes with costumes) were weekly events, and they were all at the children's initiative. An hour of sharing grew into a whole afternoon of sharing. The children loved it, and they were highly engaged in reading.

For some of the children this meant reading books they could read at their independent reading levels, which made them stronger readers. When I'd taken a job as a reading tutor one summer I had observed the positive results of practicing reading text that was familiar but also offered some challenge. So I allowed book choices that might have been considered below grade level for some children. Every child read at least 10 books a month; we kept track of this on a reading bulletin board for all to see.

I must admit I was frightened to make such drastic changes. I hoped that the principal would not make a surprise visit to my classroom during free choice reading and sharing time because I was definitely not following the prescribed reading curriculum. However, I felt accountable to my students. They loved their new reading program, and they and I could see that all students were making reading progress.

The formal proof of my students' reading interest and their reading progress was evidenced in their reading tests in the spring; their scores had improved dramatically in comparison with their scores from the previous year. Administrators took note; they also had heard positive comments from parents. I was even asked to write the curriculum for the next year. I used my observations, knowledge about reading, and love for reading to change my reading program so that I could be accountable to the children.

However, I did not change my language arts curriculum (which was thought to be separate from reading at the time). When my students wrote (usually only once a week), I chose the topic and I evaluated the product by assessing spelling, mechanics, and proper usage; I rarely considered content. Because I had no prior knowledge of writing as a process, it never occurred to me to teach it as a process. My students learned to hate writing just like I did.

Today, many teachers realize their instructional and assessment practices need to be based on more than previous instructional methods or a packaged program, and they realize their assessments need to lead learning and not just identify good readers and struggling readers. They want to change methods and assessments to be consistent with their beliefs so they can be accountable for their students' literacy learning, but they are frightened about how to do it. I understand their fearful state. Although reading and understanding current literacy research takes time, it is necessary to provide the strong support teachers need to make changes that are consistent with teachers' beliefs about learning (Routman, 2000).

All educators need to be enlightened as to why and how the young child learns to become literate. It is necessary to understand that all literacy is learned in the same manner that a child learns to talk (Cambourne, 1988; Clay, 2001). This requires knowledge of the developmental stages involved in learning literacy, especially those of writing and spelling (see chapters 1–3). A solid understanding of literacy theory is necessary for teachers to know what to assess and how to evaluate those assessments to improve instruction (Routman, 2000). It takes time to read and understand research regarding literacy, but it is necessary to make instruction, assessment, and evaluation processes consistent with beliefs about literacy education.

When students do not learn to read and write in school, they often are not successful in or beyond school. Knowing the why and how of research allows teachers to guide all students to be literate, and teachers can be accountable not only to students but also to parents, administrators, and society in general.

Being Accountable

Parents, administrators, and society expect schools to educate students to be literate. They consider this to be the primary function of schools, yet Clay (as cited in Calkins, 2001) states that 20% of U.S. students do not know how to read (or write and spell) at a level that a high school education and diploma would indicate—in fact, some of these children drop out of school and do not even get a diploma.

Employers, parents, administrators, and society in general demand accountability from their schools and their teachers. They demand this accountability in the form of standardized tests. Unfortunately, as Routman (2000) states, "[T]oo few [teachers, parents, students, and other stakeholders] understand how 'standards' are determined, how standardized tests are constructed, and what the scores mean" (p. 560). Although there is a place for well-constructed standardized tests (for example, Clay's [1993a] Dictation Test discussed later in this chapter), these tests need to be combined with other methods of assessment. Doing well on such a test is not a goal in itself; the goal is to have readers and writers who communicate and comprehend messages.

So while a test score might look good, it *must* be supported by other measures. For example, in a writing workshop, samples of writing are kept from the first day of school to the last. Real growth can be seen in these samples. (See, for example, the first three spelling samples on the Developmental Spelling Chart in Appendix C, which shows the growth of one kindergartner who couldn't even write his name in September to being able to write a self-initiated sentence in April.) When real growth is evidenced in writing samples as well as in well-constructed standardized tests, students will be able to read and write and schools will have the accountability they need to report to parents, administrators, and the public.

To be accountable for students' literacy learning in school, assessments must be made that serve the information needs of those who use them. There are three different levels or groups who use assessments (Stiggens, 2001):

1. students, their teachers, and parents;
2. decision makers who provide professional development for teachers; and
3. policymakers.

Level One: Students, Their Teachers, and Parents

The first question teachers must answer is "To whom are we accountable?" First and foremost, teachers need to be accountable to their students. From the time a student enters school, he or she looks to the teacher for evidence of success. If that early evidence shows progress and increments of success, the student develops a sense of confidence and expectation that he or she can and will learn to be literate (Stiggens, 2001). Students, teachers, and parents use the results of student assessments to guide students' improvement and to decide if the student has learned enough by measuring the level of success every quarter and ultimately at the end of the year (Stiggens, 2001). Teachers and students, as well as parents, can and will feel accountable for students' success when proper literacy assessments that lead learning are made.

Level Two: Decision Makers Who Provide Professional Development

The second level of accountability consists of instructional and resource support from the teacher's department, building, district, or beyond to help teachers in curricular and professional development. This support promotes learning about current and new literacy research from workshops, inservice sessions, and most important, from ongoing programs that hire literacy coaches to aid staff development (Routman, 2000). Ways of providing this support follow.

Literacy Coaches and Teachers Supporting Teachers

Ongoing literacy training is necessary for teachers' professional development. This training should not only provide information to teachers but also the time and the knowledge to practice the information (Routman, 2000). Thus, it is important to utilize literacy coaches, peer coaching, and teacher support groups.

As a literacy coach, I always recommend that teachers continue to read and discuss current research presented in various formats (e.g., the International Reading Association's [IRA] journal *The Reading Teacher*). I also advocate teacher support groups in which teachers meet in groups on a weekly basis to discuss successes, "snags," suggestions, and solutions that concern the teaching of literacy in writing and reading workshops. In the larger schools in which I worked, groups were made up entirely of kindergarten teachers. In the smaller schools, these groups were made up of K–2 teachers. Teachers often met during their lunch hour or after school, and some principals even provided school time for meetings.

It is important to know what books to read and where to look for reliable literacy research. Literacy coaches can be resources to teachers in this endeavor. For example, I remember a kindergarten teacher from a neighboring school district asked me what books their newly formed literacy study group should read. I recommended what I usually recommend that kindergarten and first-grade teachers read: *The Art of Teaching Writing* (Calkins, 1994) and *The Art of Teaching Reading* (Calkins, 2001). *The Foundations of Literacy* (Holdaway, 1979) is a favorite of K–1 teacher study groups, too, and to understand the acquisition of literate behavior, I recommend *Becoming Literate: The Construction of Inner Control* (although it's difficult reading; Clay, 1991) and *Change Over Time: In Children's Literate Development* (Clay, 2001).

Administrators Supporting Teachers

Currently in many schools, the principal of a school is held accountable for the results on literacy tests in the school by the policymakers in the school district. Parents also demand results that are more tangible—they want to see their children actually reading and writing. Principals have a lot at stake, and according to Routman (2000), they want teachers in their schools to teach in a way that "respects the needs and interests of students while promoting inquiry and high-level learning" (p. 590). As a literacy coach, this desire has certainly been evident to me with most of the principals with whom I have had the good fortune to work. These principals also promoted peer coaching and writing workshop in their schools.

Although I personally do not have much experience in peer coaching (i.e., when one teacher observes a peer teacher as he or she teaches, and then together they discuss ways of improvement), I firmly believe that teachers should work together in sharing ideas they have found to be useful. Many of the teachers with whom I have worked were actively involved with peer coaching, and their principals promoted it. I will, however, note that there can be two drawbacks to peer coaching: (1) Teachers have to be willing to give and receive advice in a spirit of moving forward and not take it as criticism, and (2) teachers have to be willing to learn about current research and be willing to change their thinking and not continue to do things because "that's the way it's always been done." Literacy coaches can be very helpful in overcoming these hurdles and in keeping teachers knowledgeable about current literacy.

Although I recommend peer coaching, I believe it needs to take a secondary position to writing workshop. My main concern as a literacy consultant and coach has always been making writing workshops a priority in every classroom because nothing does more to promote literacy learning—the very essence of education. The principals with whom I have worked have been very supportive of writing workshops and of me coaching it in their schools. For example, Jeff Reiche truly understood the importance of writing workshop and made it a priority during the time teachers were learning about writing workshop; in fact, no other new programs were introduced during this time. Jeff Reiche even substituted for Mrs. Clark and Mrs. Williams once a week during nap time so they could meet with me in an undisturbed setting to discuss the "why" behind what I or they had just demonstrated in their kindergarten writing workshops. Also, when these kindergarten teachers told him of their difficulties in scheduling big blocks of time in the morning for writing workshops, he told them to do the best they could that year. However, when he worked on the schedule for the following year, he consulted with these teachers first and let them have first choice of where and when to schedule the specialists coming to their school. Mr. Reiche gave these kindergarten teachers scheduling priorities because he understood that writing in the first 18 months of learning to read is of major importance to children's developing literacy (Robinson, 1973), and he agreed that a sound literacy foundation is mandatory in kindergarten for optimum future literacy development of all children (Clay, 2001).

The overwhelming majority of the more than 60 kindergarten teachers with whom I've worked support big blocks of time in the morning for writing and reading workshops; kindergartners write and read best in the morning when they are fresh. Clay (2001) agrees on the necessity of making writing as easy as possible for kindergartners because writing teaches every kind of inner control needed by the successful reader (especially to the students who struggle with literacy tasks). If a school's administration is not aware of this research (presented in chapter 1), kindergarten teachers need to present and discuss this research with them and present dated writing samples illustrating students' literacy development. If a literacy coach or consultant is available, he or she should lead teachers in this presentation.

Level Three: Policymakers

The third and final level of accountability is for policymakers (i.e., superintendents, school boards, and public officials); these are the people who usually establish literacy and other content area achievement levels. Ultimately, a school district's academic standing is based on the decisions these policymakers make. These decisions require a certain amount of testing in an area to "find out if a program is working, how students are doing nationally, or whether a student qualifies for a special program" (Routman, 2000, p. 560). Also, low literacy test scores may prohibit a school from getting state funding, result in probation, or result in principals and teachers being removed from a school (Routman, 2000). Demand for test results is understandable, but in too many cases across the United States, policymakers are making an enormous investment of time and materials into testing to meet standards that are "difficult to use" or "not equitable" or "rigorous enough" to lead to "inquiry" and the complex thinking and deeper understanding that literacy learning requires (Routman, 2000, pp. 586–587).

The Need for Performance-Based Reading and Writing Standards and Samples

Routman (2000) explains, "While there are lots of standards documents in place, there is little evidence that standards themselves are raising student performance levels in ways that involve deep and enduring understanding" (p. 586). Standards that spell out what a student should know but do not provide guidance on how to assess whether or not the student meets the standard are not too helpful (Routman, 2000). Quality literacy standards should oblige schools and teachers to focus on how well students are actually learning to read and write, not on passing one test that may not really assess a child's literacy knowledge (Finn, Petrilli, Cheney, & Vanourek, 1998; Gardner, 1998). One test on one specific day cannot truly assess a child's knowledge like keeping writing samples throughout the year can. I remember Principal Jeff Reiche asking me about a child's poor results on a literacy test because he thought the child was a good student. The child was not feeling well on the day of the test; if we had not had his writing samples to verify his progress, it would have been difficult to prove on paper. However, the child could have easily proven it in person.

According to Tucker and Codding (1998), performance-based standards are quality standards because they "enable teachers, students, and parents to judge whether a particular piece of student work actually meets the standard" (p. 56). Performance-based standards include (a) a description of what students must know and be able to do (the content standard), (b) samples that show what kind of work meets the standard, and (c) commentaries that explain the features of what that work should look like (Tucker & Codding, 1998). Tucker and Codding explain:

> Including samples of student work is the key to making the standard usable by teachers, children, and parents. Any student should be able to look at a [writing] performance standard [with its accompanying sample and commentary] and say, "I understand now. I can learn to do that." (p. 56)

(See chapter 3 for descriptions and samples of the five stages of written language in kindergarten.)

For teachers to be accountable for all their students' writing progress, teachers must determine if students are progressing. Teachers must be able to *show* that their students know more at the end of the year than at the beginning. This is the true measure of standards at any level whether it be local, state, or national.

The Need for Quality Performance Tests

Routman (2000) reports, "It is now the norm in many schools across the [United States] for teachers to focus not on teaching and learning essential concepts, but on having their students pass tests designed to measure whether standards are being met" (p. 588). In too many cases this leads to a fixation on skills. Yet "There is *no* evidence that testing and preparation for [these] tests helps to develop literacy" (Krashen, 1996, p. 444).

To select worthy tests, noted educator, professor, and writer Howard Gardner (1998) suggests that the following questions, which I have adapted, be applied to any proposed test:

- Does accepted current research recognize the focus of the test as indisputably important to learning to communicate in written language?

- Does it test students' writing knowledge and skills directly by having students write, or by other methods? (Asking students to choose the best of four writing samples presented on a test would not be considered a direct test of their writing ability.)

- Do teachers have the knowledge and training to be able to help students acquire the ability and skills to become better writers? Have they read the research? Do they know how to implement effective writing workshops?

- Could students who do well on this test do well on a different sort of exam that presumably tests the same ability or skill? (If students do well on this exam, would their daily writing samples support the exam's outcome?)

For testing the ability of students in 1st grade through 12th grade to communicate a message effectively, Routman (2000) advocates a writing performance test initiated by a standardized writing prompt. (See Routman, pp. 226–229, for more information on this prompt.) Noted middle school literacy educator and author Linda Reif (1992) agrees that this type of writing assessment is closer to the writing students experience in the classroom and the real world. I concur with Routman's and Reif's suggestions. Furthermore, I believe that teachers in grades 1–12 will find knowledge of the scoring procedures that Routman outlines beneficial for not only assessing writing tests but also in providing guidance in teachers' daily assessments of writing samples, too.

Routman (2000) outlines scoring procedures as follows: Scoring is done with a rubric; based on performance standards; and created by a district-wide, cross-grade-level scoring committee that includes at least one representative from each school and every grade level. These performance standards include the following:

- a succinct description of what students must know and be able to do,

- samples of student work to create a vivid image of what kind of work meets the standards, and

- commentaries on those samples that explain the features that cause them to meet the standards.

Routman (2000) also adds that "while a writing prompt is a good way to get started looking at the 'big picture' of writing, the most reliable and useful information comes from examining students' authentic day-to-day writing samples" (p. 229). That is why Mr. Reiche often asks kindergarten (and all his) teachers to share and discuss student writing samples with him when any student literacy test scores seem inappropriate.

To test the emergent skill level of kindergartners' writing (and reading), see the section "Formal Assessment Tools," p. 253. To test kindergartners' development in spelling as well as in communicating a message in written language, teachers should review and assess dated writing samples from the beginning of the year to the end of the year.

Comparing kindergartners' writing samples from different points in the year to the Five Stages of Written Language Development chart in Appendix

C is more appropriate than using writing prompts, which are the recommended method of writing assessment for grades 1–12. Also, to assess kindergartners' spelling development, selected samples from throughout the year could be compared to the Five Stages of Developmental Spelling chart in Appendix C. (See chapters 2 and 3 for information on developmental stages of spelling and writing.)

Testing is the avenue most policymakers and administrators take to try to ensure that literacy is being taught properly in schools. They rely on these tests because they often do not understand how the young child learns to be literate. Unfortunately, most policymakers and administrators lack university training and experience in early childhood education; therefore, they don't always choose the most appropriate forms of testing for young children. Early childhood educators need to communicate effectively about developmentally appropriate assessment and evaluation (Routman, 2000). In addition to communicating, they need to support their words with authentic evidence that students are indeed succeeding in writing, spelling, and reading (Stiggens, 2001). For example, as a literacy consultant and university instructor, I had read about and taught the values of writing workshop. I had come to believe in the theory of writing workshop, but I had never implemented one. Like my university students, I had a lot of questions about application, so in 1993, I decided to give writing workshop a try.

I made an appointment with the superintendent of my local school district to ask permission to test writing workshop in the school district. He gave me a very wise directive followed by an equally wise question: "I not only want you to teach students how to write; I want you to teach them a love of writing. I want to hear from parents that their kids are writing at home because they enjoy it. Can your writing workshop do that?"

I replied, "I'm sure it can!" (I had learned I could trust the research.) I also told him I would show him writing samples and tests at the end of the trial period to prove it.

Because I did not have any samples of my own as yet, I showed him samples that illustrated spelling progression and development in Gentry and Gillet's (1993) *Teaching Kids To Spell*, and alphabetic progression and development on Clay's (1993a) Dictation Test in *An Observation Survey of Early Literacy Achievement*. I explained the significance of these samples as I presented them. This was the hard evidence that convinced the superintendent to let me try writing workshops; words alone might not have been sufficient.

The results of my yearlong project were quite remarkable. Many children did write at home, and they brought things to school of their own accord, such as the writing by a kindergartner about his farm shown in Figure 47. I'm pretty sure this was a joint effort on the part of the boy and his parents, but what a wonderful way to learn literacy and bond at the same time!

Although writing from home is certainly a part of good assessment, I wanted something more concrete and all encompassing, so I pretested and

Figure 47. Student's Writing Sample

the cow is
EatiNg silAje.
ANd cow isWheN The
DONe
she will go
ovt side. Brandon Thurs

posttested the children from the two classrooms in which I was working (a kindergarten class and a first-grade class) using Clay's (1993a) Dictation Test and Robinson's (1973) Writing Vocabulary Test. Like the two classroom teachers who volunteered to allow me to work in their classrooms, I volunteered my time to do this action research.

The teachers were impressed with their students' progress during and at the end of the year. Dated writing samples and test results verified students' success in the classroom. The superintendent, the personnel director, and the curriculum director were impressed, too, and they asked me if I would consider coaching one elementary school the next year with pay for my consulting duties. I accepted, not because I was concerned about the payment, but because I cared deeply about proving to this school system that writing workshop is essential to students'—especially kindergarten students'—ability to read, write, and spell.

After a year, results in this elementary school were similar to my test classrooms, and the superintendent and the school board decided writing workshop should be implemented in all elementary classrooms in the district.

In 1966 I did not have the knowledge to approach anyone about my methods of teaching reading. However, in 1993 I believed my knowledge of literacy research would allow me to make useful assessments to improve the process as well as the product of students' writing, which it did. Now, in 2006, this knowledge has enabled kindergarten teachers to employ this method with their students to not only meet district expectations but also to meet standards set by the state.

Meeting standards and being accountable requires teachers to make meaningful assessments and evaluations that have an impact on instruction. Therefore, the remainder of this chapter is devoted to (a) assessment—definition, methods, criteria, purpose, and tools (informal and formal); (b) evaluation—definition, recording, and filing; and (c) reporting—to parents and administrators.

Assessment

Definition of Assessment

Assessment refers to data collection and the gathering of evidence as we take into account the individual's range of development in the process of learning (Routman, 2000). The word *assessment* is derived from the Latin term *assidere*, which means to sit beside someone. Routman (2000) explains that "By sitting right next to the child, we observe his strengths and weaknesses, how he thinks and solves problems, how he performs simple and complex tasks" in the process of learning (p. 557). Understanding this is important to choosing a proper method of assessment.

Assessment Methods

Quality assessment that measures learning isn't a single method accomplished only by viewing a finished product. No one assessment measure should be given "complete and total weight and treated as an end in itself," as so many standardized tests are (Routman, 2000, p. 561). The purpose of assessment is to know the child so well that teaching responds to the child's individual needs.

For teachers to choose the proper methods of assessments, they must know the purpose for and the target of their assessments, because there are many kinds of assessments. However, there are four basic assessment methods to analyze student proficiency in the classroom: (1) selected response, (2) essay, (3) performance-based assessment (also known as process assessment), and (4) personal communication (Stiggens, 2001). In the following sections, each of these methods is discussed with the idea of matching the testing method with its target (Stiggens, 2001).

Selected Response

This method includes all objectively scored pencil-and-paper tests formats, which include the following items: multiple choice, true or false, matching, and short answer. These tests are used to measure student mastery of facts, concepts, and sometimes generalizations, especially in the areas of history, science, vocabulary, and spelling. A problem with these tests is that although some students might have knowledge of facts and concepts, they may score poorly because they are not proficient enough in reading.

Essay

This method entails students preparing an original written answer to a specific question or questions. This method is required when the knowledge being tested is defined by larger concepts and generalizations than a simple selected response assessment can measure. This method may present difficulties in scoring because teachers must be subjective about judging quality. Also, students need to have a certain level of writing proficiency. Students may have the required knowledge but not be able to communicate it effectively in written language.

Performance-Based Assessment

In this method, students do some kind of performance task and then the teacher uses a set of scoring guides to determine the quality of achievement demonstrated. Performance-based assessments can be based on observations of the process when students are demonstrating it as they work at the task, or in the evaluation of the product created. Stiggens (2001) states, "The best way to assess writing proficiency is to rely on performance assessment and have students create written products" (p. 94). However, the problem in using performance-based assessment by itself in assessing writing is that the match between performance and mastery of content knowledge is not always a strong one. For example, a child might understand the concept of word but might not demonstrate it in his or her writing with spaces. I recall such an instance when I first noticed a child's written product had dots between the words. I asked the child about the dots and discovered this was the child's creative way of separating her words. Therefore, the key point to remember when using performance-based assessment is that the teacher needs to combine this method with another type of assessment (preferably personal communication assessment) in order to understand why a student may have failed to adequately communicate or demonstrate his or her actual knowledge in writing (Stiggens, 2001). Calkins (1994), Clay (2001), Cudd and Roberts (1994), Graves (1994), and a host of other researchers state that the process of writing as well as the product of writing needs to be analyzed to make quality instructional changes that will ultimately improve both product and process.

Personal Communication Assessment

One of the most common methods teachers use to gather information about their students is to talk to them and ask them questions. Typically, teachers don't think of this as assessment, but it is a primary source of assessment in job interviews, conferences, and even conversations (Stiggens, 2001). It is necessary to add direct personal communication assessment to performance-based assessment to determine the reasons students are excelling or struggling when they are involved in the process of completing a product. Teachers need to use personal communication in writing conferences to determine not only why but also how to help the child. Stiggens (2001) states that "a primary reason why large-scale standardized assessments, whether objective tests or performance assessments, have historically had so little impact on teachers in classrooms is that they do not provide the teacher with the reasons for student failure" (p. 96), and they fail to suggest actions the teacher can follow to help the student improve. They only reveal a score.

For writing to progress, assessment must be based on process as well as product. When the assessment goal is to find out if students can demonstrate the performance level that written language requires, teachers must observe students while they are exhibiting writing behaviors and make judgments as to the effectiveness of these behaviors. Teachers also must take into account each student's range of development in the process of learning to write (Routman, 2000). Performance-based assessment of the writing process and product followed by personal communication is not done solely in writing workshop but any time the child writes during the day—and it includes anything else that a teacher might observe about the child that would be helpful in "knowing the child" (as in the "Butterflies" example that opened this chapter).

To know children requires that personal communication assessment be used along with performance-based assessment because the best assessments ask young children to explain and justify their work, not just do it. Talking to and questioning the child allows teachers to know what knowledge the child has and how the child is using it as he or she tries to write (Stiggens, 2001). Personal communication assessment is especially important in writing workshops on those days in the week that the teacher cannot observe a child's process of writing. By looking at the product and using personal communication to question the child about something in the product, the teacher can gain an understanding of the child's thinking process. An example follows:

Near the end of conferring time, the kindergarten teacher notices that one child has little work on his paper except for a circle and the letter *P*, which he is tracing over and over again. Thinking he might be wasting time, the teacher asks the child in a kindly and curious manner why he is making his *P* so black. He replies, "I'm showing the 'big' noise my balloon made when it popped!" After applauding his creativity, his teacher shows him another way to show strong feeling by demonstrating an exclamation mark on a sticky note, which she gives to him to keep.

In addition to revealing deep and creative thinking, another advantage to using personal communication assessment is that it teaches the child to ask questions of him- or herself. Young authors need to learn to anticipate readers' questions to progress as writers (Harwayne, 2001). An example follows:

Near the end of the kindergarten year, Mrs. Clark hears a young author say, "Oops, I forgot to put my dog's name in. I know the kids will ask me that." Thinking about readers' questions is crucial to good writing and is a good strategy to learn. Mrs. Clark records this comment (strategy), and along with the sample, saves it in the child's writing portfolio.

Saving writing samples that only show final results with no understanding of how those results came to be or what they mean to future writing progress is not being accountable to students, parents, or administrators. Performance-based assessment and personal communication assessment are designed to probe what students actually do as they write—the decisions they make and the strategies that they use—rather than only making a judgment on the final product (Tompkins, 1994).

To be able to make good performance and personal communication assessments concerning children's writing development, it is necessary to know what criteria are important to the development of communicating messages in written language.

Assessment Criteria

Table 9 lists some of the concise instructional and assessment writing criteria that kindergarten teachers such as Mrs. Clark and Mrs. Williams have used as a basis for their assessments. This list is based on the research of Calkins (1994), Clay (1991), Gentry and Gillet (1993), Graves (1994), Harste and colleagues (1981), Morrow (1989), and Temple and colleagues (1988). It is neither inclusive nor exclusive. For the most part, the same criteria used for instructional purposes also should be used for assessment. Therefore, these criteria are grouped in the same categories as in the minilessons in chapter 6: procedures, content, strategies, and skills.

The list of criteria is so comprehensive that it would prove too cumbersome to use for assessment in its natural state. All the criteria listed are worthy targets, but kindergarten teachers need to know which target to focus on at any given time. In addition to knowing which developmental stages of writing and spelling the child is in and to make unbiased, sound judgments in the classroom that lead learning, Stiggens (2001) recommends teachers' assessments arise from having the following:

- a clear sense of purpose (setting a dominant focus),
- clear and appropriate targets (devising developmentally appropriate checklists and rubrics), and
- samples of dated student's writing (that support the assessment and provide the best view of a student's writing strengths and needs).

Table 9. Writing Assessment Criteria

I. Content
Picture is identifiable
Picture has detail or added information
Picture communicates or informs
Picture and writing communicate the same message
Writing has voice (child tells of own experiences, not Pokémon's or Scooby Doo's)
Writing sounds natural, like speech
Writing makes sense, is about one thing, has focus
Writing has good sequence (order); flows (could it happen that way?)
Writing shows good word choice
Writing has some interesting, descriptive, big words (shows risk taking)
Good conclusion linked to message
If being published, has an interesting title linked to its content

II. Procedures
Writes name and date on writing sample
Follows writing rules
Uses only one side of the paper
Manages time wisely
Keeps a neat writing folder
Finds writing folder quickly and gets to work
Enjoys writing and finds it rewarding; sometimes writes at home
Is helpful to others in explaining procedures
Listens carefully and asks good questions about others' stories (in classroom and Author's Chair)

III. Strategies
Chooses topics easily
Chooses topics by listening to others
Uses books for inspiration in writing
Uses writing to communicate; has a sense of what writing can do
Uses different genres (introduced or not)
Uses "Alphabet Song" and ABC strip to find letters of alphabet
Attempts to read his or her writing in Author's Chair
Can read his or her kid writing; has one-to-one matching of spoken word to printed word
Finger points as he or she reads writing
Rereads writing and writes for sense
Knows writing is for an audience
Can read some published pieces, including classmates'

Uses word wall to spell some words
Uses "Look, Cover, Write, Check" strategy when trying to write high-frequency words introduced in minilessons and displayed on word wall
Confers well and purposefully with others
Is beginning to understand how to evaluate his or her writing
Revisits old pieces of writing to add more or look for ideas

IV. Skills and Conventions
Demonstrates good language abilities such as proper pronunciation and usage, uses some "big words" (Teachers should make note of any health problems that affect auditory discrimination of sounds, words, and sentence structure, as well as slowness to acquire speech.)
Can write name
Good pencil grip (small motor skills)
Can write some names and words correctly
Can write and identify some letters, usually uppercase
Can write and identify some lowercase letters
Can write and identify some digraphs (e.g., *sh, wh, th,* and *ch*)
Willing to spell unknown words by taking risks
Demonstrates phonemic awareness (beginning, end, middle sounds)
Demonstrates that print can represent oral language
Demonstrates understanding and use of the alphabetic principle
Can point to a word in own writing
Recognizes words from own writing in other contexts
Beginning to realize that a word's spelling is always the same
Can locate some spelling references within the room, such as on the word wall
Can spell some high-frequency words correctly
Demonstrates using concepts of print such as:
  • Orientating the page correctly to start writing
  • Managing the overall space of piece of writing paper
  • Demonstrating directionality of top to bottom and left to right
  • Demonstrating use of punctuation marks (e.g., period, question mark, exclamation mark, quotation marks) and capitalizing first letter of word at beginning of sentence
  • Demonstrating concept of word by leaving dots or spaces between words
  • Writing one or more sentences and representing parts of words, such as common endings (e.g., *s* and *ed*) and vowels

A Clear Sense of Purpose
Boyd-Batstone (2004) suggests teachers establish an initial dominant focus based on the content standards of written language in order to provide a clear sense of purpose when conferring with students during writing conferences; this will help resolve two issues: (1) preparing a quality record for standards-based authentic assessment and (2) aiding teachers' limited recording time.

Reviewing content standards to choose a dominant focus will not only help teachers to provide a quality record for standards-based assessment but also to stay focused and avoid distractions not directly related to this focus during writing conferences (Boyd-Batstone, 2004). Once an initial writing focus has been decided on based on a content standard, Boyd-Batstone suggests teachers borrow "key verbs from the content standard" to record data observed during writing conferences; this will save time with on-the-spot composing of anecdotal records (p. 232). For example, key verbs from Wisconsin's state content standards are *communicates* and *writes*. Thus, the initial and ongoing dominant writing focus for kindergartners in this state and most states could be "Communicates messages in written language" or "Writes messages that communicate."

When teachers guide students to write messages that communicate in any way they can, teachers must keep adjusting their assessment and instructional decisions to their students' development in the various stages of written language and spelling (see chapters 2 and 3). To aid in the development of "skills" within these stages so kindergartners' written messages become readable print, teachers also must realize the necessity of teaching and guiding writers to interrelate Clay's (1991) four emergent behaviors (see chapter 1).

The primary emphasis for teachers in conferences should be on helping each student communicate a message that eventually becomes readable and not on recording every criterion. Having a dominant focus and using meaningful verbs on a daily basis (e.g., "chooses topics easily" or "hears beginning sounds") enables teachers to stay on track and keep conferences relatively short as they record their observations using informal assessment tools, which are outlined later in the chapter.

Clear and Appropriate Targets

To help their students write messages that communicate, teachers need to be able to select clear and appropriate targets for each child from the numerous criteria that could be used for writing assessment (see Table 9). Knowing which criteria to target so each kindergartner can communicate a written message effectively is dependent on what standards of performance all kindergartners need to learn and when they need to learn them to effectively communicate written messages (Routman, 2000).

As Mrs. Williams and Mrs. Clark worked toward developing checklists and rubrics, their anecdotal records became a resource for deciding on which criteria to target and when to target them within the kindergarten year. Maintaining a list of clear and appropriate writing targets that have guided teacher observations over a period of weeks or the quarter is recommended (Boyd-Batstone, 2004). For many teachers this listing takes the form of a checklist or rubric. (These forms are discussed in detail in the next section, "Writing Assessment Tools.")

When Mrs. Clark and Mrs. Williams first began to record anecdotal records, they looked for strengths in the child's ability to communicate "content" in his or her written message, and they looked for strengths in the "skills" involved in interrelating Clay's (1991) four emergent reading behaviors. They recorded these strengths.

Then they observed which developmental stage of written language and spelling the child was in and tried to determine which procedure, strategy, skill, or content criterion was most needed at the moment to help the child progress toward the next stage in communicating a message. They recorded this need in the child's anecdotal record.

At the end of a quarter, as these teachers reviewed, analyzed, and interpreted their children's anecdotal records, they began to see a clearer picture of which criteria were most important and when these criteria were important within the quarter. For example, procedural criteria such as following writing rules were very important in the beginning of the first quarter for most children, but strategy criteria such as choosing topics and using the "Alphabet Song" and strip became more important near the end of the first quarter.

As Mrs. Clark and Mrs. Williams became more experienced in analyzing their anecdotal records for "what makes good writing" throughout the year, they began to get a sense of which criteria might define and describe the knowledge and the skills expected of kindergartners at different times in the year. When Mrs. Williams and Mrs. Clark itemized these criteria (performance standards), they developed quarterly checklists and eventually a rubric to aid not only in assessment but also in their future instruction.

Writing Assessment Tools

Teachers use assessment tools to record and compare kindergartners' writing performance to certain standards of writing and to inform the selection of instructional procedures, strategies, and skills to improve content. These tools can be categorized as informal and formal assessments. Informal assessment tools refer to performance-based and personal communication assessments, which include anecdotal records used on a daily or weekly basis and checklists or rubrics normally used on a quarterly basis in kindergarten. Formal assessment tools refer to literacy tests, which are usually administered twice a year: in January and May.

Informal Assessment Tools

Anecdotal Records

When teachers observe their students striving to communicate messages in written language, they make observational notes about their students' writing process and progress. As teachers sit next to the child in a writing conference, they record their observations of the author's writing strengths, weaknesses, and confusions, and how he or she thinks and solves writing problems (Routman, 2000). These notes are called anecdotal records, and according to Boyd-Batstone (2004), focused anecdotal records that "use the lens of content standards for an initial focus" can be a tool for standards-based authentic assessment (p. 230). A yearlong collection of anecdotal records provides a comprehensive picture of a student's writing development (Tompkins & Hoskisson, 1995).

Being a writing teacher calls for developing skill in observing children as they write, deciding what to record, and how to mange this recording (Boyd-Batstone, 2004). It takes one to two years for a teacher to develop assessment skills. Having some insight as to how other kindergarten teachers have handled this task in the past is helpful.

Where to record: Teachers use different organizational schemes to record anecdotal notes. Some teachers write notes on 3" by 5" index cards and make a card file with dividers for each child, some teachers divide a spiral-bound notebook into sections and assign one section per child, and other teachers record comments on sticky notes or forms and place them in folders or portfolios (Tompkins & Hoskisson, 1995).

When to record: As a literacy coach, I advise taking no notes when working with the child. After a writing conference (on my way to the next conference), I briefly record only those things that I feel the writing sample might not remind me of later (Harwayne, 2001). Sometimes it is necessary to quickly jot down a few words that will help me transcribe the child's kid writing on a sticky note when I am still conferring with the child. If the child asks me what I'm doing as I write a transcription of his or her writing, I have found the following comment useful: "What you told me was so interesting, I didn't want to forget it, so I took a few notes." Then I show the child my notes in cursive.

Out of respect for the author's work, it is important not to write on the front of the paper where the child's work is displayed. As Mrs. Clark leaves a conference, she lightly records in pencil on the back of the writing paper what the child said he or she wrote (if it is unreadable). Mrs. Clark prefers copying transcriptions directly on the paper because, in her experience, sticky notes can be difficult to photocopy and often get lost.

How to record: Ideally, young authors' writing should be assessed and evaluated every day. However, as a literacy coach, I recommend doing only a few conferences and assessments on any given day to make conferring manageable; this will give teachers one written assessment per student per week. (Adjustments that include additional conferences and assessments each week may have to be made for students who are struggling.)

Remember the formula I use for conferring? Kindergarten teachers take the number of students in their class (20), divide by the number of days in a week (5), and the answer (4) is the number of students with whom the teacher confers on any given day in a week's time (Crafton, 1991). Some kindergarten teachers preselect the students they will work with on any given day; other teachers do not like to preselect students until there are only a few students remaining. Many teachers prefer to take a quick walk around the room to ensure that all students are busy and then make choices about who they will meet with.

Boyd-Batstone (2004) suggests dividing the students into groups, too, but he suggests dividing the total number of students in the room by four days, so Friday can be a day "to observe the students who were absent or require further observation" (p. 231). Mrs. Clark divides her class into four days of conferences because she likes to use Friday's writing workshop session to guide her kindergartners in choosing their best work for the week to save for quarterly reporting (see "Identifying Good Writing Traits," p. 215, and "Choosing My Best Writing," p. 218). Mrs. Williams, on the other hand, confers with a few students on Friday and has her children pick their best work for the week that day, too. How the teacher divides the class, or even if he or she divides the class, is up to the teacher's discretion.

What to record: All recordings should describe only what has been observed without evaluation or interpretation (Boyd-Batstone, 2004). Initially, it is easy to record too much. That is why it is essential that teachers keep their initial dominant focus (communicating a message) and its byproduct (interrelating Clay's [1991] four emergent reading behaviors) in mind. Once a child's developmental writing and spelling stages are determined, the teacher's anecdotal notes should communicate what a child knows and can do and any confusion the child might have as he or she writes messages that communicate. If it concerns the progress of this dominant focus, the following also could be recorded:

- the "levels of engagement, curiosity or motivational factor" on the part of a child (Boyd-Batstone, 2004, p. 230);
- things that surprise the teacher that he or she wouldn't be able to see from just looking at the product later on (e.g., if the child refers to letters of the alphabet as numbers); and
- the author's management of writing procedures and materials in the classroom.

Once the initial dominant focus has been determined, Boyd-Batstone (2004) recommends using the following considerations for recording assessments:

- Write observable data (what was the student doing?).
- Borrow the key verb from the content standard you've selected.
- Use significant abbreviations.
- Write records in the past tense.
- Don't use the c-word, *can't*; it is enough to record the child "didn't."

- Avoid redundancy (sentences are unnecessary; begin phrases with verbs).
- Support records with examples of evidence.
- Remember "lean is clean: wordy is dirty" (p. 235). Keep your focus.

When teachers have a dominant focus in mind for their assessments, anecdotal notes can also pinpoint problems that need the teacher's direct instruction. This will require choosing clear and appropriate targets that enhance students' writing of messages that communicate.

Checklists

A written language checklist is a list of the objectives and criteria that a teacher and children think are necessary for the children's writing to develop and progress (Morrow, 1989). It is also used to monitor a student's writing progress (Tompkins & Hoskisson, 1995). A checklist is established *before* the children's work is undertaken so the teacher and children know the goal they are working toward and can evaluate work in the process as well as when completed (Routman, 1991).

Although Routman (1991) prefers anecdotal records and narratives to checklists, she suggests that checklists work well "for checking early literacy behaviors—letter–sound knowledge, basic sight words, and print concepts" (p. 321). She also likes checklists when they help put students "in charge of their own learning" (p. 321). For example, students can use checklists to determine if specific content or skills are present in their writing samples before choosing their best work for parent conferences or publishing. (See "Identifying Good Writing Traits," p. 215.)

The problem with teachers filling out a checklist on a daily basis is that most of their time is spent focusing on the list rather than on the children's writing needs. Routman (1991) cautions that checklists devised by someone else never quite fit the teacher or his or her students' needs. This is why Mrs. Williams makes her own checklists—one per quarter (see Appendix E). She uses them to set instructional performance standards and to make judgments to see if her students are on course as she prepares for quarterly reporting. The checklist shown in Appendix E was devised in the first quarter of the 2003 school year and was Mrs. Williams's first attempt at making one. As Mrs. Williams writes anecdotal records this school year and in the future, she carefully thinks about her students' writing progress and notes any criteria that might be necessary to change or add to her quarterly checklists. She also refers to her students' Good Writing Charts (see p. 216).

Checklists developed over time help set performance standards (clear and appropriate targets) that are necessary for children to develop as writers; however, the checklists usually need to be revised throughout the year to assess different levels of writing proficiency and to prevent limiting a teacher's focus. (For this reason, Mrs. Williams prepares a different checklist for each quarter of the school year.)

Rubrics

Fountas and Pinnell (2001) define a rubric as

> A scoring guide used to evaluate the quality of a student's performance. Typically rubrics list written criteria that describe the levels of proficiency on a task. The written descriptions define the task with great specificity and are a useful guide to proficiency. Rubrics may be holistic, or segmented to measure components or traits of a process. (p. 486)

Written language rubrics generally assess writing content and conventions. After using checklists during the first year she implemented writing workshop, Mrs. Clark designed a writing rubric to use with writing workshop because the same writing rubric—one that is carefully developed and evaluated over time—can focus sharply on the right achievement targets as children gain different levels of proficiency in the writing process (Routman, 2000; Stiggens, 2001). (See Appendix E for a sample writing rubric.) Like checklists, rubrics are established *before* the children's work is undertaken, so the teacher and children know the goal they are working toward and can evaluate work in process as well as completed work (Routman, 1991).

According to Stiggens (2001), the targets or criteria of a quality rubric include the following four performance attributes:

1. It is described vividly and understandably.

2. It is well-organized and makes sense, and levels of proficiency progress from weak to strong.

3. It is described clearly with samples to illustrate each level of quality.

4. It yields a consistent rating—that is, if two evaluators judge the same work independently, the same level of proficiency is seen.

For rubrics to provide sound assessment, rubric performance criteria must be complete and compelling:

- Criteria should center on what literacy experts consider important and not simply be a matter of opinion.

- Nothing that experts consider to be key criteria should be left out.

- It should be clear to an evaluator why criteria are included; trivial or unrelated aspects of writing performance should be left out.

- Criteria should be balanced but the most important aspects should be weighed more heavily (Stiggens, 2001).

Although children can give input to help the teacher develop a quality rubric, most kindergarten teachers feel a rubric is too difficult for kindergarten children to use on their own. Routman (2000) suggests the young child develop an informal sheet listing what he or she can do (see "Triangular Conferences," p. 264).

As teachers attempt to select clear and appropriate targets (procedure, content, strategy, and skill criteria) necessary for young authors' writing to progress, they analyze anecdotal records and develop checklists and rubrics that are helpful to assessment and instruction. Checklists and rubrics developed over time by the kindergarten teacher can help the teacher to know which criteria to target at any given time. Standardized writing checklists or rubrics, sometimes furnished by a school district, cannot do this and should not take the place of teacher-developed ones (Calkins, 1994).

Whether a checklist or a rubric is used, teachers need to make their own assessment tool for it to be effective in guiding their instruction. Although looking at someone else's assessment tool may be useful as a catalyst for making one's own, most teachers resist a form that someone else has made (Bomer, 1995), which is actually positive because the value of classroom writing assessment comes from teachers having a deep understanding of research concerning writing processes and instruction, thinking diagnostically, and using assessment information on an ongoing basis to guide their own instruction (Black & William, 1998; Place, 2002; Shepard, 2000).

It is important to remember that *all* forms of informal assessment—anecdotal records and checklists or rubrics—need to be accompanied by the students' dated writing samples. These samples provide visual, concrete support so they are understandable to parents, administrators, and other teachers who might need to see them. These writing samples should not only support the teacher's assessments but also provide the best possible view of each student's writing strengths and developmental needs. In addition to using assessment tools accompanied by dated writing samples, kindergarten teachers also should use formal assessment tools in the form of tests.

Formal Assessment Tools

Formal assessment tools refer to literacy tests that are usually given twice a year: once in January and again in May. Well-constructed tests—such as Clay's Concepts of Print Test, Clay's Letter Identification Test, Robinson's Word Test, and Clay's Dictation Test—assess the child's literacy knowledge, ability to perform the skills involved with writing (and reading) readable print, or both. (These tests are discussed next and can be found in Clay's [1993a] *An Observation Survey of Early Literacy Achievement*.) Many kindergarten teachers or reading teachers give these tests twice during the year because testing in January gives the teacher important assessment data to guide instruction so significant progress can be seen in May's testing results.

Clay's Concepts of Print Test (approximately 10 minutes per child): This test identifies some of the print concepts children should know, such as

- print can represent oral language;
- print has directionality;
- the concepts of letters, words, and punctuation.

This test is given individually and requires one of the following two booklets to complete the test: *Sand* (Clay, 1972a) or *Stones* (Clay, 1972b). To administer the test, the teacher explains to the child that he or she is going to read a story (either *Sand* or *Stones*) and wants the child's help. The teacher asks the child to point to certain features in the book as he or she reads it.

There are 24 items on this test. Some of the items in which the order of the letters or words have been changed are particularly sensitive to changes in the children's visual attention to detail in print. Also, items 12 to 14 increase in difficulty; for example, children should notice the changed word order before a change in first and last letters, or a change in middle letters or letters buried within the word. To score the test, the teacher awards a point for each correct answer; a perfect score is 24 points.

Clay's Letter Identification Test (approximate time, 10 minutes per child): This test checks what letters of the alphabet (both upper- and lowercase) the child knows and can identify. It is not enough to say the child knows some letters; teachers must know exactly what letters are known for instructional purposes. This test consists of showing a child a chart of all the letters, both upper- and lowercase, printed in random order (not alphabetical). The child is asked to read across the lines on the chart. To introduce the task, the child is asked, "What do you call these?" and "Can you find some you know?"

The teacher then points to a letter and asks "What is this one?" Correct responses for the letter *b* would include any of the following:

- the alphabetical name of letter *b;*
- a sound that is acceptable for the letter *b;*
- a response in which the student says, "It begins like...," and then gives a word (e.g., *bat*) that begins with the targeted letter.

Prompting questions that might prove helpful include the following: "Do you know its name?" "What sound does it make?" or "Do you know a word that starts like that?"

The teacher scores the test by awarding one point for every correct letter identified, which includes the two variant forms of *a* and *g* (i.e., a, g), so a total of 54 points is possible.

Robinson's Writing Vocabulary Test (approximate time, 10 minutes per child): This test asks the child to list all the words the child knows how to write beginning with his or her name. The teacher simply tells the child, "Write all the words you know." Prompting of words is allowed, and each completed word scores one point if correctly spelled, with the exception of any words the child might accidentally write and cannot read. For example, if the teacher prompts the word *am* and the child accidentally writes the word *and*, even though it is a word, it would not be counted. To be able to discern this mix-up takes one-on-one testing or a very small group for testing.

Clay's Dictation Test (approximately 10 minutes per child): This test checks a child's ability to hear individual sounds in words (i.e., phonemic awareness). However, it also tests the child's ability to remember the letters of the alphabet, so, in essence, this is a test that checks the child's understanding of the alphabetic principle (sound-to-letter relations).

Figures 48A and B and 49 show two different samples of Clay's Dictation Test: The test was administered in the beginning of the kindergarten year and at the end of the kindergarten year. (Normally, kindergartners are not tested in the beginning of the year; however, for research purposes I needed to test in September, and I also needed to use the same test for a pretest and posttest.)

As Clay's Dictation Test was administered individually to each of these kindergartners, they attempted to write what they heard as the following sentence was read aloud very slowly:

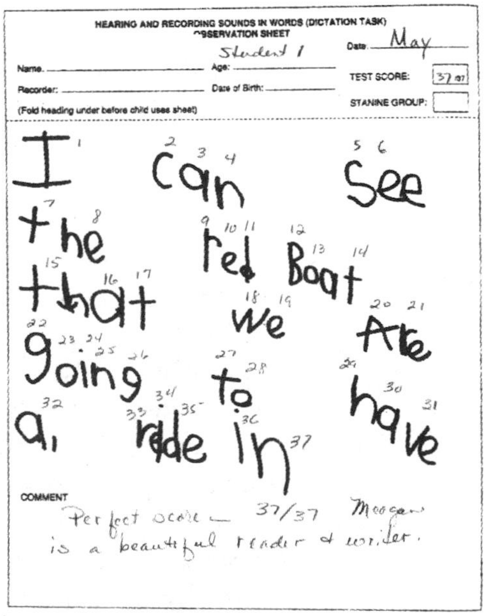

I can see the red boat that we are going to have a ride in.

One point is scored for each *sound* heard and recorded appropriately as a letter. A perfect score is 37.

Figure 48. Clay's Dictation Test: Beginning and End of the Year

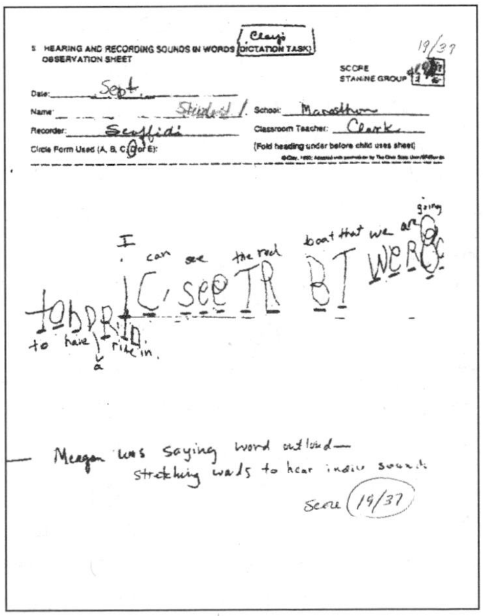

A

B

Figure 49. Clay's Dictation Test: End of the Year

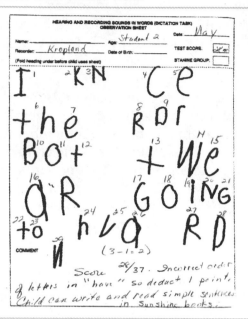

Upon entry to kindergarten, the first student could write her name and had some prior knowledge of the alphabetic principle; this child scored the highest of the class (19/37) at the beginning of the year and at the end of the year had a perfect score (37/37).

The second student could not write his name and made no attempt to record letters for sounds on his first test (which is why no test for the beginning of the year is shown here; the teacher simply wrote the following comment: *Does not hear sounds as yet and has no concept of letters—confuses with numbers*). He scored one of the lowest of the class (0/37) in the beginning of the year, and again at the end of the year (28/37). Yet notice the progress that both students made.

Because kindergarten teachers' time is limited, some teachers administer Robinson's Word Test to the whole class; however, it's best done one on one. Teachers often get a substitute to come in for a day so they can administer (and later score) Clay's Dictation Test and Letter Identification Test individually. Administrators are usually supportive of individual testing when the value of these tests is shown and explained. However, if only one half day can be allotted to testing, many reading teachers (including myself) recommend giving Clay's Dictation Test because it helps teachers know if the child needs work on hearing sounds, learning letters, or both.

If the district requires the reading teacher or reading specialist to administer literacy tests, then the teacher should meet with the test giver and get feedback on each individual's testing process.

These tests carry great weight with administrators as far a documenting kindergartners' writing progress. The results of these tests are considered valid because they are the same no matter who administers the test (provided the tester is knowledgeable about administrating and scoring it). I believe these tests fit Routman's (2000) definition of "standardized" because all students receive the same test, under the same conditions, at approximately the same time (within the same half day), and scoring must be done in the same way.

Analyzing writing tests and writing samples that measure student progress is mandatory to planning useful instruction for both the near future and long range (Miller-Power, 1996). When teachers determine what they need to do to help children move forward, assessment becomes part of evaluation.

Evaluation

Assessment "must serve the learner" (Routman, 2000, p. 559); otherwise, it is pointless. Assessment becomes part of the evaluation process when teachers summarize and interpret data they've collected to make professional judgments that translate into actions to improve their teaching (Routman, 2000). As noted throughout this book, the ongoing focus of assessment in kindergarten is to have young authors write messages that communicate and are readable. Assessments made with this focus in mind must then be evaluated so appropriate instruction can be determined; Figure 50 illustrates the cyclical nature of this process.

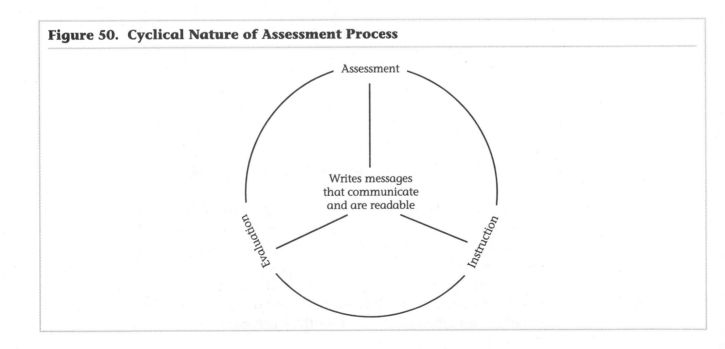

Figure 50. Cyclical Nature of Assessment Process

Two questions that educator Andrea Butler (as cited in Routman, 1991) uses to guide her assessments to become evaluations are, "What do I want to know?" and "How am I going to find out?" (p. 307).

To enable teachers to keep track of their responses to these questions, Mrs. Clark, Mrs. Williams, Mrs. Kropland, a first-grade teacher, and I created some evaluation forms that we thought would be beneficial to teachers. Once teachers fill out these forms, they file them in portfolios. We refer to these two evaluation forms as (1) the CID (pronounced "kid") form, which stands for what the Child knows, what I know, and what I will Do and (2) the Weekly Conference and Instructional Guidesheet (WCIG; see Appendix E for templates for both of these forms). The following section provides in-depth explanations of these two forms and portfolios.

Using the CID Form for Evaluation

The purpose of assessment and evaluation is to know the child so well that teaching responds to the child's individual needs. The most effective assessment and evaluation requires the teacher to work from a child's strengths to teach to his or her individual needs, "known to unknown" (Routman, 1991, p. 144). Routman (1991, 2000), Graves (1994), and Calkins (1994) strongly advise teachers to know their students. This means teachers should get to know the child outside school as well as in school, which requires

- knowing the child inside out (their literacy background, likes, and dislikes);

- knowing the child's process of thinking as he or she writes; and

- guiding the child to be able to assess his or her work for improvement.

Mrs. Williams and Mrs. Clark like to use a CID form to record their weekly anecdotal assessments and evaluations of writing samples; I adapted this form from a K-W-L chart (Ogle, 1986; see Appendix E for a CID template). The CID form has three columns:

1. Child knows and demonstrates (writing strengths);

2. I know child needs to know (writing needs or weaknesses);

3. What I will do to guide child's writing progress (instruction).

Mrs. Clark makes note of any conference observations directly on her CID form under the "Child knows" and "I know" headings at the time of the conference to preserve anything important that might potentially be forgotten when she reviews the writing samples later. Then, when she has time later in the day, under these two headings she adds any other assessment that she feels is necessary and also decides on the best instruction, which she places under the third heading, "What I will do."

Some teachers, like Mrs. Williams, prefer to write assessment notes on sticky notes and then rewrite them on their CID forms later on in the day. Other teachers simply tape or staple their notes to the CID form. Normally only the teacher sees this form, so it just needs to be readable by him or her.

After a conference (later in the school day or even after school), Mrs. Williams and Mrs. Clark make photocopies of the writing samples from the children with whom they conferred that day for their records. If it is necessary to record on a sticky note what the child wrote, the note is attached to or photocopied onto the back of the child's paper.

In addition to looking at the child's writing sample and reviewing writing conference observational notes, Mrs. Williams scans her checklist or even looks at a more detailed list of criteria important to writing development (see Table 9, p. 246). These lists help her remember important assessment data while the memory of the conference is still fresh in her mind (Karelitz, 1993). As she reviews these lists, she keeps the child's developmental stages of writing and spelling in mind. Then she finishes filling out the CID forms for the children with whom she conferred that day.

Mrs. Clark scans her rubric when filling out her children's CID forms to aid her observations. She also reviews the criteria to aid her observations. If she finds or thinks of something that needs to be assessed that isn't listed on her rubric, she changes her rubric to reflect that thinking. (Mrs. Clark also reflects and makes changes on her checklists in this manner.)

Mrs. Williams and Mrs. Clark realize the necessity of spending their time recording on their CID forms *only* those assessments helpful to improving present instruction. Assessment needs to lead evaluation; it is not an entity in itself (Routman, 2000).

Once Mrs. Williams and Mrs. Clark have recorded the assessment data that is necessary, they evaluate it to guide their instruction. They look for a pattern of error concerning the student's ability to communicate a written message because only one thing can be the focus of instruction at a time. When they have decided on one instructional guideline, they write it under the "What I will do" column on the CID form.

Transferring Information to the WCIG Form

Because teachers should use the information from the "What I will do" column on the CID form to guide immediate instruction, they need to transfer any recorded instructional guidelines to their WCIG forms. As previously mentioned, the WCIG form is kept on a clipboard that teachers carry as they confer with students; it reminds teachers which students to confer with and what specific instruction (derived from a previous conference) to implement.

The following example illustrates how Mrs. Clark uses the CID and WCIG forms for such purposes. (Refer to Billy's and Kara's writing conferences in chapter 5 to better understand how Mrs. Clark evaluates and guides Billy's and Kara's writing processes.)

Keeping writing's dominant focus (communicating a message) and its byproduct (Clay's [1991] four emergent reading behaviors) in mind, Mrs. Clark looks for strengths and weaknesses in Billy's and Kara's writing and decides on one weakness to address that will most help each child write a meaningful message and another weakness that addresses writing readable messages. See Figures 51 and 52. Because the anecdotal records or notes on Billy and Kara have been provided as samples, they are more detailed than Mrs. Clark would normally write. Her notes consist of only a few words and usually begin with key verbs (Boyd-Bastone, 2004). Things that are known about the child's background that affect the child's writing are considered in her assessment but are rarely recorded. For example, Mrs. Clark knows, but does not find it necessary to record, whether or not the child comes from a literate home, uses nonstandard dialects, speaks English as a second language, or has a speech or hearing problem. This knowledge aids Mrs. Clark's assessments and decisions as to what is developmentally appropriate instruction for the child. (The important thing in assessment is that the teacher uses his or her time wisely in determining *suitable instruction* to address an *immediate* concern, and not waste time recording information that he or she already knows and does anyway.)

The immediate concerns Mrs. Clark has for Billy and Kara are transferred from each of these children's "What I Will Do" boxes on their CID forms to Mrs. Clark's WCIG form. She briefly records on her WCIG form in Billy's name box, *Topic? Write? Praise*, and in Kara's name box, *Running home in rain*.

Mrs. Clark also records on next week's WCIG form in Kara's box, "Needs work on focus." (Kara's need for focus and, later, extension of her writing are not immediate needs, but they provide direction for Mrs. Clark in Kara's near future.) In Billy's case, Mrs. Clark plans a brief check to see if he has some form of writing along with his picture during tomorrow's conference time, and as long as necessary after that.

The essential point when doing instructional "rechecks" after a prior writing conference is that they should be quick. They should not take time away from the children who were selected for more comprehensive conferences on that day. If extensive time is needed to work with a child, it must be done at another time (e.g., lunch, recess, and so forth). Some teachers use a portion of nap time for this purpose or train tutors (e.g., aides, parents, or older students) to help.

Mrs. Clark did not tackle everything in her evaluation assessment for instruction; she only focused on a main problem important to her dominant writing focus or goal. Her major concern in evaluating assessment for instructional purposes is that instruction is developmentally appropriate

Figure 51. CID Form for Billy

Child (Billy) knows (strengths)	I know (needs)	What I will do
• Draws beautifully • Uses interesting words (*roughhouse*) • Likes dogs	• Try procedures • Needs work on hearing sounds and learning letters • Needs work on writing first name (writes first letter now)	• Check on Billy briefly for topic and work (praise him) • Review different forms of writing rules in teacher demonstration time and remind Billy, if necessary; provide a model of Billy's first name on a separate sheet of paper for "sign-in" time each day until he can sign his name to the class attendance sheet • "Getting Ready" and Writing Workshop will probably help Billy's developing alphabetic principle (if he falls behind, give him special help)

Figure 52. CID Form for Kara

Child (Kara) knows (strengths)	I know (needs)	What I will do
• Wrote first name and last • Chose topic easily; seemed to enjoy writing about personal family experience • Was talkative—strong language skills • Hears some beginning sounds and represents them	• Writing needs focus—one thing • Said she knows her ABCs—observe for lowercase • Used *me* for *my*—probably isn't looking at all the letters yet	• Kara said in Author's Chair, "I'm gonna write about running home in the rain." Check tomorrow to see if she wants to add this • Guide Kara to keep focus on topic in future (as she learns to extend her writing beyond simple labeling and develop voice) • Address improper language usage (*me*) if seen in publishable work

(see chapters 2 and 3 for a description of the developmental stages of spelling and writing) and that the child develops the ability to write messages that *communicate* and eventually become *readable* through interrelating Clay's (1991) four emergent reading behaviors.

Writing Portfolios

No single behavior, strategy, activity, or test can provide a comprehensive picture of students' writing progress. Only a variety of measures, examined carefully over a period of time, can give an accurate, detailed, and complete picture of a student's writing needs and strengths (Routman, 1991). This variety of measures can be kept in a writing portfolio.

Writing portfolios are systematic and meaningful collections of students' writing samples and anything else the teacher thinks shows students' effort and progress in writing over a period of time (De Fina, 1992). The portfolio is designed to reveal what the child knows and needs to know at any given point in time; each saved assessment should provide dependable information about the child's writing proficiency and expand the view of the child as a writer (Routman, 2000; Stiggens, 2001).

Some kindergarten teachers use a three-ring binder for their Writing Assessment and Evaluation Portfolio with a pocket folder for each child. For ease in locating each child's name, colored tabs can be put on the pocket folders. Other teachers use large envelope-type folders. Teacher preference and whatever holds the necessary assessments and evaluations dictate the structure or type of portfolio needed.

Teachers need to make deliberate choices when organizing writing portfolios so portfolios do not become overwhelmed with samples and ultimately have no purpose or structure. A good place to start when compiling writing portfolios is to include the author's writing samples and informal and formal writing assessments and evaluations. Mrs. Clark's writing portfolio holds each kindergartner's weekly CID form attached to the dated writing sample it corresponds to. It also holds the weekly writing sample of "best work" that each child selected. This self-selected sample does not need to have a CID form attached; every item does not need to be assessed or evaluated in a portfolio. Mrs. Clark also includes a rubric for each child and 10-line summary (see p. 263) for each quarter of the year.

Other important assessment materials that the teacher or the child deems worthy to telling the complete story about the child's writing progress can be included. For example, Mrs. Clark saves and dates any notes or stories the child has written outside of writing workshop (e.g., at school or home) that have been given to her.

Portfolio collections should reflect what the child has learned about writing in writing workshop *and* across the curriculum (Tompkins & Hoskisson, 1995).

Reporting Evaluations to Parents

Typically, teachers are required to have conferences with parents several times a year so they can keep them informed of their child's progress in school. As a literacy consultant, I noticed reporting was generally done on a quarterly basis throughout the year. In one of the schools in which I worked, the kindergarten teachers filled out 10-line summaries to report on the writing progress of their kindergartners. They also pointed out for parents where their children were on developmental spelling and written language charts and discussed ways the parents might help their children become better writers. In this school, conferences were always led by the teacher, but in some schools, students become involved in reporting to parents—for example through Triangular Conferences and an Author's Party (see pp. 264–267).

However, teachers should note that observational notes or anecdotal assessments and CID forms are only meant to be seen by the teacher; these forms are used only as guides for the teacher's assessments and evaluations of students' writing. At the end of a quarter, in preparation for parent conferences, Mrs. Clark and Mrs. Williams complete their respective rubric and checklist forms for each child. Completing these forms helps them interpret and summarize data gleaned from their students' CID forms for writing narrative reports for parents. They rarely show these rubrics and checklists to parents, however, because the lengthy explanations required are not usually warranted.

10-Line Summary

Mrs. Clark and Mrs. Williams have found that a 10-line summary for each child—based on assessments and evaluations derived from the child's anecdotal records (CID forms) and rubric or checklist—along with the writing samples that support the summary, to be most successful for sharing information with parents (Clay, 2001). This 10-line summary, which is written in narrative form, highlights the child's writing progress, including the child's strengths and weaknesses; it also includes recommendations to the parents (Clay, 2001).

Writing samples that the child has chosen as his or her best weekly writing sample are looked at by teachers, too, and anything noteworthy is added to the summary and pointed out to the parents during conferences. Usually in the beginning of the year, the children's writing on these best samples cannot be read, but by viewing the sequence of the samples over a quarter and over the entire year, teachers, students, parents, and administrators get an overall idea of the student's writing growth. (Some teachers hold brief conferences with the child to determine why a piece was saved.)

Students need to understand how assessment can help them establish a plan of action to improve; therefore, they need to be able to explain and assess their own work. Three good questions kindergartners can ask themselves in regard to their writing include the following: (1) What can I do well? (2) What do I need to work on? (3) What am I doing better? (Routman, 1991). With these questions in mind, Fisher (1991) recommends going over kindergartners' writing portfolio samples with the students before parent–teacher conferences; she regards this review as "a celebration of what each child can do and a way of validating their progress" (p. 133). As teacher and student review writing samples together, growth is pointed out, goals are decided on, and student input is noted.

When Mrs. Clark and Mrs. Williams write 10-line summaries to share with parents, they use the sandwich technique. They begin with the child's strengths; next they focus on the learning achievements the student has demonstrated since the beginning of the year; then, with an idea in mind and input from the parents, they map out a plan of action for parents to encourage continued literacy growth, especially in areas of weakness. Last, the 10-line summary ends on a complimentary note. So writing progress can be seen at year's end, all of the child's weekly photocopied samples (one conferred with and the one chosen as student's best) along with CID forms throughout the year are kept in Mrs. Clark's and Mrs. Williams's writing portfolios after the conferences.

When writing assessments are discussed with kindergartners and their parents, teachers show the student's current writing samples in comparison to writing and spelling developmental charts (see Appendix C). This serves two purposes: (1) It shows how the child has progressed from the beginning of the year and (2) it shows the child's potential growth. It also answers the question so many parents ask, "So how is my child doing?"

When spelling developmental charts are shown to parents, teachers also should explain the importance of using invented spelling, or kid spelling, in learning the alphabetic principle and learning how to spell in developmental stages. (See Appendix C for a letter to parents explaining developmental spelling.)

Mrs. Clark and Mrs. Williams explain to the parents how they can help their child to be more literate by reading to the child at home and pointing to the words as they read. Parents are reminded that reading should be done as often as possible (e.g., bedtime is a good time). They are also given a list of good books to read aloud, including nursery rhymes, especially rhymes set to song (see Appendix B for booklists). Both of these teachers encourage parents to take the children to the library and get a library card, and to write little notes to their children in conventional spelling to encourage their children to write notes back to them in kid spelling. Labeling some things in sentences in the children's rooms or in their homes is also suggested to help the children learn certain high-frequency and other sight words. Furthermore, parents are encouraged to take every opportunity to point out and read environmental print—that is, print in the child's surroundings (e.g., restaurant signs, household item labels, and so forth). (Teachers could print a list of these suggestions prior to conferences so they can be handed out to parents.)

Triangular Conferences

Although I have discussed teacher-led conferences where the only participants are the teacher and the parents, many school districts require that one conference during the school year be a triangular conference, which means a student must be present with the parents (Routman, 2000). I believe this is a good idea in kindergarten if done later in the year and if the teacher leads the conference. The teacher can provide commentary on the child's writing progress as writing samples and tests are shown to the child and his or her parents. The child could read the list of things he or she can do in writing (content and mechanics) from his or her "I Can Do" list recorded on the front of the student's writing folder. The student also could point out those things he or she can do in his or her writing samples. Filling out a simple photocopied checklist from the class's "Good Writing Chart" prior to the conference might be useful in this endeavor, too (see p. 216). Mrs. Clark keeps a supply of these photocopied checklists accessible on Fridays for the children to use at their discretion when they choose their best work.

Prior to a triangular conference, Routman (2000) recommends the following suggestions to possibly reduce the time frame that they take (up to 45 minutes):

- Have students and parents come 20 minutes early before their scheduled conference. Parents, with their child, can preview the writing portfolio ahead of time and jot down any questions.

- Schedule spring "open house" as a portfolio evening. Students come with their families and share their portfolios. Families can ask questions, and if privacy is an issue, a private triangular conference could be scheduled.

Author's Party

Another way children can show parents their literacy progress is to have an Author's Party (Calkins, 1994). Children pick their best piece of writing to share and then practice reading their best piece until the teacher and the children feel confident that they can read the piece. Students make and send invitations to their parents to come to their Author's Party. (Ask parents to RSVP so a parent substitute can be found in case a parent can't come. I've seen principals, cooks, and janitors lend their aid in this endeavor.) The children entertain the parents with their stories, and then they serve refreshments they've helped to prepare. (Making a grocery list and reading recipes for refreshments are meaningful literacy tasks, too.)

I have seen teachers handle an Author's Party in two ways: In one school, the teacher had numbered stations with eight chairs in each station: four chairs (decorated with balloons) were for the authors, and four chairs (facing the authors' chairs) were set up for parents. Extra chairs for extra visitors were available if needed. The children had been divided into groups of four and were seated in a particular station when the parents entered. Parents were asked to sit in the station where their child was, and they stayed there for the duration of all the kindergartners' readings. However, when the four authors had finished their readings and received praise, they moved from the station their parents were in to the next higher numbered station and began reading again until they had made the rounds of every station (see Figure 53).

In the other school, the teacher and children set up enough chairs for the parents to sit in a huge circle of chairs. Then the children formed an inner circle inside the circle of chairs (see Figure 54).

Each student read his or her story in front of his or her parent(s). When the young author was finished, he or she moved counterclockwise to the

Figure 53. Author's Party Setup Option 1

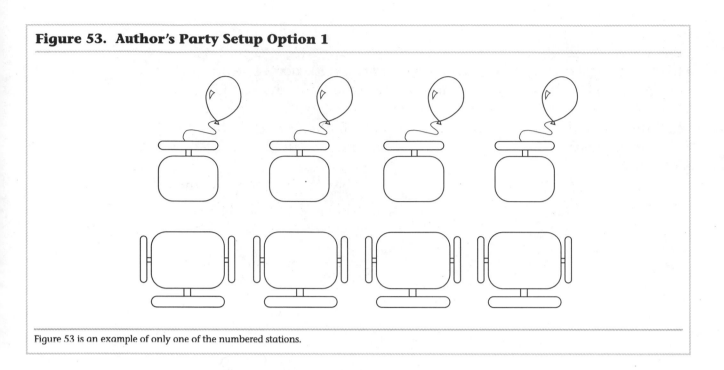

Figure 53 is an example of only one of the numbered stations.

Figure 54. Author's Party Setup Option 2

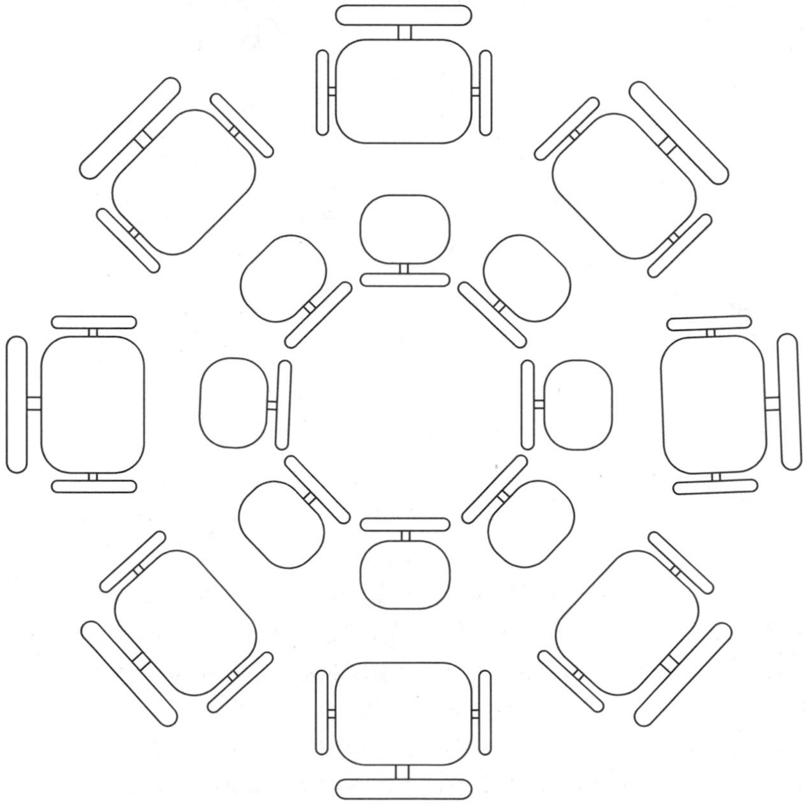

next set of parents. The author gets a lot of practice reading this way and remains active. The parents get to relax and get the opportunity to show their appreciation to each young author.

It is a good idea to attach a note to parental invitations to an Author's Party, explaining children's need to hear appreciation for their writing; compliments are greatly appreciated and needed when each author is finished reading.

Mrs. Clark and Mrs. Williams have found parents and members of their school districts to be very enthusiastic about this type of assessment and evaluation reporting. In fact, most parents preferred this type of reporting. Which writing samples and how many samples are saved for assessment and evaluation purposes depends on a school district's requirements and the teacher's discretion. However, Mrs. Clark's and Mrs. Williams's districts have found the following to be helpful: two dated writing samples per week (one based on the student's choice and one piece from a student–teacher conference), CID form, formal tests (if the teacher has administered any), quarterly checklists or rubrics, and quarterly 10-line summaries with recommendations for improvement.

Reporting Evaluations to Administrators

As I was addressing a group of K–5 teachers in a school where I would soon be serving as a literacy coach, the principal asked the following questions: "Can we start this session with assessment? Shouldn't all learning start with assessment?" I agreed with him, as long as assessments are used to lead learning and do not simply label it. Assessments should help determine whether or not the goals (standards) we have in mind before we begin to teach are met and let us know what has to be done yet (Routman, 2000). This requires assessing process as well as product.

Administrators desire and need to see kindergartners' writing processes and progress as shown in the January and May scores on Clay's (1993a) Dictation Tests (formal assessment) and in dated yearly writing samples (informal assessment). Mr. Reiche, Mrs. Clark's and Mrs. Williams's principal, requests that they (and all his teachers) share and discuss daily writing samples with him for any students whose formal literacy test results are questionable.

If administrators are not knowledgeable about performance-based assessment, teachers should inform them of its value to literacy progress. When teachers provide commentaries on these performance assessments and explain the features that help them to meet state standards, administrators, colleagues, and parents are able to judge for themselves that students' work actually does meet the standards (Routman, 2001; Tucker & Codding, 1998).

For example, observers easily can see the writing progression and progress made by the student noted earlier in the chapter (see p. 256) who was not able to write anything on his first test but performed remarkably on his second test. This student's daily writing samples also confirm his test results. (See the first three student samples on "Five Stages of Developmental Spelling" chart in Appendix C. They belong to the same student.)

Because policymakers and administrators often do not understand the active and constructive nature of the young child's mind as he or she becomes literate, they do not understand kindergarten teachers' needs when they only talk to administrators about students' literacy progress. Administrators want accountability in the form of concrete informal and formal performance assessments. They also want these assessments explained with current, accepted research. Kindergarten teachers can show their administrators that they are sufficiently accountable for their students' learning through knowing the research and showing and explaining the process of students' growth in writing samples and with improved scores on Robinson's and Clay's tests.

Summary

Children are like butterflies. Teachers can guide and encourage children's literacy development, so like butterflies, they can shed their cocoons and take flight on their own—*if* teachers become knowledgeable about literacy research and realize that assessment must serve children's individual processes of learning. Or by not recognizing children's development and continuing to assess only their finished products with no understanding of how they came to be, teachers can choose to allow children to remain in their cocoons.

When teachers are knowledgeable about current literacy research, they can explain and justify their instructional methods to students, parents, and administrators through students' dated writing samples and test scores. This accountability will empower teachers to have input into how their literacy teaching needs can best be met by staff and policymakers, and administrators may change from authoritative roles to collaborative ones.

When knowledgeable literacy teachers' assessments are used as a means of evaluation, then assessment, evaluation, and instruction go hand in hand. Understanding this cycle allows teachers to connect the goal of writing to effective writing practice, so children can become readers through writing.

Reflections on Writing Workshop in Kindergarten

In this final chapter, I share some of my personal reflections as well as some reflections and reactions from teachers, administrators, and students concerning the successful implementation of a writing workshop in kindergarten. I begin with an observation I made from my years of coaching writing workshop.

> When I first began to help teachers set up their writing workshops, management was the most important issue. The simple predictable structure of writing workshop and utilizing Cambourne's (1988) seven conditions of learning language (especially time, demonstration, expectation, responsibility, and positive response) addressed this issue most appropriately. Once management was under control, the main issue became advancing the teacher's ability to recognize what each student's writing strengths and needs were as he or she attempted to communicate in writing and learn the alphabetic principle. This required an understanding of literacy research, what each child knew about literacy, and what was developmentally appropriate to teach to each child.

Although this book provides most of the research necessary to implement a quality writing workshop, if teachers would like to delve deeper, I suggest reading portions of the sources that have been cited throughout this book as necessary.

The more the teachers with whom I worked read and understood the research, the more capable they became at implementing a writing workshop. In fact, in one district, one teacher won an outstanding elementary teacher of the year award, and writing workshop was cited as a major contributor. In other districts, these teachers were asked by their administrators, after seeing the amazing progress in children's daily writing samples and in scores on Clay's (1993a) Dictation Test, to lead other kindergarten teachers (or, in one small district, all elementary teachers) in the implementation of writing workshops.

Kindergarten Teachers' Reflections on Writing Workshop

The reflections presented in this section are from kindergarten teachers whom I coached in the implementation of writing workshops over the past

13 years, except for the last two reflections. The last two reflections are from kindergarten teachers whom I did not personally coach but who followed my book in its rough draft form. All these teachers' reflections provided direction for my coaching and writing.

The reflections that follow include both verbal and written comments directed to me as a writing workshop coach. I have written the oral comments as best as I can recall them since many were made before I had any intention of writing a book.

As teachers know, we are all stretched to our limits. Each year we are asked to do more and more. We are asked to try new "programs" and methods. We must be able to demonstrate our students' learning with measurable results, regardless of their experiences and learning prior to entering kindergarten. Despite these expectations, our teaching time is structured by the many subjects we are to teach and by our school's scheduling of lunch, recess, and "specials" such as physical education, art, library, guidance, and computer lab. Each year we wonder, "How can I do it all?" We must set priorities and work within our limits.

Since beginning writing and reading workshops in kindergarten, I have had to examine my priorities. What do I really feel is important for my students to learn? When first introduced to writing workshop in 2003 by Arlene, I wondered how I could devote a whole hour every day to it. But I felt that if I was going to "Give it a try!" as Arlene suggested, I would find a way to do it as well as I could. I made writing workshop a priority and, to my delight, it became a priority to my students as well. If for some reason we couldn't have writing workshop, both my students and I would miss it!

The children looked forward to this enjoyable time every day, and in the morning they came into the classroom excited about what they would write about that day. I watched as my children went from drawing simple pictures to writing three-page stories, which included a title, marvelous illustrations, and a sentence or two on each page. They were able to publish some of these stories with me on the computer. All proudly took their stories home to share with family members. All the children learned to relish their time in the Author's Chair. All the children quickly saw themselves as readers and writers, even the little girl who, on the second day of school, said, "Wait a minute, I can't read!"

—Karen Clark

I am so proud of my kindergarten students! They really grew as writers and readers this year. I feel that I have gotten to know each child better than I ever have with these workshops. I taught letter of the week for many, many years. It was a bit scary to change, but I would never go back to it. Writing and reading workshops really complement each other and really work!

—Teri Williams

When you first came that September, I decided I would give writing workshop a try, but I would continue to do "Letter of the Week," too. By November, I realized I didn't need to do "Letter of the Week" anymore. Writing workshop was not only teaching the alphabetic principle, but my children were becoming writers and readers! Now, 10 years later, I only have an aide for a half-hour a day. So in the beginning of the year I scheduled my aide to help with writing workshop because writing workshop has become a priority in my classroom.

—Cyndi Lentz

I love the way my students are learning to communicate in writing. They are so proud when I praise them for using writing strategies like checking their alphabet song and strip to identify a letter or rereading their work to make sense. They all are becoming writers and readers and they really love writing workshop! In fact, if they have extra time, they will often ask if they can do a writing workshop. I only wish I'd had your book sooner; it is a wonderful book!

—Joan Schier

Although I'd heard of writing workshop, I didn't know how to implement one. Chapter 5 told me how. I wish I'd had your book last year in college because I've found that writing is essential to kindergartners' literacy learning. And they love it!

—Amy Neuenfeldt

Other Kindergarten Teachers' Comments

The following comments from kindergarten teachers were made to me over the past 13 years while working as a literacy consultant and coach. I've always remembered these comments because for me they validate the importance of writing workshop. Although I am unable to include specific names here, I would like to share their comments.

Writing workshop pushes my bright students, and I've found it's absolutely essential for those slower, struggling students. At the end of the year, I feel good that I have taught all my students literacy to the best of their and my ability with writing and reading workshops.

What I love about writing workshop is the way it gets kids thinking! They love it and they really learn this way.

My children were a lot smarter than I gave them credit for. I used to think I had to tell them everything, but I found out telling was not the way to teach. Children learn best when I demonstrate and they do. They already know a lot. It was my challenge to find out what they knew about literacy and what they were trying to learn so I could guide them. Writing workshop allowed me to do this.

I was surprised that some of my children who knew quite a lot about print when they entered school did not write easily at first. I hadn't realized how complex learning to be literate was until we discussed [the work of] Clay. It takes several years to learn all the details of letters because the child has to figure out each new letter by checking it against those letters he already knows. Now I see that while letters can be learned in isolation, this knowledge doesn't transfer to the process of real writing and reading. For children to learn to use print meaningfully, it has to be taught meaningfully within writing and reading workshops.

I understand why writing personal stories is important to getting kids writing, but some of my children wanted more variety. I'm glad different genres of writing were introduced; some of my boys, especially, preferred note writing.

I expected my kids to write with invented spelling right away. I was disappointed with writing workshop when I first tried it on my own because they didn't. However, when you came and we started reading and discussing the research, I realized what I had been doing was just journaling; I was not really teaching writing. Once I learned about writing process and developmental stages of writing and spelling, I understood why changes took place so slowly and that each child had to develop in his or her own way. When I worked with my children on an individual basis, guiding them in their process of learning to write, invented spelling did happen for all my children. That had never happened before!

I questioned the value of invented spelling at first, but now I see that writing with invented spelling is absolutely the best way to practice phonemic awareness! Writing workshop provides the interest (and the pace) for children to be totally engaged in working with sound-to-letter correspondences because they want to communicate.

Writing helps kids to think about how reading should make sense because they learn that their own writing must make sense, just as they've learned that their talking must make sense. It is true that writers become readers!

In addition to the kindergarten teachers' reflections and comments above, I worked with one special education teacher and one learning disabilities teacher. They both liked the individual approach and the self-esteem a writing workshop provided for their students. The learning disabilities teacher especially appreciated the way writing kept her students engaged and focused on communicating and learning more about print. The special education teacher was impressed that all of her students were able to think of a story and write the words with invented spelling, except for one student who had severe physical disabilities and had to be helped with the actual writing. All the children's stories were published with help from the special education teacher and proudly read in Author's Chair. Some of the stories even had complex sentences in them.

Isolated skill and drill work doesn't work any better for these special children than for those in a regular classroom. Research does indicate that teaching the writing process has a positive effect on the writing abilities of learning disabled students (Hallenbeck, 1995; Lewis et al., 1996; Morocco et al., 1992; Storeyard et al., 1993) and students who are intellectually challenged (Stires, 1991). I certainly witnessed this growth with the students with whom I worked in these two classes, and what I especially liked was the way these children truly enjoyed writing workshop. In addition to learning more about literacy, they were able to increase their self-esteem.

Reading Teachers' Reflections on Writing Workshop

When you first introduced writing workshop in the fall, I thought this would never work. But when I saw what Robert and the other kindergartners could do in the spring, I knew it worked!
—Joy Haehlke

My own child had reading difficulty until I put him into a Reading Recovery program at the end of first grade that promoted writing as well as reading. Even though I had read to him as a preschooler and we had a literate home, he had difficulty because he'd never properly focused on the print. The Reading Recovery teacher discovered that he was attempting to read words from right to left. Writing cleared up his reading problem. I realize now how a writing workshop in kindergarten and first grade would have helped him to discover how speech and written language were related.

Happily, Reading Recovery recovered my son! Because it is an early intervention program, my child's reading problem was diagnosed and solved before bad habits were ingrained. In fact he won a writing contest in the sixth grade!

—Linda Scaffidi

I couldn't believe that kindergartners could achieve scores as high as Mrs. Clark's and Mrs. Williams's kindergartners did at the end of the school year when I tested them with Clay's Dictation Test. I rushed to tell our principal the good news—writing workshop was doing the job.

—Kathy Kropland

Administrators' Reflections on Writing Workshop

All the principals with whom I have worked within three different school districts in north central Wisconsin have been very supportive of a writing workshop approach to teaching literacy. The literacy progress of each kindergartner could be easily seen by looking at their dated writing samples from the beginning of the year to the end of the year; Clay's (1993a) tests also corroborated this progress.

Several administrators' positive comments and reactions to writing workshop can be found throughout my book; however, I am especially grateful to the following two administrators who took the time to put their thoughts in writing.

For an experienced teacher to change his or her method of teaching is a difficult task. However, once teachers gave writing workshop a try, and read and understood the research, they were very pleased with the results. It works!

—John Ader

Writing workshop is indeed a powerful instructional practice. If you spend any time at all with a child of age 5 or 6, you very quickly discover they have a lot to tell. Yet prior to the implementation of writing workshop, seldom did we provide the structure or opportunity for students to "tell" us in writing. We had often overlooked or underestimated the ability of our very youngest students to communicate their stories, their messages, in writing. We have not set aside precious time in our daily school schedules for writing and we have, at times, insisted these young ones master some set of prerequisite skills (letter formation, mastery of spellings of basic sight words, etc.) before we allow them to try their hand at becoming an author.

As a building principal, I am seeing and hearing firsthand the difference that this approach is making for our students as a result of our teachers learning and being coached "on the job" in writing workshop. Now teachers see the powerful impact writing workshop has on their students' literacy development and make time to model writing, provide writing time for their students, and conference with them, and to celebrate their literacy words in progress through Author's Chair.

Teachers comment on the incredible capacity young children do indeed have to write. Students become increasingly fluent, skilled, and confident in their abilities to communicate their "tellings" in writing. This, in turn, builds their capacity to become fluent, independent, and confident readers.

—Karen Wendorf-Heldt

Kindergartners' Reflections on Writing Workshop

Mrs. Clark asked her students to share their feelings about writing workshop in class one day. The following are some of their wonderfully insightful reflections:

You think—get ideas in your head. A good idea is something you really did.

You get to read your stories again after you haven't read them for a while.

You can look through your stories and put more details in if you don't have details.

You get to show your teacher your picture and read your own words—tell everything in the story.

You can ask your friends for help because they are teachers, too.

Sometimes the words you need to write are in the classroom—on the word wall, in a pocket chart, in books, or on posters. If you need help spelling your name, it's right there—on the poster and your desk.

You get to publish. You get to take it home and read it to your family like a real book!

You can write about seeing each other somewhere [a parade]. It's really exciting to make a story with each other and publish it.

And one final comment often overheard by Mrs. Clark that illustrates the self-confidence children build as writers and readers in a writing workshop approach is the following:

Can I take your book home to read it? I really liked it when you read it in Author's Chair.

My Final Thoughts

Initially, because most teachers I coached did not think of writing as approximation, or a process, they did not understand how writing could lead to conventional reading. A big concern was giving up an hour of their instructional day to implement an approach they were unsure of and that was entirely different from anything they had seen or tried. They questioned whether writing workshop would really help them teach emergent literacy in the best possible way and if literacy testing would support this approach.

Understanding these teachers' misconceptions about writing firsthand and realizing that it takes time to see progress, I asked all of these kindergarten teachers to simply give writing workshop a try for a semester. Then they could decide if they wanted to continue using it or not. At the end of the semester, their students' literacy knowledge was not only easily seen in their day-to-day classroom work but also in their literacy test results. Test scores were dramatically higher than they had ever been before! To my knowledge, all the kindergarten teachers with whom I worked are still implementing a writing workshop.

Educators often expect immediate results, but learning to be literate doesn't happen that way. It is a very complex and slow process. However, Clay (1991) suggests that observant teachers who are knowledgeable about literacy learning can speed up the writing and reading process somewhat with the following two "shortcuts":

1. Implement a writing workshop as well as a reading workshop, because these workshops not only provide the proper conditions to engage children in meaningful self-directed experiences with print but also lead them to literacy independence. As the more competent children become more independent, the teacher is freed to help those who need more assistance.

2. Know what each child knows about literacy, so the teacher can guide the child's strengths to teach his or her needs when the child is engaged in composing and writing a simple message or reading simple continuous text.

Each child has to follow his or her own path to writing and reading just as he or she did when learning to speak. However, children need guidance from a knowledgeable literacy teacher at their point of need, similar to the guidance they received from proficient language users in their preschool years. As well as being immersed in the process of reading in kindergarten, children need to be immersed in the process of meaningful writing where the proper conditions of learning language are valued. Children's primary need to communicate their thoughts in writing in any way they can at first (i.e., their approximations) should be encouraged within a writing workshop structure. For when they are, the child writer becomes a reader.

Phonemic Awareness Activities and Additional Minilesson Topics

Instruction in Phonemic Awareness 278

    Sound Matching Activities...279

    Sound Isolation Activities..281

    Sound Substitution Activities..285

    Sound Blending Activities...288

    Sound Segmentation Activities 292

Additional Kindergarten Minilesson Topics...295

Additional Content Minilessons With Brief Descriptions............................297

Instruction in Phonemic Awareness

Teachers should prepare students for phonemic awareness activities by using listening and rhyming activities that include literature and songs that stress identifying rhyming words. Activities that help students develop an understanding of syllables and recognize the letters of the alphabet are important, too. In addition to singing the "Alphabet Song" and tracking the letters on an alphabet chart, playing games that focus on visualizing letters of the alphabet can be helpful.

When using the following phonemic awareness activities or trying to devise your own, think about the desired result of the activity. Initially phonemic activities should just be about isolating and hearing the beginning consonant sound in a word. When isolating and hearing sounds prove difficult, Elkonin sound boxes (see chapter 4) and iteration (like stuttering) are helpful. When children can isolate and hear the beginning sound in a spoken word and they know how to find letters of the alphabet on an alphabet chart, they can attempt to match the beginning sound to the letter in these phonemic awareness activities.

Finally, and most important, think about making the activity as enjoyable as possible. Use many sources of playful language—songs and nursery rhymes are especially good sources. Don't forget to capitalize on the teachable moment—that is, when an opportunity arises—to explore sounds and their relations to letters. Phonemic awareness activities should be done with a sense of playfulness and fun to develop positive feelings and curiosity in the child toward his or her language.

A good introductory book that can be read before beginning phonemic awareness activities is *The Ear Book* (Perkins, 1968), which is about listening. It might help to remind children that when they really want to listen carefully, it helps to close their eyes.

Unless otherwise indicated, I devised the phonemic activities that follow. Since their inception in 1992, hundreds of kindergarten teachers have successfully used these activities and enjoyed them. Although I suggest working with isolating ending and middle sounds as well as beginning sounds in some of these activities, I have found that it is not necessary to work with ending and middle sounds because children transfer the knowledge they learn from working with beginning sounds to ending and middle sounds (Bear et al., 2000). Furthermore, it is best to present short vowels in their word families (phonograms) to kindergartners and beginning first graders, because they are not yet developmentally ready to hear isolated short-vowel sounds (Routman, 1991, 2000). The activities are presented in order of their developmental progression from the easiest to the most difficult. Most children should experience some success in one level before moving to the next. The activities are arranged into the following categories:

- Sound Matching Activities
- Sound Isolation Activities

- Sound Substitution Activities
- Sound Blending Activities
- Sound Segmentation Activities

Sound Matching Activities

The objective of a sound matching activity is for children to find a word that matches a targeted isolated sound (phoneme) instructed by the teacher. When beginning sound matching activities, it is best to target only beginning consonant sounds because consonant sounds at the beginning of words are usually the easiest to hear.

1. Play with children's names. To the tune of "Jimmy Cracked Corn and I Don't Care" or "Skip to My Lou," ask the children to say a classmate's name that begins with the sound you target. Use as many of the children's names as time or interest allows. (Some names begin with vowels and digraphs. These are the only vowel and digraph sounds that should be addressed with phonemic awareness activities in kindergarten and the beginning of first grade. Use these names after going through the names that begin with consonant sounds.)

   Begin singing the "Name Song" (text should be in large print on chart paper and laminated). Children join in the singing when they can.

   Who has a name that starts with /m/?
   Who has a name that starts with /m/?
   Who has a name that starts with/m/?
   Please tell me the name now.

   (Mary) has a name that starts with /m/.
   (Mary) has a name that starts with /m/.
   (Mary) has a name that starts with /m/.
   (Mary) is your/my name.

   Always use the same terminology when talking about the beginning sound in a word. Based on my experience, kindergartners respond to the word *start* better than the word *beginning*.

   Also, the "Name Song" can be used to have children generate a sound and a word that begins with that sound by changing the words to the "Word Song" as follows:

   Who has a /d/ word to share with us? [repeat three times]
   It must start with the /d/ sound!
   (Dog) is a word that starts with /d/. [repeat three times]
   (Dog) starts with the /d/ sound. (Yopp, 1992, pp. 699–700)

2. To the tune of "Frere Jacques," sing about the parts of the body that begin with the same letter. Stand up and sing the song, and point with both

hands to the targeted parts of the body in a pronounced fashion, overarticulating the beginning sound.

Fingers, face, forehead
Fingers, face, forehead
Give me another /f/ word
Give me another /f/ word
It's on my body
It's on my body
It's my (feet) [If students need a hint, sing "look down below" and point.]
It's my (feet)

Other verses can focus on the following:

knees, neck, knuckles (nose or nails; Hints: It's on my face or it's on my hands.)
teeth, tongue, tummy (toes; Hints: Look down below.)
head, hand, heart (hair or heel; Hints: It grows on my head or it's part of my foot.)
elbow, ear, eyebrow (eye; Hint: They show me where to go.)

3. Target the /w/ sound in "Willoughby Wallaby Woo" or the /b/ sound in "Baa, Baa Black Sheep"; have the children clap every time they hear the targeted sound. Both of the songs are available on the audiotape *Singable Songs for the Very Young* (Raffi, 1976).

4. Target any repetitive beginning consonant sounds found in nursery rhymes; have children clap their hands when they hear the sound. Have them generate new words with the targeted sound, too. Ask them to look around the room for things that start with that sound if they need help in generating their own words. Good source books for nursery rhymes and nursery rhymes put to song include *The Classic Mother Goose* (Eisen, 1988) and *The Mother Goose Songbook* (Glazer & McHail, 1990).

5. Use *Animalia* (Base, 1986) to match sounds with pictures. Ask the children to listen carefully to the targeted sound on a particular page. After proper modeling by the teacher, ask the children to volunteer names of objects and things illustrated on the page that match the targeted beginning sound. (*Animalia* is a good source of alliteration). This same technique can be used with other books such as *Dr. Seuss's ABC: An Amazing Alphabet Book!* (1996).

6. Using tongue twisters, have the children identify the repeated sound. Then have them suggest other things that might begin with that same sound. You might read some tongue twisters and ask the children to clap or jump up and down when they hear a different beginning sound other than the one targeted. Children enjoy making up their own tongue twisters, especially when their names are included. This also is a good time to introduce nonsense words; it might be easier to generate new tongue twisters that way. (Try writing out some simpler tongue twisters with invented spelling when children can use the alphabet chart to find most letters.) A good source for tongue twisters is *Busy Buzzing Bumblebees and Other Tongue Twisters* (Schwartz & Abrams, 1992).

7. Show several items on a tray. Pick a targeted beginning sound and an object that has that beginning sound. Have the children identify the other items on the tray that begin with the same sound.

8. In this simple activity, say, "I went to the store and bought butter, beans, and blocks." Have the children volunteer other words with the same beginning sound.

9. This activity can be used any time of the day when the children must line up. Ask students to do any of the following:

   • anyone who has a name that starts with /p/ can line up

   • anyone who has a name that starts with /j/ can line up

   • anyone who has a name beginning with the same sound as *monkey* can line up

   You can improvise using these basic examples.

10. Show three different picture cards to the children at the same time. Students must pick the two cards depicting objects that begin with the same sound. As the children become more skilled at this, more than three picture cards can be added to choose from. (TREND makes a set of "Alphabet Match-Me" cards that can be used for this purpose.)

    When the children demonstrate success with matching beginning sounds, try adaptations of some of these activities to match end and middle sounds (in that order); however, Bear and colleagues (2000) state it is relatively easy for children to transfer their knowledge of beginning sounds to ending—and eventually middle—sounds, so you may wish to spend limited time on this and then move on to sound isolation activities.

Sound Isolation Activities

The objective of a sound isolation activity is to ask children to isolate or separate a phoneme from a word the teacher targets. When beginning sound isolation activities, it is best to target only beginning consonant sounds because consonant sounds at the beginning of words are usually the easiest to hear. When you isolate all sounds in a word, you are segmenting the word, which is addressed at the end of this appendix.

1. To the tune of "Jimmy Cracked Corn and I Don't Care" or "Skip to My Lou," use the words from the first step in sound matching (p. 279) but leave out the sound at the end of each line for children to complete to isolate sounds. (It is a good idea to begin each new level of phonemic awareness activities with the same opening activity as used in the preceding level.)

2. If some children experience difficulty with hearing the beginning consonant sound, practice iteration (which is similar to stuttering). Sing the "K-K-K-Katy Song," and substitute children's names and the word *handsome* or *good-looking* for *beautiful* when using boys' names.

> K-K-K-Katy, beautiful Katy,
> You're the only, /g/-/g/-/g/-girl that I adore.
> When the /m/-/m/-/m/-moon shines
> over the [/m/-/m/-/m/-mountain].
> I'll be waiting for you at the /k/-/k/-/k/-kitchen door.
>
> —Geoffrey O'Hara (1882–1967)

Other songs (see Glazer & McHail, 1990) that can be adapted for the iteration process include the following:

- "Pop Goes the Weasel," iterate the /p/-/p/-/p/-pop in the final line of the song
- "Down by the Station," iterate the /p/-/p/-/p/-poof in the last line of the song, and later in the year the digraph /ch/-/ch/-/ch/-chug
- "Baa, Baa, Black Sheep," iterate the /b/-/b/-/b/-baa in the beginning of the song
- "To Market, To Market," iterate the /j/-/j/-/j/-jog in the song
- "The Bear Went Over the Mountain," iterate the /b/-/b/-/b/-bear and /m/-/m/-/m/-mountain
- "I'm a Little Teapot," iterate /sh/-/sh/-/sh/-short and /st/-/st/-/st/-stout (do this at end of year when you see children using digraphs in writing workshop)

Digraphs (e.g., *ch*, *sh*, and *th*) should not be addressed early in the year unless they begin a child's name. Later, when you see children having need of digraphs in their writing, they can also be addressed.

3. Use the book *In a Dark, Dark Wood* (Carter, 1991) to isolate beginning and final positions of the repeated word *dark*. This is a good book to use when first beginning to isolate sounds with the children.

4. To the tune of "The Wheels on the Bus Go Round and Round," use the words below to isolate a beginning sound.

> I went to the store to buy
> butter, beans, blocks
> butter, beans, blocks,
> butter, beans, blocks,
> The things I bought start with /b/, /b/, /b/
> That's what I bought at the store.

5. To the tune of "The Wheels on the Bus Go Round and Round," use the words below to isolate beginning sounds.

> The chicks on the farm go
> peep, peep, peep
> peep, peep, peep
> peep, peep, peep
> The sound they make starts with /p/, /p/, /p/
> That's the sounds they make.

Other animal names and their sounds can be used: horse (neigh), pig (grunt), dog (woof), cat (meow), sheep (baa), owl (hoot), snake (hiss), hen (cluck), duck (quack), and so forth.

6. To the tune of "Old MacDonald Had a Farm," use the words below to isolate sounds. A single sound may be emphasized throughout the entire song, or each verse may focus on a different sound.

> What's the sound that starts these words:
> Turtle, time, and teeth?
> [wait for a response from the children]
> /t/ is the sound that starts these words
> Turtle, time, and teeth.
>
> With a /t/, /t/ here, and a /t/, /t/ there,
> Here a /t/, there a /t/, everywhere a /t/, /t/.
> /t/ is the sound that starts these words:
> Turtle, time, and teeth! (Yopp, 1992, p. 700)

The words *turtle, time,* and *teeth* can be changed to other words such as *chicken, chin,* and *cheek,* and of course the sound made would be /ch/; or *daddy, duck,* and *deep* with the sound of /d/.

The following examples focus on medial and final sounds:

Medial	Final
What's the sound in the middle of these words?	What's the sound that ends these words?
[Focus on middle sound]	[Focus on ending sound]
Leaf and deep and meat?	Duck and cake and beak?
[wait for a response]	[wait for a response]
/ee/ is the sound in the middle of these words:	/k/ is the sound that ends these words:
Leaf and deep and meat.	Duck and cake and beak.
With an /ee/, /ee/ here, and an /ee/, /ee/ there	With a /k/, /k/ here, and a /k/, /k/ there
Here an /ee/, there an /ee/, everywhere an /ee/, /ee/	Here a /k/, there a /k/, everywhere a /k/, /k/. (Yopp, 1992, p. 700)

A positive ending to these verses that helps students' self-esteem is "You all did great, so clap your hands!" [Clap, clap, clap, clap, clap] (Yopp, 1992, p. 700).

7. Isolate the beginning sounds of tongue twisters. When tongue twisters have repetitive sounds in the medial and final positions, target those positions for isolating, too. Use *Busy Buzzing Bumble Bees and Other Tongue Twisters* (Schwartz & Abrams, 1992).

8. Use Raffi's rendition of "Willoughby Wallaby Woo" (1976) as one of the beginning activities for isolating sounds. Ask the children to name the beginning sound in "Willoughby Wallaby Woo"; you might have them clap every time they hear the /w/ in the song. Raffi's rendition of "Spider on the Floor" (1976) is especially fun for children to work with. Isolate the beginning and final sounds in all the repeated words: *spider, floor, leg, stomach, neck, face,* and *head.*

9. Limericks are especially good for isolating medial and final sounds. In kindergarten and the beginning of first grade, only isolate long vowels in the medial position. Use the following limerick for isolation of the medial sound /i/ in the rhyming words at the end of the lines:

> There was a young lady of Niger
> Who smiled as she rode on a tiger:
> They came back from the ride
> With the lady inside
> And the smile on the face of the tiger.
> Anonymous (Ferris, 1957, p. 360)

10. Target repetitive sounds in the beginning and final positions of rhyming words in nursery rhymes. If you want to include medial sounds, only target long-vowel sounds, not short ones. For example,

- Target the beginning sound of /p/ in "Peter Piper Picked a Peck of Pickled Peppers"
- Target the medial sound of /e/ in *teapot* of "I'm a Little Teapot"
- Target the final sound of /g/ in *pig* of "To Market, To Market"

11. The poems "The Yak" and "The Giggling, Gaggling of Geese" found in *Zoo Doings* (Prelutsky, 1983) are useful in isolating beginning sounds. Target the repetitive beginning sounds.

Also, use the poem "Galoshes" (found in *Sing a Song of Popcorn*, de Regniers, Moore, White, & Carr, 1988) to target the beginning sound /g/.

When trying to think of tunes and the proper number and placement of words within the rhythm of a tune, *Piggyback Songs* (Warren & Ekberg, 1990) is useful.

Sound Substitution Activities

The objective of a sound substitution activity is to teach children that sounds or phonemes can be manipulated to form new words—these can be conventional words or nonsense words. With kindergartners and beginning first graders, it is best to only substitute beginning sounds, which is the easiest form of substitution.

1. To the tune of "Jimmy Cracked Corn and I Don't Care," use the words below to substitute sounds:

   > Mary is a name that starts with /m/.
   > Mary is a name that starts with /m/.
   > Mary is a name that starts with /m/.
   > Mary is your/my name.
   > [Explain that you want someone to "loan" you the first sound of their name].
   > /n/ary is a name that we don't know.
   > /n/ary is a name that we don't know.
   > /n/ary is a name that we don't know.
   > This is fun, it's so.

   As an adaptation, use other children's names in the first verse.

2. The section of the song "I've Been Working on the Railroad" that begins with "Dinah" adapts itself quite well to substitution. "Fe-Fi-Fiddly-i-o" can become "Se-Si-Siddly-i-o" and so forth.

   > I have a song that we can sing
   > I have a song that we can sing
   > I have a song that we can sing
   > It goes something like this:
   > Fe-Fi-Fiddly-i-o
   > Fe-Fi-Fiddly-i-o
   > Fe-Fi-Fiddly-i-o
   > Now try it with the /z/ sound!
   > Ze-Zi-Ziddly-i-o
   > Ze-Zi-Ziddly-i-o
   > Now try it with the /br/ sound! (Yopp, 1992, p. 701)

   Keep substituting different sounds.

   Many songs can be used for sound substitution as the following examples show:

   - The "Ee-igh, ee-igh, oh" sections of "Old MacDonald Had a Farm" can be changed to "Fee-figh, fee-figh, foh" and so forth.

   - "Happy Birthday" may be sung as "Bappy Birthday bo boo" or simply sung on the same syllable—"Ta" or "Pa," for example—all the way through the song. (Yopp, 1992).

"Here We Go Looby Loo" and "The Musicians" are good for substitution, too. Children love nonsense words, and they readily contribute sounds for substitutions.

3. "The Name Game" is very popular. Many children may already know it. Sing it together, substituting the name of a different child on every round.

> Sam Sam Bo Bam, Banana Fanna Bo Fam, Fee Fi Mo, Mam, Sam!
> Kaitlyn Kaitlyn Bo Baitlyn, Banana Fanna Bo Faitlyn, Fee Fi Mo, Maitlyn, Kaitlyn!

"Miss Mary Mack" (found in *Miss Mary Mack and Other Children's Street Rhymes* [Cole & Calmenson, 1990]) is good for substitution, too. Many of the other rhymes in this book also can be used.

4. Using the traditional folk song "Fiddle-I-Fee" and "The Barnyard Song" (Glazer, 1973) children can make interesting and fun substitutions.
   Children can make the following additions to the song: goose, honk; horse, neigh; sheep, baa; cow, moo.

5. Read *The Hungry Thing* (Slepian & Seidler, 1967). For extra motivation, introduce a large stuffed animal as the "Hungry Thing" and hang a sign around its neck that says, "Feed Me" on the front and "Thank You" on the back.
   Also, print on large notecards the part of the words that remains the same (e.g., *ickles*) in a series of three words, such as with the two nonsense words (e.g., *sickles* and *fickles*) and the one real word (*pickles*). Place this card (e.g., *ickles*) in front of the children as it comes up in the story. As the word in the story changes, change the first letters that have been preprinted on small notecards (e.g., *s, f, p*) to the appropriate letters. Attach the letter of the real word on the larger notecard. Last, ask one of the children to "feed" the real word to the Hungry Thing. Also, let a child turn Hungry Thing's sign from "Feed Me" to "Thank You."
   The same type of activities can be done with *The Hungry Thing Returns* (Slepian & Seidler, 1990) and you can add a "baby" Hungry Thing.

6. Read *Hairy Bear* (Cowley, 1990). Have the children substitute different beginning sounds into the various series of nonsense words found in the story. For example, "bim-bam-bash-em" might become "dim-dam-dash-em." These substitutions could be written on sticky notes and placed over the author's words.

7. Read *Henny Penny* (Galdone, 1984). Substitute beginning sounds for the names in the story: Henny Penny, Goosey Poosey, Cocky Locky, and Foxy Woxy. Children enjoy putting the beginning sounds of their names in place of the beginning sounds of the animal's names. They enjoy making up their own silly rhyming names, too (e.g., Airy Mary).

8. Use Raffi's (1976) tune "Willoughby Wallaby Woo." Listen to the entire song first; then point out the substitution of /w/ for the beginning sounds of the children's names. Listen again. Improvise on the tune with your children's names. Let the children take turns singing the verses and generating new names for their classmates. For example, one child sang "Willoughby Wallaby Wustin, an elephant sat on Justin"; then Justin sang the same verse inserting a different name, "Willoughby Wallaby Wanya, an elephant sat on Tanya"; and so on. (It takes a little practice to get children to this point of self-generating new names in verses, but they love the learning and the final result.)

9. Discuss the substitutions made within the following two poems:

> Eletelephony
> Once there was an elephant.
> Who tried to use the telephant—
> No! No! I mean an elephone
> Who tried to use the telephone—
> (Dear me! I am not certain quite
> That even now I've got it right.)
> Howe'er it was, he got his trunk
> Entangled in the telephunk;
> The more he tried to get it free,
> The louder buzzed the telephee—
> (I fear I'd better drop the song
> Of elephop and telephong!)
> Laura E. Richards (1850—1943)

> Once a Big Molicepan
> Saw a bittle lum,
> Sitting on the sturbone
> Chewing gubble bum.
> "Hi!" said the molicepan.
> Better simmie gum."
> Tot on your nintype!"
> Said the bittle lum.
> Anonymous (Ferris, 1957, p. 360)

(For this poem, teachers will need to discuss tintype old-fashioned photography.)

Nursery rhymes can be adapted easily to substitutions; substitute the beginning sounds of the rhyming words. For example, substitute the /f/ of *fiddle* with the /d/ of *diddle* in "Hey Diddle, Diddle."

10. Read *Don't Forget the Bacon* (Hutchins, 1976). This book plays with manipulation of phonemes in words to make totally new words. For example, "a cake for tea" becomes a "cake for me" and finally "a rake for leaves." The story is about a little boy sent to the grocery store with a "mental" shopping list from his mother. He gets the list all mixed up but

manages to come home with most of the items. After reading the book once and writing the grocery list on the board, reread the story. Have the children raise their hands every time the boy makes a substitution. Write the substitution exactly under the original request. (Make sure you allow plenty of space under each of the original requests to allow for this). Discuss the substitutions. Also, children could make up their own grocery lists (one item or more) and make substitutions.

11. The teacher may designate a certain sound to be used as the "Sound of the Day" (Yopp, 1992). The teacher can take attendance by substituting the "chosen" sound in place of the beginning sounds of the children's names. The children can be encouraged to do this type of substitution with their classmates' names, too.

Sound Blending Activities

The objective of a sound blending activity is to teach children that individual sounds can be blended to form a word; sound blending is an activity that is closely related to the skill of reading. In sound blending activities, the teacher slowly says the individual sounds in a word (at a rate of approximately one sound every one half-second), and then asks the children to blend the sounds together into the word.

However, in the case of kindergartners and first graders, a caveat is needed. When I first wrote these activities, I did not realize that kindergartners and first graders could not hear isolated short-vowel sounds (Routman, 1991), so I said words in their isolated forms. I noticed many children had difficulty figuring out the words. After reading and understanding the appropriate research, I say short vowels in children's names and other words within their rime (Johnston, 1999).

For example, when saying the word *cat*, say /c/-/at/. The /c/ is said slowly at the rate of one half-second, with a full separation between the /c/ and the /at/ rime. The /at/ also is said slowly by giving the /a/ one half-second, but holding the sound and sliding it into the /t/: a-a-a-a-t. Sliding the sound like this also is necessary when saying blends like /cl/ in *clop*. In the case of words where the vowel sound is long like *boat*, it is not necessary to slide the vowel sound into its rime or word family. Instead, the word can be said in its isolated form /b/-/o/-/t/, because young children can hear long vowels.

When doing the sound blending activities that follow, try to target words with *no more than* three sounds, even though the words may have more than three letters. For example, the word *boat* has four letters but only three sounds, so it is a good choice for blending.

1. To the tune of "Jimmy Cracked Corn and I Don't Care" use the words below to blend the sounds of the name, Jim.

/j/ -/im/ is a name that you all know. [Say the individual sounds of the name
slowly in approximately half-second intervals.]
/j/-/im/ is a name that you all know.
/j/-/im/ is a name that you all know.
Whose name is it?
[Wait for a response.]
Jim is a name that we all know. [Say the name as you normally would.]
Jim is a name that we all know.
Jim is a name that we all know.
He's (She's) our friend, that's so!

2. The game "What Am I Thinking of?" (Yopp, 1992) can be adapted quite
   well to blending. Tell the children you are thinking of a particular
   category (e.g., animal); then slowly articulate the separate sound
   segments of the chosen word (e.g., /g/-/o/-/t/). The children then blend the
   separate sounds together to answer the question. Yopp suggests using a
   grab bag with real objects in it to increase motivation. When using the
   grab bag idea, peek into the bag, and say, "I see a /b/-/a/-/t/ in here."
   When the children blend the separate sounds into the word, show the
   children the stuffed toy bat (e.g., Stella Luna) that is in the bag.

3. To the tune of "If You're Happy and You Know It, Clap Your Hands" use
   the words below to help you isolate or segment sounds so the children can
   blend them back together into words.

   If you think you know this word, shout it out!
   If you think you know this word, shout it out!
   If you think you know this word,
   Then tell me what you've heard,
   If you think you know this word, shout it out!
   [Teacher says a segmented word such as /k/-/a/-/t/, and the children respond by
   saying the blended word] (Yopp, 1992, p. 701)

4. Play "Mystery Picture" game. In preparation for the game, the teacher
   should find some individual pictures of words that have no more than
   three phoneme sounds (e.g., *web*, *goat*, or *cake*). To play the game, the
   teacher hides the pictures behind his or her back and targets them one by
   one. To begin the game, say, "Children, I have a picture of something
   behind my back, and I want you to try to guess what it is. I will help you
   by saying its name in a *secret* language. Are you ready?" Say the name of
   the word in segmented fashion, and then the children guess the word by
   blending the sounds together again. When they guess correctly, show
   them the picture and give some form of appropriate praise (e.g., "You did
   that so quickly" or "I'm so proud of you").

   Teachers may want to use the following song to enhance this activity. If
   the teacher writes the song and points to the words, it can help increase
   children's sight vocabulary, too. The song is sung to the tune of "Oh Dear,
   What Can the Matter Be?"

Oh, oh what can the picture be?
Oh, oh what can the picture be?
Oh, oh what can the picture be?
I know it is a /w/-/eb/.

When I first played this game with the children, many of them were having difficulty with guessing those words that had short vowels in them because I isolated all the sounds (e.g., /w/-/e/-/b/). Sometimes the entire class had problems, and I had to give additional hints. Once I started saying short-vowel sounds within their rimes (e.g., /eb/ in /w/-/eb/), additional hints were not necessary.

5. Nursery rhymes, because they are familiar, are good to use as an introduction to blending activities. Target the rhyming words as done below, and then have the children blend the sounds into a word. For example,

   Jack and /j/-/il/
   went up the /h/-/il/...

   Baa, baa black sheep, have you any /w/-/ul/?
   Yes sir, yes sir, three bags /f/-/ul/...

6. Poetry, chants, and finger plays can be adapted into blending activities, too. In the poem "Jump or Jiggle," the rhyming words can be isolated by the teacher so they can be blended together orally by the children. The rhyming words also could be creatively dramatized for better comprehension.

   Frogs jump   Mice creep
   Caterpillar's hump (/h/-/um/-/p/)   Deer leap (/l/-/e/-/p/)
   Worms wiggle   Puppies bounce
   Bugs jiggle (/j/-/ig/-/l/)   Kittens pounce (/p/-/ou/-/s/)
   Rabbits hop   Lions stalk—
   Horses clop   But
   I walk! (/w/-/aw/-/k/)   I walk!
   Snakes slide
   Sea gulls glide (/gl/-/i/-/d/)

   —Evelyn Beyer (1907)

In the chant "Five Little Monkeys," the rhyming words (*head*, *bed*, and *said*) can be isolated for blending.

   Five little monkeys bouncing on the bed
   [Let fingers of one hand bounce on the other]
   One fell off and bumped his head.
   [Hold head]
   Mama called the doctor and the doctor said,
   [Dialing motions or hold phone receiver to ear]
   "No more monkeys bouncing on the bed."
   [Shake finger]

Four little monkeys bouncing on the bed [etc.]

—Anonymous

In the chant and finger play "Jack-in-the Box," the words *tight*, *light*, *still*, *out*, and *will* can be isolated for blending.

Jack-in-the-box shut up tight
[Curl up tightly on floor]
Not a breath of air, not a ray of light.
[Tuck head down]
How tired we must be all down in a heap.
[Freeze]
I'll open the lid
And up you'll leap.
[Fling arms and pop out]

—Anonymous (Cromwell, Hibner, & Faitel, 1976, p. 110)

7. Use *Brown Bear, Brown Bear, What Do You See?* (Martin & Carle, 1983) to isolate color names so that children can blend them together. As an extended activity, put the children into groups of three or four. Give each group a box of approximately 1" by 12" strips of construction paper in the colors mentioned in *Brown Bear*. (Within each group, the teacher can choose to give enough color strips of the various colors for each group or for each child in the group.) Direct the children to pick up the correct color as you read it in isolated form from the following poem:

We can play a color game
Here are the colors we can name
Red, yellow, green, and blue.
There's orange and brown,
And purple, too.
Hold up the red strip,
Raise it high.
Now hold up yellow
To the sky.

Then hold up the card that's blue,
Now orange, then brown
And purple, too.
Now put down the card that's blue.
Then yellow, red, and purple, too.
Now the colors green, orange, and brown.
Now all the colors should be down.

—Anonymous (Cromwell, Hibner, & Faitel, 1976, p. 110)

After reading the poem, ask the children to paste their color strips on a sheet of paper in any design they choose. (Those groups that had enough color strips for each child will produce individual designs; those groups who didn't will produce one cooperative effort design.)

8. Read *Alphabet Soup* (Banks, 1988) to the children. Isolate the highlighted words found in the soupspoon. As an extending activity, you might want to bring in a box of Alpha-Bits cereal (or use plastic letters); let the children reenact the story by spelling some words with these letters using invented spelling. (It would be best to group the children in small groups of three or four for this activity if teaching a large class.)

9. The following books can be read in a similar manner as *Alphabet Soup* and *Brown Bear*. Using these books, target certain words that start with phoneme sounds that correspond quite closely to the letters that stand for them:

- *Willy O'Dwyer Jumped in the Fire* (de Regniers & Montresor, 1968)
- *Chicken Soup With Rice: A Book of Months* (Sendak, 1986)
- *Little Red Hen* (Galdone, 1985; target some of the animal names)
- *The Hide-and-Seek Book of Animals* (Wood, Wood, & Holmes, 1988). (Target the "hiding" animals. You might change the form of the animals' names to make it easier, such as using *cat* for *kitten*.)

Also use Raffi's audiotape (1976). There are many songs that work for blending, such as "Down by the Bay" and "Spider on the Floor."

10. Use the song "I Know an Old Lady" (found in *Shrieks of Midnight*, Brewton & Brewton, 1969). Isolate the following words from the first verse: *fly*, *die*, and *spider*. As the additional verses are added, isolate the additional words *bird*, *cat*, *dog*, and *horse* for the children to blend together. This song is fun to do innovations with, too.

When choosing appropriate picture books, songs, nursery rhymes, poetry, riddles, and the like for the purpose of isolating and then blending, pick words that are relatively short and have easily detected consonant phonemes.

Sound Segmentation Activities

The objective of a sound segmentation activity is to isolate all the sounds heard in a word. Segmentation (i.e., totally isolating all the sounds in a word) is a skill closely related to the skill of reading or decoding words.

Teachers should not ask kindergartners and beginning first graders to segment words of more than three sounds or phonemes. Also, initially teachers should not include words with short vowels, and when short vowels are introduced, they should be introduced in the context of their pattern or rime (i.e., /at/ in *cat*). (See introduction to "Sound Blending" in this appendix for information on how to do this.)

1. To the tune of "Jimmy Cracked Corn and I Don't Care," use the words below to segment some of the children's names that can easily be segmented:

Jim is a name that we all know.
Jim is a name that we all know.
Jim is a name that we all know.
Let's say his (her) name real slow.

/J-/im/ is a name that we all know. [Say the name here in its isolated sounds in half-second intervals.]
/J/-/im/ is a name that we all know.
/J/-/im/ is a name that we all know.
He's (She's) our friend, that's so!

2. Say the children's names with the iteration process. For example, Jim is said as /J/-/J/-/J/-Jim and Mary is said as /M/-/M/-/M/-Mary. Exaggerating sounds is an easier way of focusing attention on them. It is a good way to begin isolation and segmentation.

3. Because segmentation is difficult, it is best to limit targeted words to no more than three phonemes. The following song, sung to the tune of "Twinkle, Twinkle Little Star," is useful for teaching the complete segmentation of words:

Listen, listen
To my word
Then tell me all the sounds you heard: *race*
(slowly)
/ r/ is one sound
/a/ is two
/s/ is the last in *race*
It's true.

Thanks for listening
To my words
And telling all the sounds you heard! (Yopp, 1992, p. 702)

4. Several tunes on Raffi's tape (1976) can be used for iteration and segmentation of two- and three-phoneme words. They include the following:

• "Baa, Baa Black Sheep" has some easy words for segmentation—*dame* and *lame*.

• "Brush Your Teeth," which is good for iteration of the digraph /ch/-/ch/-/ch/. After singing the song, make up a list of /ch/ words.

• "Five Little Frogs" is good for iteration of the /um/ pattern in *yum*, and it has several other good patterns that can be segmented orally—*frog, log, bug, yum, pool,* and *cool.*

• "Five Little Pumpkins" has some easy words for segmentation; for example, the *ate* pattern in *gate* and *late*, the *un* pattern in *run* and *sun*, and the *ight* pattern in *light* and *sight.*

After orally segmenting some words in one of these songs, it might be fun to have the children draw a picture of something that interested them in the song. Have them also write a caption beneath the picture in invented spelling.

5. Simple poems are good for segmentation. Following are some examples:

Sound of a Poem
Whenever I hear
Up in the sky,
Zzz zzz uuu mmm
I know an airplane
is flying by,
Zzz uuu mmmm mmmmm.
[This poem could be lengthened by adding more verses such as *car goes ppp ppp uuu ttt, train goes ch ch ch ooooo*, and so forth.]

Where Have You Been?
Little Old Toad
Little Old Toad
Where have you been?
I've been up the road
That's where I've been
[The rhyming words *toad* and *road* can be segmented.]
Adapted from Margaret Wise Brown (Ferris, 1957, p. 127)

6. Rhymes, riddles, and nursery rhymes are good for segmentation activities. In addition, children enjoy making up riddles. The answers can be segmented but should only have three phonemes. Following are a few samples of riddles for young children. Have them segment the answers.

When the band comes down the street, you will hear marching _____. (feet)
Which do you like most, pancakes or French _____? (toast)
Alice wanted to be cool, so she jumped into the _____. (pool)

Nursery rhymes used in the form of riddles or oral cloze activities can be fun to segment. Have students guess the missing word and segment it.

Jack and ___?____ went up the ___?____.
Little Bo___?____ has lost her ___?____.
Rain, rain, go away; come again another ___?_____.

7. Segment the following words in the song "I Know an Old Lady": *fly* and *die*. As the additional verses are added, isolate the additional words *bird*, *cat*, *dog*, *cow*, and *horse*.

8. Use the two finger plays "Five Little Monkeys" and "Jack-in-the-Box" (see "Sound Blending" for these finger plays) to segment the rhyming words at the ends of the lines.

9. Read the scratch-and-sniff book *Little Bunny Follows His Nose* (Howard, 1971). Then tell the children that you are going to reread the story. Every time you say the name of a special "scented" rhyming word (e.g., *rose*, *pine*, and *peach*), have students tell you all the sounds they hear in the

word. As additional motivation for segmentation, use the following song, which is sung to the tune of "Oh, Dear What Can the Matter Be?"

> Oh, oh what can that smell be?
> Oh, oh what can that smell be?
> Oh, oh what can that smell be?
> It must be a "rose." [Segment this word, and the other "scented" words.]

This book and song can be adapted easily to sound blending and should be used in the sound blending section, too.

10. Other books that adapt well to segmentation include the following:

- *Alphabet Soup*, Banks, 1988 (Target the highlighted words in the spoon.)
- *Little Red Hen*, Galdone, 1985 (Target the animal names.)
- *The Hide-and-Seek Book of Animals*, Wood, Wood, & Holmes, 1988 (Target the "hiding" animals. You might change the form of the animals' names to make it easier, such as using *cat* for *kitten*.)

Additional Kindergarten Minilesson Topics

When choosing their own topics for writing workshop minilessons, veteran kindergarten teachers share three pieces of advice: First, do not assume that children know information that you have not demonstrated in a minilesson; second, minilessons are supposed to be about one thing and they should be brief; and third, know what developmental stages of written language and spelling the children are in.

Procedures

- Demonstrate singing a nursery rhyme, or a variation of a nursery rhyme, for children to quietly sing as they gather in community circle; for example, sing (to the tune of "All Around the Mulberry Bush") "This is the way we come to circle, come to circle, come to circle,/ This the way we come to circle with quiet mouths and feet."
- Demonstrate and discuss covering markers so they don't dry out
- Demonstrate how to ask for and share markers
- Demonstrate and discuss using soft voices and being respectful
- Discuss where to keep writing tools
- Demonstrate using only one side of the paper (students normally use both sides) to save pictures for possible posting or publishing

Strategies

- Demonstrate choosing topics by hearing other writers' pieces
- Demonstrate rereading your work

- Role-play and discuss what you and other children do when they're stuck
- Discuss what you and other children have done to become better writers
- Discuss what do you do when you are writing about one thing and get a new idea
- Discuss or demonstrate using a good book to give you an idea
- Discuss writing at home (e.g., Is it different from writing in school?)
- Demonstrate using the top half of the page for drawing and the bottom half for writing
- Demonstrate "reading posted rhymes" and "word wall" for correcting spelling if publishing (of if child wishes to)
- Demonstrate using a notebook to record writing ideas from daily life
- Demonstrate using different paper in minilessons
- Demonstrate how to use "rimes" or digraphs, already taught and posted on word wall, to spell another word (/c/-/at/; to /b/-/at/)
- Demonstrate how to use the "Look, Cover, Write, Check" strategy to help with spelling high-frequency words *already taught and highlighted* on the word wall, rather than simply copying them

Skills

- Demonstrate using proper pencil grip
- Demonstrate directionality of word, line, and page
- Demonstrate using uppercase letters for names and sentence beginnings
- Demonstrate and discuss managing space: words are too big (two or three to a page) or words are too little and all run together
- Demonstrate and discuss changing "me and my friend" to "my friend and I" (compound subjects)
- Demonstrate using *ing* endings

Content

- Demonstrate a picture and writing telling the same story
- Demonstrate using words that make "pictures in your head"
- Demonstrate writing sentences that have good sequence (order)
- Demonstrate adding or deleting something for clarity (most kindergartners can add and cross out; a few can "cut" and "paste" when revising with the teacher's guidance)
- Demonstrate writing in a different genre and explain why you chose that genre

- Discuss the importance of not using a story that has already been written (e.g., Pokémon); possibly demonstrate plagiarizing a story like *Goldilocks and The Three Bears* to aid discussion

- Demonstrate crossing out extra *ands*

- Demonstrate writing about small moments in life

- Demonstrate fleshing out a "bare-bones" piece

Additional Content Minilessons With Brief Descriptions

Shelly Harwayne (2001), early education teacher, consultant, and administrator, suggests the following minilessons to enhance the quality or content of kindergartners' writing. This list can be as extensive or limited as your children's needs dictate. This list will ultimately be based on how responsible children are in following classroom procedures and helping each other.

Help children recognize when writing is too sparse.

Explain to children that when you take their papers home and read them, some of the papers make you feel very "hungry" and some make you feel full. But what you are hungry for isn't a sandwich; you are hungry for more information. Next (with children's permission), read a few "bare-bones" pieces, and demonstrate what makes you hungry for more. Then, invite the class to reread their previous work to determine whether or not they have enough information.

Help children expand on their writing.

Use movement to show students when they can expand on their writing. Harwayne tells her students, "There's a line in [the movie] *Grease* that keeps playing in my head when I read some of your work. It goes, 'Tell me more, tell me more [she invents the next part] when I tap on the floor.'" Then (having asked permission) she reads a work and asks, "Can you tell me where I hear these words?" Children also can tap on the floor during Author's Chair when they hear places where the writer needs to add more.

Help children make better use of verbs.

Young writers are not familiar with the word *verb*, but they can understand that certain action words give more information than others. For example, the teacher could write *I went to school* and change the verb *went* to *jogged* and discuss the change.

Help children elicit sensory responses in writing.

Discuss with students what they have learned about the five senses in science class. Then say, "Today I am going to read some of the writing you've done, and I want you to tell me if the authors put any of your five senses to work. In other words, did our friends make you see, hear, smell, feel, or taste anything with the words they've written?" Read the samples and discuss students' responses to them.

Help children appreciate "surprising" elements in their writing.

Begin by saying, "Yesterday during writing workshop, I felt like I was attending a few surprise parties. Those are parties you don't expect that someone gives for you. You've probably seen people jump up and yell, 'Surprise!' when the guest of honor opens the door. As I walked around the room yesterday, many of you surprised me with your writing. I'm going to begin our writing workshop by telling you about all the wonderful surprising things I discovered in your writing because all good writers want to surprise their readers." Then, share some of the children's unusual topics, clever formats, and interesting words choices.

Booklists

Children's Books That Aid Prediction...300

    Wordless Picture Books..300

    Pattern Books Set to Song....................................301

    Pattern Books That Rhyme....................................302

    Classic Pattern Books..305

Children's Books and Additional Resources by Genre.................307

    ABC Books..307

    Beast Folk Tales...307

    Cumulative Folk Tales...308

    Information..308

Recommended Guided Reading Books.................................311

Children's Books That Aid Prediction

The predictive processes dominate reading and writing. To make prediction easier for the emergent reader and the early reader, texts that have pictures, rhythm, rhyme, and repetition are initially preferred. These predictable supports in a text greatly aid the emergent and early reader in handling the challenges of reading. Books of this nature are called predictable books. Repetition in predictable books is usually achieved by repeating language patterns or story patterns or by using familiar sequences such as numbers, the days of the week, or hierarchical patterns. Texts that repeat patterns are called pattern books.

The four predictable booklists that follow include the following categories: (1) wordless picture books, (2) pattern books set to song, (3) pattern books that rhyme, and (4) classic pattern books.

Wordless Picture Books

Pictures greatly aid the predictive processes; the first book list is of picture books that tell a story without words. Wordless picture books are a good way to initially introduce kindergartners to reading and the use of pictures as a prediction strategy.

Aliki. (1995). *Tabby: A story in pictures*. New York: HarperCollins.

Anno, M. (1977). *Anno's journey*. Cleveland, OH: Collins World.

Banyai, I. (1995a). *Zoom*. New York: Penguin.

Banyai, I. (1995b). *Re-zoom*. New York: Penguin.

Blake, Q. (1996). *Clown*. New York: Henry Holt.

Briggs, R. (1978). *The snowman*. New York: Random House.

Carle, E. (1971). *Do you want to be my friend?* New York: Crowell.

Collington, P. (1995). *The tooth fairy*. New York: Knopf.

Crews, D. (1980). *Truck*. New York: Greenwillow.

Day, A. (1990). *Carl's Christmas*. New York: Farrar, Straus and Giroux.

Day, A. (1991). *Good dog, Carl*. New York: Farrar, Straus and Giroux.

Day, A. (1992). *Carl goes shopping*. New York: Farrar, Straus and Giroux.

Day, A. (1998). *Follow Carl!* New York: Farrar, Straus and Giroux.

dePaola, T. (1991). *Pancakes for breakfast*. New York: Scholastic.

Handford, M. (1997). *Where's Waldo? The wonder book*. Cambridge, MA: Candlewick.

Hoban, T. (1995). *Colors everywhere*. New York: Greenwillow.

Hutchins, P. (1971). *Changes, changes*. New York: Macmillan.

Jenkins, S. (1995). *Looking down*. Boston: Houghton Mifflin.

Keats, E.J. (1973). *Skates*. New York: Franklin Watts.

Keats, E.J. (1982). *Clementina's cactus*. New York: Viking Press.

Krahn, F. (1977). *The mystery of the giant footprints*. New York: Dutton.

Mayer, M. (1969). *Frog, where are you?* New York: Dial Books for Young Readers.

Mayer, M. (1973). *Bubble, bubble*. Roxbury, CT: Troll.

Mayer, M. (1976). *Ah-choo*. New York: Dial Books for Young Readers.

Mayer, M., & Mayer, M. (1971). *A boy, a dog, a frog, and a friend*. New York: Dial Books for Young Readers.

Mayer, M., & Mayer, M. (1975). *One frog too many*. New York: Dial Books for Young Readers.

McCully, E.A. (1984). *Picnic*. New York: Harper & Row.

McCully, E.A. (1987). *School*. New York: Harper & Row.

McCully, E.A. (2001). *Four hungry kittens*. New York: Dial Books for Young Readers.

Oxenbury, H. (1991). *Good night, good morning*. New York: Dial Books for Young Readers.

Rankin, L. (1991). *The handmade alphabet*. New York: Dial Books for Young Readers.

Schories, P. (1991). *Mouse around*. New York: Dial Books for Young Readers.

Sis, P. (1992). *An ocean world*. New York: Greenwillow.

Sis, P. (2000). *Dinosaur!* New York: Greenwillow.

Turkle, B. (1976). *Deep in the forest*. New York: Puffin.

Weitzman, J.P. (1998). *You can't take a balloon into the Metropolitan Museum*. Ill. R.P. Glasser. New York: Dial Books for Young Readers.

Wiesner, D. (1988). *Free fall*. New York: Lothrop, Lee & Shepard.

Wiesner, D. (1999). *Sector 7*. New York: Clarion Books.

Wilson, A. (1999). *Magpie magic: A tale of colorful mischief*. New York: Dial Books for Young Readers.

Pattern Books Set to Song

Pattern books that have been set to song add the predictable element of the tune's rhythm to the book's repetitive pattern. Many of the song pattern books in the following list also add the predictable element of rhyme, and these are the best songs to sing and select for display in the classroom. Children can learn many sight words in a meaningful way if words are pointed to as these songs are sung frequently. It is a good idea to print the words (or chorus) of these selected songs in enlarged print on chart paper and keep the charts posted in the classroom. Song pattern books that rhyme are beneficial for hearing and playing with sounds in words (phonemic awareness), too, and they are the easiest of pattern books with print for kindergartners to practice approximated reading with.

Adams, P. (1974). *This old man*. New York: Child's Play.

Aliki. (1974). *Go tell Aunt Rhody*. New York: Macmillan.

Carle, E. (1993). *Today is Monday*. New York: Philomel Books.

Child, L.M.F. (1993). *Over the river and through the wood: A Thanksgiving poem*. Ill. C. Manson. New York: North-South Books.

Galdone, P. (1967). *London bridge is falling down!* Ill. P. Spier. New York: Doubleday.

Galdone, P. (1985). *Cat goes fiddle-I-fee* [set]. Ill. P. Galdone. New York: Clarion Books.

Hale, S.J. (1995). *Mary had a little lamb*. Ill. S. Mavor. New York: Orchard Books.

Kellogg, S. (1998). *A hunting we will go!* New York: Morrow Junior Books.

Langstaff, J.M. (1957). *Over in the meadow*. Ill. F. Rojankovsky. New York: Harcourt.

O'Brien, J. (2000). *The farmer in the dell*. Honesdale, PA: Boyds Mills Press.

Pearson, T.C. (1984). *Old MacDonald had a farm*. New York: Dial Books for Young Readers.

Peek, M. (1985). *Mary wore her red dress and Henry wore his green sneakers*. New York: Clarion Books.

Quackenbush, R.M. (1973). *She'll be comin' round the mountain*. Philadelphia: Lippincott.

Raffi. (1999). *Down by the bay*. Ill. N.B. Westcott. New York: Holiday House.

Raffi & Wickstrom, S.K. (1990). *Wheels on the bus*. New York: Random House.

Russell, B. (1993). *Spider on the floor*. Ill. T. Kelley. New York: Crown.

Spier, P. (1961). *The fox went out on a chilly night: An old song*. Ill. P. Spier. Garden City, NY: Doubleday.

Stevens, J. (1981). *Animal fair*. New York: Morrow Junior Books.

Taylor, J. (1992). *Twinkle, twinkle, little star*. Ill. M. Hague. New York: Morrow Junior Books.

Trapani, I. (1993). *The itsy bitsy spider*. New York: Whispering Coyote Press.

Watson, W. (1990). *Wendy Watson's frog went a-courting*. New York: Lothrop, Lee & Shepard Books.

Pattern Books That Rhyme

Pattern books that rely heavily on rhythm and rime add these two predictive elements to the books' repetitive pattern. When children are read an abundance of rhyme, they develop sensitivity to rhyme early and easily. Children love to recite and have rhymes read to them in a "sing-song" manner that emphasizes the rhythm of the rhymes. (In fact, children usually do not like rhymes read straight with no rhythm.)

The ability to recite rhymes in kindergarten is one of the best indicators of how well kindergartners will learn to read. Rimes (i.e., the rhyming portion of a word) are the basic units for reading and spelling by analogy. For example, a child using the analogy strategy spelled and read the new word *rat* from knowing how to read and spell *cat*. Using the analogy strategy aids early readers in becoming fluent readers because they do not have to sound out every letter in a word.

After pattern books set to song, pattern books that rhyme are the easiest books for kindergartners to approximate reading with. Mother Goose and Dr. Seuss are extremely helpful in this endeavor. See "Children's Books by Genre" in this appendix for a listing of Mother Goose nursery rhyme books.

Ahlberg, J., & Ahlberg, A. (1986). *Each peach pear plum*. New York: Puffin.

Barchas, S. (1975). *I was walking down the road*. Ill. J. Kent. New York: Scholastic.

Battaglia, A. (1972). *Old Mother Hubbard*. New York: Golden.

Brown, M.W. (1975). *Goodnight moon*. Ill. C. Hurd. New York: HarperTrophy.

Cameron, P. (1961). *"I can't" said the ant*. New York: Scholastic.

Christelow, E. (1989). *Five little monkeys jumping on the bed*. New York: Clarion Books.

Cowley, J. (1990). *Dan the flying man*. San Diego, CA: The Wright Group.

de Regniers, B. (1968). *Willy O'Dwyer jumped in the fire: Variations on a folk rhyme*. Ill. B. Montresor. New York: Atheneum.

de Regniers, B. (1989). *May I bring a friend?* Ill. B. Montresor. New York: Alladin Books.

Dr. Seuss. (1940). *Horton hatches the egg*. New York: Random House.

Dr. Seuss. (1953). *Scrambled eggs super!* New York: Random House.

Dr. Seuss. (1955). *On beyond zebra*. New York: Random House.

Dr. Seuss. (1964). *The cat in the hat beginner book dictionary by the cat himself and P.D. Eastman*. New York: Random House. (Although this beginning picture dictionary is not one of Dr. Seuss's rhyming books, kindergartners and first graders find it enjoyable to use and look at, especially when publishing.)

Dr. Seuss. (1965). *Fox in socks*. New York: Beginner Books.

Dr. Seuss. (1985). *The cat in the hat*. New York: Random House.

Dr. Seuss. (1987). *Green eggs and ham*. New York: Beginner Books.

Dr. Seuss. (1991). *Hop on Pop*. New York: Beginner Books.

Dr. Seuss. (1996). *Dr. Seuss's ABC: An amazing alphabet book!* New York: Random House.

Dr. Seuss. (1997). *I can lick 30 tigers today: And other stories*. New York: Random House.

Ehlert, L. (1995). *Snowballs*. San Diego, CA. Harcourt Brace.

Einsel, W. (1962). *Did you ever see?* New York: Scholastic.

Emberley, B. (1967). *Drummer Hoff.* New York: Simon & Schuster.

Gelman, R. (1984). *More spaghetti, I say!* Ill. J. Kent. New York: Scholastic.

Guarino, D. (1989). *Is your mama a llama?* Ill. S. Kellogg. New York: Scholastic.

Hoberman, M. (1988). *A house is a house for me* [kit]. Ill. B. Frazer. New York: Puffin.

Hutchins, P. (1976). *Don't forget the bacon.* New York: Greenwillow.

Janovitz, M. (1996). *Can I help?* New York: North-South Books.

Krauss, R. (1948). *Bears.* New York: Scholastic.

Kraus, R. (1970). *Whose mouse are you?* Ill. J. Aruego. New York: Macmillan.

Martin, B., Jr. (1970). *The haunted house.* New York: Holt, Rinehart and Winston.

Martin, B., Jr. (1992). *Brown Bear, Brown Bear, what do you see?* Ill. E. Carle. New York: Henry Holt.

Martin, B., Jr. (1996). *Fire! Fire! Said Mrs. McGuire.* Ill. R. Egielski. San Diego, CA: Harcourt Brace.

Martin, B., Jr., & Archambault, J. (1986). *Barn dance!* Ill. T. Rand. New York: Henry Holt.

Martin, B., Jr., & Archambault, J. (1989). *Chicka chicka boom boom.* Ill. L. Ehlert. New York: Henry Holt.

Marzollo, J. (1985). *Three little kittens.* Ill. S. Thorton. New York: Scholastic.

Paparone, P. (1995). *Five little ducks: An old rhyme.* New York: Scholastic.

Patrick, G. (1970). *A bug in a jug and other funny rhymes.* New York: Scholastic.

Peters, S. (1988). *Rub-a-dub-suds.* Mahwah, NJ: Troll.

Prelutsky, J. (1970). *The terrible tiger.* Ill. A. Lobel. New York: Macmillan.

Riley, L. (1997). *Mouse mess.* New York: Blue Sky Press.

Sendak, M. (1991). *Chicken soup with rice: A book of months.* New York: Margaret K. McElderry.

Serfozo, M. (1988). *Who said red?* Ill. K. Narahashi. New York: Margaret K. McElderry.

Shaw, N. (1986). *Sheep in a jeep.* Ill. M. Apple. Boston: Houghton Mifflin.

Shaw, N. (1989). *Sheep on a ship.* Ill. M. Apple. Boston: Houghton Mifflin.

Slate, J. (1996). *Miss Bindergarten gets ready for kindergarten.* Ill. A. Wolff. New York: Dutton.

Snow, P. (1985). *Eat your peas, Louise.* Ill. M. Venezia. Chicago: Children's Press.

Thomas, P. (1990). *"Stand back," said the elephant, "I'm going to sneeze!"* Ill. W. Tripp. New York: Lothrop, Lee & Shepard.

Wells, R. (1997). *Noisy Nora.* New York: Dial Books for Young Readers.

Classic Pattern Books

Most of the books in the list that follows are pattern books that rely on some form of repetition. Many have stood the test of time and are considered classics. This list represents some of kindergarten teachers' and kindergartners' favorite read-aloud books.

Adams, P. (2000). *This is the house that Jack built*. Auburn, ME: Child's Play.

Brett, J. (1990). *Annie and the wild animals* [kit]. Boston: Houghton Mifflin.

Barrett, J. (1970). *Animals should definitely not wear clothes*. Ill. R. Barrett. New York: Atheneum.

Baum, A., & Baum, J. (1962). *One bright Monday morning*. New York: Random House.

Brown, M.W. (1956). *The big red barn*. Ill. R. Hartman. New York: Young Scott Books.

Brown, M.W. (1984). *Home for a bunny*. Ill. G. William. New York: Golden.

Brown, M.W. (1990). *Four fur feet*. Ill. R. Charlip. New York: Dell Publishing.

Carle, E. (1984). *The very busy spider*. New York: Philomel Books.

Carle, E. (1987). *The very hungry caterpillar*. New York: Philomel Books.

Cleveland, D. (1978). *The April rabbits*. Ill. N. Karlin. New York: Coward, McCann & Georghegan.

Cooke, T. (1994). *So much*. Ill. H. Oxenbury. Cambridge, MA: Candlewick Press.

Cowley, J. (1997). *Greedy cat is hungry*. Huntington Beach, CA: Learning Media.

Cowley, J. (1999). *Mrs. Wishy-Washy*. Ill. E. Fuller. New York: Philomel Books.

Crews, D. (1998). *Night at the fair*. New York: Greenwillow.

dePaola, T. (1975). *Strega Nona: An old tale*. New York: Simon & Schuster.

Dewan, T. (1994). *Three billy goats gruff*. New York: Scholastic.

Eastman, P.D. (1988). *Are you my mother?* New York: Random House.

Elting, M., & Folsom, M. (1980). *Q is for Duck: An alphabet guessing game*. Ill. J. Kent. New York: Houghton Mifflin.

Ets, M.H. (1976). *Play with me*. New York: Puffin Books.

Fox, M. (1988). *Hattie and the fox*. Ill. P. Mullins. New York: Bradbury Press.

Gag, W. (1928). *Millions of cats*. New York: Putnam.

Galdone, P. (1968). *Henny Penny*. New York: Clarion Books.

Galdone, P. (1972). *The three bears*. New York: Seabury Press.

Galdone, P. (1975). *The gingerbread boy*. New York: Clarion Books.

Ginsburg, M. (1972). *The chick and the duckling*. Ill. J. Aruego & A. Aruego. New York: Macmillan.

Guilfoile, E. (1961). *Nobody listens to Andrew*. Ill. M. Stevens. New York: Scholastic.

Heller, R. (1981). *Chickens aren't the only ones*. New York: Grosset & Dunlap.

Heller, R. (1982). *Animals born alive and well*. New York: Grosset & Dunlap.

Hutchins, P. (1968). *Rosie's walk* [kit]. New York: Macmillan.

Hutchins, P. (1971). *Titch*. New York: Macmillan.

Hutchins, P. (1972). *Good night, Owl!* New York: Macmillan.

Hutchins, P. (1986). *The doorbell rang*. New York: Greenwillow.

Keats, E.J. (1974). *The snowy day* [kit]. New York: Viking Press.

Kellogg, S. (1971). *Can I keep him?* New York: Dial Books for Young Readers.

Kent, J. (1971). *The fat cat: A Danish folktale*. New York: Parent's Magazine Press.

Kirk, D. (1994). *Miss Spider's tea party*. New York: Callaway Editions.

Kraus, R. (1971). *Leo, the late bloomer*. Ill. J. Aruego. New York: Simon & Schuster.

Littledale, F. (1985). *The magic fish* [kit]. Ill. W.P. Pels. New York: Scholastic.

Lionni, L. (1988). *Frederick*. Barcelona, Spain: Editorial Lumen.

Lobel, A. (1979). *A treeful of pigs*. Ill. A. Lobel. New York: Scholastic.

Mack, S. (1974). *Ten bears in my bed: A good night countdown*. New York: Pantheon.

Marshall, J. (2000). *The three little pigs*. New York: Grossett & Dunlap.

Mayer, M. (1973). *What do you do with a kangaroo?* New York: Scholastic.

McGovern, A. (1967). *Too much noise*. Ill. S. Taback. Boston: Houghton Mifflin.

Numeroff, J. (1985). *If you give a mouse a cookie*. Ill. F. Bond. New York: Harper & Row.

Numeroff, J. (1998). *What Mommies do best/ What Daddies do best*. New York: Simon & Schuster.

Piper, W. (2002). *The little engine that could* (Rev. ed.). Ill. G. Hauman & D. Hauman. New York: Platt & Munk.

Polushkin, M. (1978). *Mother, Mother, I want another*. Ill. D. Dawson. New York: Crown.

Roy, R. (1979). *Three ducks went wandering*. Ill. P. Galdone. New York: Seabury Press.

Sendak, M. (1963). *Where the wild things are*. New York: HarperCollins.

Shaw, C.G. (1947). *It looked like spilt milk*. New York: HarperCollins.

Sherman, I. (1973). *I do not like it when my friend comes to visit*. New York: Harcourt Brace Jovanovich.

Tolstoy, A.N. (1968). *The great big enormous turnip*. Ill. H. Oxenbury. New York: F. Watts.

Van Allsburg, C. (1987). *The Alphabet Theatre proudly presents the Z was zapped: A play in twenty-six acts performed by the Casion Players*. Boston: Houghton Mifflin.

Viorst, J. (1989). *Alexander and the terrible, horrible, no good, very bad day*. New York: Aladdin Books.

Wood, A. (1984). *The napping house*. Ill. D. Wood. San Diego, CA: Harcourt Brace Jovanovich.

Zolotow, C. (1958). *Do you know what I'll do?* Ill. G. Williams. New York: Harper & Row.

Zolotow, C. (1969). *The hating book*. Ill. B. Shecter. New York: HarperTrophy.

Children's Books and Additional Resources by Genre

Kindergartners enjoy writing in various forms or genres—for example, notes, personal recounts, and reports. To provide engagement for young authors so they want to try writing in a different genre, Calkins (1994) suggests teachers find an example of the genre "that knocks...[their] socks off" and read and discuss it with their class (p. 364). Thus, the following list presents books that I have used for this purpose as well as magazines.

ABC Books

Crosbie, M. (2000). *Arches to zigzags: An architecture ABC*. Photos. S. Rosenthal & K. Rosenthal. New York: Abrams.

Duke, K. (1983). *The guinea pig ABC*. New York: Dutton.

Knox, B. (2003a). *ABC under the sea: An ocean life alphabet book*. Mankato, MN: Capstone Press.

Knox, B. (2003b). *Animal babies ABC: An alphabet book of animal offspring*. Mankato, MN: A+ Books.

Schuette, S. (2003). *An alphabet salad: Fruits and vegetables from A to Z*. Mankato, MN: Capstone Press.

Beast Folk Tales

Brett, J. (1991). *Berlioz the Bear*. New York: Putnam.

Brett, J. (1997). *The hat*. New York: Putnam.

Dewan, T. (1994). *Three billy goats gruff*. New York: Scholastic.

Murdock, H. (1985). *The three little pigs*. Ill. L. Grundy. Lewiston, ME: Ladybird Books.

Parkes, B., & Smith, J. (1987). *Musicians of Bremen*. New York: Rigby.

Rockwell, A. (1975). *The three bears and 15 other stories*. New York: Crowell.

Rockwell, A. (1988). *Puss in Boots and other stories*. New York: Macmillan.

Schmidt, K. (1984). *The little red hen*. New York: Grosset & Dunlap.

Cumulative Folk Tales

Carle, E. (1987). *The very hungry caterpillar*. New York: Philomel Books.

Galdone, P. (1961). *The house that Jack built*. New York: McGraw-Hill.

Galdone, P. (1975). *The gingerbread boy*. New York: Clarion Books.

Hutchins, P. (1968). *Rosie's walk* [kit]. New York: Macmillan.

Kent, J. (1971). *The fat cat: A Danish folktale*. New York: Parent's Magazine Press.

Taback, S. (1999). *Joseph had a little overcoat*. New York: Viking Press.

Tolstoy, A.N. (1968). *The great big enormous turnip*. Ill. H. Oxenbury. New York: F. Watts.

Wood, A. (1984). *The napping house*. Ill. D. Wood. San Diego, CA: Harcourt Brace Jovanovich.

Information

Magazines

Your Big Backyard (12 issues a year) is about animals and their habitats; it is for ages 3–6. Published by National Wildlife Federation, 8925 Leesburg Pike, Vienna, VA 22184, USA.

Zoobooks (12 issues a year) can be especially helpful to inquiry reporting. Published by Wildlife Education, Ltd. 12233 Thatcher Court, Poway, CA 92064-6880, USA.

Books

Demarest, C. (2000). *Firefighters A to Z*. New York: Margaret K. McElderry.

Demarest, C. (2003). *Hotshots!* New York: Margaret K. McElderry.

DuTemple, L. (1996). *Tigers*. Photos. L. M. Stone. Minneapolis, MN: Lerner.

Gibbons, G. (1991). *From seed to plant*. New York: Holiday House.

Gibbons, G. (2000a). *My football book*. New York: HarperCollins.

Gibbons, G. (2000b). *Rabbits, rabbits, and more rabbits*. New York: Holiday House.

Gorman, J.L. (2002). *Bus driver*. Photos. G. Anderson. Milwaukee, WI: Weekly Reader Early Learning Library.

Gordon, S. (2001a). *Hearing*. New York: Children's Press.

Gordon, S. (2001b). *Seeing*. New York: Children's Press.

Gordon, S. (2001c). *Smelling*. New York: Children's Press.

Gordon, S. (2001d). *Tasting*. New York: Children's Press.

Gordon, S. (2001e). *Touching*. New York: Scholastic.

Hewitt, S. (1999). *Growing up*. New York: Children's Press.

Hoban, T. (1998). *So many circles, so many squares*. New York: Greenwillow.

Johnston, G., & Cutchins, J. (1991). *Slippery babies: Young frogs, toads, and salamanders*. New York: Morrow Junior Books.

Lewis, J. (2001). *Dinosaur 123 ABC*. Markham, ON: Scholastic Canada.

Magloff, L. (2003). *Frog*. New York: DK Publishers.

Patent, D.H. (1982). *Spider magic*. New York: Holiday House.

Rockwell, A. (2002). *My pet hamster*. Ill. B. Lum. New York: HarperCollins.

Rosenberg, M. (1991). *Brothers and sisters*. Photos. G. Ancona. New York: Clarion Books.

Titherington, J. (1986). *Pumpkin, pumpkin*. New York: Greenwillow.

Labels

Anholt, C., & Anholt, L. (1995). *What makes me happy?* Cambridge, MA: Candlewick.

Appelt, K. (1993). *Elephants aloft*. Ill. K. Baker. New York: Crown.

Bridwell, N. (1990). *Clifford's word book*. New York: Scholastic.

Gibbons, G. (1982). *The post office book: Mail and how it moves*. New York: Crowell.

Gibbons, G. (1995). *The reasons for the seasons*. New York: Holiday House.

Rockwell, A., & Rockwell, H. (1979). *The supermarket*. New York: Macmillan.

Spanyol, J. (2001). *Carlo likes reading*. Cambridge, MA: Candlewick.

Sweeney, J. (1999). *Me and my amazing body*. Ill. A. Cable. New York: Crown.

Lists

Bottner, B., & Kruglik, G. (2004). *Wallace's lists*. Ill. O. Landstrom. New York: Katherine Tegen Books.

Hoban, T. (1978). *Is it red? Is it yellow? Is it blue? An adventure in color*. New York: Greenwillow.

Hutchins, P. (1976). *Don't forget the bacon*. New York: Greenwillow.

Lobel, A. (1971). A list. In *Frog and Toad together* (pp. 4–17). New York: HarperCollins.

Stewart, S. (1997). *The gardener*. Ill. D. Small. New York: Farrar, Straus and Giroux.

Tyron, L. (1999). *Albert's birthday*. New York: Atheneum.

Notes and Letters

Ahlberg, J., & Ahlberg, A. (1986). *The jolly postman or other people's letters*. Boston: Little, Brown.

Caseley, J. (1991). *Dear Annie*. New York: Greenwillow.

Danneberg, J. (2003). *First year letters*. Ill. J. Love. Watertown, MA: Charlesbridge.

Edwards, P.D. (2003). *Dear Tooth Fairy*. Ill. M. Fitzpatrick. New York: Katherine Tegan Books.

Harrison, J. (1994). *Dear Bear*. Minneapolis, MN: Carolrhoda Books.

Hoban, L. (1976). *Arthur's pen pal*. New York: Harper & Row.

Jackson, K. (1985). *First day of school*. Ill. J.E. Goodman. Mahwah, NJ: Troll.

James, S. (1991). *Dear Mr. Blueberry*. New York: Margaret K. McElderry.

Lobel, A. (1975). The letter. In *Frog and Toad are friends* (pp. 53–64). New York: HarperCollins.

Number Books

Carle, E. (1968). *1, 2, 3 to the zoo*. New York: World Publishing.

Hargreaves, R. (1981). *Count worm*. Windermere, FL: Rourke Interprises.

Hoban, T. (1985). *1, 2, 3*. New York: Greenwillow.

Reiss, J. (1987). *Numbers: A book*. New York: Aladdin Books.

Nursery Rhymes

Baxter, L. (1997). *Mother Goose: The children's classic edition*. Ill. L. Baxter, G. Percy, G. Rees, K. Widdowson, & J. Williams. Philadelphia: Courage Books.

Chorao, K. (1994). *Mother Goose magic*. New York: Dutton.

dePaola, T. (1985). *Tomie dePaola's Mother Goose*. New York: Putnam.

Edens, C. (1988). *The glorious Mother Goose*. New York: Atheneum.

Lobel, A. (1997). *The Arnold Lobel book of Mother Goose*. New York: Knopf.

Marshall, J. (1986). *James Marshall's Mother Goose*. New York: Farrar, Straus and Giroux.

Opie, I. (1996). *My very first Mother Goose*. Ill. R. Wells. Cambridge, MA: Candlewick.

Opie, I. (1999). *Here comes Mother Goose*. Ill. R. Wells. Cambridge, MA: Candlewick.

Wildsmith, B. (1965). *Brian Wildsmith's Mother Goose: A collection of nursery rhymes*. New York: Watts.

Wright, B.F. (1994). *The real Mother Goose*. New York: Scholastic.

Wonder Folk Tales

Daniels, P. (1991). *Beauty and the Beast*. Ill. A. Large. Austin, TX: Raintree Children's Books.

Grimm, J., & Grimm, W.K. (1964). *Rapunzel*. Ill. F. Hoffman. New York: Harcourt, Brace & World.

Grimm, J., & Grimm, W.K. (1983). *Little Red Riding Hood*. Ill. T. Schart Hyman. New York: Holiday House.

Grimm, J., & Grimm, W.K. (1984). *The goose girl*. Ill. P. Perret. Mankato, MN: Creative Education.

Grimm, J., & Grimm, W.K. (1989). *The fisherman and his wife*. Ill. A. Marks. (Trans. A. Bell). Saxonville, MA: Picture Book Studio.

Grimm, J., & Grimm, W.K. (1993). *Fairy tales*. Ill. G. Hildebrandt. Morris Plains, NJ: Unicorn Publishing.

Grimm, J., & Grimm, W.K. (1998). *The elves and the shoemaker*. Ill. M. Walty. New York: Barefoot Books.

Nemerson, R. (1997). *Grimm's fairy tales*. New York: Baronet Books.

Provensen, A. (1971). *The Provensen book of fairy tales*. Ill. A. Provensen & M. Provensen. New York: Random House.

Ross, T. (1994). *Hansel and Gretel*. Woodstock, NY: Overlook Press.

Stamper, J. (1997). *The three wishes*. Ill. R. Fritz. New York: Scholastic.

Tarrant, M. (1978). *Fairy tales*. New York: Crowell.

Zelinsky, P. (1997). *Rumpelstiltskin*. New York: Scholastic.

Recommended Guided Reading Books

In guided reading, students read a text with their teachers' guidance. Guided reading is usually done with small groups of children who read at about the same level. Therefore, in addition to needing multiple copies of a text for everyone in a reading group, guided reading also requires that books be at a certain level of readability. To help teachers choose an appropriate series for their guided reading sessions, I suggest the following series of books be reviewed when choosing a series.

Discovery Links
Newbridge Educational Publishing
PO Box 6002
Delran, NJ 08370-6002, USA
800-867-0307

This collection was developed for guided reading and has been well received. It introduces science concepts, has lovely pictures, and shows a diversity of cultures. Emergent and early reading levels each have 32 titles; the fluent level has 24. All titles are available in Spanish as well as English.

Oxford Reading Tree
Oxford University Press Education
PO Box 1550
Woodstock, IL 60098, USA
888-551-5454

There are 8 wordless books and 55 books with text in this series. Routman (2001) recommends this set of books for the developing reader. These books are about real-life stories with engaging characters that reappear in several of the books, and the books have colorful, culturally diverse pictures.

PM Collection
Rigby Publishers
PO Box 797
Crystal Lake, IL 60039-0797, USA
800-822-8661

This collection is highly recommended by kindergarten and first-grade teachers for guided reading. This series of books has been carefully leveled. The stories are based on children's oral language and provide good practice with basic vocabulary.

The PM Collection is divided into two sets: PM Starters (40 titles) that range from captions for pictures to simple repetition of sentences, and PM Story Books (168 titles) that range from simple to more complex sentences. Nonfiction titles have been added recently, too.

Books for Young Learners
Richard C. Owen Publishers, Inc.
PO Box 585
Katonah, NY 10536, USA
800-335-5588

This series is a great addition to any kindergarten or first-grade classroom. It includes many beautiful photographs and illustrations that support the text. There are 41 titles, and they are divided into three sets as follows: emergent (14 titles), early (20 titles), and fluent (7 titles). Twenty-two of these titles are available in Spanish. The publisher provides a leveling bar on the backs of these books suggesting levels for shared, guided, and independent readings of each book.

Letters and Charts

Letters

    Letter to Parents: Making an ABC Book...314

    Letter to Parents: Developmental Spelling..315

    Letter to Parents: Writing Nonfiction Reports..317

Charts

    Five Stages of Spelling Development 318

    Five Stages of Written Language Development...319

Letter to Parents: Making an ABC Book

Dear Parents and Guardians,

Learning the alphabet well enough to write any letter at random from memory is a lengthy learning process for your child. To help your child in this endeavor, please guide him or her in making an ABC book in which the alphabet can be printed in sequence, with a drawing for each letter that your child knows.

Directions: Guide your child to write the letters he or she knows (and only these), one to a page, leaving blank pages for letters yet to be learned. Your child should use the form of the letter he or she knows, whether it is uppercase or lowercase. Also, have your child draw (or cut and paste) on each page a key picture that he or she identifies the letter with already.

Keep this book in a handy place so your child can continue to add letters (and key pictures) as he or she learns more letters.

Advanced Learning of the Alphabet
When your child has good control of letter knowledge, practice sequencing the alphabet by getting him or her to say the next letter in the alphabet before you turn your attention to that letter.

Example:
Parent (points):   "a - apple"
Child (anticipating):   "b - balloon"
Turn the page
Parent (points):   "c - cat"
Child (anticipating):   "d - dog"

Note: Avoid saying "a is for apple" because many children try to find a printed sign for "is for."

I would like to invite your child to bring his or her completed ABC book to school to share with classmates.

Thank you for being a partner in your child's learning,

Mrs. Clark

This activity is recommended by Clay, M.M. (1993b). *Reading recovery: A guidebook for teachers in training.* Portsmouth, NH: Heinemann (pp. 26–27).

Letter to Parents: Developmental Spelling

Dear Parents and Guardians,

I want you to know that the teachers at Spring Valley School take spelling very seriously, but current research has informed us that the way spelling was taught in the past is not consistent with the way spelling should be taught. This information will probably not come as a surprise to you. Remember those spelling books and the weekly spelling tests you took? How many of those words can you spell today without a dictionary?

Spelling is not simply rote memorization, unless one has a visual gift. Spelling requires thinking. It is learned in the same manner that your child learned to talk—through experimentation—and it occurs in developmental stages as your child tries to communicate meaningfully to fulfill his or her needs.

The best way for young children to learn to talk is one on one with a proficient language user as they try to communicate their needs; however, children do not simply imitate what they hear. Children experiment with and actively construct language as they try out different sounds. Children save and reuse the sounds (and eventually words) that caregivers reinforce with their smiles and delight, and children eliminate those sounds that were not useful because they were ignored.

In trying to get language just right, young children's attempts are often far from perfect. For example, you were probably not alarmed when your toddler made statements like "Dat Daddy cup." You probably did not say, "No, that's wrong; you left out the verb *is* and the possessive *s* and you mispronounced the word *that*. Now say after me: 'That is Daddy's cup.'" How many children would want to learn how to talk after such negative feedback? Yet that is what we do with young children's initial attempts to spell.

The same kind of patient, supportive guidance that teaches children how to move through developmental language stages is needed to guide children through developmental spelling stages. Children learn to spell while attempting to write messages that are meaningful to them with the teacher's guidance, just as they learn to talk while participating in meaningful conversations with the guidance of parents and caregivers.

Let's take a look at two spelling samples written by the same kindergarten child to better understand how spelling develops through meaningful writing. In the beginning of the year, a kindergartner wrote the following:

ThEbiskITwLSHTOLMGTU.

At first glance, this may look like a lot of letters with no meaning, when indeed it is a well-thought out, developmentally appropriate piece of work that is meant to convey a message! This child knows that writing is supposed to communicate and mean something, and he knows exactly what this message means: *The bus is coming. It will stop here to let me get on.*

Almost every letter stands for a word in this sentence.

ThE b is k   IT wL S   H   TO L M GT U.
The bus is coming. It will stop here to let me get on.

Some developmental stages come before this one and some come after. (See attached chart of "Five Stages of Spelling Development.") From this sample, we can see that the child knows

- print proceeds in a straight line from left to right,
- print is made up of letters,
- letters come in upper- and lowercase, and
- letters stand for sounds in words.

(continued)

Letter to Parents: Developmental Spelling (continued)

Midyear, this same child was able to write about a personal experience that meant a great deal to him. His teacher, who was used to reading developmental spelling, was able to read the message without any help from the child. His message read:

My Gampa diyd Frim hirt Prblms FriDa.
(My Grampa died from heart problems Friday.)

In this writing sample, we see that the child has learned

- writing is made up of words separated by spaces;
- each word between spaces stands for one word in speech;
- written words are made up of different letters;
- there are a number of letter–sound combinations in each word (both beginning and ending sounds are included here);
- if you can't spell a word, you can use what you do know about letters and sounds to say what you mean until you learn the dictionary spelling;
- you self-correct your own writing when it doesn't look right to you, just as you did when you were learning to talk and something didn't sound right; and
- punctuation is a part of written language.

This child's spelling is developing, as is his ability to communicate his ideas in writing, which is the main purpose for writing and spelling. Spelling is only a tool that writers use to communicate. Readers do not buy novels for their spelling; ideas are what sell. If young students are only allowed to write the words they can spell, or if the teacher spent all of his or her energy in correcting temporary spellings, children would learn that spelling is more important than writing; it would severely limit their creativity. They would not only lose their natural desire to write but also their natural curiosity to experiment with and learn spelling patterns and rules.

There is a time to teach spelling. As spelling "needs" are noted in the children's writing, teachers guide whole-class and individual conferences that address those needs with spelling pointers and strategies. Also, when children publish their writing, their spelling needs to be corrected. (When kindergartners publish, the teacher helps the child make corrections.) As children become more experienced, they begin to take responsibility for this editing work themselves.

In a period of three to four years, your child has mastered the exceedingly complex system of your native language. Your child has learned to talk from talking. He or she could understand sentences never heard before and create sentences never said before. In the same developmental manner, your child's spelling will look conventional around fourth grade, if he or she is allowed to write "rough drafts" of his or her choice with "approximated" spellings and receive spelling guidance from his or her teacher at points of need. Expert conventional spelling requires effort, time, and instruction at point of need. It develops over years of reading, writing, and word study because it is as complex as learning to talk.

If you have any further questions about developmental or temporary spelling, I will gladly discuss them with you if you'll kindly make an appointment with me. Also, I would like to invite you to visit our classrooms during writing workshop and word study time to see how we are teaching spelling that transfers from the classroom to everyday writing.

Yours in education,
Principal Jeff Reiche

The letter is adapted from Routman, R. (1991). *Invitations: Changing as teachers and learners, K–12.* Portsmouth, NH: Heinemann, pp. 101b–102b.

Letter to Parents: Writing Nonfiction Reports

Dear Parents and Guardians,

Kindergartners are very curious about their worlds, as you well know. Our kindergarten class is about to begin a unit of study that will combine science and writing and allow your child to study an animal of his or her choice. Your child has this coming week to think about an animal that he or she knows something about but would like to know more about. Then, next week, on _____, your child should bring the live animal to school in an appropriate cage or container, if possible. If this is not possible, your child should bring a good picture of the animal that shows a lot of detail. Please help your child to remember to do this.

Next week, I will show the children how to closely observe their animals or pictures of their animals, and I will guide them to write a "big" question about their animal. Then the children will go to our school library to try to find books that will answer their "big" questions. They will be guided to write their answers to their questions in their own "words"; their answers will not be copied from a book. Total understanding is the goal.

It would be very helpful to your child if you would take him or her to the children's section of the public library and help your child find picture books about his or her animal. Not only might these books prove helpful in answering your child's "big" question, but also your child would get good experience in using the library as a resource.

Thank you for your interest in your child's education,

Mrs. Williams

Five Stages of Spelling Development

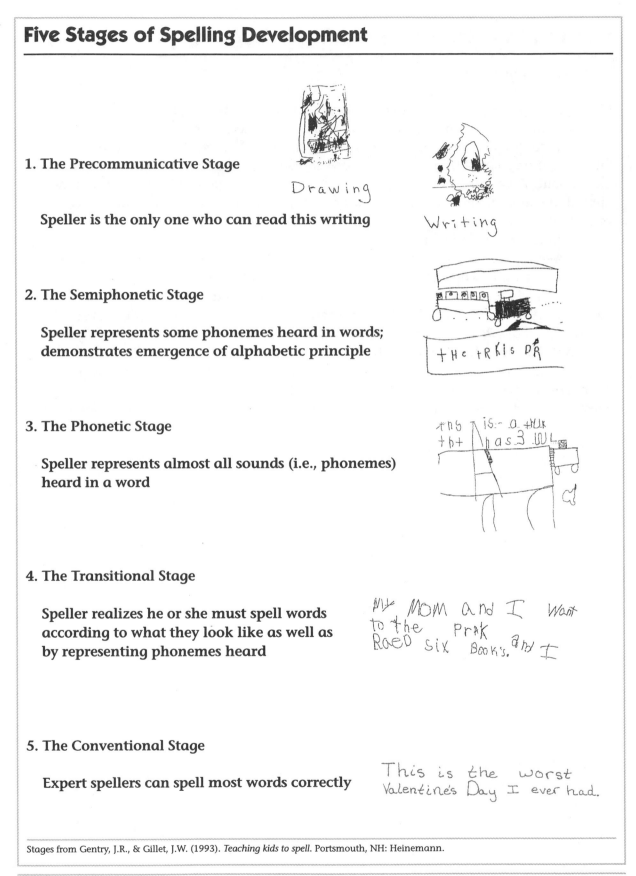

1. **The Precommunicative Stage**

   Speller is the only one who can read this writing

2. **The Semiphonetic Stage**

   Speller represents some phonemes heard in words; demonstrates emergence of alphabetic principle

3. **The Phonetic Stage**

   Speller represents almost all sounds (i.e., phonemes) heard in a word

4. **The Transitional Stage**

   Speller realizes he or she must spell words according to what they look like as well as by representing phonemes heard

5. **The Conventional Stage**

   Expert spellers can spell most words correctly

Stages from Gentry, J.R., & Gillet, J.W. (1993). *Teaching kids to spell*. Portsmouth, NH: Heinemann.

Five Stages of Written Language Development

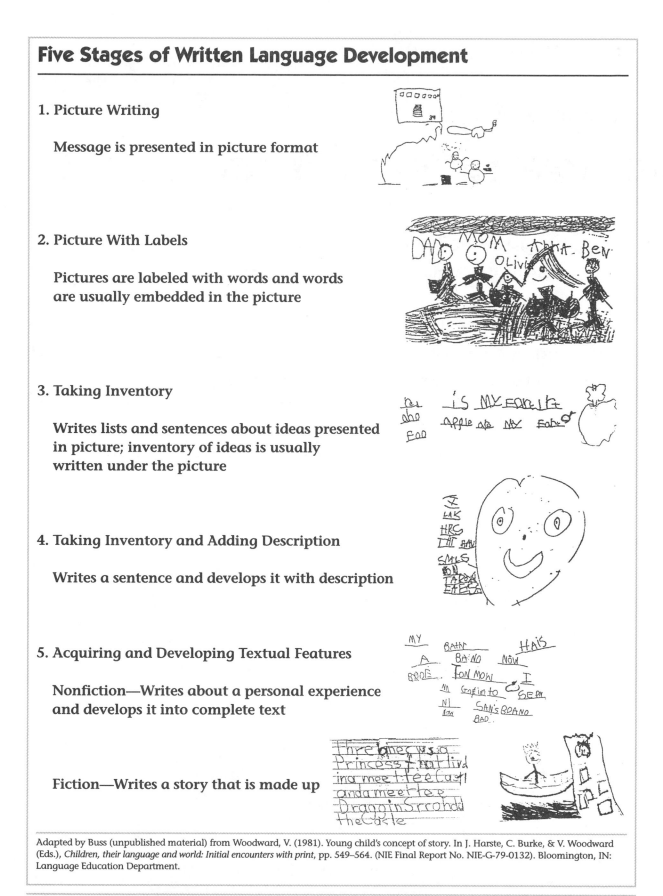

1. Picture Writing

   Message is presented in picture format

2. Picture With Labels

   Pictures are labeled with words and words
   are usually embedded in the picture

3. Taking Inventory

   Writes lists and sentences about ideas presented
   in picture; inventory of ideas is usually
   written under the picture

4. Taking Inventory and Adding Description

   Writes a sentence and develops it with description

5. Acquiring and Developing Textual Features

   Nonfiction—Writes about a personal experience
   and develops it into complete text

   Fiction—Writes a story that is made up

Adapted by Buss (unpublished material) from Woodward, V. (1981). Young child's concept of story. In J. Harste, C. Burke, & V. Woodward (Eds.), *Children, their language and world: Initial encounters with print*, pp. 549–564. (NIE Final Report No. NIE-G-79-0132). Bloomington, IN: Language Education Department.

Common Lists
and How to Teach Them

High-Frequency Words 321

List of High-Frequency Words for Kindergartners and First Graders 323

Wordo Directions 324

Be a Mind Reader Directions 324

Thirty-Seven Common Rimes Within Word Families or Phonograms 325

List of 37 Common Rimes Within Word Families
or Phonograms 326

Representative Word Families 329

List of Representative Word Families..330

High-Frequency Words

Words commonly found in the English language have been ranked in frequency of order and are thus known as high-frequency words. Fry's (1980) research has identified words based on frequency of occurrence in school texts and trade books, and the result is referred to as "The New Instant Word List." The first 100 words of the list on page 323 have become well known because they make up about half of all written material (Graves, 1994). Also, according to Pinnell and Fountas (1998), there are 22 italicized words on this list that can be easily learned by kindergartners as they write and read.

McCarrier, Pinnell, and Fountas (2000) explain that because high-frequency words appear often in text, children who know how to read and write them quickly will be able to concentrate on message. Also, half of the high-frequency words have patterns that can serve as models for reading and spelling other words. For example, knowing the *at* pattern can be helpful in reading and spelling *sat, fat, bat*, etc.

According to McCarrier and colleagues (2000), four words from the list (*the, do, is*, and *it*) can be learned by simply engaging kindergartners in meaningful writing and reading. The other words in the list may require further word study. It is a good idea to introduce the high-frequency words slowly throughout the year when you observe need in children's writing.

Gaskins and colleagues (1997) confirm Ehri's (1992) earlier research, which suggests that rote memorization of words is not the most effective way to learn sight words. The most effective way for children to retain a sight word is to fully analyze the sounds in the spoken word and then match those sounds to the letters in the printed form of the word (as is done in invented spelling). For students to analyze and match, teachers need to provide them with a model of how to analyze and talk about the words they are learning. First, Gaskins and colleagues (1997) suggest that the teacher pronounce the word as students fully analyze the sounds because hearing the word without seeing it makes it easier to hear and identify the number of sounds in it. Next, the teacher should show students the word and discuss the following:

- sound–letter matches,
- possible patterns,
- what is known about the vowel, and
- another word that has the same vowel sound.

Cunningham (2000) also states that abstract, high-frequency words must "be associated with meaning" and be practiced both briefly on the spot and daily in meaningful reading and writing (p. 57). An example of how this research was applied to teach a high-frequency word follows:

Mrs. Clark notices that children in the Semiphonetic spelling stage are having difficulty with the sight word *he* in their writing, so she teaches a minilesson to study it. Mrs. Clark tells the children they are going to play "Word Detective" to learn how to spell *he*. She invites the children to listen closely to hear how many sounds are in the word as she slowly pronounces it. James says he hears two sounds; the other children agree. (If students have difficulty with this, use the Elkonin sound box strategy in chapter 4, p. 122.) Mrs. Clark then displays the word *he* in context of the posted song "There Was a Little Turtle" (Prelutsky, 1986). After the children read the word *he* in context, she isolates the word by removing it from the text. (She'd written the word *he* on an index card earlier and used adhesive to stick the card to the text.) Next, she places the card containing the word *he* on the chalkboard tray. As the children look at the word *he* on the card, they count two letters and match them to the two sounds they hear. The children easily hear and identify *e* with its letter name. When Mrs. Clark asks if there is another word that sounds like or rhymes with *he*, several children answer *me*. Mrs. Clark writes *me* under *he* and asks the children what is the same about these two words. The children respond that they both end with *e*. Then Mrs. Clark asks Jeremy to underline the part that is the same. A brief discussion about both words having the same ending (rime) ensues. Then the children identify *h* as the "tricky" part because its sound in the word *he* has no similarity to its letter name *H* (pronounced ai-ch). Mrs. Clark asks the children if there is some way they might remember the sound /h/ in words like *he*. Julie says she will look at the "turtle song" if she has trouble. Mrs. Clark agrees that looking at the *he* in the turtle song would be a good idea. (Later, after reading *The Little Red Hen* [Galdone, 1985], Mrs. Clark discusses the sound /h/ in the word *hen* with the children. Then she puts a picture of a hen on the word wall under the letter *H* to help children remember the sound /h/ in words like *hen*.)

For immediate practice, Mrs. Clark asks the children to chant aloud the letters in the word *he* as they write them in the air. Then, she asks the children to look closely at the word again. Next, she covers the word with her hand and asks them to write it from memory on their dry-erase boards. Finally, she asks them to check their spelling as she uncovers the word. Those children who get it right are congratulated and the others are kindly reminded to practice the strategy "Look, Cover, Write, Check" (see chapter 4, p. 121) whenever they want to write a studied word like *he*.

Both the introduction and the practice just described took less than four minutes to do. Once a word has been studied as described, it is added to the kindergarten word wall and highlighted in context in the room.

List of High-Frequency Words for Kindergartners and First Graders

Words 1–25	Words 26–50	Words 51–75	Words 76–100
the	or	will	number
of	one	_up_	_no_
and	had	other	way
_a_	by	about	could
_to_	word	out	people
_in_	but	many	_my_
_is_	not	then	than
you	what	them	first
that	all	these	water
_it_	were	_so_	been
_he_	_we_	some	call
was	when	her	who
for	your	would	oil
on	_can_	make	now
are	said	_like_	find
as	there	him	long
with	use	into	down
his	_an_	time	day
they	each	has	did
_I_	which	look	get
_at_	_she_	two	come
be	_do_	more	made
this	how	write	may
have	their	_go_	part
from	if	_see_	over

Words that kindergartners can easily learn are noted in italics and underlined.
Reprinted from Fry, E. (1980). The new instant word list. *The Reading Teacher, 34*(3), p. 286.

Once high-frequency words are introduced, the best practice of them is with meaningful writing and reading. In addition, word hunts—using familiar text and in the classroom—are a good idea. There are two word wall practice ideas that kindergartners enjoy: "Wordo" and "Be a Mind Reader" (Cunningham, 2000, p. 70).

Wordo Directions

When 9 of the 22 high-frequency words that kindergartners can learn have been introduced and have been displayed on the word wall, the game "Wordo" can be played to reinforce learning of these words.

Wordo is a variation of the popular Bingo game. It is recommended by Gentry and Gillet (1993) and Cunningham (2000). The kindergarten teachers with whom I have worked also like to use this game on bad weather days during recess or lunch hour as a enjoyable way to reinforce the learning of high-frequency words.

Materials needed per player: One photocopied Wordo sheet (see Appendix E) and 9 small objects such as hard kernels of field corn.

Directions: Call on students to choose words from the word wall that they want included in the game. As each word is chosen, children should write it on their Wordo sheets in any blank block they choose, and the teacher will write it on an index card. (Make sure that children spell the words correctly on their sheets and that they understand that, unlike Bingo, players will ultimately have all the same words that are called out. Because they will have written them in different places, however, there will still be winners. Unfortunately, one cannot play for a full card.)

When all students have filled their sheets with the nine words called out, you are ready to play the game. The teacher shuffles his or her index cards and calls the chosen nine words out one at a time. Children should chant the spelling of each word and then cover it with a small object. The first student to have a complete row covered wins (diagonals do not count). The winner should tell the teacher and other players the words he or she has covered to be sure the words were actually called. Students can then clear their sheets and play again. Winners can become callers when the game is thoroughly understood, and the teacher can play the winner's card.

Be a Mind Reader Directions

Once there are enough words posted on the word wall (so that guessing a displayed word is a challenge), children enjoy playing "Be a Mind Reader" with their teacher.

Directions: The teacher thinks of a word on the wall and gives students five clues to that word's identity, such as telling students

1. It is one of the words on the wall.
2. It has three letters.
3. It begins with /th/.
4. It includes the vowel *e.*
5. It begins the sentence, _____ door is open; please close it.

Clues can be any features of the word the teacher wants students to notice.

Early in the year, this game is played orally, but later in the year, children can write their answers as the teacher gives clues. To do the latter, students should number their papers one to five before playing. After clue five, the teacher shows the children the word she wrote and says, "I know you all have the word next to number five, but who has it next to number four? Three? Two? One?" Some students will have read the teacher's mind from the beginning and will be very proud they are "mind readers."

Thirty-Seven Common Rimes Within Word Families or Phonograms

Knowing the 37 common rimes on p. 326 helps students to spell and read 500 basic words by analogy (Adams, 1990; Routman, 2000). Rather than teach complicated phonic and decoding rules with many exceptions that children will not understand, Johnston (1999) recommends introducing word families or phonograms when students consistently demonstrate the use of beginning and ending consonants in their written words.

To begin, teach one word family at a time. It is best to begin with short-vowel families rather than long-vowel families because kindergartners spell by sound and aren't aware of silent letters that represent most long vowels yet. Although there is no particular order, possibly begin with the short /a/ family because it is so prevalent.

The *at* pattern is a good family to begin with. After reading *Cat Sat on the Mat* (Wildsmith, 1983), the teacher explains, "We say these words—*cat, sat,* and *mat*—belong to the same family of words because they all end in the same two letters, *a* and *t.*" Then the teacher and children generate a list of words containing the *at* pattern. As children read other books, they can hunt for *at* words and add them to their posted *at* word list, too. (Children should be encouraged to initial their entries to provide ownership and interest; however, the teacher should be consulted on a word's authenticity and spelling before children add their words to the list.)

The next day, the teacher prepares an index card for each word he or she chooses to use from the class *at* list. After reading the chosen *at* word cards with the class, the teacher cuts the *at* rime off each word card. Then he or she puts the rimes in a column on a pocket chart and places the onsets in scrambled order at the bottom of the pocket chart. Next, volunteers are asked to come up and make a word such as *cat.* All onsets and rimes are put

List of 37 Common Rimes Within Word Families or Phonograms

ack	ank	eat	ill	ock	ump
ail	ap	ell	in	oke	unk
ain	ash	est	ine	op	
ake	at	ice	ing	ore	
ale	ate	ick	ink	ot	
ame	aw	ide	ip	uck	
an	ay	ight	it	ug	

Reprinted from Wylie, R., & Durrell, D. (1970). Teaching vowels through phonograms. *Elementary English, 47*(6), 787–791.

back together again in the pocket chart. The teacher might also say, "What if I wanted to spell another word such as *fat*; what letters would I need? What about *rat*?" (These words would be added to the *at* list, too.)

After this group work, children can work independently with a handout containing *at* words and corresponding *at* pictures such as *hat, cat, rat, bat, mat,* and *sat.* The children match the correct *at* word to its picture.

The following activity helps students master spelling phonogram or word family words. The teacher holds up each picture (cut from teacher-created handout mentioned above) and asks different children to spell the matching word on the chalkboard (with chalk or magnetic letters). Children should spell words in one vertical column, so the same rime can be seen easily. Children can also be asked to underline or point out the part that "is the same." Later, this activity can be done independently as each child writes the word on his or her own paper.

Another good activity that helps reinforce spelling and reading words by analogy is making and using word family wheels or flipcharts (see Figure D.1). Children enjoy playing with these wheels and charts independently or with partners. A word wheel can be made by cutting out two 6" circles and fastening them together in the middle with a brass fastener to make two circular wheels. Cut a wedge from the top circle and write the rime on the top circle to the right of the missing wedge, so the onsets on the bottom circle can be seen as the bottom circle is turned. Flipcharts or books can be made by using a piece of tagboard for the bottom or base page of the chart or book. The rime is written on the right-hand side of the base page. Then,

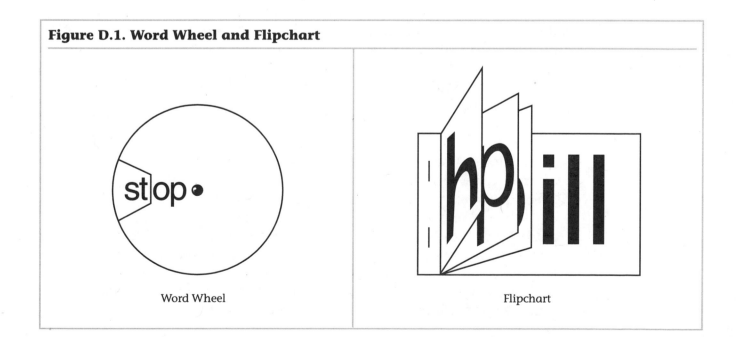

Figure D.1. Word Wheel and Flipchart

Word Wheel   Flipchart

pages half the length of the base page are stapled to the left-hand side of the base page and onsets are written on each one of these half pages.

Once two word families that have the same short vowel (e.g., *at* or *an*) have been studied in the manner described above, word sorts that contrast the same short vowel can be introduced. For example, after placing the words *cat* and *man* as headers on a pocket chart, the teacher says, "Today, we're going to compare (sort) some of the words you've been studying. Here is a word from the *at* family (*cat*), and here is a word from the *an* family (*man*)." Then the teacher holds up the word *sat* and says, "I am going to place *sat* under *cat*." Next he or she says, "Listen, *cat*, *sat*; these words go together." This procedure is repeated with the words *can* and *man*. Then volunteers are asked to do other words taken from the class *at* and *an* word family lists. Each time a child puts a word up, he or she is asked to read the other words in the chosen column to check for the "sound" as well as the "look" of the pattern; then the entire class reads all the words in the child's chosen column, too.

One teacher, Mrs. Reiche, has her children sing such a list to the theme song of the television show *The Addams Family*. For example: "There's *cat*, and there's *mat*, there's *sat* and there's *bat*, there's *fat* and there's *hat* in the *at* family." Then, the children clap their hands twice, and snap their fingers twice. They love doing this; it makes repetition fun.

In addition, when introducing the *an* pattern, teachers may wish to use *Dan the Flying Man* because it focuses on this pattern.

Johnston (1999) also recommends (as do I) follow-up word sorts with a partner; they also can be used as a center activity. Sorting can be done in many ways, but Johnston suggests doing "sound sorts." If children simply do visual sorts, they might do the sort merely by looking at the letters (especially the middle vowel when it comes to sorting families with different short vowels later on). Because it is important to form associations between the visual patterns read and the sounds used to spell the rimes, sound sorts are necessary. When teachers first present sound sorts, they should model them as follows: Using a pocket chart and the same headers (*cat* and *man*) as used to originally sort *at* and *an* families, the teacher pulls some *at* and *an* word cards from the two stacks of cards. Next, the teacher selects a word and reads it aloud without showing it to the group. Children then take turns identifying where each word the teacher read would go on the basis of sound alone. After placing each word in either the *at* column or the *an* column under its proper header (*cat* or *man*), the teacher asks the children to check the word visually to make sure it belongs there.

When doing sound sorts with partners, the teacher has one child (the reader) pick some words he or she knows from the word families being targeted. Then the reader reads aloud one of the chosen words without letting his or her partner see the word. The partner indicates the header under which the word goes. Then the reader lays the card under the header and the partner immediately sees if he or she is right.

Sometimes, children do "writing sorts," too. One child reads the words while the partner writes them in columns according to the ending rime. The writer receives immediate feedback by seeing the word after writing it. When students are able to sort without problems, it's time to move on to other word families. When choosing word families, the teacher should look for words children know from their reading.

After introducing and comparing the *at* and *an* word families individually and at length as described, the teacher can introduce word families that share the same vowel in sets of two, three, or even four families. As these families are introduced, they can be sorted in similar fashion.

If children show evidence of using but confusing short vowels in their writing (usually in the Phonetic spelling stage), word families with different short vowels (e.g., *at*, *ut*, and *it*) can be compared by word sorting.

Representative Word Families

It is not necessary to teach every word family; children's constructive minds will make many intuitive analogies (Johnston, 1999). However, it is wise to observe children's writing for problems with certain families.

If teachers observe several students using but confusing any of the following word families, teachers should help students study them in the manner described by Johnston in this appendix.

List of Representative Word Families

ab	aim	an	are	at
ace	ain	ance	ark	atch
ack	air	and	arm	ate
act	ait	ane	arn	ave
ad	ake	ang	arp	aw
ade	alk	ank	art	ax
aft	all	ant	ase	ay
ag	alt	ap	ash	aze
age	am	ape	ask	
aid	ame	ar	ass	
ail	amp	ard	ast	

ead	eat	een	elp	esk
eak	eck	eep	elt	ess
eal	ed	eer	em	est
eam	eed	eet	en	et
ean	eek	eg	end	etch
eap	eel	ell	ent	ew
ear	eem	elm	ep	

ib	ig	ince	irt	itch
ibe	ike	ind	is	ite
ick	ile	ine	ise	ive
id	ill	ink	ish	ix
ide	ilt	int	isk	ize
ife	im	ip	iss	izz
iff	ime	ipe	ist	
ift	in	ire	it	

oach	obe	oll	oop	orn
oad	ock	om	oor	ort
oak	od	ome	oot	ose
oal	ode	on	op	ot
oam	oft	one	ope	otch
oan	og	oof	or	ote
oap	oid	ook	orb	ow
oast	oil	ool	ord	owe
oat	oke	oom	ore	ox
ob	ole	oon	ork	oy

ub	ug	ume	ur	ush	uff
ube	uge	un	ure	usk	um
uck	ule	und	urn	uss	up
ud	ull	une	urt	ust	use
ude	ult	unk	us	ut	ute	uzz

Reprinted from Gentry, J.R., & Gillett, J.W. (1993). *Teaching kids to spell.* Portsmouth, NH: Heinemann, p. 91.

Reproducible Forms

Getting Ready and Writing Workshop Lesson Plan Form............................332

CID Form for Daily Assessment and Evaluation..333

Weekly Conference and Instructional Guidesheet (WCIG) Form..................334

Directions for WCIG Form 335

Kindergarten Writing Rubric Sample..336

Kindergarten Writing Checklist Sample..337

Friendly Letter Form 338

Friendly Letter Form With Labels..339

Wordo Form...340

A Different Alphabet Form..341

Getting Ready and Writing Workshop Lesson Plan Form

Date: _____

I.   Getting Ready for Writing Workshop

        A. Alphabet Study

            1. "Alphabet Song"

            2.

        B. Phonemic Awareness Activities

            1. Name Song

            2.

II.   Writing Workshop

        A. Teacher Demonstration and Minilesson

        B. Teacher Confers and Students Write

        C. Student Authors Share Work in Author's Chair

CID Form for Daily Assessment and Evaluation

Writing Assessment Evaluation   Name _____   Date _____

Teacher:

What Child Knows	What I Know	What I Will Do

Weekly Conference and Instructional Guidesheet (WCIG) Form

Days	Monday	Tuesday	Wednesday	Thursday	Friday
Ideas	Minilesson	Minilesson	Minilesson	Minilesson	Minilesson
Review					
New					

I = Instruction
S = Shared This Day
C = Conference
P = Published This Day

Directions for WCIG Form

The WCIG form is used to remind teachers which student he or she is meeting with on any given day and what specific instruction, derived from previous conferences, to implement.

This form has been designed for kindergarten teachers who divide the number in their class (15 to 20) by the days in a week (5) to determine the number of students (4) that can be conferenced with on any given day. Select four children to conference with on Monday and write their names in the Monday column, one name to a box. However, if possible, on Friday, schedule less than four students to allow time for each child to choose his or her best work for the week. If this is not possible, allot extra time on Friday to discuss the "Good Writing" chart, to add to it, and to have students choose their best work.

To save on recording time, using initials proves very helpful. Some common initials teachers use are presented in the key (with definitions) on the guidesheet. An example of using these initials follows:

> In Andrew's box, Mrs. Clark places a *C* because Andrew is present and she did have a conference with him on Monday. He did not share his work in Author's Chair so she does not place an *S* in his box. Mrs. Clark writes *Check for writing* next to an *I* in his box to remind her to ensure that Andrew has some writing along with his drawing on Tuesday. She determines this instructional need from her assessment and evaluation of Andrew's writing conference on Monday.

The bottom two rows on the form, "Review" and "New," are for any need that the teacher noticed during conferences that requires reteaching ("Review") or teaching ("New").

Kindergarten Writing Rubric Sample

Name: Date: Teacher:

Writes Name	attempts	first letter	first name	last name	1st and last name
Chooses Topic	needs encouragement	most of the time	has own voice	sense of audience	brainstorms other topics
Concepts of Print	print carries message	directionality	uses letters	uses punctuation correctly	uses spaces
Visual Attending to Graphic Cues	uppercase letters	lowercase letters	names/words	blends/cues	short vowels
Phonological Awareness	hears words	hears rhyme	hears syllables	hears some individual sounds	hears beginning/ middle/ ending sounds
Phonemic Awareness (hearing sounds in words)	no sounds	match beginning	isolate beginning	isolate beginning and ending	isolate middle
Writing Stages	Picture Writing	Picture with Labels	Taking Inventory	Taking Inventory and Description	Acquiring and Developing Textual Features of Nonfiction and Fiction
Follows Writing Rules	needs encouragement	sometimes	most of the time	consistent	helps others
Voice					
Focus					
Sequence					
Spelling Stage	Pre-communicative	Semiphonetic	Phonetic	Transitional	Conventional
Reads Own Writing	no attempt	attempts immediately	attempts to read next day	reads own writing	reads others' writing
Writing Posture	positions paper correctly	positions arm and wrist correctly	holds pencil at correct angle	control on lines	control on circle

Kindergarten Writing Checklist Sample

Name _____ Date _____

	Not Yet	Sometimes	Consistently
Interest in writing			
Writes first name			
Chooses topic easily			
Drawing tells about a personal experience			
Reads back own writing			
Uses own voice			
Follows writing rules (idea, draw, write)			
Uses "Alphabet Song" and chart			
Uses some lowercase letters			
Can spell some high-frequency words			
Good language abilities			
Understands that print can stand for language			
Can hear some individual sounds in words			
Uses directionality			
Pencil pressure/grip			

Writing stage _____

Spelling stage _____

Friendly Letter Form

Name _____ Date _____

Dear _____

_____

_____

_____

_____

_____

_____

_____

_____

_____

_____

_____,

_____

Friendly Letter Form With Labels

Greeting

Name _____   Date _____

Dear _____

_____

_____

_____

_____

_____

Body

_____

_____

_____

_____

_____

_____

Greeting

Closing

_____,

_____

Wordo Form

WORDO

A Different Alphabet Form

This page of print has proven useful to understanding a child's initial perception of the alphabet in print, and what an extraordinary undertaking it is for him or her to learn not only the alphabet but also the alphabetic principle.

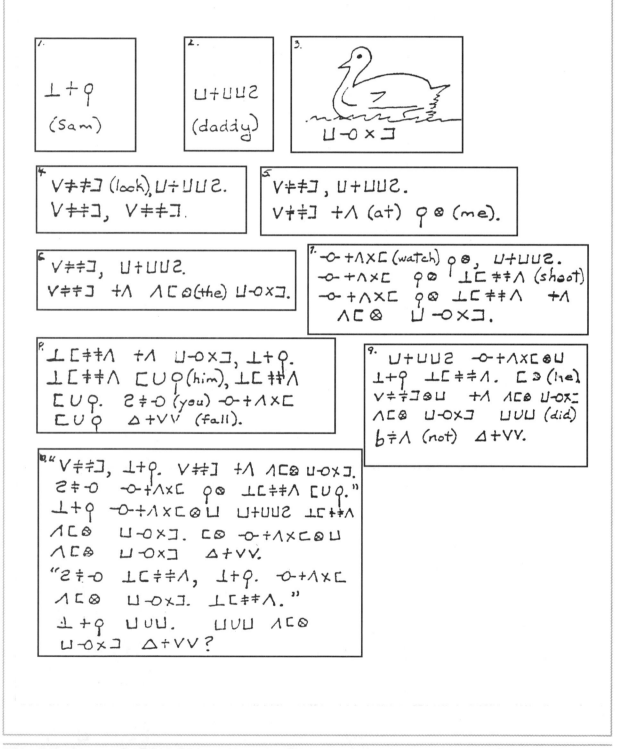

REFERENCES

Adams, M. (1990). *Beginning to read: Thinking and learning about print*. Cambridge, MA: MIT Press.

Anderson, R.C., Hiebert, E.H., Scott, J.A., & Wilkinson, I.A.G. (1985). *Becoming a nation of readers: The report of the Commission on Reading*. Washington, DC: National Institute of Education.

Angelillo, J. (2002). *A fresh approach to teaching punctuation*. New York: Scholastic.

Ashton-Warner, S. (1963). *Teacher*. New York: Simon & Schuster.

Atwell, N. (1987). *In the middle: Writing, reading, learning with adolescents*. Portsmouth, NH: Heinemann.

Avery, C. (1993). *...And with a light touch: Learning about reading, writing, and teaching with first graders*. Portsmouth, NH: Heinemann.

Ball, E.W., & Blachman, B.A. (1991). Does phoneme awareness training in kindergarten make a difference in early word recognition and developmental spelling? *Reading Research Quarterly, 26*(1), 49–66.

Bear, D., Invernizzi, M. Templeton, S., & Johnston, F. (2000). *Words their way: Word study for phonics, vocabulary, and spelling instruction*. Upper Saddle River, NJ: Prentice Hall.

Birnbaum, J.C. (1982). The reading and composing behavior of selected fourth- and seventh-grade students. *Research in the Teaching of English, 16*, 241–260.

Black, P., & William, D. (1998). Assessment and classroom learning. *Assessment in Education, 5*(1), 7–74.

Bomer, R. (1995). *Time for meaning: Crafting literate lives in middle and high school*. Portsmouth, NH: Heinemann.

Boyd-Batstone, P. (2004). Focused anecdotal records assessment: A tool for standards-based, authentic assessment. *The Reading Teacher, 58*(3), 230–239.

Bradley, L., & Bryant, P.E. (1983). Categorizing sounds and learning to read: A causal connection. *Nature, 301*, 419–421.

Britton, J. (1970). *Language and learning*. London: Allen Lane.

Buss, K., & Karnowksi, L. (2000). *Reading and writing literary genres*. Newark, DE: International Reading Association.

Buss, K., & Karnowksi, L. (2002). *Reading and writing nonfiction genres*. Newark, DE: International Reading Association.

Calkins, L.M. (1986). *Lessons from a child: On the teaching and learning of writing*. Portsmouth, NH: Heinemann.

Calkins, L.M. (1994). *The art of teaching writing*. Portsmouth, NH: Heinemann.

Calkins, L.M. (2001). *The art of teaching reading*. New York: Addison-Wesley, Longman.

Calkins, L., & Oxenhorn, A. (2003). *Small moments: Personal narrative writing*. Portsmouth, NH: Heinemann.

Cambourne, B. (1987). Language, learning and literacy. In A. Butler & J. Turbill (Eds.), *Towards a reading-writing classroom* (pp. 5–9). Portsmouth, NH: Heinemann.

Cambourne, B. (1988). *The whole story: Natural learning and the acquisition of literacy in the classroom*. Auckland, New Zealand: Ashton Scholastic.

Chall, J.S. (1983). *Stages of reading development*. New York: McGraw-Hill.

Chapman, M.L. (1995). The sociocognitive construction of written genres in first grade. *Research in the Teaching of English, 29*, 164–191.

Chomsky, C. (1971). Invented spelling in the open classroom. *Word, 27*, 499–518.

Chomsky, C. (1979). Approaching reading through invented spelling. In L.B. Resnick & P.A. Weaver (Eds.), *Theory and practice of early reading* (Vol. 1–2, pp. 43–65). Hillsdale, NJ: Erlbaum.

Chomsky, N. (1975). *Reflections on language*. New York: Pantheon Books.

Clark, M.M. (1976). *Young fluent readers: What can they teach us?* London: Heinemann.

Clay, M.M. (1967). The reading behavior of five-year-old children: A research report. *New Zealand Journal of Education Studies, 2*(1), 11–31.

Clay, M.M. (1972a). *Sand*. Auckland, New Zealand: Heinemann.

Clay, M.M. (1972b). *Stones*. Auckland, New Zealand: Heinemann.

Clay, M.M. (1975). *What did I write?* Portsmouth, NH: Heinemann.

Clay, M.M. (1979). *Reading: The patterning of complex behaviour* (2nd ed.). Portsmouth, NH: Heinemann.

Clay, M.M. (1991). *Becoming literate: The construction of inner control*. Portsmouth, NH: Heinemann.

Clay, M.M. (1993a). *An observation survey of early literacy achievement*. Portsmouth, NH: Heinemann.

Clay, M.M. (1993b). *Reading Recovery: A guidebook for teachers in training*. Portsmouth, NH: Heinemann.

Clay, M.M. (2001). *Change over time: In children's literate development*. Portsmouth, NH: Heinemann.

Cordeiro, P. (1988). Children's punctuation. An analysis of errors in period placement. *Research in the Teaching of English, 22*(1), 62–72.

Covington, M. (1992). *Making the grade: A self-worth perspective on motivation and school reform*. New York: Cambridge University Press.

Crafton, L. (1991). *Whole language: Getting started...moving forward*. Katonah, NY: Richard C. Owen.

Cudd, E., & Roberts, L. (1994). A scaffolding technique to develop sentence sense and vocabulary. *The Reading Teacher, 47*(4), 346–349.

Cunningham, A.E. (1990). Explicit vs. implicit instruction in phonemic awareness. *Journal of Experimental Child Psychology, 50*, 429–444.

Cunningham, P. (2000). *Phonics they use: Words for reading and writing*. New York: Addison Wesley Longman.

Cunningham, P.M., & Allington, R.L. (1994). *Classrooms that work: They can all read and write*. New York: HarperCollins.

Dahl, K.L., & Farnan, N. (1998). *Children's writing: Perspectives from research*. Newark, DE: International Reading Association.

De Fina, A.D. (1992). *Portfolio assessment: Getting started*. New York: Scholastic.

Dickerson, D. (1982). A study of use of games to reinforce sight vocabulary. *The Reading Teacher, 36*(1), 46–49.

Downing, J. (1970). The development of linguistic concepts in children's thinking. *Research in the Teaching of English, 4*, 5–19.

Durkin, D. (1966). *Children who read early*. New York: Teachers College Press.

Durkin, D. (1987). *Teaching young children to read* (4th ed.). Boston: Allyn & Bacon.

Dyson, A.H. (1986). Children's early interpretations of writing: Expanding research perspectives. In D. Yoden & S. Templeton (Eds.), *Metalinguistic awareness and beginning literacy*. Exeter, NH: Heinemann Educational Books.

Dyson, A.H. (1989). *Multiple worlds of child writers: Friends learning to write*. New York: Teachers College Press.

Dyson, A.H., & Freedman, S.W. (1991). *Critical challenges for research on writing and literacy: 1990–1995* (Technical Rep. No. 1B). Berkeley, CA: Center for the Study of Writing.

Ehri, L.C. (1992). Reconceptualizing the development of sight word reading and its relationship to decoding. In P. Gough, L. Ehri, & R. Trieman (Eds.), *Reading acquisition* (pp. 107–143). Hillsdale, NJ: Erlbaum.

Ehri, L.C. (2002). Phases of acquisition in learning to read words and implications for teaching. In R. Stainthorp & P. Tomilinson (Eds.), *Learning and teaching reading* (pp. 7–28). London: British Journal of Educational Psychology.

Elbow, P. (1973). *Writing without teachers*. London: Oxford Press.

Elkonin, D.B. (1973). U.S.S.R. In J. Downing (Ed.), *Comparative reading* (pp. 551–580). New York: Macmillan.

Emig, J.A. (1971). *The composing processes of twelfth graders*. Urbana, IL: National Council of Teachers of English.

Ferreiro, E. (1981). The relationship between oral and written language: The children's viewpoints. In Y. Goodman, M. Haussler, & D. Strickland (Eds.), *Oral and written language development research: Impact on the schools* (pp. 47–56). Urbana, IL: National Council of Teachers of English.

Ferreiro, E., & Teberosky, A. (1982). *Literacy before schooling*. Portsmouth, NH: Heinemann.

Finn, C.E., Petrilli, M.J., Cheney, L.V., & Vanourek, G. (1998, November 22). Commentary. The state of state standards. Four reasons why most don't cut the mustard. *Education Week, 39,* 56.

Fisher, B. (1991). *Joyful learning: A whole language kindergarten.* Portsmouth, NH: Heinemann.

Fletcher, R.J. (1993). *What a writer needs.* Portsmouth, NH: Heinemann.

Fountas, I.C., & Pinnell, G.S. (2001). *Guiding readers and writers, grades 3–6: Teaching comprehension, genre, and content literacy.* Portsmouth, NH: Heinemann.

Fry, E. (1980). The new instant word list. *The Reading Teacher, 34*(3), 284–289.

Galda, L., Cullinan, B.E., & Strickland, D.S. (1997). *Language, literacy, and the child* (2nd ed.). Fort Worth, TX: Harcourt Brace.

Gardner, H. (1998, December 4). What do tests test? *The New York Times,* A29.

Gaskins, I.W., Downer, M.A., Anderson, R.C., Cunningham, P.M., Gaskins, R.W., & Schomer, M. (1988). A metacognitive approach to phonics: Using what you know to decode what you don't. *Remedial and Special Education, 9,* 36–41.

Gaskins, I.W., Ehri, L.C., Cress, C., O'Hara, C., & Donnelly, K. (1997). Procedures for word learning: Making discoveries about words. *The Reading Teacher, 50*(4), 312–327.

Gentry, J.R., & Gillet, J.W. (1993). *Teaching kids to spell.* Portsmouth, NH: Heinemann.

Gere, A.R. (1985). Introduction. In A.R. Gere (Ed.), *Roots in the sawdust: Writing to learn across the disciplines* (pp. 1–8). Urbana, IL: National Council of Teachers of English.

Gibson, E.J., Osser, H., Schiff, N., & Smith, J. (1963). *An analysis of critical features of letters tested by a confusion matrix* (Cooperative Research Project, No. 639). Ithaca, NY: Cornell University.

Gillet, J.W., & Temple, C. (1990). *Understanding reading problems: Assessment and instruction* (3rd ed.). Glenview, IL: Scott Foresman.

Glazer, S.M. (1980). *Getting ready to read: Creating readers from birth to six.* Englewood Cliffs, NJ: Prentice Hall.

Goldstein, A., & Carr, P. (1996). *Can students benefit from process writing?* (NAEP Facts, 1, Report No. NCES-96-845). Washington, DC: U.S. Department of Education, National Center for Education Statistics. (ERIC Document Reproduction Service No. 395320)

Gough, P.B., & Tunmer, W.E. (1986). Decoding reading and reading disability. *Remedial Special Education, 7*(1), 6–10.

Graves, D. (1975). An examination of the writing processes of seven-year-old children. *Research in the Teaching of English, 9,* 227–241.

Graves, D. (1981). *A case study observing the development of primary children's composing, spelling, and motor behaviors during the writing process* (Final Report No. NIE-G-78-0174. ED 218-653). Durham, NH: University of New Hampshire.

Graves, D. (1983). *Writing: Teachers and children at work.* Portsmouth, NH: Heinemann.

Graves, D. (1994). *A fresh look at writing.* Portsmouth, NH: Heinemann.

Griffith, P.L., & Olson, M.W. (1992). Phonemic awareness helps beginning readers break the code. *The Reading Teacher, 45,* 516–523.

Gundlach, R., McLane, J.B., Scott, F.M., & McNamee, G.D. (1985). The social foundations of children's early writing development. In M. Farr (Ed.), *Advances in writing research, Volume I: Children's early writing development* (pp. 1–58). Norwood, NJ: Ablex.

Gunning, T.G. (1995). Word building: A strategic approach to the teaching of phonics. *The Reading Teacher, 48*(6), 484–488.

Haley-James, S. (1991). *Perspectives on writing in grades 1–8.* Urbana, IL: National Council of Teachers of English.

Hallenbeck, M. (1995, April). *The cognitive strategy in writing: Welcome relief for adolescents with learning disabilities.* Report presented at the Council for Exceptional Children Annual Convention, Indianapolis, IN. (ERIC Document Reproduction Service No. 381 981)

Halliday, M. (1978). *Language as social semiotic: The social interpretation of language and meaning.* Baltimore: University Park Press.

Harste, J.C., Burke, C.L., & Woodward, V.A. (1981). *Children, their language and world: Initial encounters with print* (Final Report No. NIE-G-79-0132). Bloomington, IN: Language Education Department.

Harste, J.C., Burke, C.L., & Woodward, V.A. (1983). *The young child as writer-reader, and informant* (Final Report No. NIE-G-89-0121). Bloomington, IN: Language Education Department.

Harste, J.C., Burke, C.L., & Woodward, V.A. (1984). *Language stories & literacy lessons.* Portsmouth, NH: Heinemann Educational Books.

Harwayne, S. (2001). *Writing through childhood: Rethinking process and product.* Portsmouth, NH: Heinemann.

Heath, S.B. (1983). *Ways with words: Language, life, and work in communities and classrooms.* Cambridge, England: Cambridge University Press.

Henderson, E. (1990). *Teaching spelling* (2nd ed.). Boston: Houghton Mifflin.

Hillocks, G. (1986). *Research on written composition: New directions for teaching.* Urbana, IL: National Council of Teachers of English.

Holdaway, D. (1979). *The foundations of literacy.* New York: Ashton Scholastic.

Huck, C., Hepler, S., Hickman, J., & Kiefer, B. (1997). *Children's literature in the elementary school* (6th ed.). Boston: McGraw-Hill.

Hudson, R., Mercer, C.D., & Lane, H. (2000). *Exploring reading fluency: A paradigmatic overview.* Unpublished manuscript. University of Florida, Gainesville.

Invernizzi, M. (1992). The vowel and what follows: A phonological frame of orthographic analysis. In S. Templeton & D. Bear (Eds.), *Development of orthographic knowledge and the foundations of literacy: A memorial Festschrift for Edmond H. Henderson* (pp. 105–136). Hillsdale, NJ: Erlbaum.

Johnston, F. (1999). The timing and teaching of word families. *The Reading Teacher, 53*(1), 64–75.

Johnston, F. (2001). Spelling exceptions: Problems or possibilities? *The Reading Teacher, 54*(4), 372–378.

Juel, C. (1991). Beginning reading. In R. Barr, M.L. Kamil, P.B. Mosenthal, & P.D. Pearson (Eds.), *Handbook of reading research* (Vol. 2, pp. 759–788). New York: Longman.

Kamberelis, G., & Sulzby, E. (1988). Transitional knowledge in emergent literacy. In J.E. Readence & R.S. Baldwin (Eds.), *Dialogues in literacy research* (37th yearbook of the National Reading Conference, pp. 95–106). Rochester, NY: National Reading Conference.

Karelitz, E. (1988). Note writing: A neglected genre. In T. Newkirk & N. Atwell, *Understanding writing: Ways of observing, learning, and teaching K–8* (2nd ed., pp. 88–113). Portsmouth, NH: Heinemann.

Karelitz, E. (1993). *The author's chair and beyond: Language and literacy in a primary classroom.* Portsmouth, NH: Heinemann.

Krashen, S. (1996). *Every person a reader: An alternative to the California Task Force Report on Reading.* Culver City, CA: Language Education Associates.

Lamme, L., & Ayris, B. (1983). Is the handwriting of beginning writers influenced by writing tools? *Journal of Research and Development in Education, 17*(1), 32–38.

Lavine, L. (1972). *The development of perception of writing in prereading children: A cross-cultural study.* Unpublished PhD dissertation. Cornell University, Ithaca, New York.

Lee, D.M, & Allen, R.V. (1963). *Learning to read through experience* (2nd ed.). New York: Meredith.

Lewis, R., Ashton, T., & Kieley, C. (1996). *Word processing and individuals with learning disabilities. Overcoming the keyboard barrier.* In Eleventh Annual Conference of Technology for People With Disabilities. Northridge, CA: California State University.

Lundberg, K., Frost, J., & Peterson, O. (1988). Effects of an intensive program for stimulating phonological awareness in preschool children. *Reading Research Quarterly, 23*(3), 263–284.

Mason, J.M., & McCormick, C. (1983, April). *Intervention procedures for increasing preschool children's interest in and knowledge about reading.* Paper presented at the American Educational Research Association, Montreal, Canada.

May, F.B. (1990). *Reading as communication: An interactive approach.* Columbus, OH: Merrill.

McCarrier, A., Pinnell, G.S., & Fountas, I.C. (2000). *Interactive writing: How language and literacy come together, K–2.* Portsmouth, NH: Heinemann.

McCaslin, N. (1990). *Creative drama in the classroom.* New York: Longman.

McCormick, C., & Mason, J.M. (1981). What happens to kindergarten children's knowledge about reading after a summer vacation? *The Reading Teacher, 35*(2), 164–172.

McGee, L., & Richgels, D. (1990). *Literacy's beginnings: Supporting young readers and writers.* Boston: Allyn & Bacon.

McGinley, W. (1992). The role of reading and writing while composing from sources. *Reading Research Quarterly, 27*(3), 226–248.

McKenzie, M. (1985). *Shared writing* (Nos. 1 & 2 of Language Matters). London: ILEA Centre for Language in Primary Education.

McNaugton, S. (1974). *Behaviour modification and reading in a special class.* Unpublished master's thesis, University of Auckland, New Zealand Library.

Miller-Power, B. (1996). *Taking note: Improving your observational note taking.* York, ME: Stenhouse.

Millie's Math House [Computer software]. (1992). San Francisco: Edmark.

Ministry of Education, New Zealand. (1992). *Dancing with the pen: The learner as a writer.* Katonah, NY: Richard C. Owen.

Morocco, C. (1987). *Final report to U.S. Office of Education.* Washington, DC: Special Education Programs, Educational Development Center.

Morocco, C., Dalton, B., & Tivan, T. (1992). The impact of computer-supported writing instruction on fourth grade students with and without learning disabilities. *Reading and Writing Quarterly: Overcoming Learning Disabilities, 8,* 87–113.

Morris, D. (1992). *Case studies in teaching beginning readers: The Howard Street tutoring manual.* Boone, NC: Fieldstream.

Morris, D., Bloodgood, J.W., Lomax, R.G., & Perney, J. (2003). Developmental steps in learning to read: A longitudinal study in kindergarten and first grade. *Reading Research Quarterly, 38*(3), 302–328.

Morrow, L.M. (1989). *Literacy development in the early years: Helping children read and write.* Englewood Cliffs, NJ: Prentice Hall.

Morrow, L.M., & Strickland, D.S. (1989). *Emerging literacy: Young children learn to read and write.* Newark, DE: International Reading Association.

Moustafa, M. (1998). Whole-to-part phonics instruction. In C. Weaver (Ed.), *Practicing what we know: Informed reading instruction.* Urbana, IL: National Council of Teachers of English.

Murray, D. (1985). *A writer teaches writing.* Boston: Houghton Mifflin.

Murray, D. (1996). *Crafting a life in essay, story, poem.* Portsmouth, NH: Heinemann.

Newkirk, T. (1987). The non-narrative writing of young children. *Research in the Teaching of English, 21*(2), 121–144.

Newkirk, T., & Atwell, N. (1988). *Understanding writing: Ways of observing, learning, and teaching K–8* (2nd ed.). Portsmouth, NH: Heinemann.

Nineo, A., & Bruner, J. (1978). The achievement and antecedents of labeling. *Journal of Child Language, 5,* 1–14.

Ogle, D. (1986). K-W-L: A teaching model that develops active reading of expository text. *The Reading Teacher, 39,* 564–570.

Papandropoulou, I., & Sinclair, H. (1974). What is a word? Experimental study of children's ideas on grammar. *Human Development, 17*(4), 241–258.

Parry, J., & Hornsby, D. (1985). *Write on: A conference approach to writing.* Portsmouth, NH: Heinemann.

Pinnell, G.S., & Fountas, I.C. (1998). *Word matters: Teaching phonics and spelling in the reading/writing classroom.* Portsmouth, NH: Heinemann.

Place, N.A. (2002). Policy in action: The influence of mandated early reading assessment on teachers' thinking and practice. In D.L. Schallert, C.M. Fairbanks, J. Worthy, B. Malock, & J.V. Hoffman (Eds.), *Fiftieth Yearbook of the National Reading Conference* (pp. 45–58). Oak Creek, WI: National Reading Conference.

Purcell-Gates, V. (1989). What oral/written language differences can tell us about beginning instruction. *The Reading Teacher, 42,* 290–294.

Ray, K., & Cleaveland, L. (2004). *Writing workshop with our youngest writers.* Portsmouth, NH: Heinemann.

Read, C. (1975). *Children's categorization of speech sounds in English.* Urbana, IL: National Council of Teachers of English.

Reid, J. (1966). Learning to think about reading. *Educational Research, 9,* 56–62.

Reif, L. (1992). *Seeking diversity: Language arts with adolescents.* Portsmouth, NH: Heinemann.

Richgels, D. (1995). Invented spelling ability and printed word learning in kindergarten. *Reading Research Quarterly, 30*(1), 96–109.

Robinson, S.E. (1973). *Predicting early reading progress.* Unpublished master's thesis, University of Auckland, New Zealand.

Rog, L., & Burton, W. (2002). Matching texts and readers: Leveling early reading materials for assessment and instruction. *The Reading Teacher, 55*(4), 348–356.

Roth, F., Speece, D., & Cooper, D. (2002). A longitudinal analysis of the connection between oral language and early reading. *Journal of Educational Research, 95,* 259–274.

Routman, R. (1991). *Invitations: Changing as teachers and learners, K–12.* Portsmouth, NH: Heinemann.

Routman, R. (2000). *Conversations: Strategies for teaching, learning and evaluating.* Portsmouth, NH: Heinemann.

Sammy's Science House [Computer software]. (1994). San Francisco: Edmark.

Sampson, M. (1986). *The pursuit of literacy: Early reading and writing.* Dubuque, IA: Kendall/Hunt.

Schickendanz, J. (1990). *Adam's righting revolutions: One child's literacy development from infancy through grade one.* Portsmouth, NH: Heinemann.

Schiefele, U. (1991). Interest, learning, and motivation. *Educational Psychologist, 26*(3/4), 299–323.

Schwartz, S., & Pollishuke, M. (1991). *Creating the child-centered classroom.* Katonah, NY: Richard C. Owen.

Shanahan, T. (Ed.) (1990). *Reading and writing together: New perspectives for the classroom.* Norwood, MA: Christopher-Gordon.

Shanahan, T., & Lomax, R. (1986). An analysis and comparison of theoretical models of the reading-writing relationship. *Journal of Educational Psychology, 78*(2), 116–123.

Shepard, L. (2000). The role of assessment in a learning culture. *Educational Researcher, 29*(7), 4–14.

Sitton, R. (1996). Achieving spelling literacy: A no-excuses approach. *California Reader, 30*(1), 7.

Smith, J., & Elley, W. (1997). *How children learn to write.* Auckland, New Zealand: Addison-Wesley Longman.

Snow, C.E. (1977). The development of conversation between mothers and babies. *Journal of Child Language, 4*(1), 1–22.

Stauffer, R. (1970). A reading teacher's dream come true. *Wilson Library Bulletin, 45,* 282–292.

Stennett, R., Smithe, P., & Hardy, M. (1972). Developmental trends in letter-printing skill. *Perceptual and Motor Skills, 34,* 183–186.

Stiggens, R. (2001). *Student-involved classroom assessment* (3rd ed.). Upper Saddle River, NJ: Merrill Prentice-Hall.

Stires, S. (1991). *With promise: Redefining reading and writing for "special" students.* Portsmouth, NH: Heinemann.

Storeyard, J., Simmons, R., Stumpf, M., & Pavloglou, E. (1993). Making computers work for students with special needs. *Teaching Exceptional Children, 26,* 22–24.

Sulzby, E. (1985). Kindergartners as writers and readers. In M. Farr (Ed.), *Advances in writing research, Vol. I: Children's early literacy development.* Norwood, NJ: Ablex.

Taylor, D. (1983). *Family literacy: Young children learning to read and write.* Exeter, NH: Heinemann Educational Books.

Teale, W. (1982). Toward a theory of how children learn to read and write naturally. *Language Arts, 59*(6), 555–570.

Teale, W., & Sulzby, E. (1986). *Emergent literacy: Writing and reading.* Norwood, NJ: Ablex.

Temple, C., Nathan, R., Burris, N., & Temple, F. (Eds.). (1988). *The beginnings of writing* (2nd ed.). Boston: Allyn & Bacon.

Templeton, S. (1980). Young children invent words: Developing concepts of "word-ness." *The Reading Teacher, 33*(4), 454–459.

Tompkins, G. (1994). *Teaching writing: Balancing process and product* (2nd ed.). New York: Macmillan College Publishing.

Tompkins, G., & Hoskisson, K. (1995). *Language arts: Content and teaching strategies* (3rd ed.). Englewood Cliffs, NJ: Prentice Hall.

Trachtenburg, R., & Ferruggia, A. (1989). Big books from little voices: Reaching high risk beginning readers. *The Reading Teacher, 42*(4), 284–289.

Treiman, R. (1993). *Beginning to spell: A study of first-grade children.* New York: Oxford University Press.

Trelease, J. (1982). *The new read-aloud handbook.* New York: Penguin.

Tucker, M., & Codding, J. (1998, February 18). Raising our standards for the standards movement. *Education Week, 17*(23), 37–38.

Venezky, R., & Massaro, D. (1979). The role of orthographic regularity in word recognition. In L.B. Resnick & P.A. Weaver (Eds.), *Theory and practice of early reading* (Vol. 1–2, pp. 85–107). Hillsdale, NJ: Erlbaum.

Vygotsky, L.S. (1978). *Mind in society: The development of higher psychological processes* (M. Cole, V. John-Steiner, S. Scribner, & E. Souberman, Eds. & Trans.). Cambridge, MA: Harvard University Press. (Original work published 1934)

Vygotsky, L.S. (1986). *Thought and language* (A. Kozalin, Trans.). Cambridge, MA: MIT Press. (Original work published 1934)

Wagstaff, J.M. (1998). Building practical knowledge of letter-sound correspondences: A beginner's word wall and beyond. *The Reading Teacher, 51*(4), 298–304.

Weaver, C. (1982). *Reading in the content areas*. Kalamazoo, MI: Western Michigan University Mimeo.

Weaver, C. (1988). *Reading process and practice: From socio-psycholinguistics to whole language*. Portsmouth, NH: Heinemann.

Wheat, L.B. (1932). Four spelling rules. *Elementary School Journal, 32*(9), 697–706.

Woodward, V.A. (1980, May). The young child's concept of story. Paper presented at the Annual Convention of the International Reading Association, St. Louis, Missouri.

Woodward, V. (1981). Young child's concept of story. In J. Harste, C. Burke, & V. Woodward (Eds.), *Children, their language and world: Initial encounters with print* (NIE Final Report No. NIE-G-79-0132). Bloomington, IN: Language Education Department.

Wotherspoon, T. (1974). *Modification of writing behaviour in a special class*. Unpublished master's thesis, University of Auckland, New Zealand.

Wylie, R., & Durrell, D. (1970). Teaching vowels through phonograms. *Elementary English, 47*(6), 787–791.

Yopp, H.K. (1992). Developing phonemic awareness in young children. *The Reading Teacher, 45*(9), 696–703.

Zinsser, W. (1980). *Writing well* (2nd ed.). New York: Harper & Row.

Zinsser, W. (1998). *On writing well: The classic guide to writing nonfiction* (6th ed.). New York: HarperCollins.

Children's Literature References

Ahlberg, J., & Ahlberg, A. (1986). *The jolly postman, or, other people's letters*. Boston: Little, Brown.

Banks, K. (1988). *Alphabet soup*. New York: Alfred Knopf.

Base, G. (1986). *Animalia*. New York. Harry Abrams.

Bottner, G., & Kruglik, B. (2004). *Wallace's lists*. Ill. O. Landstrom. New York: Katherine Tegen Books.

Brewton, S., & Brewton, J. (1969). *Shrieks of midnight* [audiotape]. New York: Thomas Crowell.

Bridwell, N. (1990). *Clifford's word book*. New York: Scholastic.

Cannon, J. (1993). *Stella Luna*. New York: Harcourt.

Carle, E. (1968). *1, 2, 3 to the zoo*. New York: World Publishing.

Carle, E. (1987). *The very hungry caterpillar*. New York: Philomel Books.

Carter, D. (1991). *In a dark, dark wood*. New York: Simon & Schuster.

Cole, J. (1993). *Six sick sheep: 101 tongue twisters*. New York: Scholastic.

Cole, J., & Calmenson, S. (1990). *Miss Mary Mack and other children's street rhymes*. Ill. A. Tiegreen. New York: Morrouno.

Cowley, J. (1990). *Hairy bear*. Bothell, WA: Wright Group.

Cromwell, L., Hibner, D., & Faitel, J. (1976). *Finger frolics: Finger plays for young children*. Livonia, MI: Partner Press.

de Regniers, B. & Montresor, B. (1968). *Willy O'Dwyer jumped in the fire*. New York: Atheneum.

de Regniers, B., Moore, E., White, M., & Carr, J. (1988). *Sing a song of popcorn*. New York: Scholastic.

Dewan, T. (1994). *Three billy goats gruff*. New York: Scholastic.

Dr. Seuss. (1985). *Cat in the hat*. New York: Random House.

Dr. Seuss. (1996). *Dr. Seuss's ABC: An amazing alphabet book!* New York: Random House.

Edwards, P.D. (2003). *Dear tooth fairy*. Ill. M. Fitzpatrick. New York: Katherine Tegan Books.

Eisen, A. (1988). *The classic Mother Goose*. New York: Running Press.

Ferris, H. (Ed.). (1957). *Favorite poems old and new*. New York: Doubleday.

Galdone, P. (1984). *Henny Penny*. Boston: Houghton Mifflin.

Galdone, P. (1985). *The Little Red Hen*. Boston: Houghton Mifflin.

Glazer, T. (1973). *Eye Winker, Tom Tinker, Chin Chopper*. New York: Doubleday.

Glazer, T., & McHail, D. (1990). *The Mother Goose songbook*. New York: Doubleday.

Grace, P. (1988). Butterflies. In *Electric City* (p. 15). New York: Penguin.

Hyman, T.S. (1983). *Little Red Riding Hood*. New York: Holiday House.

Hoban, L. (1976). *Arthur's pen pal*. New York: Harper & Row.

Hoban, T. (1978). *Is it red? Is it yellow? Is it blue? An adventure in color*. New York: Greenwillow Books.

Hoban, T. (1985). *1, 2, 3*. New York: Greenwillow Books.

Howard, K. (1971). *Little Bunny follows his nose*. Racine, WI: Western Publishing.

Hutchins, P. (1968). *Rosie's walk* [kit]. New York: Macmillian.

Hutchins, P. (1976). *Don't forget the bacon*. New York: Greenwillow Books.

Hyman, T.S. (1983). *Little Red Riding Hood*. New York: Holiday House.

Knox, B. (2003a). *ABC under the sea: An ocean life alphabet book*. Mankato, MN: Capstone Press.

Knox, B. (2003b). *Animal babies ABC: An alphabet book of animal offspring*. Mankato, MN: A+ Books.

Lobel, A. (1971). A list. In *Frog and Toad together* (pp. 4–17). New York: HarperCollins.

Lobel, A. (1975). A letter. In *Frog and Toad are friends* (pp. 53–64). New York: HarperCollins.

Lobel, A. (1997). *The Arnold Lobel Book of Mother Goose*. New York: Knopf.

Martin, B., Jr., & Archambault, J. (1989). *Chicka chicka boom boom*. Ill. L. Ehlert. New York: Henry Holt.

Martin, B., & Carle, E. (1983). *Brown Bear, Brown Bear, what do you see?* New York: Henry Holt.

Milton, J. (1993). *Bats: Creatures of the night*. Ill. J. Moffat. New York: Grosset & Dunlap.

Murdock, H. (1985). *The three little pigs*. Ill. L. Grundy. Lewiston, ME: Ladybird Books.

Nemerson, R. (1997). *Grimm's fairy tales*. New York: Baronet Books.

Obligado, L. (1983). *Faint frogs feeling feverish and other terrifically tantalizing tongue twisters*. New York: Viking.

Opie, I. (1996). *My very first Mother Goose*. Ill. R. Wells. Cambridge, MA: Candlewick Press.

Parkes, B., & Smith, J. (1987). *Musicians of Breman*. New York: Riby.

Perkins, A. (1968). *The ear book*. New York: Random House.

Prelutsky, J. (1983). *Zoo doings*. New York: Greenwillow Books.

Prelutsky, J. (1986). *Read-aloud rhymes for the very young*. Ill. M. Brown. New York: Knopf.

Raffi. (1976). *Singable songs for the very young* [audiotape]. Universal City, CA: MCA Records.

Rockwell, A. (1975). *The three bears and 15 other stories*. New York: Crowell.

Ross, T. (1994). *Hansel and Gretel*. Woodstock, NY: Overlook Press.

Schmidt, K. (1984). *The little red hen*. New York: Grosset & Dunlap.

Scieszka, J. (1996). *The true story of the three little pigs! as told by A. Wolf*. Ill. L. Smith. New York: Puffin.

Schwartz, A., & Abrams, K. (1992). *Busy buzzing bumblebees and other tongue twisters*. Ill. P. Meisel. New York: HarperCollins.

Sendak, M. (1991). *Chicken soup with rice: A book of months*. New York: Scholastic.

Shaw, N. (1989). *Sheep on a ship*. Ill. M. Apple. Boston: Houghton Mifflin.

Slepian, J., & Seidler, A. (1967). *The hungry thing*. New York: Scholastic.

Slepian, J., & Seidler, A. (1990). *The hungry thing returns*. New York: Scholastic.

Spanyol, J. (2001). *Carlo likes reading*. Cambridge, MA: Candlewick Press.

Tolstoy, A.N. (1968). *The great big enormous turnip*. Photos. H. Oxenbury. New York: F. Watts.

Vachel, L. (1986). There was a little turtle. In J. Prelutsky (Ed.), *Read-aloud rhymes for the very young* (p. 20). New York: Knopf.

Vollmer, D. (1988). *Joshua disobeys*. Kansas City, MO: Landmark Editions.

Warren, J., & Ekberg, M. (1990). *Piggyback songs*. Everett, WA: Warren Publishing House.

Wildsmith, B. (1983). *The cat on the mat*. New York: Oxford University Press.

Wood, J., Wood, T., & Holmes, S. (1988). *The hide-and-seek book of animals*. New York: Derrydale Books.

Zelinsky, P. (1997). *Rumpelstiltskin*. New York: Scholastic.

Note: Page numbers followed by *f* and *t* indicate figures and tables, respectively.

A

ABC BOOKS, 83, 84f, 307; letter to parents on, 314

ABC CENTER, 116–117

ABCs: manipulating, 124

ABRAMS, K., 132, 280, 284

ACCOUNTABILITY, 234; and assessment, 232–242

ADAMS, M., 56, 151, 325

ADMINISTRATORS: accountability to, 236–237; reporting evaluations to, 267–268; on writing workshop, 273–274

AHLBERG, A., 87

AHLBERG, J., 87

ALLEN, R.V., 105

ALLINGTON, R.L., 61

ALPHABET: forms for, 341; walk, 124

ALPHABETIC PRINCIPLE, 18; in kindergarten, x

ALPHABET SONG, 149, 151–152

ALPHABET STRIP, 164, 164f; using, 215

ALPHABET TIME: lesson plan for, 150–152

ANDERSON, R.C., 20, 103

ANECDOTAL RECORDS, 248–251; on conferences, 167–168

ANGELILLO, J., 223

APPROXIMATED SPELLING. *See* invented spelling

APPROXIMATION: encouraging, 168–169; and language learning, 22–23; teachers and, 148

ARCHAMBAULT, J., 124

ARTICULATION: modeling, 128–129

ASHTON, T., viii, 272

ASHTON-WARNER, S., 131

ASSESSMENT, 231–268; criteria for, 245–248, 246t; as cyclical, 257f; definition of, 242; methods of, 242–245; of spelling, 53–54; tools for, 248–257; users of, levels of, 234; in writing workshop, examples of, 169–171

ATWELL, N., 8, 60, 77, 90, 181, 187

AUTHOR'S CHAIR, 13–14, 149, 159, 159f, 173–179; guidelines for, 173; time limits for, 177

AUTHOR'S PARTY, 265–267; setups for, 266f

AVERY, C., 5, 181, 184, 190

AYRIS, B., 164

B

BALL, E.W., 40, 156

BANKS, K., 291, 295

BASE, G., 280

BE A MIND READER: directions for, 324–325

BEAR, D., 11, 16, 34–35, 38–43, 45, 51, 107, 131–132, 141, 155–156, 183, 278, 281

BEAST TALES, 96, 307

"BE" THE ALPHABET, 123

BIG BOOK, 103

BIRNBAUM, J.C., 5, 63

BLACHMAN, B.A., 40, 156

BLACK, P., 253

BLOODGOOD, J.W., 17

BOMER, R., 182, 253

BOOK ORIENTATION CONCEPTS, 14

BOOKS: by genre, 307–311; making, 201–202; for prediction, 300–307

BOTTNER, G., 86

BOYD-BATSTONE, P., 246–247, 249–250, 260

BRADLEY, L., 17

BREWTON, J., 292

BREWTON, S., 292

BRIDWELL, N., 85

BRITTON, J., 79

BRUNER, J., 98

BRYANT, P.E., 17

BURKE, C.L., 2, 6, 16, 31, 33, 40, 62–63, 65, 78, 110, 135, 181, 232, 245

BURRIS, N., 2, 8, 13, 16, 19–20, 29, 31, 34–36, 38–40, 42–43, 46–47, 51, 55, 66–67, 79–81, 100, 110, 123, 127, 131, 135, 141, 155, 172–173, 179, 183, 213, 226, 245

BURTON, W., 136

BUSS, K., 80, 93

C

CALKINS, L., 166, 183, 189, 195, 197–198, 206, 208, 210–212

CALKINS, L.M., vii, viii, 1, 5–6, 8–10, 20, 25, 34, 64, 67–69, 71, 74, 76, 80, 82, 100–103, 109, 124, 134, 136, 138–139, 144, 147, 158, 164, 167, 173, 178, 181–184, 186, 217–219, 226, 229, 234–235, 243, 245, 258, 265, 307

CALMENSON, S., 286

CAMBOURNE, B., vii, viii, ix, xi, 1, 18, 21, 24–26, 30, 68, 74, 101, 134, 140, 147,

158, 181, 233, 269

CANNON, J., 91

CARLE, E., 84, 96, 291

CARR, J., 284

CARR, P., 6

CARTER, D., 282

CARTOON CHARACTERS: and topic selection, 188

CENTER TIME, 114–118; possibilities for, 115f

CHALL, J.S., 18

CHANTS, 290–291

CHAPMAN, M.L., 82

CHARACTERS, CARTOON: and topic selection, 188

CHARTS: good writing, 216t; pocket, 110–111, 112f; word family, 327, 327f

CHECKLISTS, 251; sample, 337

CHENEY, L.V., 237

CHILD-CENTERED CLASSROOM, 114

CHILDREN SHARE: in reading workshop, 140

CHOICE: and center time, 117; and language learning, 23–24; in writing workshop, 25–26

CHOMSKY, C., 2, 18, 36, 53, 62, 155

CHOMSKY, N., 232

CID FORM, 165; reproducible, 333; samples, 261f; using, 258–259

CLAPPING: for Author's Chair, 177; syllables, 141

CLARK, M.M., 98, 100

CLASS NEWSPAPER, 144–145

CLASSROOM: child-centered, 114; print-rich environment in, 120; teacher and environment of, 182

CLAY, M.M., viii, ix, x, xi, 1–6, 9–11, 13–21, 23–27, 29–34, 40, 47, 51, 62–63, 65, 67, 83–84, 101–102, 110, 119, 122, 125, 127, 135–136, 144, 147–148, 155–157, 163–164, 166, 172–173, 180, 183, 232–235, 237, 240–241, 243, 245, 247–248, 250, 253–256, 260–261, 263, 267, 269, 273, 275, 314

CLAY'S CONCEPTS OF PRINT TEST, 253–254

CLAY'S DICTATION TEST, 255–256, 255f–256f

CLAY'S LETTER IDENTIFICATION TEST, 254

CLEAVELAND, L., xi, 25, 27, 69, 181

CLOZE PROCEDURE, 100, 105, 143; for group prediction, 140

CODDING, J., 238, 267

COLE, J., 131, 286

COMMUNITY CIRCLE, 111

CONCEPT OF WORD, 15–16, 126–127; versus concept of letter, 126; demonstration of, 127–128, 128f; in Semiphonetic stage, 41

CONCEPTS OF PRINT, 10, 11f, 14–17

CONCLUSIONS: interesting, 208–212

CONFERENCES, 147, 158, 158f, 163–173; examples of, 168–171, 169f, 171f; procedure for, 165–171; teacher materials for, 165; triangular, 264–265

CONFIDENCE: feedback and, 24

CONSOLIDATED ALPHABETIC STAGE, 19

CONSONANT BLENDS: Phonetic stage and, 47

CONTENT: minilessons on, 190, 202–212, 296–298

CONTEXT: using words in, 119–120; and written language development, 65–66

CONVENTIONAL STAGE, 38, 54–57, 318; terminology for, 39t

CONVENTIONS. See skills

COOPER, D., 13

COPYING: from classroom print, 214; importance of, 181; letters, drawbacks of, 32–33

CORDEIRO, P., 225

CORE WORD LIST, 53

COVINGTON, M., 24

COWLEY, J., 286

CRAFTON, L., 249

CREATIVE DRAMATICS, 94, 95f

CRESS, C., 20, 44, 321

CROMWELL, L., 291

CUDD, E., 78, 243

CULLINAN, B.E., 10, 13–14, 21–22

CUMULATIVE TALES, 96, 308

CUNNINGHAM, A.E., 18

CUNNINGHAM, P., 44, 49, 115, 121, 123, 125, 130, 148, 151, 321, 324

CUNNINGHAM, P.M., 20, 61

D

DAHL, K.L., 5, 9, 70, 220

DALTON, B., viii

DATE STAMP, 158, 166; introduction of, 160; minilesson on, 191–192

DECISION MAKERS: accountability to, 235–237

DE FINA, A.D., 262

DEMONSTRATION(S): importance of, 181–183; and language learning, 22; sample, 190–229; in writing workshop, 158, 160–163. See also minilessons

DE REGNIERS, B., 284, 292

DERIVATIONAL RELATIONS STAGE. See Conventional stage

DEWAN, T., 96

DICKERSON, D., 130

DIGRAPHS: initial consonant, 131–132; in names, 154; Phonetic stage and, 47

DIRECTIONAL CONCEPTS: development of, 125–126; on page, 127

DONNELLY, K., 20, 44, 321

DOWNER, M.A., 20

DOWNING, J., 16

DRAMATICS: creative, 94, 95f

DRAWING: to excess, minilesson on, 188–189; importance of, 7

DURKIN, D., 9, 16, 98, 100–101, 135

DURRELL, D., 48, 326
DYSON, A.H., 2, 5, 63

E

EARLY PHONEMIC STAGE. *See* Semiphonetic stage
EARLY STAGE, 10–11
EDITING, 70–71
EDWARDS, P.D., 88
EHRI, L.C., 19, 20, 44, 321
EISEN, A., 280
EKBERG, M., 284
ELBOW, P., 71
ELKONIN, D.B., 122, 155–156
ELKONIN SOUND BOXES, 122–123, 123f, 155; for making words, 125
ELLEY, W., viii
EMERGENT LITERACY, 1–6
EMERGENT READING BEHAVIORS, 10, 11f, 12–21
EMERGENT STAGE: of reading, 10. *See also* Precommunicative stage
EMIG, J.A., 6
EMPLOYMENT: and language learning, 23
ENDINGS: classic, 93, 94f; interesting, 208–212
ENGLISH-LANGUAGE LEARNERS: labeling and, 86
ESSAY, 243
EVALUATION, 257–262; reporting, 262–268
EXPECTATION: and language learning, 24–25
EXPLICIT INSTRUCTION: in phonemic awareness, 18; in writing workshop, 26
EXTENSIVE WRITING, 6

F

FAILURE ACCEPTORS, 24
FAITEL, J., 291
FAMILY. *See* parents
FARNAN, N., 5, 9, 70, 220
FEEDBACK: and language learning, 24
FERREIRO, E., xi, 1–3, 5, 62, 98, 170, 232
FERRIS, H., 284, 287, 294
FERRUGGIA, A., 104
FICTION: development of textual features of, 79–81, 81f, 319; for kindergarten, 93–96
FINGER PLAYS, 290–291
FINGER POINTING, 141; remediation for, 141–142
FINN, C.E., 237
FISHER, B., 69, 75, 110, 120, 141, 144, 158, 161, 181, 189, 202, 263
FLANNEL BOARD, 94
FLETCHER, R.J., 79
FLIPCHART, 327, 327f
FLUENCY: development of, 20
FLUENT STAGE, 11–12
FOCUS: and anecdotal records, 250; and assessment, 246–247; in conferences, 166; minilesson on, 206–208
FOLDERS: "I'm Working On," 192–193; writing, 193–195, 195f

FOLK TALES, 95–96; cumulative, 308
FORMAL ASSESSMENT TOOLS, 253–257
FOUNTAS, I.C., 106, 112, 117, 252–253, 321
FREEDMAN, S.W., 5
FRIENDSHIP CIRCLE, 145
FROST, J., 17–18, 157
FRY, E., 321, 323
FULLY ALPHABETIC STAGE, 19

G

GALDA, L., 10, 13–14, 21–22
GALDONE, P., 286, 292, 295, 322
GARDNER, H., 237–238
GASKINS, I.W., 20, 44, 321
GENRE(S): books in, 307–311; for kindergarten, 82–96
GENRE DEVELOPMENT STAGE, 79–81, 80f–81f, 319
GENTRY, J.R., xi, 20, 31, 34–35, 37–39, 42–43, 45, 49, 51, 53–55, 58, 67, 102, 121, 124–125, 141–143, 155, 183, 214, 240, 245, 318, 324, 330
GERE, A.R., 107
GETTING READY, 147–157; form for, 332; overview of, 118; schedule for, 148t; structure of, 148–149
GIBSON, E.J., 31
GILLET, J.W., xi, 18, 20, 31, 34–35, 37–39, 42–43, 45, 49, 51, 53–55, 58, 67, 102, 121, 124–125, 141–143, 155, 183, 214, 240, 245, 318, 324, 330
GLAZER, S.M., 13
GLAZER, T., 280, 282, 286
GOLDSTEIN, A., 6
GOUGH, P.B., viii, 5, 18
GRACE, P., 231
GRAPHIC SYSTEM, 10, 11f, 18–21
GRAPHOPHONICS, 10
GRAVES, D., vii, 1–2, 6–9, 25, 31, 36–37, 60, 72, 76, 79–81, 90–91, 102, 147, 160, 165–167, 172–174, 177–178, 181–183, 187–188, 190, 195, 199, 204, 206–208, 213, 217, 222–223, 243, 245, 258, 321
GRIFFITH, P.L., 18
GRIP POSITION, 187
GUIDED READING, 133–143; books for, 311–312; questions and statements for, 138–139
GUNDLACH, R., 61
GUNNING, T.G., 43

H

HALEY-JAMES, S., 71
HALLENBECK, M., viii, 272
HALLIDAY, M., 13
HARDY, M., 31
HARSTE, J.D., 2, 6, 16, 31, 33, 40, 62–63, 65, 78, 110, 135, 181, 232, 245
HARWAYNE, S., 181–182, 244, 249, 297
HEATH, S.B., 98

HELP PAPER, 187
HENDERSON, E., 44, 54, 56
HEPLER, S., 90, 95–96
HIBNER, D., 291
HICKMAN, J., 90, 95–96
HIDE A WORD, 143
HIEBERT, E.H., 103
HIGH-FREQUENCY WORDS, 321–323; invented spelling and, 37; tent cards for, 129–130, 130f; on word wall, 120–122
HIGH-RISK CHILDREN: print-rich environment for, 100
HILLOCKS, G., 6
HOBAN, L., 88
HOBAN, T., 84, 87
HOLDAWAY, D., viii, 4, 10, 21, 26, 29–32, 63, 98, 100–101, 103–105, 131, 139–140, 143–144, 151, 156, 160, 181, 190, 212, 232, 235
HOLMES, S., 292, 295
HOME: and reading, 98–100, 99f; writing from, 240, 241f. See also parents
HORNSBY, D., 8
HOSKISSON, K., 10, 12, 14, 20–21, 27, 62, 67, 69, 71–72, 89–90, 93, 102–103, 106, 114, 249, 251, 262
HOUSEKEEPING CENTER, 115
HOWARD, K., 294
HUCK, C., 90, 95–96
HUDSON, R., 11
HUTCHINS, P., 86, 96, 145, 287
HYMAN, T.S., 96

I

IDEAS: generating, 161–162, 178, 221–222
"I'M DONE" WRITING: minilesson on, 199–201
"I'M FINISHED" folders, 194
IMMERSION: and language learning, 22
"I'M WORKING ON" folders: minilesson on, 192–193
INDIVIDUALIZED INSTRUCTION: importance of, 29–30
INFORMAL ASSESSMENT TOOLS, 248–253
INFORMATIONAL TEXTS, 308–311
INITIAL CONSONANT DIGRAPHS: working with, 131–132
INQUIRY: teacher and, 57
INTENTION: and writing, 6, 63–64, 64f
INTERACTIVE WRITING, 106–107
INVENTED SPELLING, 18, 36–37, 67, 68f; demonstration of, 162–163; minilesson on, 226–228
INVERNIZZI, M., 11, 16, 34–35, 38–43, 45, 47, 51, 107, 131–132, 141, 155–156, 183, 278, 281
ITERATION, 153, 282, 293

J

JOHNSTON, F., 11, 16, 19, 34–35, 38–45, 47–49, 51–53, 55–56, 107, 129, 131–132, 141, 155–156, 183, 278, 281, 288, 325, 328–329
JOURNALING, 27
JUEL, C., 19

K

KAMBERELIS, G., 8
KARELITZ, E., 87, 205, 259
KARNOWSKI, L., 80, 93
KID-WRITING. See invented spelling
KIEFER, B., 90, 95–96
KIELEY, C., viii, 272
KINDERGARTEN: fictional stories in, 81; genres appropriate for, 82–96; stages of written language in, 73–81; teachers of, on writing workshop, 269–272; writing in, 1–28; writing workshop in, vii–xiv, 1–28
KINDNESS: modeling, 168–169, 173, 177, 179, 189
KNOX, B., 83
KRASHEN, S., 232, 238
KRUGLIK, B., 86

L

LABELING: shared, 125. See also Picture and Label Writing stage
LABELS: books with, 309; writing, 84–86, 85f
LAMME, L., 164
LANE, H., 11
LANGUAGE ABILITY, 10, 11f, 12–14
LANGUAGE DEVELOPMENT CONDITIONS, 21–25; in writing workshop, 25–27
LANGUAGE EXPERIENCE APPROACH, 105–106
LAVINE, L., 31
LEARNING LOGS, 107–108
LEE, D.M., 105
LEFT-HANDED STUDENTS, 187
LESSON PLANS: forms for, 332; for Getting Ready, 149–157; for writing workshop, 158–179
LETTER CONCEPTS, 15; versus concept of word, 126; directionality, development of concept of, 126
LETTER FORMATION: developmental, 29–59; impediments to, 31
LETTER–NAME STAGE. See Phonetic stage; Semiphonetic stage
LETTERS: books with, 309–310; characteristics of, 89t; form for, 338–339; to parents, 314–317; to student, 115, 116f; terminology with, 156; writing, 62–63, 88–90, 89f
LEVELED TEXTS: for reading workshop, 136–138
LEWIS, R., viii, 272
LIMERICKS, 284

LINING UP: by sounds, 123
LISTENING: center, 117; for same and different sounds, 122
LISTS: books with, 309; of class names, 124; for instruction, 320–330; Things I Can Do, 220; writing, 86f, 86–87
LITERACY COACHES, 235
LITERACY DEVELOPMENT: writing and, 1
LITERACY INSTRUCTION: approaches to, 102–108; effective, requirements for, 21–27
LITERACY PROGRAM: Center Time in, 114–118; importance of, ix; opening activities in, 110–114; planning, 98–146
LOBEL, A., 86, 88, 95
LOMAX, R., 5
LOMAX, R.G., 17
LOOK-COVER-WRITE-CHECK STRATEGY, 121
LUNDBERG, K., 17–18, 157

M

MAIL: in classroom, 62–63, 88–90, 89f, 115, 116f
MANAGEMENT: reflections on, 269
MANIPULATION: of ABCs, 124
MARKERS, 164
MARTIN, B., 291
MARTIN, B., JR., 124
MASKING DEVICES: in shared reading, 104–105, 104f
MASON, J.M., 65, 98
MASSARO, D., 53
MATCHING WORDS IN PRINT, 142
MAY, F.B., 10
MCCARRIER, A., 106, 112, 117, 321
MCCASLIN, N., 94
MCCORMICK, C., 65, 98
MCGEE, L., 31, 33–34
MCGINLEY, W., 5
MCHAIL, D., 280, 282
MCKENZIE, M., 106
MCLANE, J.B., 61
MCNAMEE, G.D., 61
MCNAUGHTON, S., 5
MEDIA CHARACTERS: and topic selection, 188
MERCER, C.D., 11
MESSAGE: conferences on, 166; importance of, 182; reading for, 100
MILLER-POWER, B., 257
MILTON, J., 91
MILLIE'S MATH HOUSE, 109t
MINILESSONS, 163, 181–230; categories of, 190; definition of, 184; developmental stages and, 185–186; formats for, 189–190; importance of, 181–183; purpose of, 183–184; in reading workshop, 133–134; repeating and reinforcing, 184; sample, 190–229; topics for, additional, 295–298; whole-class versus small-group, 186–187

MINISTRY OF EDUCATION, NEW ZEALAND, 10
MISTAKES: dealing with, 164
MODELING: articulation, 128–129; kindness, 168–169, 173, 177, 179, 189; and letter formation, 32–34
MONTRESOR, B., 292
MOORE, E., 284
MORNING MESSAGE, 111–113
MOROCCO, C., viii, 272
MORRIS, D., 17, 44, 48
MORROW, L.M., 10, 22, 30, 32, 40, 60–61, 79–80, 98, 100–101, 112, 115, 121, 158, 181, 214, 245, 251
MOUSTAFA, M., 43
MR. BUNNY, 62–63
MURDOCK, H., 96
MURRAY, D., 9, 63, 182, 204
"MY BEST WRITING," 219; selection of, 218–221
MYSTERY PICTURE GAME, 289–290

N

NAME(S): cards, 164; with iteration, 293; lists, 124; sorting, 124; wall, 120–122, 121f; on word wall, using, 213–214; on writing, 160
NAME GAME, 286
NAME SONG, 149, 149f, 152–155, 279
NARRATIVE TEXT, 93–96
NATHAN, R., 2, 8, 13, 16, 19–20, 29, 31, 34–36, 38–40, 42–43, 46–47, 51, 55, 66–67, 79–81, 100, 110, 123, 127, 131, 135, 141, 155, 172–173, 179, 183, 213, 226, 245
NEEDS: minilessons and, 163, 183, 186
NEGATIVE SPACE: and concept of word, 16
NEGATIVISM: dealing with, 168–169
NEMERSON, R., 96
NEWKIRK, T., 60, 77, 84, 90, 187
NEWSPAPER: class, 144–145
NINEO, A., 98
NONFICTION: development of textual features of, 79–81, 80f, 319; for kindergarten, 82–93
NOTEBOOKS: for topic ideas, 183
NOTES: books with, 309–310; to student, 115, 116f; writing, 87–88, 87f, 128, 129f
NUMBER BOOKS, 84, 310
NURSERY RHYMES, 94–95, 290, 294, 310; innovations in, 141

O

OBLIGADO, L., 131
OGLE, D., 258
O'HARA, C., 20, 44, 321
OLSON, M.W., 18
OPEN HOUSE, 265
OPIE, I., 95

Osser, H., 31
Oxenhorn, A., 166, 183, 189, 195, 197–198, 206, 208, 210–212

P

Papandropoulou, I., 15
paper: Help, 187; unlined, 158
parents: accountability to, 234–235; letters to, 314–317; and reading, 98–100, 99f; reporting evaluation to, 262–267
Parkes, B., 307
Parry, J., 8
Partial Alphabetic stage, 19
partners: writing, 195–199; and writing selection, 220
pattern books: classic, 305–307; rhyming, 302–304; with song, 301–302
Pavloglou, E., viii, 272
peer coaching, 236
performance-based assessment, 243
performance-based standards: need for, 237–238
periods: minilesson on, 223–225
Perkins, A., 278
Perney, J., 17
personal communication assessment, 243–245
Peterson, O., 17–18, 157
Petrilli, M.J., 237
phonemic awareness, 10, 11f, 17–18; activities, 295; in Getting Ready, 149; instruction in, 278–279; lesson plan for, 152–157
Phonetic stage, 38, 45–51, 46f, 318; reading workshop activities for, 142–143; terminology for, 39t; writing workshop activities for, 129–133
phonics: versus phonemic awareness, 17
phonograms, 278
phonological awareness, 17
Picture and Label Writing stage, 75–77, 76f, 319; reading workshop activities for, 141–142; writing workshop activities for, 124–129
picture books: wordless, 300–301
Picture Writing stage, 74–75, 75f, 319; reading workshop activities for, 140–141; writing workshop activities for, 119–124
Pinnell, G.S., 106, 112, 117, 252–253, 321
Place, N.A., 253
pocket charts, 110–111, 112f
poetry, 290, 294
policymakers: accountability to, 237–242
Pollishuke, M., 114
portfolios, 261–262
Prealphabetic stage, 19
Precommunicative stage, 37–40, 39f, 318; reading workshop activities for, 140–141; terminology for, 39t; writing workshop activities for, 119–124

prediction strategy, 100, 105, 143; group, 140
Prelutsky, J., 144, 284, 322
Prephonemic stage. See Precommunicative stage
prewriting, 68–69
principals: accountability to, 236–237; reporting evaluations to, 267–268; on writing workshop, 273–274
print: directionality of, development of concept of, 125. See also concepts of print
print-rich environment, 100, 120
prior knowledge, 10
procedures: minilessons on, 190–202, 295
process: time frame of, 275; writing as, 6–9, 160–162, 183; written language development as, 63–65
professional development: providers of, accountability to, 235–237
progressive exposure technique, 139
publishing, 71–73; formal, 73f; informal, 72f
punctuation: minilessons on, 223–226
puppetry, 94
Purcell-Gates, V., 144

Q

questions: for Author's Chair, 173, 178–179; for conferences, 165, 167; for guided reading, 138–139; for student writing teachers, 196–197; on texts, 238–239; on writing criteria, 217
Quick Draw, 188–189
Quick Share, 75, 177–178
quotation marks: minilesson on, 225–226

R

Raffi, 280, 284, 287, 292–293
Ray, K., xi, 25, 27, 69, 181
Read, C., 36, 62
reading: cues of, 10; definition of, 9; shared, 103–105; stages of, 9–12; teachers of, on writing workshop, 272–273
reading aloud, 103, 143–144; at home, 264
reading centers, 135
reading development: writing and, 1, 233
reading workshop, 103, 133–143
rebus print, 132
reflections: on spelling progress, 57–59; on writing workshop, 269–275
reflexive writing, 6
rehearsing, 68–69
Reid, J., 16
Reif, L., 239
repeated reading, 139
report(s): characteristics of, 91t; informal, 90–93, 92f; letter to parents on, 317
reporting: to administrators, 267–268; to parents, 262–267

RESEARCH: on literacy, coaches and, 235; on writing development, 1–6
RESPONSE: and language learning, 24
RESPONSIBILITY, 110; and language learning, 23–24; reminders of, 184–185, 185f; and text selection, 138; and writing process, 70–71; in writing workshop, 8, 166, 168
REVERSALS: pointing out, 131
REVISING, 69–70
RICHGELS, D., 18, 31, 33–34
RIDDLES, 294
RIMES, 19–20, 43–44; common, 325–329
RISK TAKING: and spelling, 35; and written language development, 66–67
ROBERTS, L., 78, 243
ROBINSON, S.E., 3, 102, 236, 241
ROBINSON'S WRITING VOCABULARY TEST, 254–255
ROCKWELL, A., 96
ROG, L., 136
ROLLER MOVIES, 232
ROSS, T., 96
ROTH, F., 13
ROUGH DRAFT, 69
ROUTMAN, R., 18, 20, 26, 29–30, 34, 37, 40, 45, 49, 51–53, 55–56, 69, 71, 82, 106–108, 110, 113, 118, 121, 134–136, 143–144, 154, 161, 163, 166, 177, 187, 204–206, 212, 217, 220, 223, 233–240, 242, 244, 247, 249, 251–252, 257–259, 261–265, 267, 278, 288, 316, 325
RUBRICS, 252–253; definition of, 252; sample, 336; scoring, 239

S

SAMMY'S SCIENCE HOUSE, 109t
SAMPSON, M., 5, 101–102
SANDWICH TECHNIQUE, 263–264
SCHEDULE: for Author's Chair, 177; for Getting Ready and writing workshop, 148t; for literacy program, 108–110, 109f, 237; in morning message, 111–113; for triangular conferences, 265
SCHICKEDANZ, J., 20
SCHIEFELE, U., 25
SCHIFF, N., 31
SCHMIDT, K., 96
SCHOMER, M., 20
SCHWARTZ, A., 132, 280, 284
SCHWARTZ, S., 114
SCIENCE CENTER, 117–118
SCIESZKA, J., 106
SCORING: for performance tests, 239
SCOTT, F.M., 61
SCOTT, J.A., 103
SCRIBES, 199
SEIDLER, A., 286
SELECTED RESPONSE, 242
SELECTIVE-CUE STAGE, 19

SEMANTICS, 10
SEMIPHONETIC STAGE, 37, 40–45, 41f, 318; reading workshop activities for, 141–142; terminology for, 39t; writing workshop activities for, 124–129
SENDAK, M., 292
SENSORY RESPONSES: minilesson on, 297–298
SENTENCES: reconstructing, 142
SEQUENCING, 198
SEUSS, DR., 44, 280
SHANAHAN, T., 1, 5
SHARED LABELING, 125
SHARED READING, 103–105
SHARED WRITING, 106
SHARING: book reviews, 232; in reading workshop, 140. *See also* Author's Chair; Quick Share
SHAW, N., 132
SHEPARD, L., 253
SHORT VOWELS: different, word family study on, 132; isolation of, 288; in names, 154–155; same, word family study on, 129
SHOWING WHAT YOU KNOW, 113–114
SIGHT WORDS: building vocabulary of, 131; reviewing, 131
SIGN-IN, 110–111, 111f
SIMMONS, R., viii, 272
SINCLAIR, H., 15
SITTON, R., 53
SKETCHING: minilesson on, 188–189
SKILLS: minilessons on, 190, 223–229, 296; tests and, 238
SLEPIAN, J., 286
SMALL-GROUP MINILESSONS, 186–187
SMITH, J., viii, 31, 307
SMITHE, P., 31
SNOW, C.E., 98
SOCIAL STUDIES CENTER, 117
SONGS: pattern books with, 301–302
SOUND ACTIVITIES: blending, 288–292; isolation, 281–284; matching, 279–281; segmentation, 292–295; substitution, 285–288
SOUNDS: of the day, 288; lining up by, 123; same and different, 122; terminology with, 156
SPACES: minilesson on, 228–229
SPANYOL, J., 85
SPEECE, D., 13
SPEECH BUBBLES: minilesson on, 225–226
SPELLING: developmental, 34–37; instruction in, recommendations for, 58–59; invented, 18, 36–37; letter to parents on, 315–316; stages of, 37–57, 318; terminology in, 38, 39t; vacillation in stages of, 49, 50f
STANDARDIZED TESTS, 234

STANDARDS: performance-based, need for, 237–238

STARTS WITH: term, 155

STAUFFER, R., 105

STENNETT, R., 31

STICKY NOTES, 165

STIGGENS, R., 24, 166, 234–235, 240, 242–245, 252, 262

STIRES, S., viii, 272

STOOL: for conferences, 165

STOREYARD, J., viii, 272

STORIES: types of, 93

STRATEGIES: introduction of, 135; Look-Cover-Write-Check, 121; minilessons on, 190, 212–222, 295–296; prediction, 100, 105, 140, 143; for writing, 7

STRICKLAND, D.S., 10, 13–14, 21–22

STRUGGLING WRITERS: time for, 166; writing workshop and, 271

STUDENTS: accountability to, 234–235; achievement targets for, selection of, 247–248; and writing selection, 218–221; as writing teachers, 195–199; on writing workshop, 274

STUMPF, M., viii, 272

SULZBY, E., 8, 63, 98

SURPRISE: minilesson on, 298

SYLLABLES: clapping, 141

SYLLABLES AND AFFIXES STAGE. See Transitional stage

SYNTAX, 10

T

TABLET, 165

TAKING INVENTORY AND ADDING DESCRIPTION STAGE, 78–79, 78f, 319; reading workshop activities for, 142–143; writing workshop activities for, 129–133

TAKING INVENTORY STAGE, 77–78, 77f, 319; reading workshop activities for, 141–142; writing workshop activities for, 124–129

TALKING MARKS: minilesson on, 225–226

TARGETS: for student achievement, selection of, 247–248

TAYLOR, D., 61, 98

TEACHER(S): accountability to, 234–235; conferring, 158, 158f, 163–173; and learning environment, 182; in reading workshop, 133; on spelling progress, 57–59; students as, 195–199; on writing workshop, 269–273; on written language development, 62–63

TEALE, W., 63, 98

TEBEROSKY, A., xi, 2–3, 5, 62, 98, 170

TEMPLE, C., 2, 8, 13, 16, 18–20, 29, 31, 34–36, 38–40, 42–43, 46–47, 51, 55, 66–67, 79–81, 100, 110, 123, 127, 131, 135, 141, 155, 172–173, 179, 183, 213, 226, 245

TEMPLE, F., 2, 8, 13, 16, 19–20, 29, 31, 34–36, 38–40, 42–43, 46–47, 51, 55, 66–67, 79–81, 100, 110, 123, 127, 131, 135, 141, 155, 172–173, 179, 183, 213, 226, 245

TEMPLETON, S., 11, 15–16, 34–35, 38–43, 45, 51, 107, 131–132, 141, 155–156, 183, 278, 281

10-LINE SUMMARY, 263–264

TENT CARDS, 129–130, 130f; name, 164

TEXT SELECTION: for reading aloud, 144; for reading workshop, 136–138

TEXTUAL FEATURES DEVELOPMENT STAGE, 79–81, 80f–81f, 319

TIME. See schedule

TITLES: engaging, 202–203

TIVAN, T., viii

TOLSTOY, A.N., 96

TOMPKINS, G., 10, 12, 14, 20–21, 27, 62, 67, 69, 71–72, 89–90, 93, 102–103, 106, 114, 245, 249, 251, 262

TONGUE TWISTERS, 280, 284

TOPICS: inappropriate, 189; repeated, minilesson on, 187–189; selection of, 182–183, 212–213

TRACHTENBURG, R., 104

TRANSITIONAL STAGE, 38, 51–54, 52f, 318; terminology for, 39t

TREIMAN, R., 36

TRELEASE, J., 144

TRIANGULAR CONFERENCES, 264–265

TUCKER, M., 238, 267

TUNMER, W.E., viii, 5, 18

U

UNLINED PAPER, 158

USE: and language learning, 23

V

VACHEL, L., 141

VANOUREK, G., 237

VENEZKY, R., 53

VERBS: minilesson on, 297

VERY OWN WORDS, 131

VISUAL REMINDERS, 131, 132f

VOICE, 76; development of, 203–206; encouraging, 178–179; responsibility and, 23–24

VOLLMER, D., 200

VYGOTSKY, L.S., 26, 118

W

WAGSTAFF, J.M., 120

WALK THE WORDS, 142

WARREN, J., 284

WEAVER, C., 49, 105

WEEKLY CONFERENCE AND INSTRUCTIONAL GUIDESHEET (WCIG), 165; directions for, 335; reproducible, 334; transferring